Schott's
Almanac

2 0 0 6

LIBER PRAETERITORUM ET POSTERITATIS CARMEN

Everyone spoke of information overload,
but what there was, in fact, was a non-information overload.
— RICHARD SAUL WURMAN, *What-If, Could-Be,* 1976

Schott's Almanac 2006 ™ · Schott's Almanac ™
Schott's Annual Astrometer ™ © 2006

Published by Bloomsbury Publishing Plc.
36 Soho Square, London, W1D 3QY, UK

www.schottsalmanac.com · www.benschott.com

3 4 5 6 7 8 9 10

NOTE · Information included within is believed to be correct at
the time of going to press. Neither the author nor the publisher
can accept any responsibility for any error or subsequent changes.

ISBN 0-7475-8307-2 · ISBN-13 9780747583073 [see p.153]

A CIP catalogue record for this book is available from the British Library.

Designed and typeset by BEN SCHOTT
Printed in Great Britain by CLAYS Ltd., ST IVES Plc.

*   *   *   *

Also by BEN SCHOTT
Schott's Original Miscellany
Schott's Food & Drink Miscellany
Schott's Sporting, Gaming, & Idling Miscellany
Schott's Miscellany Diary (with Smythson of Bond St.)

Schott's Almanac

2 0 0 6

· *The book of things past and the song of the future* ·

Conceived, edited, and designed by

BEN SCHOTT

assistant editor

Claire Cock-Starkey

BLOOMSBURY

Preface

A calendar, a calendar! look in the almanack;
find out moonshine, find out moonshine.
— A Midsummer Night's Dream, III i

Schott's Almanac offers a biography of the year. Its aim is to record the events of the past, and give a calendar of events to come. In the modern information age, however, the role of the almanac has changed. Just as C20th almanacs were less concerned with astronomical and ecclesiastical data than their C18th–C19th predecessors, so the C21st almanac must adapt to its time. *Schott's Almanac* reflects the age in which it has been written: an age where information is plentiful, but selection and analysis are more elusive. So, while *Schott's Almanac* hopes to include all of the essential data one would expect to find in such a volume, it has not attempted to be comprehensive. Perhaps in contrast to some of its venerable forerunners [see p.6], rather than presenting encyclopaedic listings, *Schott's Almanac* aspires to provide an informative, selective, and entertaining analysis of the year.

— *Schott's* is an almanac written to be read.

──────────── THE ALMANAC'S YEAR ────────────

In order to be as inclusive as possible, the *Schott's Almanac* year runs until mid-September.

Data cited in *Schott's Almanac* are taken from the latest sources available at the time of writing.

──────────── ERRORS & OMISSIONS ────────────

Every effort has been taken to ensure that the information contained within *Schott's Almanac* is both accurate and up-to-date, and grateful acknowledgement is made to the various sources used. However, as Goethe once said: 'error is to truth as sleep is to waking'. Consequently, the author would be pleased to be informed of any errors, inaccuracies, or omissions that might help improve future editions.

Please send all comments or suggestions to the author, care of:

Bloomsbury Publishing Plc, 36 Soho Square, London, W1D 3QY
or email *editor@schottsalmanac.com*

Readers are invited to subscribe to future annual editions of *Schott's Alamanc* via:

www.schottsalmanac.com

Contents

EARLY ALMANACS OF NOTE

Solomon Jarchi *c.*1150	Regiomontanus (at Nuremberg) . 1474
Peter de Dacia *c.*1300	Zainer (at Ulm) 1478
Walter de Elvendene 1327	Richard Pynson.................. 1497
John Somers (Oxford) 1380	Stoffler (in Venice) 1499
Nicholas de Lynna 1386	Poor Robin's Almanack 1652
Purbach 1150–1461	Francis Moore's Almanack 1698–1713
After the invention of printing	Almanach de Gotha.............. 1764
Gutenberg (at Mainz) 1457	Whitaker's Almanack............. 1868

ALMANAC vs ALMANACK

The spelling and etymology of 'almanac' are the subject of some dispute. The *Oxford English Dictionary* notes the very early use of 'almanac' by Roger Bacon in 1267, though Chaucer used 'almenak' in *c.*1391; and Shakespeare, 'almanack' in 1590. Variations include almanach(e), amminick, almanacke, almanack, &c. A number of etymologies for *almanac* have been suggested: that it comes from the Arabic *al* [the] *mana(h)* [reckoning or diary]; that it comes from the Anglo-Saxon *al-moan-heed* 'to wit, the regard or observations of all the moons', or from the Anglo-Saxon *al-monath* [all the months]; or that it is linked to the Latin for sundial, *manachus*. In 1838, *Murphy's Almanac* made the bold prediction that 20 January that year would be 'Fair, prob. lowest deg. of winter temp'. When, on the day, this actually turned out to be true, *Murphy's Almanac* became a best seller.

SYMBOLS & ABBREVIATIONS

> .... greater than	km............................ kilometre
≥ .... greater than or equal to	m .... metre
< .... less than	mi .... mile
≤ .... less than or equal to	'/" .... feet/inches
♂ .... male/men	C................. Century (e.g. C20th)
♀ .... female/women	ONS ..... Office of National Statistics
c. ... circa, meaning around or roughly	Crown © .... Crown Copyright

Throughout the *Almanac,* some figures may not add to totals because of rounding.

'AVERAGES'

With the following list of values: 10, 10, 20, 30, 30, 30, 40, 50, 70, 100 = 390

MEAN or AVERAGE	the sum divided by the number of values..............	39
MODE	the most popular value	30
MEDIAN	the 'middle' value of a range, here: (30+30)/2	30
RANGE..................	the difference between the highest & lowest values ...	90

Chronicle

To every thing there is a season, and time to every purpose under the heaven:
A time to be born, and a time to die.
— ECCLESIASTES 3:1–8

―――――――― SOME AWARDS OF NOTE ――――――――

TIME Magazine Man of the Year [2004] · GEORGE W. BUSH
'For sticking to his guns (literally [sic] *and figuratively), for*
reshaping the rules of politics to fit his ten-gallon-hat leadership style
and for persuading a majority of voters that he deserved to be in
the White House for another four years…'

Tipperary international peace prize	Margaret Hassan
Woodrow Wilson award for public service	John Howard [Australian PM]
Robert Burns humanitarian award	Archbishop Pius Nicube
Australian of the year	Dr Fiona Wood (plastic surgeon)
BP portrait award	Dean Marsh for *Giulietta Coates*
Airline of the year [Skytrax]	Cathay Pacific
Airport of the year [Skytrax]	Hong Kong International
Car of the year [*What Car?*]	Land Rover Discovery TDV6 S auto
Barrister of the year [*The Lawyer*]	David Kitchin QC, 8 New Square
Young geographer of the year [RGS]	James Cohen, The Judd School
Prison officer of the year [HM Prison Service]	Terry Blane (HMP Exeter)
Master builder of the year [FMB]	DITT Construction Ltd, Lerwick
International engine of the year	BMW 5-litre V10 (M5, M6)
Cmsn. for Racial Equality's media personality	Thierry Henry
Sexy Specs Wearer	Penny Lancaster
Charity of the year [Charity Awards]	Beatbullying
GQ woman of the year	Charlotte Church
Menu of the year [The Cateys]	Bohemia, St Helier, Jersey
Guild Food Writers food book of the year	Matthew Fort, *Eating Up Italy*
W.C. Handy blues entertainer of the year	B.B. King
Annual Ernest Hemingway look-alike award	Bob Doughty, USA
Pet slimmers of the year	Mischief, the cat [lost 5kg]; Max, the dog [lost 22kg]
Rears of the year	Nell McAndrew; Will Young

―――――――― PLAIN ENGLISH CAMPAIGN ――――――――

Boris Johnson won the Plain English Campaign's 2004 'Foot in Mouth Award' for

'I could not fail to disagree with you less'.

——— MISC. LISTS OF 2005 ———

GREATEST AMERICAN
c.2·5m voted in an AOL Discovery Channel poll for 'greatest American':

1 .... Ronald Reagan
2 ...... Abraham Lincoln
3 Martin Luther King Jr
4 ... George Washington
5 .... Benjamin Franklin
6 .... George W. Bush
7 .... Bill Clinton
8 .... Elvis Presley
9 .... Oprah Winfrey
10 Franklin D Roosevelt

GREATEST PAINTING IN BRITAIN
As voted for by listeners to Radio 4's Today Programme

The Fighting Temeraire tugged to her last berth to be broken up, 1838
J.M.W. Turner, 1839

MADAME TUSSAUDS
New waxworks for 2005 in the London museum

Robbie Williams
Jamie Oliver
Simon Cowell
Sharon Osbourne
Louis Walsh
Justin Hawkins
(*The Darkness*)
Prince William
Andy & Lou
(played by Matt Lucas
and David Walliams in
Little Britain)
Elton John
(made of Cadbury's
chocolate)

GREATEST PHILOSOPHER
Voted by listeners to Radio 4's In Our Time

1 .... Karl Marx
2 .... David Hume
3 .. Ludwig Wittgenstein
4 .... Friedrich Nietzsche
5 .... Plato
6 .... Immanuel Kant
7 .... St Thomas Aquinas
8 .... Socrates
9 .... Aristotle
10 .... Karl Popper

TOP DOG WALKS
Britain's top 5 dog walk locations, according to the Good Dog Campaign

Camel Estuary
(North Cornwall)
Footscray Meadows
(Bexley)
Jesus Green
(Cambridge)
Malvern Hills
(Cotswold's)
Newton by the Sea
(Mid Northumberland)

GREATEST FRENCHMAN
According to the viewers of France 2 TV

1 ...... Charles de Gaulle
2 .... Louis Pasteur
3 .... Abbé Pierre
4 .... Marie Curie
5 .... Coluche
6 .... Victor Hugo
7 .... Bourvil
8 .... Molière
9 Jacques-Yves Cousteau
10 .... Edith Piaf

——— 2006 WORDS ———

The following words celebrate anniversaries in 2006, based upon the earliest cited use traced by the venerable *Oxford English Dictionary*:

{1506} *arsenal* (a naval dockyard and store of arms) · *Venice* (the city state) · {1606} *circum-ambulation* (walking around) · *devirginating* (deflowering a virgin) · *fashionable* (good looking or stylish) · *has been* (someone whose days are over) · {1706} *pseudonymous* (writing under an assumed name) · *snigger* (to laugh immaturely) · {1806} *croûton* (small cubes of fried bread) · *dementia* (the failing of mental powers) · *washroom* (lavatory) · {1906} *lowbrow* (that considered intellectually inferior) · *paedophilia* (sexual desire for children) · *teddy bear* (stuffed children's toy) · {1956} *fluffer* (one who removes fluff and dirt from railway tunnels) · *meta-text* (a text outside another) · {1966} *cherry-pick* (to select only the best) · *hokey-cokey* (the dance) · {1976} *chocoholic* (one overly fond of chocs) · *megastar* (world famous celeb) · *Thatcherite* (like the PM) · {1986} *McJob* (a low-paid, repetitive, unskilled service job).

——— SOME SURVEY RESULTS OF 2005 ———

%	result	source & month
82	of adults back Anti-Social Behaviour Orders	[MORI; Jun]
82	want immigrants screened for HIV, TB, and hepatitis	[Populus/*News OTW*; Feb]
80	of workers think some of their colleagues underperform	[Investors in People; Aug]
75	think GP surgeries are more important than walk-in centres	[MORI/BMA; Apr]
75	of Russians fear their own police force	[Levada Centre; Aug]
69	of teachers in England & Wales back abortion education	[*Times Educational Sup.*; Feb]
66	agree that voluntary euthanasia should be legal	[Populus/*The Sun*; Jun]
66	do not want the Queen to abdicate	[Populus/*The Times*; Mar]
65	of British Muslims believe clerics should preach in English	[BBC/MORI; Aug]
63	of Chinese have 'very bad' or 'not very good' impressions of Japan	[Peking Uni.; Aug]
59	support an independent inquiry into Iraqi war casualties [see p.20]	[MORI; Feb]
55	think GB will be at a greater security risk hosting the 2012 Olympics	[Harris; Aug]
52	do not think nuclear power should be a future energy source	[BBC/ICM; May]
50	of women prefer to make love in the dark	[Populus/*The Sun*; Jan]
48	associate the Rotary Club logo with their charity work	[MORI; Feb]
46	of adults think Anti-Social Behaviour Orders effective	[MORI; Jun]
46	prefer team to individual sports	[YouGov/*Telegraph*; Jan]
46	of men prefer brunette women (30% prefer blondes)	[Populus/*The Sun*; Jan]
44	'strongly agreed' with Bluewater's policy to ban 'hoodies' [see p.11]	[ICM; May]
42	of Americans believe in creationism over evolution [see p.178]	[Pew Forum; Aug]
42	of adults find a sea view conducive to relaxation	[Hoegaarden; Jul]
42	of women think about sex while on the London Underground	[Viacom Outdoors; Jul]
38	of British people take pride in Big Ben as a British symbol	[YouGov/*Telegraph*; Jul]
33	believe contact with or by the dead is possible	[Populus/*The Sun*; Jun]
32	of OAPs think means testing social security benefits is 'demeaning'	[MORI; Feb]
32	think journalism does not make a positive contribution to GB	[YouGov/*UKPG*; Jan]
30	of Plymouth Hospital staff do not want care in their hospitals	[Healthcare Cmsn; Jun]
30	of London teenagers are distracted by mobiles when crossing roads	[Think!; Aug]
25	think Prince Harry's Nazi costume was as acceptable as any	[ICM/*Sun Mirror*; Jan]
23	have 'never trusted Tony Blair'	[Populus/*The Sun*; Apr]
22	14-year-old girls have had sex (of whom 65% had unprotected sex)	[*Bliss*; Mar]
22	of men think about sex while on the London Underground	[Viacom Outdoors; Jul]
21	of 13–19-year-old girls have been hit by their boyfriends	[NSPCC; Mar]
21	of drivers think speeding acceptable if there is little other traffic	[Direct Line; Aug]
18	think the Monarchy should end with the Queen	[Populus/*The Times*; Apr]
15	of Welsh do no housework at all	[BBC; Apr]
14	of pensioners regularly feel lonely	[Help the Aged; Mar]
14	of badgers found dead by the roadside had tuberculosis	[Defra; Aug]
12	of Italians believe that Jews lie about the Holocaust	[*Corriere della Sera*; Jan]
10	failed to identify Nelson as the British admiral at Trafalgar	[YouGov/*Telegraph*; Aug]
10	children (5–16) have a clinically recognisable mental disorder	[Dept. Health; Aug]
9	think enough is being done to protect children from sex offenders	[ICM; Jun]
8	are interested in the sport of wrestling	[YouGov/*Telegraph*; Jan]
6	of women buy jewellery on impulse (1% of men do)	[Harris/*The Grocer*; Apr]
1	of women are happy with their shape	[National Slimming Survey; Jun]

WORDS OF THE YEAR

COUNSELOR · the enigmatic final word Hunter S. Thompson typed in the centre of a sheet of paper before he committed suicide [see p.48].

CELEBUTANTE · tenuous conflation of celebrity and débutante, used for luminaries like Paris Hilton [see p.112].

HAPPY SLAPPING · (aka BANGING OUT) · the disturbing trend of capturing acts of random violence against strangers on video phones and texting these clips to friends [see p.28].

ASTROTURFING · political jargon for filling out empty press conferences with party workers, a practice popular during the 2005 election.

ENCORE PRESENTATION · a media euphemism for a TV repeat; similar to a 'classic episode of…'.

VLOG · a blog containing video.

MOBISODES · a movie trailer, or television show, condensed into a short film clip suitable for playing on 3G mobile phones.

TURKEY TWIZZLER · curious turkey-based snack [see p.87].

PAJAMAHIDEEN · a word-play on Mujahideen, used to deride a class of political Bloggers who comment on the world from the comfort of their homes, presumably in the comfort of their pajamas. Adopted by some activists as a badge of honour.

CHUGGER · charity 'muggers' who work the streets.

INTEXTIFICATION · texting drunk.

MAN DATE · a platonic date between two heterosexual men. MANDALS · male sandals. MURSE · a male purse.

CRUNK · a form of raw, unrefined Southern American party hip-hop popularised by *Lil' Jon & The East Side Boyz*, et al. Also, a C19th term for a short, harsh cry or croak.

SANTO SUBITO · roughly translates as 'immediate sainthood' – chanted by tens of thousands in St Peter's Square after the death of Pope John Paul II.

DEFERRED SUCCESS · euphemistic term proposed to replace 'failure'.

YEPPIES · questionable new acronym for Young Experimental Perfection Seekers who eschew money and status, and browse for jobs and relationships.

FREAKONOMICS · the title of a book by 'gonzo' economist Steven Levitt, freakonomics is the use of economic methodology to explore 'real life' questions, such as 'Why Do Drug Dealers Still Live with Their Moms?'.

RENDITION · a euphemism for sending prisoners from a country where torture is illegal to a country where it is not. It is alleged that US intelligence 'outsources torture' by rendering terror suspects to countries such as Egypt and Syria for interrogation.

COURAGE · the enigmatic and somewhat pretentious word that CBS newsanchor Dan Rather sometimes used to end broadcasts, and indeed his last ever show on 9 March 2005.

DESHOPPING · buying goods, using them, and then returning them.

WORDS OF THE YEAR cont.

BRITISH-ASIAN, INDIAN-BRITISH · much derided new multicultural terms mooted by the Home Office.

OPERATION KRATOS · code-name for the UK police's policy of 'shoot-to-kill-to-protect' when confronting suspected suicide bombers. The strategy is said to be based on tactical advice from Israel's security forces. Kratos was introduced after 9/11, but became public after the accidental shooting of Jean Charles de Menezes on 22 July 2005. [Kratos ('might') was the son of Pallas and the River Styx. He and his brother Bia ('force') were ordered by Zeus to chain Prometheus to the rock of Caucasus as punishment for giving fire to mankind. Kratos' other siblings were Zelus ('zeal'), and Nike ('victory').]

OPERATION SASSOON · code-name for the plan for mass evacuation of any part of London in an emergency.

AFFLUENZA · the collection of problems confronting those, like lottery winners, who suddenly acquire wealth.

ISRAELISATION · [1] the pervasive influence of the Arab-Israeli conflict on world politics; [2] the fact that post-9/11, Madrid, and 7/7, Western states now also live with the reality of suicide attacks; [3] the adoption of Israeli tactics for tackling terrorism.

BODY SPAM · undesirable physical contact by strangers, such as that suffered by waitresses, or commuters on buses or the Underground.

TAPPING UP · footballing term for the outlawed act of rival clubs approaching players under contract with other teams without first obtaining permission from their current employers.

HOODIES · a 'moral panic' that hit the frontpages, relating to youths wearing hooded tops (allegedly to conceal their identities from CCTV cameras). In May 2005, the Bluewater shopping centre in Kent issued a code of conduct that banned the wearing of hoodies and baseball caps.

BARIATRIC · the medical treatment of obese patients; derived from 'baros', the Greek for weight (as in geriatric).

CLEANSKINS · security service term for individuals with no previously known links to terrorist or criminal activities; used to describe the 7/7 bombers. (Also LILLYWHITES.)

LONDONISTAN · half-joking term to describe the apparent popularity of London amongst 'Islamic' terrorists, and the supposed laxity of UK security laws in comparison to other countries.

BOUNCEBACKABILITY · the ability (of a sports team) to recover from defeat.

MEDAL · used as a verb by athletes to describe achieving a medal-winning position: *'I medalled in Athens'.*

CRACKBERRY · used to describe the addictive nature of PDAs [see p.185] such as the BlackBerry. SLACKBERRY · using your BlackBerry incompetently, or at inappropriate times (a wedding or a funeral). SMACKBERRY · hitting someone with your PDA.

BATHROOM BREAK · during a UN summit, George W. Bush was snapped by a Reuters' photographer writing a note to his Secretary of State, Condoleezza Rice: 'I think I may need a bathroom break? Is this possible?'

2004 INDIAN OCEAN TSUNAMI

DATE: Sunday, 26 December 2004 · TIME: 07:58:53 at epicentre
QUAKE MAGNITUDE: 9·3 Richter Scale [see p.67] · DEPTH: 30km (18·6 miles)
LOCATION: off the west coast of northern Sumatra
255km SSE of Banda Aceh, Sumatra, Indonesia · 310km W of Medan, Sumatra, Indonesia
1260km SSW of Bangkok, Thailand · 1605km NW of Jakarta, Java, Indonesia
[source: US Geological Survey]

The world's fourth greatest earthquake since 1900 tore up the sea floor off NW Sumatra, at the interface of the India and Burma tectonic plates. The resulting tsunami sped at *c.*500mph thousands of miles across the Indian Ocean with wave heights of *c.*20m. Sumatra was the first landmass hit, just half an hour after the quake; the city of Banda Aceh was destroyed within minutes. The waves ran northeast to Thailand, west to Sri Lanka, southwest to the Maldives, and on to Somalia and Kenya. In all, thirteen countries were severely affected. With no tsunami warning systems in the area and no effective coastal defence, more than 300,000 were killed, and at least 1·3m were left homeless or dispossessed. Even nine months after the waves hit, the scale of the environmental and human disaster was unclear.

As images of devastation played across the globe, their contrast to Christmas festivities was graphic. The public's response was instant and overwhelming. In the UK, the *Disasters Emergency Committee* appeal was inundated with donations [see below], and across the world the public's generosity consistently outstripped the sums pledged by national governments. Yet reports soon emerged about the disparity between money pledged and money given, and about the misdirection of aid once it had reached the affected countries.

The UN estimated that it might take up to 5 years to revive the region – although much will depend on the ability of aid organisations to work effectively in challenging local conditions, and the willingness with which tourists from around the world return to the region.

DEC Appeal Landmarks		
28·12·04	*opened*	£5·3m
29·12·04		£20m
31·12·04		£32m
01·01·05		£60m
04·01·05		£76m
06·01·05		£109m
07·01·05		£138m
14·01·05		£200m
26·02·05	*closed*	£300m

─────── POPES JOHN PAUL II & BENEDICT XVI ───────

Karol Józef Wojtyla · Ioannes Paulus PP. II · Pontificate 16·10·1978–2·4·2005
Born *near Krakow, Poland* 8·5·1920 · Died *The Vatican* 2·4·2005

At 9·37pm on 2 April 2005, John Paul II, the 264th Pope, died. Archbishop Leonardo Sandri declared to those massed in St Peter's Square: 'Our Holy Father John Paul has returned to the house of the Father'. The crowd responded with a traditional Italian sign of respect: applause. ❧ John Paul II's 27 year reign, the third longest in history, was punctuated by political upheavals, like the end of apartheid and the fall of the Berlin Wall, matched only by advances in science and technology. ❧ For those with an '*à la carte*' attitude to morality, JPII's unflinching defence of the sanctity of life was problematic. Many who condemned war, euthanasia, and cloning, took more liberal lines on the 'choices' of divorce, IVF, homosexuality, and contraception. For JPII these were all part of a 'culture of death' that represented a 'contempt for human life'. JPII's refusal to relax his opposition to condoms proved increasingly controversial as AIDS swept across Africa. (It is claimed that this stance prevented him from being awarded the Nobel Peace Prize.) ❧ Yet, few would disagree that JPII demystified the Papacy, taking his highly personal ministry to 117 countries and creating theatrical images like kissing the airport tarmac. JPII was the first Pope to visit a synagogue or a mosque, the first to visit Britain or Ireland, and the first to apologise for the sins of the Church. At his death, JPII was one of a handful of people who had global recognition. But his charisma was not enough to stem a fall in vocations and congregations in the West, or the growth of 'alternative' Churches. Nor for some was it enough to pacify anger caused by sexual abuse scandals within the Church. ❧ As Pope, JPII made 104 pastoral visits abroad and 146 in Italy. In addition to 5 books, he wrote 14 encyclicals, 15 apostolic exhortations, 11 apostolic constitutions, and 45 apostolic letters. He presided at an unprecedented 147 beatifications (1,338 Blesseds) and 51 canonization ceremonies (482 Saints). It is estimated that at more than 1,160 General Audiences during his Papacy JPII spoke to more than 17·5m people.

The election of Joseph Ratzinger as the 265th Pope was announced with the traditional plume of white smoke, and the newly-adopted tolling of bells, on 19 April 2005. It took the College of Cardinals only 2 days and 4 votes to elect Benedict XVI, the first German Pope since Victor II (1055–57). ❧ Most describe BXVI as fiercely intelligent and religiously conservative. He is fluent in eight languages, including Latin, and is an accomplished pianist. Yet, nicknames like 'God's Rottweiler' more than hint at a theological hard-line. Ratzinger's previous attacks on birth control, women's ordination, abortion, euthanasia, homosexuality, and 'liberation theology', dismayed many hoping for a liberal Papacy. However, some detected a conciliatory tone in his 24 April inaugural homily: 'My real programme of governance is not to do my own will, not to pursue my own ideas, but to listen, together with the whole Church, to the word and the will of the Lord.'

2005 UK GENERAL ELECTION

	LABOUR	Conservative	Lib Dem	Others
No. of Seats	356 (-47)	197 (+33)	62 (+11)	30 (+3)
Votes	9,556,183	8,772,598	5,982,045	2,821,501
Share of Vote	35·2% (-5·5)	32·2% (+0·6)	22·0% (+3·7)	10·5% (+1·4)
Share of Seats	55·2%	30·5%	9·6%	4·7%

Labour MAJORITY = 67 (167 in 2001; 179 in 1997)
SWING from Labour to Conservative = 3·0% · TURNOUT 61·3% (+2%)
FEMALE MPs = 125 (+6) [98 Lab; 17 Con; 10 Lib Dem]
At the time of going to press, some of the above figures were tentative or disputed.

On 5 May 2005, Tony Blair's 'New' Labour party won an historic third term in government, though with the lowest share of the vote since 1832 and with its majority cut from 166 to 67. Despite the fact that nine post-war governments have ruled with majorities smaller than 67, New Labour, accustomed to landslide victories, was chastened. In his acceptance speech in Sedgefield, Blair said 'I have listened and I have learned. And I think I have a very clear idea of what the British people now expect'. ❦ The election was characterised by a number of issues including the economy, the provision of public services, and controls on immigration. The latter was controversially championed by the Tories in a so-called 'dog-whistle' campaign that sought to chime with voters' unspoken concerns. However, the prominent issue of the election was the Iraq conflict – both because the war was so divisive, and because it allowed Blair's style, judgement, and honesty to be questioned. When the Attorney-General's advice on the legality of the war was partially leaked and then finally published, Michael Howard took the unprecedented step of calling the PM a liar.

Tony Blair

In the face of criticism, Blair persevered with a 'masochism strategy' that saw him facing stern public criticism on television and radio to draw the sting of public disappointment and anger. ❦ In an attempt to end relentless speculation about the Blair-Brown relationship, the PM and his Chancellor regularly appeared side by side offering each other generous tributes. This had the benefit of highlighting the economy, which was perceived as a Labour 'positive'. ❦ The Lib Dems positioned themselves as the 'Real Alternative', and saw their opposition to the war rewarded with 11 new MPs. Yet, some claimed that Charles Kennedy had wasted a unique opportunity fully to capitalise on anti-war feeling. ❦ Despite running what was widely seen as an agenda-setting campaign, and winning 33 seats, Michael Howard's inability to present the Tories as a valid alternative led him to resign as party leader a day after the election. ❦ Blair returned to No. 10 having secured a place in electoral history, yet with doubts surrounding his future. As he admitted on election night, 'it seems that the British people wanted the return of the Labour Government with a reduced majority'.

NOTES ON THE 2005 GENERAL ELECTION

Galloway vs Paxman

Ex-Labour MP George Galloway ousted Blairite MP Oona King from *Bethnal Green & Bow*, after a bitter fight that focused on the Iraq war. Standing for his party, *Respect*, Galloway polled 15,801 votes. His BBC1 interview was the highlight of the TV coverage: *Jeremy Paxman* – 'Mr Galloway, are you proud of having got rid of one of the very few black women in Parliament?' *George Galloway* – 'What a preposterous question. I know it's very late in the night, but wouldn't you be better starting by congratulating me for one of the most sensational election results in modern history?'

Twigg's Downfall

Stephen Twigg, whose astonishing victory over Michael Portillo in 1997 defined Blair's landslide, was beaten by the Tories in *Enfield Southgate*. An 8·7% swing to the Tories meant David Burrowes was returned as MP.

Scots & Welsh Nats

Plaid Cymru lost 1 MP leaving them with 3; its share of the vote fell 0·1% to 0·6%. The *SNP* gained MPs, from 4 to 6, although its share of vote fell 0·3% to 1·5%.

Northern Ireland

David Trimble's *Ulster Unionist Party* suffered defeats across Northern Ireland, losing 4 MPs; leaving them with only 1. Trimble lost his *Upper Bann* seat, and resigned as leader the next day. Ian Paisley's *Democratic Unionist Party* gained 4 MPs. *Sinn Féin's* share of the vote fell slightly (-0·1%), but they gained an extra seat. The *SDLP* lost and gained a seat, retaining 3 MPs; their share of vote fell 0·1%.

Supermarginals

A range of 43 new *supermarginal* constituencies emerged where Labour would lose with a swing of just 2·5%. In *Crawley*, Labour had a majority of 0·1% – or just 37 votes.

Kilroy, Veritas, & UKIP

Robert Kilroy-Silk was humiliated in *Erewash*, polling just 2,957 votes (5·8%). His party *Veritas* polled just 40,481 votes nationwide. ❦ The party he left, *UKIP*, saw a 0·7% rise in its vote, polling 605,973 votes. However they lost their deposit in 451 seats at a cost of £225,500. Unlike in 2001, Europe was not a strong electoral issue, since all three major parties had committed to holding a referendum.

Blair vs Keys

15 candidates stood against Blair in *Sedgefield* – including Reg Keys (the father of a military policeman killed in Iraq) who polled 10·25%. To the clear embarrassment of Blair, Keys' denunciation of the Iraq war was televised live: 'I hope in my heart that one day the Prime Minister will be able to say sorry, that one day he will say sorry to the families of the bereaved. And one day the Prime Minister may be able to visit wounded soldiers in hospital'.

British National Party

The *BNP* saw its share of vote increase by 0·5% to 0·7%, polling 192,850 nationwide. In *Barking*, the *BNP* won its highest ever share of the vote, 28 votes short of beating the Tories into second place behind Margaret Hodge.

Muslim MPs

Together, the three main political parties fielded 48 Muslim candidates, of whom 4 were elected – all for Labour.

By-election

Only 645 out of 646 Parliamentary seats were contested at the election, after the death of a candidate in *Staffordshire South* [see p.258].

—————————— 31st G8 SUMMIT · GLENEAGLES ——————————

The G8 summit at Gleneagles opened on 6 July 2005 – four days after the global Live8 concerts; the day on which London was awarded the 2012 Olympics; and one day before the first suicide bomb attacks across London. Against this dramatic political backdrop, public expectation ran high for equally dramatic agreements.

The Group of Eight (G8) began as the G6 in 1975 when France, Japan, USA, UK, Germany, and Italy met to discuss key economic issues. In 1976 Canada made the G7; in 1998 Russia made the G8. Unlike other world bodies, the G8 has no formal structure or administration; the country that holds the Presidency, which rotates yearly, hosts the annual summit and sets its agenda. Although the G8 does not bind its members, talks have proved decisive over global issues like AIDS and TB; making safe Russian nuclear facilities; alleviating debt; &c. Yet, being associated with the capitalist first world, summits have become targets of anti-globalisation action. And, while many countries and groups send delegates to summits, the fact that China, India, Africa and Latin America are excluded from G8 membership is controversial.

Tony Blair announced the UK's G8 Presidency would address the challenges of Africa and climate change. After 3 days of debate, the final communiqué agreed:

❦ An additional £29bn in aid by 2010 (compared to 2004 figures) including doubling African development aid to £25bn. ❦ 100% debt cancellation for 18 eligible African 'Heavily Indebted Poor Countries'. ❦ Provide 'as close to universal' access to treatment for HIV /AIDS by 2010. ❦ Step-up fight against malaria to reach 85% of those at risk – potentially saving *c.*600,000 lives by 2015. ❦ Support the eradication of polio and tackle TB. ❦ No targets for reducing carbon emissions, but the US *appears* to be recognising the risks of global warming; commitment to open dialogue between G8 and emerging countries over climate change. ❦ Set a 'credible date' for talks to end export and agricultural subsidies. ❦ Train a further 20,000 African peacekeeping troops to work in Africa. ❦ Donate $3bn a year, over the next 3 years, to help the Palestinian Authority build institutions and infrastructure. ❦

Unusually, Tony Blair asked the G8 heads (and the EU's delegate) to sign the final communiqué, declaring they would collectively be 'held by this, bound by this'.

Tony Blair · UK

Gerhard Schroeder · Germany

Vladimir Putin · Russia

Junichiro Koizumi · Japan

Jacques Chirac · France

George W. Bush · USA

Paul Martin · Canada

Silvio Berlusconi · Italy

José Manuel Barroso · EU

——31st G8 SUMMIT · GLENEAGLES · SOME REACTION——

Greenpeace · *The G8 has committed to nothing new but at least we haven't moved backwards on the environment.*

Oxfam · *The world's richest nations have delivered welcome progress for the world's poorest people, but the outcome here in Gleneagles has fallen short of the hopes of the millions around the world campaigning for a momentous breakthrough.*

Friends of the Earth · *Bush appears to have effectively stalled all progress. The action plan, without any targets or timetables, will deliver very little...*

Global Call to Action Against Poverty *The people have roared but the G8 has whispered.*

Bob Geldof · *To save lives is never a whisper. People were screaming before, a whisper is not a bad thing. Please! Perspective! Never before have so many people forced a change of policy onto a global agenda. Today is a great day for those 10m people [who will be saved]... 10 out of 10 on aid, 8 out of 10 on debt.*

Tony Blair · *It isn't all everyone wanted, but it is progress.*

——————MAKE POVERTY HISTORY & LIVE8——————

The pressure group *Make Poverty History* (MPH) is a collective of charities, trade unions, church groups, celebrities, and members of the public, initially formed to lobby world leaders before the 2005 G8 summit. The group's aim is to focus world attention on the plight of Africans, through rallies, marches, email campaigns, and wearing the white MPH wristband [see p.80]. One of the figureheads of MPH is Bob Geldof. Despite stating that a sequel to the 1985 Live Aid concerts would take place over his 'dead body', Geldof changed his mind, claiming that the Gleneagles summit presented a unique opportunity 'to gather again, this time not for charity but for political justice'. On 6 July 2005, concerts took place in ten venues across the globe, featuring world-famous artists and some local celebrities, including:

LONDON · *Coldplay, Dido, Pink Floyd, The Who, U2, R.E.M., Annie Lennox, Sting, Madonna, Elton John, Robbie Williams, Paul McCartney*

PHILADELPHIA *Bon Jovi, Def Leppard, Stevie Wonder, Maroon 5, Black Eyed Peas, Jay-Z, Destiny's Child*

BERLIN · *A-ha, Sasha, Green Day, Roxy Music, Chris de Burgh, Brian Wilson, Faithless, Crosby, Stills and Nash*

TOKYO · *Bjork, McFly*

MOSCOW · *Pet Shop Boys*

BARRIE · *Bryan Adams, Barenaked Ladies, Deep Purple, Run DMC*

JOHANNESBURG *Oumou Sangare, Zola, Orchestra Baobab*

CORNWALL · *Daara J, Youssou N'Dour, Thomas Mapfumo,*

PARIS · *The Cure, Craig David*

ROME · *Duran Duran, Zucchero, Renato Zero*

In all, 260 acts performed worldwide, watched by a live audience of 1·1m, and a television audience of 2bn (5m watched online). 26m sent texts of support.

LONDON BOMBINGS · 7/7 & 21/7

52 were killed and *c.*700 injured when 4 bombs hit London's transport system at the height of morning rush hour on Thursday 7 July 2005: the second day of the G8 conference, and one day after London had been awarded the 2012 Olympics.

1. 8:50am	**2.** 8:50am	**3.** 8:50am	**4.** 9:47am
Bomb explodes on Circle Line train as it leaves Edgware Rd for Paddington.	*Bomb explodes on Piccadilly Line train in tunnel between King's X and Russell Sq.*	*Bomb explodes on Circle Line train in tunnel between Liverpool St. and Aldgate.*	*Bomb explodes on the top deck of a Number 30 bus as it travelled south into Tavistock Sq.*
6 killed	26 killed	7 killed	13 killed

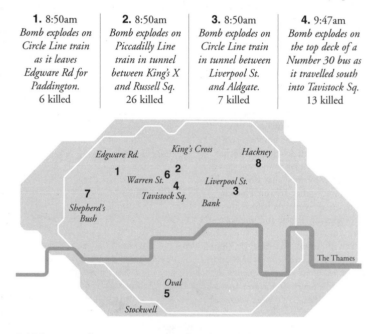

Initial reports of power surges across the Underground were quickly revised as it transpired that London had suffered an organised terrorist attack. Within hours of the bombs, the Tube and bus networks were shut; swathes of London were sealed off; armed police patrolled outside Buckingham Palace; the FTSE fell 200pts; and London turned to the media for any news. The G8 leaders in Gleneagles declared a unanimous resolve to withstand the threat of terror, and Tony Blair flew back to London by military helicopter. The emergency services put into action their much-rehearsed 'major incident' plans, and London's hospitals began to fill with the many wounded. Underground, the grim and dangerous task commenced of extracting the dead from tunnels up to 70' deep; above ground, desperate searches began for the many missing. As the days passed, London reacted with stoicism to 7/7 – hardened perhaps by a long history of terrorism, and an acceptance that attacks on the capital were almost inevitable.

> *This was not a terrorist attack against the mighty and the powerful. It was not aimed at presidents or prime ministers. It was aimed at ordinary working-class Londoners, black and white, Muslim and Christian, Hindu and Jew, young and old.*
> — KEN LIVINGSTONE

—————— LONDON BOMBINGS · 7/7 & 21/7 cont. ——————

Early speculation that the attacks 'bore the hallmarks' of Al-Qaeda intensified as a number of 'Islamic' terrorist groups claimed responsibility on the internet. However, there was widespread shock when, on 12 July, the police revealed that each of the four explosions was detonated by a British-born 'suicide bomber':

1. Mohammad	**2.** Germaine	**3.** Shehzad	**4.** Hasib Mir
Sidique Khan, 30	Lindsay, 19	Tanweer, 22	Hussain, 18
from Dewsbury	*from Aylesbury*	*from Leeds*	*from Leeds*

The scale of the security operation, which saw police raids on dozens of addresses across the country, was matched by an unprecedented political and religious condemnation of the first suicide attacks on British soil. On 14 July, a two-minute silence was held in memory of the victims. Three days later, a CCTV image was released showing the bombers setting off to London from Luton station – all four were carrying rucksacks. On 18 July, the British Muslim Council issued a 'fatwa' condemning violence and suicide attacks to be read at Mosques that Friday, and Pakistan confirmed that three of the bombers had visited the country in 2004. ❦ Two weeks after 7/7, on Thursday 21 July 2005, four more bombs hit London's transport network. As before, they were spread across the capital and, as before, three were on Tubes, and one was on a bus. All four failed to detonate properly:

5. *c.*12:30pm	**6.** *c.*12:30pm	**7.** *c.*12:30pm	**8.** *c.*1:05pm
report of attempted	*report of attempted*	*report of attempted*	*report of attempted*
explosion on	*explosion on*	*explosion on Ham.*	*explosion on No.*
Northern Line	*Victoria Line tube*	*& City Line tube*	*26 bus travelling*
tube near Oval.	*near Warren St.*	*near Shepherd's B.*	*down Hackney Rd.*

Although no one was injured in the 21/7 attacks, the police claimed that the devices were designed to kill, and the assumption was that four suicide bombers were at large. Britain's largest ever manhunt was launched and in the following days dozens of addresses were raided and arrests made. On 22 July, the police shot dead 27-year-old Brazilian Jean Charles de Menezes in Stockwell tube, only later to admit that he was not linked to terrorism [see p.11]. On 24 July, a device similar to those used on 21/7 was found on Wormwood Scrubs, leading to speculation about a fifth bomber. On 28 July, a week after 21/7, police were on high alert to deter further attacks and reassure commuters. The next day, the police announced that all of the suspected bombers were in custody. Four had been arrested in London and Birmingham, and a fifth had been held in Rome after his movements across Europe were tracked via his mobile phone. At the time of writing, 14 of the 39 detained under the Terrorism Act had been charged, and one suspect was facing extradition from Italy. ❦ In the wake of the bombs, the pressure intensified on Muslim communities, and reports of attacks against those perceived as Muslims soared. Equally under pressure was the Government, whose policy in Iraq was seen by some as a catalyst for the attacks – despite Tony Blair's vehement denials. On 1 September, a video was aired of Mohammad Sidique Khan 'explaining' his act: *'We are at war and I am a soldier. Now you too will taste the reality of this situation.'*

Schott's Almanac 2006

IRAQ BODY COUNT

For obvious political and practical reasons, figures relating to civilian casualties in Iraq are hotly contested. A report, published in October 2004 in the respected medical journal *The Lancet*, claimed that 98,000 was the 'most likely' figure for Iraqi civilians killed as a result of the US-led invasion. The report also claimed that the risk of violent death for civilians in Iraq was 58 times higher than before the war. The British and American governments were critical of *The Lancet*'s report – citing instead Iraqi Ministry of Health figures for July–December 2004:

Terrorist acts 1,233 killed; 4,115 injured · *Military acts* 2,041 killed; 8,542 injured

The main obstacle to finding conclusive data is that neither British nor US forces calculate civilian deaths (or, if they do, decline to publish the figures). The Foreign Office states there is no obligation under the Geneva Convention to keep a tally of civilian casualties, and General Tommy Franks is quoted as saying 'we don't do body counts'. Filling this vacuum of official data are many independent organisations who piece together casualty figures from military and press reports. One of these is Iraq Body Count [IBC], a group of academics and peace activists who published in July 2005 a detailed *Dossier of Civilian Casualties 2003–05*. Figures from this report are cited below. However, as IBC itself notes: 'any parties to this conflict will have an interest in manipulating casualty figures for political ends. There is no such thing (and will probably never be such a thing) as a "wholly accurate" figure, which could accepted as historical truth by all parties'.

Category	killed	% of total
US-led forces alone	9,270	37·3
Anti-occupation forces alone	2,353	9·5
Both US-led and anti-occupation forces involved	623	2·5
Iraqi Ministry of Health-defined 'military actions'	635	2·5
Iraqi Ministry of Health-defined 'terrorist attacks'	318	1·3
Predominantly criminal killings	8,935	35·9
Unknown agents	2,731	11·0
TOTAL CIVILIAN DEATHS (2003–05)	24,865	100%

Of these 24,865 civilians killed, the IBC provide age and gender data for 13,811:

Babies	51	0·4%	Adult women	1,198	8·7%
Children	1,281	9·3%	Adult men	11,281	81·7%

Figures relating to the number of Coalition military personnel killed in Iraq are easier to find, since many Coalition military authorities publish running totals:

US	1,896	Bulgaria	13	Estonia	2	*figures at*
UK	96	Spain	11	Netherlands	2	13 September 2005
Italy	27	Slovakia	3	Denmark	1	Sources:
Ukraine	18	El Salvador	2	Hungary	1	icasualties.org;
Poland	17	Thailand	2	Kazakhstan	1	UK & US forces

HURRICANE KATRINA · 2005

Hurricane Katrina formed from a tropical wave off W. Africa. She became a tropical depression 175 miles SE of Nassau on 23 August, and a tropical storm the next day [see p.66]. *On 25 August, Katrina hit Miami as a Category 1 hurricane, and swept across Florida. Crossing into the Gulf of Mexico, Katrina rapidly acquired strength and was classed as 'catastrophic' Cat. 5 on 28 August. That day, wind speeds of 175mph were recorded and the air pressure fell to 902mb, the 4th lowest on record. On 29 August, at 6·10am, Katrina made landfall in Louisiana with Cat. 4 winds of 140mph. Four hours later she hit the Louisiana/Mississippi border with Cat. 3 winds of 125mph.*

As the storms hit Louisiana those who had not fled sought shelter where they could. On 30 August, it became clear that the system of levees that protected New Orleans from the Mississippi River on one side and Lake Pontchartrain on the other had been breached; within hours, *c.*80% of the city was under several feet of water. As the administration of New Orleans was evacuated, and reports emerged of looting, assault, carjacking, murder, and rape, President Bush returned to Washington from his holiday. On 31 August, as attempts to plug gaps in the levee failed, a public health emergency was declared. Conditions deteriorated in the Superdome and Convention Centre, where *c.*25,000 were sheltering, and many were left for days in vile conditions with little water, food, or medicine. On 1 September, Mayor Ray Nagin issued 'a desperate SOS' as parts of New Orleans sunk into anarchy and 'urban warfare'. In the days that followed, the devastation Katrina wrought became clearer – as did the failures of State and Federal agencies. President Bush called the relief efforts 'not acceptable', and said 'citizens simply are not getting the help they need'. After a delay of several days, thousands of troops were drafted in to enforce martial law and to aid humanitarian missions, and the largest airlift

in US history began. ❧ The rest of America and the world looked on with astonishment, as the superpower that so easily extended its influence across the globe proved unable to cope with a domestic natural disaster that had for many years been so accurately predicted. For several days Federal authorities misjudged the scale of the disaster which, at *c.*90,000 sq. miles, was roughly the size of Britain. Many noted that while many rich (white) residents of New Orleans had escaped before the storm, the majority of those left to fend for themselves were the (black) poor who had no transport and little money. Some were critical that American 'Homeland Security' seemed focused more on foreign terror than domestic threats, and that cuts in Federal funding for hurricane defences were linked to the costly 'war on terror' in Iraq. ❧ At the time of writing, the full scale and long-term effects of Katrina are not known. The death toll looks likely to be several thousands; at least 1m are displaced in other States; many hundreds of thousands have lost belongings, property, and jobs; and the rebuilding of lives and cities looks likely to take years. Katrina's wider impact on the economy, America's attitude towards the environment, the fortunes of President Bush, and the American psyche are equally unclear.

─────── US HOMELAND SECURITY, BIKINI, & JTAC ───────

In response to the terrorist outrages of 11 September 2001, President George W. Bush created the Department of Homeland Security to 'anticipate, pre-empt and deter' terrorist and other threats. The Department employs a five-point, colour-coded Security Advisory System to indicate the perceived level of risk – the higher the 'threat condition' the greater the risk of an attack in probability and severity:

Threat	*Colour*	GUARDED..........Blue	HIGH............Orange
LOW ....Green		ELEVATED........Yellow	SEVERE.............Red

The threat condition was established at YELLOW; since then its changes have been:

Period	*shift*	*cause*
10·09·02–24·09·02	yellow–orange	*1st anniversary of the 11 September attacks*
07·02·03–27·02·03	yellow–orange	*the time of the Muslim Hajj*
17·03·03–16·04·03	yellow–orange	*start of allied military attacks on Iraq*
20·05·03–30·05·03	yellow–orange	*intelligence reports of potential attacks*
21·12·03–09·01·04	yellow–orange	*intelligence reports of holiday season attacks*
01·08·04–10·11·04	yellow–orange	*specific warning for East coast financial areas*
07·07·05–12·08·05	yellow–orange	*specific mass-transit warning after London bombs*

There is no equivalent *public* security status in Britain, though British forces across the world and some Government departments use the Bikini status to indicate the perceived level of terrorist threat at specific locations. The Bikini alert states are:

WHITE .... *no specific threat; the minimum security given the potential risks*
BLACK......................... *possibility of an attack with no defined target or time*
BLACK SPECIAL ..... *increased likelihood of an attack with no defined target or time*
AMBER......................... *substantial threat to a target within a specified period*
RED......... *imminent attack on a specific target or area (e.g. a suspect device found)*

In 2003, the Joint Terrorism Analysis Centre (JTAC) was established, with members of various bodies (MI5, MI6, GCHQ, &c), to assess intelligence relating to terrorism and produce threat assessments. Although unconfirmed, it seems that Government departments and agencies have adopted JTAC's seven-step risk status:

Negligible · Low · Moderate · Substantial · Severe General · Severe Defined · Critical

The London Underground has two alerts: *Code Amber* where trains are driven to the next station before passengers are 'de-trained'; and *Code Red* where the entire network is shut down and passengers are evacuated from tunnels. Most countries have some form of security alert status, although many, like Britain, choose not to make the status public. France uses the *Plan Vigipirate* – four colour-coded steps (*Jaune; Orange; Rouge; Ecarlate*), each signalling a greater degree of threat. In the wake of the London bombings (as with 9/11), alert statuses escalated around the world. France went from *Orange* to *Rouge*; and Britain, it is claimed, moved from a recently relaxed position of *Substantial* to its highest ever status of *Severe Defined*.

—PROFILE: PRESIDENT NIYAZOV OF TURKMENISTAN—

In 2005, President (for life) Niyazov of Turkmenistan extended his personality cult by ordering the construction of a vast zoo to hold 300 species of birds and animals (including penguins) in the Kara Kum desert. This is not Niyazov's first major project. In 2000, he announced that a 2,000 km² artificial lake was to be built in the desert, and in mid-2004 he demanded a giant ice-palace be erected in the mountains, despite average temperatures of 30°C. ❦ Turkmenistan is a landlocked republic (independent from Russia since 1991), about twice the size of the UK, with a population of *c.*5m. It shares borders with Uzbekistan, Kazakhstan, Iran, and Afghanistan, and adjoins the Caspian Sea. Much of the country is arid (*c.*80% desert) and, apart from cotton, the country's most important resources are oil and gas. ❦ In 1990, Saparmurat Niyazov was elected President, and in 1999 he declared himself President for life. Since then, Niyazov has ruled with an unusual ruthlessness. A number of human rights groups have condemned the exercise of imprisonment, exile, and a capricious use of authority. In 2000, for example, the fine for smoking in state buildings equalled a month's wages, and in 2002 the army was placed in charge of the traffic police. (In 2003, unpaid traffic fines doubled every 12 hours, and after 3 days men were sent to collect the money in person.) Religious tolerance is non-existent, opposition parties are illegal, and the media are strictly controlled – to the point of re-censoring official Russian broadcasts.

President Niyazov

I am attempting to have a logical kind of freedom ... otherwise freedom will turn into irregularity and destroy the essential of the state

❦ Although his official biography claims Niyazov is 'a lover of poetry, philosophy, history and music', in 2001 he banned opera and ballet calling them 'unnecessary', and prohibited theatre stating that it had 'exhausted its creative life'. He has similarly banned car radios, outlawed gold fillings, forbidden young men from having long hair or beards, and limited ownership of cats and dogs. ❦ In 2001, he published the *Ruhnama* – a moral and spiritual guide – 'written with the help of inspiration sent to my heart by God'. The *Ruhnama* is afforded respect equal to the Koran, and is required reading for all those taking the driving test. ❦ In 2002, Niyazov renamed the days of the week and the months of year, naming January after himself, and April after his mother. The President also redefined the stages of life, decreeing, for example, that adolescence ends at 25. The cities of Turkmenistan are awash with portraits and statues of the President (and his mother), including the 12-metre Arch of Neutrality, and a giant gold-leaf statue of Niyazov that revolves through 360 degrees every 24 hours. ❦ In 2004, 15,000 medical staff were replaced with army conscripts, and in 2005 Niyazov closed all hospitals outside the capital. A few months later, he banned recorded music from being played on television and at all public events, including weddings. ❦ Niyazov has regularly hinted that Presidential elections might be held in 2008 (or in 2010, when he turns 70), stating 'one man cannot remain President forever'.

─────── OTHER MAJOR STORIES IN BRIEF ───────

Sudan Peace Accord

On 10 January 2005, a peace deal was signed between the Sudanese government and southern rebels, led by John Garang. This supposedly ended a 21-year civil war between the Muslim north and the animist and Christian south, that has claimed >1·5m lives. The deal set terms for sharing jobs and oil wealth, and gave the south autonomy for six years, from July 2005, after which a referendum would decide secession. Despite early optimism, the deal was placed in doubt in August when Garang, newly appointed Vice-President of Sudan, died in a helicopter crash, and >130 were killed in the rioting that ensued. Garang's replacement, Salva Kiir, pledged to abide by the peace deal, but tension in the region, not least over lucrative oil deals, remains high. The effect of the peace deal on the crisis in the western Darfur region is also unclear. Since 2003, >180,000 have died and >2m have been displaced in fighting between black Africans in Darfur and the Arab Janjaweed militia, who seem to be backed by government forces. It has been suggested that the January peace deal might presage a similar deal for a form of autonomy in Darfur.

Iran's Nuclear Programme

Iran's longstanding game of cat and mouse with the international community over its nuclear programme grew tenser when Mahmoud Ahmadinejad won Iran's Presidential elections in June 2005. Then, Ahmadinejad called Iran's search for nuclear power 'irreversible'; speaking to the UN General Assembly in September, he said Iran had an 'inalienable right' to seek nuclear power, and that the country's religious principles prohibited it from seeking nuclear weapons. However, he warned that if Iran was threatened with sanctions or invasion, it would 'reconsider [its] entire approach to the nuclear issue'. The US and the EU, fearing Iran does seek nuclear bombs, is engaged in negotiation and coercion. Many are watching America's stance in particular in light of its 'axis of evil' and 'outposts of tyranny' statements [see p.60]. At the time of writing the International Atomic Energy Agency [IAEA] had adopted a resolution to report Iran to the UN Security Council, which can impose sanctions.

Niger Food Crisis

In November 2004, after a severe drought and swarms of locusts had ruined Niger's August harvest, the UN appealed for aid – few pledges were forthcoming. By February 2005, many had run low on food, especially in the southern regions of Zonder and Maradi [see p.80], and the World Food Programme [WFP] launched an operation to feed 0·5m. In May, a UN appeal for $16m went largely unanswered, and Niger's leaders dismissed calls from their own people for food. In the months that followed, the WFP warned that 2·5m (c.25% of the population), including 32,000 children, urgently required food and medicine. In response, Niger's President Tandja admitted that his country was experiencing a 'food crisis', but denied as 'false propaganda' and 'deception' reports of severe malnutrition. Niger's crisis has highlighted wider fears of 'compassion fatigue', exacerbated by the 2004 tsunami. In August, when an $88m UN appeal to prevent famine in Africa received no pledges after ten days, the UN's humanitarian chief, Jan Egeland, noted 'it seems we are losing

——————— OTHER MAJOR STORIES IN BRIEF cont. ———————

the battle for the world's attention to help these vulnerable people'.

End to the IRA's Armed Campaign
On 28 July 2005, the IRA announced an end to their armed struggle. A statement, signed by P. O'Neill [see p.152], declared: '...*All IRA units have been ordered to dump arms. All volunteers have been instructed to assist the development of purely political and democratic programmes through exclusively peaceful means. Volunteers must not engage in any other activities whatsoever ...We believe there is now an alternative way to achieve this and to end British rule in our country ... We reiterate our view that the armed struggle was entirely legitimate ...*' The statement was met with optimism tempered by the knowledge that similar pledges had been made in the past. As the Irish PM Bertie Ahern said, 'if the IRA's words are borne out by verified actions, it will be a ... historic development'. As a sign of good faith, the army dismantled observation posts in South Armagh, and the British Government outlined plans to scale-down their military presence.

Israel's Withdrawal from Gaza
On 11 September 2005, Israeli forces completed their unilateral withdrawal from the Gaza Strip, ending 38 years of military occupation. Ariel Sharon's abandonment and destruction of the Gaza settlements was met with vocal resistance from many of the Jewish residents; and the withdrawal was delayed by a court ruling that stopped Israeli troops from destroying 26 deconsecrated synagogues. Palestinian leaders described the move as a liberation. However, Israel has kept control over Gaza's borders, airspace, and seaspace. And, Sharon has stepped up

the building of settlements in the West Bank – along with the controversial 'security fence'. At the time of writing, the security situation in Gaza was tense after an escalation of violence between Palestinian and Israeli forces.

Japanese Elections
On 11 September 2005, Japan's PM, Junichiro Koizumi, won a landslide victory in the lower house elections, after calling a snap ballot. Koizumi went to the polls when his proposals to privatise Japan's post office were blocked by rebels from his own party in the upper house. (The post office is a key element in Japan's economy, and manages the savings of *c.*85% of the population.) By hand-picking 'assassin' candidates to target rebels, Koizumi secured a two-thirds majority, and a strong mandate for reforms – though he is due to step down as PM in 2006.

German Elections
On 18 September 2005, months earlier than planned, Chancellor Schroeder took Germany to the polls in an attempt to galvanise support for the reforms of his Social Democratic Party [SPD]. For most of the campaign Angela Merkel's Christian Democratic Union [CDU] looked set to win. With unemployment >11%, and discontent over the speed of reform, opinion polls predicted Germany would vote for change and a move to the Right. Yet, a fierce campaign saw Schroeder's enthusiasm rewarded over Merkel's bluntness; and, although the CDU won 3 more seats than the SPD, it was not enough to secure victory. At the time of writing, both Schroeder and Merkel claimed the mantle of Chancellor, and intense negotiations were underway to see which party could form a coalition.

————————— CHAMPIONS LEAGUE FINAL —————————

25 May 2005 · Atatürk Stadium, Istanbul · Attendance: 65,000
LIVERPOOL 3–3 AC MILAN (AET)
1st ½: Maldini '1; Crespo '39, '44 · 2nd ½: Gerrard '54; Smicer '56; Alonso '59

LIVERPOOL WON 3–2 ON PENALTIES

At 3–0 at half-time it looked to be all over for Liverpool, but an inspired fight-back, led by captain Steven Gerrard, saw the Reds win their fifth European Cup.

AC Milan: Dida; Cafu, Stam, Nesta, Maldini; Seedorf (Serginho 86), Gattuso (Rui Costa 112), Pirlo, Kaká; Crespo (Tomasson 86), Shevchenko

Liverpool: Dudek; Finnan (Hamann 46), Hyypia, Carragher, Traoré; García, Alonso, Gerrard, Riise; Baros (Cissé 84), Kewell (Smicer 23)

	1st Half		2nd Half		extra time	
Team	ACM	LFC	ACM	LFC	ACM	LFC
Possession	50%	50%	50%	50%	64%	36%
Goals	3	0	0	3	0	0
Shots on target	4	1	3	5	3	1
Shots off target	3	3	5	3	3	0
Blocked shots	2	1	2	0	0	2
Corners	2	1	5	1	3	2
Passes	249	254	238	236	198	109
Successful passes	78%	78%	79%	81%	82%	69%
Crosses	6	11	9	7	19	4
Successful crosses	67%	27%	22%	29%	21%	25%
Tackles	31	34	17	31	3	17
Successful tackles	61%	29%	76%	55%	33%	59%
Fouls	8	7	4	10	4	6
Offsides	5	1	0	3	2	2
Cards	0	0	2Y	0	0	0

*We were massive underdogs at the beginning of the competition and I'll
put my hands up and say I didn't think we were going to go all the way.
But, as you can see, we are never beaten.* — STEVEN GERRARD

THE PENALTY SHOOT-OUT

Serginho shoots high and wide.... 0–0
Hamann scores..................... 0–1
Dudek saves Pirlo's shot 0–1
Cissé scores....................... 0–2
Tomasson scores 1–2
Dida saves Riise's shot 1–2
Kaká scores........................ 2–2
Smicer scores...................... 2–3
Dudek saves Shevchenko's shot ... 2–3

THE 2005 ASHES

1st Test · Lord's
21–24 July 2005
Australia won the toss

Australia	190 all out
England	155 all out
Australia	384 all out
England	180 all out

Australia won by 239 runs

MOTM · G. McGrath

England's crushing defeat looked likely to set the tone for an Ashes humiliation. Despite an impressive first two sessions from England, Australia fought back with fierce determination. Seven dropped catches did not help England's cause, nor did McGrath's haul of 9 for 82. When, on the last day, England lost their last 5 wickets for 22, it seemed that an English victory against the Aussies at Lord's was as far away as ever.

2nd Test · Edgbaston
4–7 August 2005
Australia won the toss

England	407 all out
Australia	308 all out
England	182 all out
Australia	279 all out

England won by 2 runs

MOTM · A. Flintoff

Widely acclaimed as one of the greatest Tests, England fought tenaciously to see off a spirited tail-end of Warne, Lee, and Kasprowicz. The Aussies were hampered by McGrath's absence after he twisted his ankle on a stray cricket ball during a pre-match warm-up – but the tight bowling of Flintoff, Giles, and Harmison won through. The Test brought back memories of Botham's performance in 1981, and revived English hopes.

3rd Test · Old Trafford
11–15 August 2005
England won the toss

England	444 all out
Australia	302 all out
England	280 for 6 dec
Australia	371 for 9

Match drawn

MOTM · R. Ponting

A captain's innings from Ponting, and a strong last wicket stand from Lee and McGrath, saw Australia face down England's bowlers to secure a draw. At times on the last day it seemed the result could have gone any of three ways. The tension reached fever-pitch during the final overs, as Flintoff and Harmison failed to get the decisive wicket despite a seven man slip cordon. With the series 1–1, all eyes turned to Trent Bridge.

4th Test · Trent Bridge
25–28 August 2005
England won the toss

England	477 all out
Australia	218 all out
Australia (f-o)	387 all out
England	129 for 7

England won by 3 wickets

MOTM · A. Flintoff

After a solid first innings, featuring 102 from Flintoff, text-book reverse swing from S. Jones forced the Aussies to follow-on for the first time since 1988. Set just 129 to win, England looked wobbly at 57–4 and 116–7. Against the bowling of Warne and Lee, it seemed possible that England might not scrape the runs needed in the final nail-biting overs. However, England finally secured their first lead in an Ashes series since 1997.

5th Test · The Oval
8–12 September 2005
England won the toss

England	373 all out
Australia	367 all out
England	335 all out
Australia	4 for 0

Match drawn

MOTM · K. Pietersen

MOTS · Flintoff & Warne

The final Test proved a fitting end to an epic Ashes series. The first four days saw star performances from Hayden, Strauss, Warne, & Flintoff. For a time on the final day (with England on 67–3) the Aussies had a slim chance; but a bold 158 from Pietersen left Australia the goal of 342 off 18 in fading light. After a few balls the bails were removed, and the Ashes returned to England for the first time in 18 years.

—— OBJECT OF THE YEAR: THE CAMERA PHONE ——

On 20 January 2005, as George W. Bush was sworn in, Colin Powell used his mobile to take souvenir snaps of the President. In April, thousands of mourners took photos of John Paul II's coffin with camera phones held high above their heads. In the same month Prince Charles banned all mobile phones from his wedding, and Saudi Arabia proposed 1,000 lashes, 12 years in jail and a fine of SR100,000 for those who use camera phones for 'immoral' acts. Just hours after the London 7/7 bombings, grainy camera phone footage emerged of commuters escaping down smoke-filled tunnels. ❦ The rise of the camera phone has been rapid and stealthy. In 2002, 4% of mobiles sold had cameras; by 2004 it was 38%. *Strategy Analytics* predicts that by 2010 the figure will be 78%; already in Japan 97% of mobiles have cameras. When camera phones were introduced, many claimed they had no need of such a facility. Yet it seems that easy access to a technology can sometimes simply create a demand. Increasingly, mobiles are being sold as dual-purpose alternatives to digital cameras. ❦ Already, camera phones have revolutionised news photography. Nearly all of the iconic news photos of the C20th were taken by professional photographers using professional equipment: from the liberation of Buchenwald, to the lone protester in front of the tanks in Tiananmen Square. Towards the end of the C20th, other image sources entered the news: from the amateur video footage of Rodney King's assault, to the haunting CCTV images of Jamie Bulger being led to his death. However, the news photographs that have already defined the early years of the C21st have nearly all been taken by amateurs using digital cameras and camera phones: the outrages in Abhu Ghraib prison; Prince Harry in Nazi regalia; Saddam Hussein in his underwear; the horror of the London bombings, and so on. Camera phones are the ultimate tool of photojournalism – combining a compact and discreet means of taking pictures with a simple method of immediately transmitting them anywhere in the world. It is only a matter of time before the remaining issues of picture quality and image size are solved by improvements in lens and software design. ❦ The ubiquity of camera phones is not without its problems. Schools, health clubs, swimming pools and strip joints have all joined Prince Charles in banning the devices fearing breaches of privacy. A more disturbing trend is the use of camera phones to record footage of bullying, violent assaults (so-called 'happy slapping'), and even (in at least one case to date) rape. The victims of such attacks suffer the added violence of knowing that their abuse can be texted or emailed as 'entertainment'. And, as demonstrated by the execution of Ken Bigley and others in Iraq, it seems inevitable that more terrorists, kidnappers and other criminals will seek to exploit new imaging technology like camera phones – either posting images of their acts on the net, or blackmailing the media into broadcasting their pictures. ❦ Just as internet Blogs are increasingly blurring the distinction between amateur and professional journalism, it seems inevitable that camera phones will 'democratise' the news images the world sees – for good as well as ill.

—SCHEMATIC · SOME WORLD EVENTS OF NOTE · 2005—

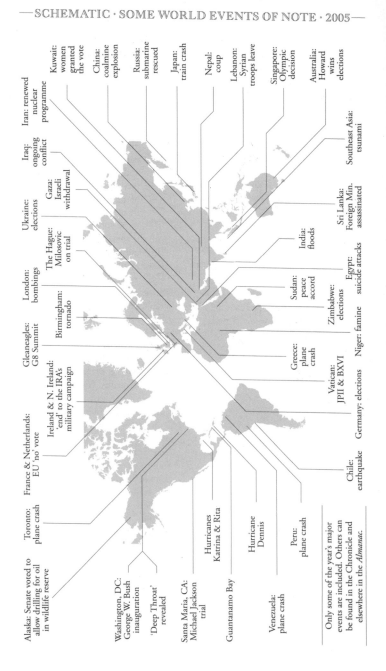

Kuwait: women granted the vote

China: coalmine explosion

Russia: submarine rescued

Japan: train crash

Nepal: coup

Lebanon: Syrian troops leave

Singapore: Olympic decision

Australia: Howard wins elections

Iran: renewed nuclear programme

Iraq: ongoing conflict

Gaza: Israeli withdrawal

Ukraine: elections

The Hague: Milosovic on trial

London: bombings

Birmingham: tornado

Gleneagles: G8 Summit

Ireland & N. Ireland: 'end' to the IRA's military campaign

France & Netherlands: EU 'no' vote

Toronto: plane crash

Southeast Asia: tsunami

Sri Lanka: Foreign Min. assassinated

India: floods

Egypt: suicide attacks

Sudan: peace accord

Zimbabwe: elections

Niger: famine

Greece: plane crash

Vatican: JPII & BXVI

Germany: elections

Chile: earthquake

Alaska: Senate voted to allow drilling for oil in wildlife reserve

Washington, DC: George W. Bush inauguration

'Deep Throat' revealed

Santa Maria, CA: Michael Jackson trial

Hurricanes Katrina & Rita

Guantanamo Bay

Hurricane Dennis

Venezuela: plane crash

Peru: plane crash

Only some of the year's major events are included. Others can be found in the Chronicle and elsewhere in the *Almanac.*

IN BRIEF · OCTOBER 2004

OCTOBER · {1st} Tony Blair recovered after a minor heart operation and stated he would stand down during his next term. ❦ At the Hartlepool by-election Labour's lead was slashed; the Tories came 4th. {3} The Tory party conference opened in Bournemouth. {4} John Lennon's murderer, Mark Chapman, was denied parole for the 3rd time. {5} The Iraq Survey Group concluded that Iraq had no Weapons of Mass Destruction [WMD]. {7} >30 were killed and >100 wounded after Egyptian tourist sites were bombed (it was thought by Al-Qaeda). {8} Ken Bigley was beheaded by Tawhid and Jihad terrorists, having been held hostage since 16 September. {9} Elections were held in Afghanistan, amidst rumours of irregularities. ❦ Australian electors returned John Howard for a 4th term. {12} A report by Adair Turner warned of a looming pensions crisis; he claimed >12m were 'not saving enough'. ❦ Foreign Sec. Jack Straw withdrew the '45 minute' WMD claim; pressure mounted on Blair to apologise. {14} Allegations that Prince Harry cheated in his art A-level exam rumbled on. {16} Boris Johnson, Tory MP and Editor of the *Spectator*, was ordered by Michael Howard to apologise to Liverpudlians for a *Spectator* editorial that claimed they had a 'flawed psychological state' and over-reacted to the 1989 Hillsborough disaster and the death of Ken Bigley. {17} The Zimbabwe Cricket Union was cleared of racism by the International Cricket Council.

Ken Bigley

We were trying to make a point about sentimentality.
– BORIS JOHNSON

{19} 'Radical Muslim' cleric Abu Hamza al-Masri was charged with 16 offences, including soliciting to murder. ❦ Margaret Hassan, a charity worker with dual English-Iraqi nationality, was kidnapped in Iraq. ❦ Alan Hollinghurst won the 2004 Booker Prize for *The Line of Beauty* [see p.152]. {20} Paul 'Gazza' Gascoigne announced his intention to change his name to 'G8'. ❦ Typhoon Tokage hit Japan killing >50. {21} Prince Harry scuffled with press photographers outside the London nightclub Pangaea. ❦ Geoff Hoon confirmed the redeployment of *c.*850 Black Watch troops to central Iraq, after a request from the USA. {22} Al-Jazeera released footage of Hassan begging for her life and urging British withdrawal from Iraq. {23} Car bombs in Iraq killed >20. ❦ A 6·8 Richter earthquake in north Japan killed >30. {25} RIP @ 65, legendary Radio 1 DJ John Peel. ❦ 5 men were convicted of sex attacks on the Pacific island of Pitcairn (total population 47). {26} Mark Thatcher appeared in a Cape Town court for questioning over a suspected Equatorial Guinea coup plot. {27} Yasser Arafat was reported to be seriously ill. {28} 9 Britons on a pilgrimage tour of Jordan were killed in a bus crash. {29} Al-Jazeera aired a video of Bin Laden admitting responsibility for 9/11. ❦ EU leaders signed the proposed new EU constitution in Rome [see p.265]. {31} Rockets were fired on a Black Watch camp south of Baghdad. ❦ Al-Jazeera broadcast a film of 3 UN workers held hostage and begging for their

───── IN BRIEF · OCTOBER – NOVEMBER 2004 ─────

lives. ❦ RIP @ 34, Staff Sgt Denise Rose – the first British female soldier to die in the Iraq conflict.

NOVEMBER · {1} RIP @ 82, businessman Lord James Hanson. ❦ 29 Labour MPs rebelled against the Government's Gambling Bill. {2} US Presidential elections held. ❦ 47-year-old Dutch director Theo van Gogh, who made a controversial film about Islamic culture, was brutally murdered in an Amsterdam street. {3} George W. Bush decisively won a 2nd Presidential term. {4} 3 Black Watch soldiers and a civilian translator were killed in a suicide attack in Iraq. {6} 7 died when the 17:35 *First Great Western* Paddington–Plymouth service hit a car on the line near Ufton Nervet, Berkshire. {8} US and Iraqi troops launched an assault on Falluja. {10} The Scottish Executive announced its intention to ban smoking in public places from Spring 2006. ❦ The US Attorney General John Ashcroft resigned. {11} RIP @ 82, Yasser Arafat, chairman of the Palestine Liberation Organisation. ❦ UK nationals fled the Ivory Coast as the civil war intensified. {12} Arafat was buried in Ramallah. ❦ John Peel was buried in Bury St Edmunds. {13} Michael Howard sacked Boris Johnson over continuing turmoil in his private life. {15} US Sec. State Colin Powell announced his resignation. {16} Condoleezza Rice was announced as next US Sec. State. ❦ Reports surfaced that Margaret Hassan had been murdered. {18} The Parliament Act

Condoleezza Rice

was invoked to force through the ban on hunting with hounds that was due to come into force in February 2005. {19} Pro-hunt campaigners mounted a legal challenge to the use of the Parliament Act. {21} The first day of the new series of *I'm a Celebrity, Get Me Out of Here!* [see p.108]. ❦ Presidential elections were held in Ukraine. {22} Electrical retailer Dixons announced that it would cease to sell analogue video players. ❦ Iran announced it would cease uranium enrichment. {23} The 3 UN workers taken hostage in October were released. ❦ In parts of Ukraine people took to the streets to protest over the result of the Presidential election. ❦ The State Opening of Parliament and the Queen's Speech. {24} Pro-opposition crowds continued to demonstrate in Kiev. {25} English cricketers flew from S. Africa to Zimbabwe after Mugabe lifted a ban on British journalists. {26} Bush offered to help secure a peace agreement in N. Ireland. {28} A gas explosion in Chenjiashan coal mine, China, killed >25. ❦ The Home Sec. David Blunkett was forced to set up an inquiry in response to allegations that he misused his position to help fast-track a visa for the nanny of

It has been my great honour and privilege to serve my nation.
– COLIN POWELL

his ex-lover, Kimberly Quinn. ❦ The Swiss voted to allow stem-cell research on surplus human embryos. {29} The 2004 version of *Do They Know It's Christmas?* went on sale. ❦ Sudan expelled the directors of *Save the Children* and *Oxfam* claiming that they made political comments about the situation in Darfur. {30} The Armed

——————— IN BRIEF · NOVEMBER – DECEMBER 2004 ———————

Forces Minister Adam Ingram announced an independent review into the alleged abuse at the Deepcut army barracks. ❦ The multi-Olympic Gold medal winning rower Matthew Pinsent announced his retirement.

DECEMBER · {1} The parliament in Ukraine passed a vote of no confidence in the government. ❦ Blunkett continued to protest his innocence in what had become called 'Nanny-Gate'. ❦ Israeli PM Ariel Sharon's coalition government was thrown into turmoil when secular parties voted against his budget. {2} George Galloway won his libel case against *The Daily Telegraph* over claims that he had received money from Saddam Hussein's regime. ❦ Gordon Brown delivered his Pre-budget Report. ❦ {3} The Ukrainian Supreme Court ruled the recent Presidential elections fraudulent, and ordered a new poll for 26 December. ❦ A protester covered controversial politician Robert Kilroy-Silk with slurry. ❦ Blunkett won the first round of a court battle to gain access to a child of Quinn that Blunkett claimed was his. {4} The Metropolitan Police Commissioner Sir John Stevens argued that householders should be able to use appropriate force to defend themselves against burglars. {5} President of Pakistan, Pervez Musharraf, admitted that Bin Laden was alive, but 'we don't know where he is'. {6} Militant gunmen killed >8 in an attack on the US Consulate in Jeddah, Saudi Arabia. ❦ Jeremy Deller won the 2004 Turner Prize [see p.157]. ❦

Viktor Yuschenko

I'm just a squeaky-voiced div.
– JOE PASQUALE

Joe Pasquale won *IACGMOOH* [see p.108]. {7} The BBC announced 2,900 redundancies and a major reorganisation of its operations. {8} Pressure intensified on Blair to investigate the number of civilian Iraqi deaths [see p.20]. ❦ Power-sharing in N. Ireland stalled when the DUP demanded photographic evidence of decommissioning; the IRA rejected the demand, claiming it would be a humiliation. {11} Allegations surfaced that the Ukrainian opposition leader, Viktor Yushchenko, had been poisoned with dioxin. ❦ Steve Brookstein won *The X Factor* [see p.112]. {15} Blunkett resigned as Home Secretary; he was replaced by Charles Clarke. {17} The EU 'opened the door' to Turkish membership [see p.264]. {19} The journalist Simon Hoggart admitted to having a 'sexual relationship' with Kimberly Quinn. ❦ >60 were killed by insurgents in Iraq. {20} A controversial Bill to introduce ID cards passed its 1st parliamentary stage. {21} Sir Alan Budd's report into the Blunkett affair was published; it linked officials working for the former Home Secretary to Quinn's nanny's visa application. ❦ >£26m was stolen from a Belfast bank in the UK's largest bank raid. {23} A crazed knifeman killed 1 and injured 6 in a series of random attacks in North London. ❦ The Czech army ended conscription. {24} Donald Rumsfeld made a surprise visit to troops in Iraq. {25} The Queen called for tolerance in her Christmas broadcast [see p.273]. {26} A massive underwater earthquake off the west coast of Northern Sumatra triggered a catastrophic tsunami [see p.12]. ❦ {27} Yushchenko emerged as the new Ukrainian President; the former president, Yanukovych, alleged fraud. ❦ In the face of the imminent ban, fox hunts across Britain reported large turnouts. ❦ >13 were killed by insurgents in Iraq. {28} Russia claimed that international monitoring of the Ukrainian elections was biased. {29} Ukrainian opposition activists renewed their blockade of Yanukovych's office. {31} Yanukovych resigned as Ukrainian President, though he refused to admit defeat. ❦ The New Year's Honours List was released [see p.277].

Prince Harry

JANUARY 2005 · {1} After the Asian tsunami, New Year's celebrations were muted around the world. {2} Rail fare increases came into force. ❦ >23 were killed by insurgents in Iraq. {3} Blair returned home from holiday, amidst claims that he should have returned earlier in response to the tsunami. ❦ >20 killed in Iraq. {4} Baghdad governor Ali al-Haidri was shot dead in a roadside ambush. {5} A 3-minutes' silence for tsunami victims was observed in countries across the world. {6} Nelson Mandela revealed that his eldest son

He realises it was a poor choice of costume.
– PALACE SPOKESMEN

had died of AIDS. ❦ 3 teenagers were charged with the murder of Damilola Taylor. {7} The Chief Constable of N. Ireland blamed the IRA for the Belfast bank robbery. {8} Sally Geeson, a Cambridgeshire girl who went missing after a New Year's Eve party, was found dead. ❦ BBC2 broadcast *Jerry Springer – the Opera*, against chorus of protest

from Christian campaigners. {9} Mahmoud Abbas claimed victory in the Palestinian elections. ❦ 3 people were killed in flooding across northern Britain. {10} The Sudanese government signed a peace accord with rebels in the south [see p. 24]. {11} The Government advised under-9s not to use mobile phones [see p.98]. {12} *The Sun* printed a front-page photo of Prince Harry at a fancy-dress party wearing Nazi uniform with a swastika armband. {13} Mark Thatcher pleaded guilty to playing a part in the Equatorial Guinea coup plot; he avoided a jail sentence. {14} A US soldier, Charles Graner, was found guilty of abusing prisoners at Abu Ghraib jail; he was sentenced to 10 years. ❦ The Cassini-Huygens probe landed on Titan [see p.181]. {15} Tory MP Robert Jackson defected to Labour. {16} The Elvis song *One Night* became the 1,000th UK Number One. {17} The Archbishop of Mosul was seized by insurgents outside his church. ❦ RIP @ 85, Zhao Ziyang. {18} The new airbus A380 was unveiled. {19} Photographs of alleged abuse by British soldiers in Iraq were released during a court-martial in Germany. {20} George W. Bush was inaugurated. {22} Militant leader Abu Musab al-Zarqawi called on Sunni Muslims to fight against the Iraqi elections. {23} RIP @ 79, Johnny Carson [see p.48]. {25} The 4 remaining British prisoners held in Guantanamo Bay were flown home. {26} The British Government announced the question that would be put to the public in any future referendum on the EU constitu-

────── IN BRIEF · JANUARY – FEBRUARY 2005 ──────

tion: '*Should the UK approve the treaty establishing a constitution for the European Union?*' ❦ Condoleezza Rice was sworn in as US Secretary of State; 13 Democrats voted against her – the most 'nays' since 1825. {27} World leaders and holocaust survivors met in Poland to commemorate the 60th anniversary of the liberation of Auschwitz. ❦ The British 'Guantanamo 4' were released without charge by the UK police. {28} Pro-hunting campaigners lost their High Court challenge to overturn the hunting ban. {29} Serena Williams beat Lindsey Davenport to win the Australian Open. {30} Iraqi elections took place with a high turnout, despite 36 dead after insurgent attacks. ❦ Chris Smith MP revealed that he had been HIV-positive since 1987. ❦ Marat Safin defeated Lleyton Hewitt in the Australian Open final. ❦ Robert McCartney, 33-year-old father of two, was murdered in a Belfast pub. {31} The trial of Michael Jackson for child molestation began. ❦ 10 died after an RAF Hercules crashed in Iraq: the greatest daily loss of British life in the conflict to date.

Ellen MacArthur

State of the Union Address, and restated his goal to end tyranny worldwide. ❦ The Provisional IRA withdrew its commitment to decommission arms. ❦ Georgia's PM Zurab Zhvania was found dead from possible carbon monoxide poisoning; no foul play was suspected. {5} The majority of G7 Finance Ministers backed British plans to write-off up to 100% of the debt of the world's poorest countries; America dissented. {7} Ellen MacArthur completed her record-breaking round-the-world challenge [see p.293]. {8} Palestinian leader Mahmoud Abbas and Israeli PM Ariel Sharon agreed a truce. {9} Islamic Jihad and Hamas stated that they were not bound by the Abbas–Sharon ceasefire. ❦ An ETA car bomb injured 31 in Madrid. ❦ England drew 0–0 with Holland in a dull friendly [see p.300]. ❦ Blair issued a public apology to the 'Guildford 4' and the 'Maguire 7'. ❦ The 25th Brit Awards [see p.130]. {10} Clarence House announced the engagement of Prince Charles and Camilla Parker-Bowles. ❦ The FTSE 100 index hit 5,000 for the first time in 2 years. {12} RIP @ 79, Arthur Miller [see p.48]. {13} Shia parties won a majority of votes in the Iraqi elections. ❦ Germany marked the 60th anniversary of the Allied bombing of Dresden. {14} Aid agencies admitted that they might struggle to spend all the money donated to Tsunami relief. ❦ Protesters and hunters clashed at the last Waterloo Cup hare-coursing event before the ban was enforced. ❦ Former Lebanese PM Rafik Hariri was assassi-

FEBRUARY · {1} A UN report condemned violence in Darfur, but stopped short of naming it genocide [see p.60]. ❦ Pope John Paul II was admitted to hospital in Rome. {2} The Crown Prosecution Service clarified householders' position in protecting their homes from intruders. ❦ The King of Nepal staged a coup. ❦ Robert Kilroy-Silk launched his new political party: *Veritas*. {3} Bush gave his annual

Unlike the old parties, we shall be honest, open and straight.
– ROBERT KILROY-SILK

IN BRIEF · FEBRUARY – MARCH 2005

nated in Beirut. {15} The International Olympic Committee arrived in Britain to evaluate the London bid. ❦ >203 people died after an explosion in a Chinese coal mine in Liaoning Province. {16} The Kyoto Protocol came into force [see p.65]. {17} The last legal fox hunts were held before the ban came into force. {18} >350 products were taken off supermarket shelves after a cancer-causing dye, Sudan I, was found in many ready-made meals. [see p.179] {19} 270 hunts across England and Wales met to challenge the new hunting laws. {20} The Beckhams' new son, Cruz, was born in Spain [see p.107]. ❦ Spain voted 'yes' to the new EU constitution by 77% [see p.265]. {22} A 6·4 Richter earthquake hit Iran, killing >500. ❦ A cold snap resulted in snow across Britain, causing the usual chaos. {23} The Queen announced that she would not attend the civil wedding of Charles and Camilla. ❦ The World Health Organisation gave a strongly worded warning that avian 'flu could result in a human pandemic [see p.96]. ❦ At a court martial in Germany, 2 British soldiers were found guilty of abusing Iraqi prisoners. {24} John Paul II was re-admitted to hospital in Rome. ❦ Maxine Carr was granted lifelong anonymity. {25} US and Canadian Anglicans were asked temporarily to leave the Anglican community after their support for gay bishops. ❦ Convictions for rape in England and Wales hit an all-time low, according to Home Office figures. ❦ Suicide bombers in Tel Aviv killed >4. {27} Clint Eastwood's *Million Dollar*

Michael Jackson

He's gorgeous, healthy and his mum is very good, so we're a very happy family.
– DAVID BECKHAM

Baby won the top Oscars [see p.146]. ❦ The family of Robert McCartney held a rally in Belfast to put pressure on the IRA to reveal his murderers. {28} The opening statements were made in Michael Jackson's trial. ❦ A car bomb in the Iraqi town of Hilla killed >100. ❦ MPs renewed the Prevention of Terrorism Act after concessions by Home Sec. Charles Clarke; the Government's majority was cut to just 14.

MARCH · {1} Lebanon's pro-Syrian government resigned after protests against Syria's involvement in the country. {3} Cleric Abu Bakar Ba'asyir was found guilty by an Indonesian court of conspiring in the 2002 Bali bombings. ❦ Gerry Adams expelled 7 Sinn Féin members over their alleged involvement in the McCartney murder. ❦ Steve Fossett became the first person to fly around the world non-stop without re-fuelling. {4} Martha Stewart was released from jail. ❦ In Iraq, US troops shot an Italian hostage and killed Nicola Calipari, her secret service rescuer. {5} DNA tests showed that Blunkett was not the father of Quinn's youngest son. {6} RIP @ 63, Tommy Vance, DJ. {8} The Registrar General dismissed 11 objections to the wedding of Charles and Camilla, made by members of the public. {9} The IRA offered to kill those responsible for the murder of McCartney; the offer was rejected by his sisters. {10} RIP @ 68, Dave Allen [see p.48]. {11} Madrid commemorated the 1st anniversary of the 2004 train

— IN BRIEF · MARCH – APRIL 2005 —

bombings. ❦ Red Nose Day 2005. ❦ The Prevention of Terrorism Act was passed after 30 hours' debate in the Lords and Commons. {14} US Senator Edward Kennedy cancelled his planned meeting with Gerry Adams because of the IRA's alleged ongoing criminal activity. ❦ The Commons' Defence Select Committee report into Deepcut criticised the army's treatment of new recruits. {15} Italy announced its intention to withdraw troops from Iraq. {16} Gordon Brown presented his 9th Budget [see p.222]. ❦ The US Senate voted to allow oil companies to drill in a remote wildlife reserve in Alaska. {17} The first Victoria Cross for 23 years was awarded to Private Johnson Beharry, who twice rescued injured comrades in Iraq. {18} 4 men were found guilty of murdering 2 teenagers at a 2003 New Year's Eve party in Birmingham. {19} Wales won the Rugby Six Nations [see p.304]. {20} A Spanish national was arrested in Slough on suspicion of involvement in the Madrid bombings. {22} A schoolboy killed 9 pupils and then himself at his Minnesota high school. ❦ The BBC announced >2,000 job cuts. ❦ A 2-day-old baby died from hospital-acquired MRSA. {24} Kyrgyzstan's President Askar Akayev was deposed after protesters stormed the parliament. {25} Conservative deputy-Chairman Howard Flight was removed from the candidates' list, after hinting the Tories had hidden tax plans. {26} The new series of *Doctor Who* attracted 10·5m viewers [see p.119]. ❦ RIP @ 92, Lord Callaghan.

Jamie Oliver

> I will take no risks with the stability of the economy.
> – GORDON BROWN

{28} An 8·7 Richter earthquake hit Indonesia, killing >1,000 and sparking fears of another tsunami. ❦ The Jackson trial judge allowed allegations of past abuse to be admitted as evidence. {29} Jonathan King was released from prison. ❦ Kofi Annan was cleared of any wrong-doing by an inquiry into the Iraqi oil-for-food programme; questions remained over the involvement of his son. ❦ A special-needs teacher was jailed for six months (reduced on appeal), after shooting near 'yobs' with a pellet gun. {30} After a TV campaign by Jamie Oliver, the Government increased funding for school lunches [see p.87]. {31} A general election was held in Zimbabwe. ❦ Terry Schiavo died after 13 days with no food or water, thereby concluding a 12-year legal battle between her husband and her parents over the removal of her feeding tube.

APRIL · {1} Anonymity ended for sperm and egg donors in the UK. {2} RIP @ 84, Pope John Paul II [see p.13]. ❦ Newcastle Utd players Lee Bowyer and Kieron Dyer brawled on the pitch during a 3–0 defeat by Aston Villa. ❦ Robert Mugabe claimed victory in Zimbabwe's elections. {4} Charles and Camilla postponed their wedding so that Charles could attend the Pope's funeral. {5} Blair called a General Election for 5 May [see p.14]. ❦ RIP @ 89, Saul Bellow. {6} RIP @ 81, Prince Rainier of Monaco. {7} A *Sun* journalist breached security at Windsor Castle, days before the royal wedding, by driving into the grounds in a white van containing a box labelled 'bomb'. ❧ A man was discovered wandering the streets of Sheerness, Kent, in a water-logged suit and tie. Although mute, he was said to 'come alive' when playing the piano. He was dubbed 'Piano Man' by the press, who appealed for help in identifying him. {8} The funeral was held of John Paul II [see p.13]. ❧ Chinese investors withdrew from negotiations with MG Rover. {9} Charles and Camilla married at Windsor Guildhall. ❧ *Hedgehunter* won the 158th Grand National. ❧ RIP @ 58, Andrea Dworkin [see p.48]. {11} The Conservatives published their election manifesto that focused on immigration, cleaner hospitals, and more police. {12} Tesco became the first British company to post profits >£2bn. ❧ Charles and Sarah Kennedy announced the birth of their son, Donald James. {13} A failed asylum seeker, Kamel Bourgass, was jailed for 17 years for a ricin poison plot; he was already serving life for killing a policeman. {14} 2 suicide car bombs killed >11 in Baghdad. {15} 17 were killed and >50 injured when a fire gutted a Parisian hotel. ❧ MG Rover finally went into administration; >5,000 were made redundant. ❧ The 60th anniversary of the liberation of Nazi death-camp Belsen. {17} Paula Radcliffe won the London Marathon in a record-breaking time [see p.294]. {18} The Papal Conclave deliberations began to elect the new Pope. ❧ Littlewoods closed their *Index* catalogue business and sacked 3,200. {19} 4 were charged with the murder of

Camilla P-B

Roberto Calvi, the Italian banker found hanging from Blackfriars Bridge in 1982. ❧ Cardinal Joseph Ratzinger was elected Pope; he styled himself Pope Benedict XVI [see p.13]. {20} Italian PM Silvio Berlusconi resigned after his coalition showed signs of collapse. {21} In a seemingly random attack, Abigail Witchells was stabbed in the neck and paralysed, as she walked with her baby in Surrey. ❧ *The Sun* backed Labour for the election by pumping red smoke from its Wapping offices, in mock homage to the Papal Conclave. ❧ Spain's lower House of Parliament approved a Bill to allow homosexuals to marry and adopt children. {22} 3 went on trial in Spain accused of planning the 9/11 attacks. ❧ Failed 'shoe-bomb' terrorist Saajid Badat was jailed for 13 years by a British court. ❧ The inquest into Harold Shipman's death concluded that he committed suicide to escape prison life and secure a full pension for his wife. {25} A train derailment in Japan killed 104 and injured >450. ❧ US investigators cleared American soldiers of any wrong-doing in the shooting of an Italian secret service agent assisting an escaped Italian hostage in Iraq. {26} Veteran Labour MP Brian Sedgemore defected to the Lib Dems. ❧ The last Syrian troops left Lebanon in compliance with UN demands. {27} Abigail Witchells began communicating with police by blinking and mouthing words. ❧ The Airbus A380 successfully completed its maiden flight. {28} After a series of leaks, the Attorney-

> *The church will miss him, the world will miss him and I will miss him.*
> — CARDINAL MURPHY-O'CONNOR

——————— IN BRIEF · APRIL – MAY 2005 ———————

General's advice to Blair on the legality of the Iraq war was released on the Downing Street website. ❧ Berlusconi was returned as PM after the Italian parliament approved his new coalition. {29} Car bombs in Baghdad killed >29. {30} 10 injured in Cairo in suicide attacks by 'Islamic' militants targeting tourists. ❧ Chelsea won the Premiership, defeating Bolton 2–0.

MAY · {1} A leaked Foreign Office memo indicated that Blair may have planned the justification for the Iraq war 8 months before it began. {2} British soldier and father of 3, Anthony Wakefield, was killed in Iraq by a roadside bomb. ❧ Shaun Murphy beat Matthew Stevens 18–16, to become the first qualifier since 1979 to win the World Snooker championship [see p.301]. ❧ Wayne Rooney was dropped from a Schools' Football Association match because of fears he might not be the ideal role model. {3} An Italian report into the shooting of secret agent Nicola Calipari by US soldiers challenged the US's exoneration of their troops. {5} The UK General Election was held [see p.14]. ❧ 2 small bombs exploded outside the British consulate in New York; no casualties were reported. ❧ The judge in the Jackson trial refused to dismiss the charges after Jackson's defence claimed the prosecution's case was too weak. {6} Blair secured an historic 3rd term with a majority of 67 [see p.14]. {8} The 60th anniversary of Victory in Europe was commemorated across the UK. ❧

It was not until 10 years after the first that I thought of doing a back story.
– GEORGE LUCAS

Prince Harry began his military training at Sandhurst. ❧ The Iraqi Government confirmed a full cabinet, three months after the election. ❧ A 16-year-old girl was found murdered in a Reading park, her friend, who had also been shot, survived. {10} Bush addressed a vast crowd of Georgians in Tbilisi's Freedom Square; he praised their peaceful 'Rose Revolution' and suggested it could inspire countries such as Iraq, Ukraine, and Lebanon. {11} >60 died in 6 separate attacks across Iraq. ❧ The Bluewater shopping centre banned hooded tops, baseball caps, and swearing in response to growing anti-social behaviour [see p.11]. {12} A US Senate report accused George Galloway of taking oil vouchers from Saddam Hussein; he eloquently denied the allegations. ❧ US tycoon Malcolm Glazer bought more Manchester Utd shares, making his acquisition of the club almost inevitable. {13} Benedict XVI initiated the beatification of John Paul II. ❧ Government troops in Uzbekistan opened fire on unarmed civilians protesting for justice and freedom; *c.*50 were killed. {15} The final *Star Wars* film, *The Revenge of the Sith*, premiered at Cannes. ❧ The final Premiership games saw tough battles to avoid relegation [see p.298]; West Bromwich beat the drop. {16} Glazer achieved the 75% stake required to take over Man. Utd. ❧ The US magazine *Newsweek* withdrew earlier claims that US troops had flushed copies of the Koran down the toilets at Guantanamo Bay. Previously,

Malcolm Glazer

the story had caused riots in many Muslim countries, and >15 were killed in Afghanistan. {17} Kylie Minogue revealed she had breast cancer. ❦ After 40 years of campaigning, Kuwaiti women were granted the right to vote and stand for election, though they were still bound by Islamic law. ❦ George Galloway gave a combative defence to the US Senate committee that had accused him of receiving oil from Saddam Hussein; Galloway used the hearing to launch a scathing attack on the Iraq war. ❦ 50 new Bills were announced in a Queen's Speech that was widely perceived to demonstrate Blair's confidence. {20} The London Eye was threatened with closure after a proposed rent increase of >1,500%. ❦ *The Sun* published photographs of Saddam Hussein in his underpants; concerns were raised that the images may have contravened the Geneva Convention. {21} Greece won the Eurovision Song Contest [see. p.132]. {23} A 24-hour strike by BBC workers over planned job cuts disrupted much live programming. {25} Liverpool beat AC Milan on penalties to win their 5th European Cup [see p.26]. {27} The clock of Big Ben stalled for 90 minutes, halting its famous chimes –

George Galloway

Supporters have saved up for weeks to come here. I am so happy to lift the cup for the fans. – STEVEN GERRARD

hot weather was blamed. {29} 3 boys died and 4 were injured in a car crash in Oxford. {30} In a referendum, the French rejected the new EU constitution: 55% voted 'non'. ❦ West Ham returned to the Premiership, beating Preston 1–0. {31} Bob Geldof announced a series of 'Live8' concerts across the world to coincide with the G8 summit [see p.16]. ❦ The French PM Jean-Pierre Raffarin resigned after the EU referendum; Dominque de Villepin replaced him. ❦ Russian former Yukos chief Mikhail Khodorkovsky was jailed for 9 years, after being found guilty of various charges, including tax evasion. ❦ Former *East 17* singer Brian Harvey was crushed under the wheels of his own Mercedes convertible in a bizarre accident.

JUNE · {1} *Vanity Fair* revealed 'Deep Throat' to be Mark Felt [see p.126]. ❦ Video of Serbian soldiers massacring Bosnian Muslims in Srebrenica was shown at Slobodan Milosevic's trial in The Hague. ❦ The FA fined Ashley Cole (£100k), Jose Mourinho (£200k), and Chelsea (£300k) over the 'tapping-up' scandal; Cole's and Mourinho's fines were reduced to £75k on appeal. {2} The Dutch returned a decisive 'no' on the EU constitution [see p.265]. ❦ 3 children were questioned over the attempted hanging of a 5-year-old boy in W. Yorkshire. ❦ The prosecution and defence offered their closing arguments in the Jackson trial. ❦ A Belfast man was charged with murder of Robert McCartney. ❦ 3 adults were found guilty of abusing an 8-year-old-girl, whom they claimed was a witch. {4} The Pentagon admitted that some abuse of the Koran did occur at Guantanamo Bay. {6} Jack Straw announced that the UK would postpone its referendum on the EU constitution. ❦ A text-message lottery opened, giving people the chance to

—————— IN BRIEF · JUNE 2005 ——————

win free Live8 tickets. ❧ The IOC released a report on the 2012 Olympic bids: Paris and London were revealed to be the front-runners. ❧ Maoist rebels bombed a bus in Nepal, killing 38. {9} A 2-day general strike began in Zimbabwe in opposition to Mugabe's regime. ❧ Alistair Darling proposed 'pay-as-you-go' road charging to replace petrol and road tax. {10} After spending a month held hostage in Afghanistan, an Italian charity-worker Clementina Cantoni was released. {11} England's women's football team was knocked out of Euro 2005 after losing 1–0 to Sweden. ❧ French journalist Florence Aubenas and her Iraqi translator Hussein Hanoun al-Saadi were released after 5 months as hostages in Iraq. {12} A row over Britain's £3bn EU rebate intensified; Jack Straw found little support from fellow Foreign Ministers. ❧ G7 Finance Ministers pledged to write-off $40bn of debt owed by 18 of the world's poorest countries. ❧ Michael Jackson was found not guilty on all charges. ❧ Mike Tyson announced his retirement after a technical knock out by Irish journeyman Kevin McBride. ❧ An Italian referendum on relaxing strict fertility laws failed after the turnout fell below the 50% required. This failure was hailed as a victory for the Vatican which had urged abstention. {13} The trial began of 80-year-old Edgar Ray Killen, who was accused of murdering 3 civil-rights workers in 1964; the events were made famous by the film *Mississippi Burning*. {14} An earthquake measuring 7·9 on

Bob Geldof

the Richter Scale hit Chile; >8 were reported dead. ❧ In Athens, Jamaican sprinter Asafa Powell set a new 100m World Record of 9·77 seconds [see. p.306]. ❧ Bob Geldof expressed outrage after free Live8 tickets were put up for sale on eBay. After a media outcry, eBay agreed to remove the tickets. ❧ President of S. Africa, Thabo Mbeki sacked his deputy Jacob Zuma, after Zuma was implicated in a corruption scandal. {15} Australian hostage Doug Wood was rescued after being held hostage for 6 weeks in Iraq. {16} A Canadian child was killed after a nursery class was taken hostage in Siem Reap, Cambodia; the remaining children were later freed. ❧ The Court of Appeal heard 4 test cases relating to so-called 'shaken-baby syndrome'. {17} The Church of England appointed John Sentamu as the first black Archbishop (of York). {18} EU budget talks collapsed; Britain refused to relinquish its rebate unless a complete reform of EU funding and agricultural subsidies was also agreed. {19} Flash-floods hit N. Yorkshire, causing serious damage, and cutting power to >2,500 homes. ❧ Michael Schumacher was gifted a win in the American Grand Prix, after a farcical race in which 7 out of the 10 teams withdrew over 'tyre safety'. ❧ The 60th birthday of Burma's pro-democracy leader Aung San Suu Kyi was celebrated; she has been under house arrest since 2003. {20} US National Guardsmen guarding Saddam Hussein in Iraq revealed details of his imprisonment, including his obsession with

I would like people to share my life, my faith, my hope.
– JOHN SENTAMU

IN BRIEF · JUNE – JULY 2005

cleanliness and a love of *Doritos*. {21} Attorney-General Lord Goldsmith announced plans to remove juries from complex fraud trials. ❦ At an employment tribunal for unfair dismissal and sexual discrimination, Faria Alam – a secretary at the FA – claimed that FA chief, David Davies, sexually harassed her. {23} Blair made a passionate pro-European speech to MEPs ahead of Britain's EU Presidency in July. ❦ Prince William graduated from St Andrews University with a 2:1 in Geography. ❦ Edgar Ray Killen, former Ku Klux Klansman, was found guilty of the manslaughter of 3 civil-rights workers in 1964, and was jailed for 60 years. ❦ Tim Henman crashed out of Wimbledon, losing to the unseeded Russian Dmitri Tursunov in the 2nd round. {24} The Glastonbury Festival opened amidst floods. {25} Hardline conservative and former Mayor of Tehran, Mahmoud Ahmadinejad, won the Iranian Presidential elections. The USA and Britain expressed doubt over the integrity of the result. ❦ 18-year-old Andrew Murray, the 'new hope' of British tennis, lost an epic 5-set match to 18th seed David Nalbandian, after suffering from cramp and exhaustion. Wimbledon's 'Henman Hill' was swiftly renamed 'Murray Mount'. ❦ A 14-year-old girl was killed by a shark off the Florida coast. {26} RIP @ 61, Richard Whiteley [see p.48]. {27} A former Israeli soldier was found guilty of manslaughter for shooting Tom Hurndall, a British peace activist in

Andrew Murray

Gaza, who was escorting children away from gunfire in 2003. ❦ The British Government continued to deport asylum seekers to Zimbabwe, despite continuing unrest in the country. ❦ The High Court began hearing the case of former Railtrack shareholders demanding £157m compensation from the Government for allegedly engineering the collapse of Railtrack. {28} The 2nd reading of the 'ID Card' Bill was passed; the Government's majority was cut to 31. ❦ Celebrations with fireworks and a naval re-enactment in Portsmouth, marked the 200th anniversary of the Battle of Trafalgar. {30} Spain passed a law legalising homosexual marriages and adoptions, thereby becoming the 3rd European state to do so (after The Netherlands and Belgium). ❦ Figures released by the Home Office indicated the presence of up to 570,000 illegal immigrants in the UK [see p.83].

JULY · {1} GB took control of the EU Presidency, amid concerns about lack of agreement over the budget. {2} Live8 concerts were held in ten cities around the world [see p.17]. ❦ *c.*225,000 marched in Edinburgh in support of 'Make Poverty History' [see p.17]. ❦ RIP @ 54, Luther Vandross [see p.48]. ❦ Venus Williams beat Lindsay Davenport in a thrilling 3-set final at Wimbledon. {3} Roger Federer won a 3rd successive Wimbledon title after a straight-set win over Andy Roddick [see p.308]. {4} Arrests were made after *c.*1,000 protesters clashed with police

We are part of a big family that should go hand-in-hand to build our proud Iran.

– MAHMOUD AHMADINEJAD

— IN BRIEF · JULY 2005 —
---

in Edinburgh ahead of the G8 summit. ❦ At a hearing for serious professional misconduct, cot-death 'expert' Roy Meadow stood by claims that the likelihood of two babies dying from cot death in one family was 1 in 73,000,000. {5} Prince Harry's former Eton art-teacher won an employment tribunal for unfair dismissal; her claims that Harry cheated in his art AS-level were rejected. ❦ During his trial, a 19-year-old German man admitted creating the destructive Sasser worm computer virus. {6} London beat Paris

Sebastian Coe

to host the 2012 Olympics [see p.292]. ❦ The *New York Times* journalist Judith Miller was jailed for refusing to reveal her sources during a case about the naming of a CIA agent. ❦ American rapper Lil' Kim was sentenced to a year in jail after perjuring herself to a grand jury about a shooting outside a radio station. {7} 4 suicide bombers struck London during the morning rush-hour [see p.18]. {8} Many commuters avoided London as the bombing death toll rose and rescue work continued. ❦ Hurricane Dennis hit Haiti and Cuba, killing >20. ❦ A 10-year-old girl was found battered to death in woods near her Manchester home. {9} >20,000 were evacuated from Birmingham city-centre after a terrorist threat. {10} 1m poppies were dropped over the Mall to celebrate 60 years since the end of WWII. ❦ 56% of Luxembourgians backed the EU constitution, giving new hope for its revival. ❦ Police appealed for camera phone photos of the terrorist attacks in London [see p.28]. ❦ Hurricane Dennis

All of us must unite in helping the police to hunt these murderers down.
– SIR IQBAL SACRANIE

hit southern USA; *c.*1·4m fled. ❦ Kyrgyzstan held democratic Presidential elections; Kurmanbek Bakiev won 89% of the vote. {11} The first victim of 7/7 to be named was 53-year-old mother of 2, Susan Levy. ❦ The Church of England changed its rules to allow female Bishops. ❦ The second trial of Sion Jenkins for the murder of his foster-daughter, Billie-Jo, collapsed after the jury failed to reach a verdict. It was announced that Jenkins would be tried for a 3rd time. ❦ Thousands joined in commemorations for the 10th anniversary of the massacre in Srebrenica. {12} Police raided houses in Leeds and announced that they knew the identity of 3 of the 4 7/7 London bombers. It emerged that some of the bombers were British-born of Pakistani origin, and that the attacks were suicide missions. ❦ 80 police were injured in rioting in N. Ireland after an Orange Order march through a Catholic area. ❦ 56 Kenyans were massacred in tribal warfare over water and grazing rights. {13} A car bomb in Baghdad killed >24, including many children. ❦ Roy Meadow was found guilty by the GMC of giving erroneous and misleading evidence in the trial of Sally Clark; he was later 'struck off' the medical register. {14} Lib Dem Mark Hunter took the Cheadle by-election, with a 3,657 majority. ❦ At midday a 2-minute silence was observed across Europe in memory of those killed on 7/7. {16} >5 killed, including 1 Irish and 1 Briton, in a suicide bomb attack on the Turkish resort of Kusadasi. ❦

The 6th Harry Potter book, *Harry Potter and the Half-Blood Prince*, went on sale at midnight. {17} Tiger Woods won his second Open [see p.301]. ❦ RIP @ 89, Edward Heath [see p.48]. {18} >150 Iraqis were reported dead after 3 days of violence across the country. ❦ A 12-year-old girl admitted causing actual bodily harm to the 5-year-old boy found hanging in W. Yorkshire woods. {19} A study by the Iraq Body Count group estimated that *c.*25,000 Iraqi civilians had been killed since the Iraq conflict began [see p.20]. {20} 3 British

J.K. Rowling

soldiers were charged with war crimes relating to abuse of Iraqi prisoners in 2003. ❦ The UN announced a food crisis in Niger; thousands were said to be facing starvation. {21} Reports emerged of minor explosions on tube trains at Warren Street, Shepherd's Bush, and Oval, and on a bus in Hackney, echoing the attacks of 7/7 [see p.18]. ❦ Play began in the first Ashes Test [see p.27]. {22} A suspected 'terrorist' was chased by police through Stockwell tube station and shot dead in a train carriage. ❦ Uncertainty remained over events surrounding the 21/7 explosions; some reports suggested that the bombs failed to detonate properly,

They killed my cousin, they could kill anyone. – ALEX PEREIRA
[cousin of Jean Charles de Menezes]

and 4 would-be suicide bombers were on the run. ❦ China revalued its currency, the Yuan; the move was welcomed by the international community, who hoped it might slow China's rapid export-led growth. {23} >88 locals and tourists were killed after a series of suicide attacks on the Egyptian resort of Sharm al-Sheikh. ❦

Police named the man they killed at Stockwell station as Brazilian electrician Jean Charles de Menezes, and admitted that he was unconnected to terrorism. {24} Lance Armstrong won his 7th *Tour de France* and announced his retirement [see p.294]. {26} A Dutch court sentenced Mohammed Boyeri to life for the murder of film-maker Theo van Gogh. ❦ The space-shuttle *Discovery* was launched – it was the first manned NASA flight since the *Columbia* disaster. {27} 4 men were arrested during dawn raids in Birmingham in connection with the London bombings; one was thought to have been involved in 21/7. ❦ A plane carrying 41 tons of aid from Save the Children departed for Niger; it was estimated that 3·6m were starving. ❦ NASA examined footage of the *Discovery* launch after debris was seen falling from the shuttle. ❦ The Healthcare Commission reported that British hospital standards had declined in previous year, with fewer trusts awarded 2 or 3-star status. {28} The IRA issued a statement pledging to end its armed conflict [see p.25]. ❦ Further arrests were made in London in connection with the 21/7 attacks. Transport Police deployed all their available officers to reassure the public and diminish the risk of further attacks. ❦ >430 reported dead in floods in Mumbai, after 26" of monsoon rain fell in 24 hours. ❦ US, China, India, South Korea, Japan, and Australia made a non-binding agreement to cut greenhouse gases [see p.65]. ❦ >20 were injured when a mini-tornado ripped

—————————— IN BRIEF · JULY – AUGUST 2005 ——————————

through Birmingham. {29} After arrests across Britain and Italy, the police claimed to have all suspected 21/7 bombers in custody. ❦ Richard Whelan was stabbed to death on a bus in N. London, after he asked a fellow passenger to stop throwing chips at his girlfriend. ❦ The British army began to dismantle security posts in South Armagh [see p.25]. {30} US astronomers identified a possible 10th planet in the solar system [see p.180]. {31} 18-year-old Anthony Walker died after a 'racially-motivated' axe attack in Liverpool.

B. Netanyahu

A UGUST · {1} 2 teenagers were arrested for the murder of Anthony Walker. ❦ RIP @ 84, King Fahd of Saudi Arabia; his half-brother Crown Prince Abdullah succeeded him. ❦ >100 died in Sudan during riots over the death of former rebel leader and Vice-President, John Garang. ❦ An Air France Airbus crashed on landing at Toronto airport; all 309 passengers escaped without serious injury before the plane burst into flames. ❦ President Bush used a constitutional quirk to force John Bolton's appointment as US ambassador to the UN, despite little support from Senators. {3} New figures revealed that religious 'hate crimes', mostly directed at those thought to be Muslims, had increased six-fold in the wake of 7/7. ❦ The *Discovery* astronaut, Stephen Robinson, successfully made a spacewalk to mend shuttle damage that could have threatened safe re-entry. {4} Mo Mowlam was reported to be criti-

cally ill in hospital. ❦ The Bank of England cut interest rates to 4·5% [see p.232]. {5} Two men were charged with the murder of Anthony Walker. ❦ A Russian mini-submarine was reported trapped with dwindling air supplies on the ocean floor near Siberia; international rescue teams were dispatched. ❦ A 19-year-old Israeli soldier killed four Arab-Israelis on a bus in Shfaram, in a protest against Israeli withdrawal from Gaza; he was killed by onlookers. ❦ A 20-year-old man was arrested over the murder of Richard Whelan. {6} The 60th anniversary of the Hiroshima atom bomb was marked around the world. ❦ The Athletics World Championships began in Helsinki [see p.307]. ❦ RIP @ 59, former Cabinet Minister Robin Cook, while hill-walking in Scotland [see p.49]. ❦ England won the 2nd Ashes Test by 2 runs. {7} Israeli finance Minister Binyamin Netanyahu resigned over planned Israeli withdrawals from Gaza [see p.25]. ❦ A British team used a remote-controlled mini-sub to cut free the crew of the trapped Russian sub. {8} *Discovery*'s re-entry was delayed for a day because of bad weather. ❦ Iran restarted its nuclear programme, thereby prompting interna-

Robin was so good that it was unwise to do without him.
– NEIL KINNOCK

tional protest. {9} *Discovery* landed safely in Los Angeles after inclement weather ruled out a return to Cape Canaveral. ❦ The 60th anniversary of the Nagasaki bomb was marked around the world. {10} Researchers from Liverpool John Moores University suggested that 1 in 25 men could unwittingly be bringing up chil-

IN BRIEF · AUGUST 2005

dren that were not their own. {11} Meals on British Airways flights were affected after strikes hit the catering firm Gate Gourmet, which had sacked 670 workers. ❦ Israeli ex-soldier Taysir Hayb was sentenced to 8 years in prison for the manslaughter of British peace activist Tom Hurndall. {12} BA was forced to ground all of its flights after wildcat Gate Gourmet strikes spread to baggage-handlers. ❦ The Home Office announced that radical 'Islamic' cleric Omar Bakri Mohammed could not return to Britain after a visit to Lebanon. ❦ Malaysia declared a state of emergency after forest fires in Indonesia enveloped Kuala Lumpur in dense smog. ❦ Politicians and friends paid tribute to Robin Cook at his funeral; racing pundit John McCirick criticised Tony Blair for not attending the service. ❦ Sri Lankan Foreign Minister Lakshman Kadirgamar was assasinated; the Tamil Tigers were blamed. ❦ Anthony Hutton won *Big Brother* 2005 [see p.108]. {14} A Cypriot plane heading for Athens crashed, killing all 121 on board; reports suggested a sudden drop in cabin pressure was to blame. ❦ VJ Day was celebrated. {15} The Iraqi parliament granted itself an extension to allow

Anthony Hutton

The eyes of the trade union movement are on this dispute.
– BRENDAN BARBER, TUC

further negotiations over its new constitution. Agreement could not be reached on a number of issues, including: the role of religion; the status of women; and the nature of local and federal powers. ❦ Israeli settlers in the Gaza Strip were presented with eviction notices by their government; vociferous protests followed. ❦ The

Indonesian government signed a truce with Aceh rebels, ending *c.*30 years of conflict. {16} 160 passengers and crew were killed after a Colombian airliner heading for Martinique crashed over Venezuela. ❦ Madonna fell from a horse at her Wiltshire estate on her 47th birthday; she broke her collar-bone, hand, and a number of ribs. {17} The deadline for settlers to leave the Gaza Strip passed at midnight; Israeli troops began evictions [see p.25]. ❦ A leaked report by the Independent Police Complaints Cmsn. alleged a startling number of errors in the shooting of Jean Charles de Menezes. ❦ One man died and another was critically wounded after a fire on a maintenance train in the Channel Tunnel. {18} The A-Level pass rate rose to 96·2%. ❦ 11-year-old school-boy Rory Blackhall was reported missing in West Lothian after failing to attend school. {19} RIP @ 55, Mo Mowlam [see p.49]. {21} The search for Rory Blackhall was called off after a body was found in woodland near his school. {22} 'Piano Man' suddenly identified himself and was flown back to his native Germany. Reports emerged that he was not a particularly gifted pianist. {23} The withdrawal of Israeli settlers from the Gaza Strip settlements was declared a success by the Israeli government [see p.25]. ❦ President Niyazov of Turkmenistan banned the playing of recorded music [see p.23]. {24} A Peruvian passenger plane crashed in the jungle, killing *c.*40 of its 100 passengers. ❦ RIP @ 78, Maurice Cowling. {25} GSCE pass-rates rose

Schott's Almanac 2006

across the country. {26} >17 people died in a fire that engulfed a block of flats in Paris. ❦ Negotiations over the Iraqi constitution stalled when Sunnis rejected the Shia and Kurdish proposals. {27} A woman holding a baby was shot dead at a christening party in Peckham. {28} England beat Australia by 3 wickets in the 4th Ashes Test. {29} Simon Harris, the man wanted in connection with the murder of Rory Blackhall, was discovered dead at his home in Livingston. Harris had also been facing charges of child abuse. ❦ Hurricane Katrina hit Louisiana, Mississippi, and Alabama [see p.21]. {30} Two males, aged 14 and 16, were charged with the shooting and robbery at the christening in Peckham. {31} As the chaos subsided it became clear that the destruction wrought by Katrina in and around New Orleans was worse than first feared. ❦ *c.*1,000 were trampled to death in northern Baghdad. The stampede of Shia pilgrims crossing a narrow bridge was prompted by rumours of a suicide bomber in the crowd. ❦ Ken Clarke launched his bid for the leadership of the Tory party, closely followed by a bid from Malcolm Rifkind.

George W. Bush

There was more than enough warning about the dangers to New Orleans.
— COLIN POWELL

S EPTEMBER · {1} 3 days of mourning began in Russia to mark the first anniversary of the Beslan siege and massacre. ❦ David Addison, a British lorry driver, was kidnapped in Afghanistan. ❦ Evacuation of New Orleans began. {2} American police implemented a shoot-to-kill policy in New Orleans in an attempt to halt looting and violence. ❦ A video by 7/7

suicide bomber Mohammad Sidique Khan 'justifying' his actions was broadcast by Al-Jazeera. {3} The first British survivors of Hurricane Katrina arrived home. ❦ British lorry driver David Addison was found dead in Afghanistan. ❦ Jacques Chirac was admitted to a Parisian hospital after a 'minor vascular incident'. {5} An Indonesian plane crashed on take-off from Medan, killing >117 passengers and >25 on the ground. ❦ The court martial began of 7 British soldiers charged with the murder of an Iraqi civilian. ❦ Petrol prices continued to rise in the wake of Hurricane Katrina, with the average cost of unleaded petrol at 94·6p a litre. ❦ At least 9 were killed in the Austrian Alps after a helicopter accidentally dropped a slab of concrete onto a cable car. {6} George W. Bush declared formal emergencies in 10 States affected by Katrina and the subsequent evacuations. ❦ Network Rail was found guilty of breaching health and safety regulations prior to the Hatfield crash. 5 executives on trial were cleared of any wrong-doing. {7} The Iraqi President Jalal Talabani claimed that Saddam Hussein had admitted to crimes during his reign and he therefore deserved to die. ❦ Egyptians went to the polls in the country's first democratic Presidential elections. ❦ England suffered a humiliating 1–0 defeat by Northern Ireland in a football World Cup qualifier; many fans and critics called for the resignation of Sven-Goran Eriksson. ❦ Average petrol prices hit 95·1p a litre [see p.198]. {8}

IN BRIEF · SEPTEMBER 2005

The final, thrilling, Ashes Test began. ❦ The Volcker Panel released its final report on the oil-for-food scandal, blaming Kofi Annan for mismanagement, although he was cleared of specific wrong-doing. It called the scheme 'illict, unethical, and corrupt'. ❦ At least 5 were reported to have died from contaminated water in New Orleans. ❦ Liam Fox announced he would run for the leadership of the Conservative party. {9} Faria Alam lost her case for sexual discrimination against the FA. ❦ Rising oil prices and shrinking domestic gas reserves caused British Gas to announce a 14% increase in prices. ❦ Ukrainian President Viktor Yushchenko sacked his entire government over in-fighting and corruption. {10} Riots broke out in N. Ireland after an Orange Order march was re-routed; >30 police officers were injured. ❦ *c.*2,000 Egyptians protested in Cairo against the re-election of President Hosni Mubarak, who had been in power for 24 years. {11} Israeli troops finally completed their withdrawal from Gaza amid Palestinian celebrations. ❦ The 4th Anniversary of 9/11 was marked around the world. {12} In Japan's snap election, the incumbent PM Junichiro Koizumi won a convincing victory in the lower house and vowed to continue his controversial reform of the post office [see p.25]. ❦ After a second night of violence in Belfast and surrounding areas, *c.*18 police were reported to have been injured. ❦ The price of unleaded petrol hit £1 a litre in areas of Britain, sparking concerns

Andrew Flintoff

I had hoped we would win a majority with our party alone, but we did even better than that – J. KOIZUMI

of blockades and protests. ❦ The new-look 'Berliner' sized *Guardian* newspaper went on sale [see p.124]. ❦ England won the Ashes [see p.27]. ❦ {14} >150 died and scores were injured after a wave of suicide attacks and shootings across Iraq; it was claimed the attacks were co-ordinated by Al-Qaeda. ❦ A couple who ran a nursing home near New Orleans were charged with manslaughter for ignoring the call to evacuate, resulting in the death of 34 of their residents. ❦ N. Ireland Sec. Peter Hain announced that the Government no longer accepted that the Ulster Volunteer Force was abiding by the ceasefire, after days of rioting. ❦ Small-scale fuel protests began at refineries across Britain. {15} Prince Harry's 21st Birthday. ❦ 7 Algerians were arrested in London and Manchester, and held under new powers to deport those considered a threat to national security. {16} 60 fuel protesters staged a go-slow on the M4. ❦ 8 men who had tried to steal £33m of gold and gems from a Heathrow airport warehouse were jailed for a total of 67 years. {18} Afghanistan held the first local and parliamentary elections for 30 years. {19} Angela Merkel won the German election by just 3 seats – not enough to secure a majority [see p.25]. ❦ During six-nation talks in Beijing, N. Korea agreed to halt its nuclear activities and re-enter the non-proliferation agreement; in return, America promised electricity and aid.

The daily chronicle will continue in the 2007 edition of Schott's Almanac.

——————— SOME GREAT LIVES IN BRIEF ———————

JOHNNY CARSON
23·10·1925–23·1·2005 (79)

One of the best known faces on US TV, Carson hosted the Tonight Show for 30 years (4,531 shows). From his first guest – Groucho Marx – Carson hosted a constellation of stars until he was replaced in 1992 by Jay Leno.

HUNTER S. THOMPSON
18·7·1937–20·2·2005 (67)

A fierce and unflinching chronicler of American counter-culture, Thompson championed 'gonzo' journalism – a crazed, stream of consciousness, highly subjective, usually drug-fuelled, and often semi-fictional style of reporting. Six months after Thompson's suicide, his friend Johnny Depp arranged for his ashes to be blown into the sky from a 150-foot high cannon.

ARTHUR MILLER
17·10·1915–10·2·2005 (89)

Widely regarded as America's greatest post-war playwright, Miller's most noted works are his dystopian vision of the 'American dream' in *Death of a Salesman*, and his caustic attack on the McCarthy trials in *The Crucible*. In 1956 he married Marilyn Monroe.

DAVE ALLEN
6·7·1936–10·3·2005 (68)

A unique comic performer, Allen combined gags, sketches, and anecdotes to rail against the absurdities of life and the tyranny of authority – especially the Church. Allen will be best remembered for his monologues, told perched on a high stool, drinking whiskey, smoking Gauloise, and flicking imaginary ash from his dark suit. He ended each performance with his catch-phrase: 'Goodnight, good luck, and may your God go with you.'

ANDREA DWORKIN
26·9·1946–9·4·2005 (58)

A powerful polemical writer, Dworkin championed a controversial strand of radical feminism in a series of works that explored her claim that men, the male state, sex, marriage, and pornography were all subjugating women.

SIR JOHN MILLS
22·2·1908–23·4·2005 (97)

Mills appeared in over 100 films, and became famous for portraying quiet, decent, loyal characters, displaying an 'English' courage and sense of fair play. In a long and distinguished career, Mills resisted the lure of Hollywood – though he did win an Oscar for best-supporting actor in *Ryan's Daughter*.

RICHARD WHITELEY
28·12·1943–26·6·2005 (61)

Whiteley achieved cult fame as presenter for 23 years of C4's teatime quiz *Countdown*. Since he also presented the Yorkshire news show *Calendar*, he often reappeared on TV – earning him the nickname 'twice-nightly Whiteley'.

LUTHER VANDROSS
20·4·1951–1·7·2005 (54)

A popular singer, discovered at the age of 23 by David Bowie, Vandross was best loved for smooth, soulful ballads like *Here and Now* – which became the most popular wedding song in America during the 1990s. Vandross sold over 25m singles, and each of his 14 albums went platinum [see p.129].

SIR EDWARD HEATH
9·7·1916–17·7·2005 (89)

Heath became the Tory's first working-class leader, and their last to have served in WWII. He ousted Wilson's government in 1970, but soon became

SOME GREAT LIVES IN BRIEF cont.

mired in industrial discontent and was forced to introduce the '3 day week' to save oil. The most notable achievement of his problematic premiership was taking Britain into the Common Market in 1972. He will be remembered for this, for his 'hinterland' hobbies of yachting and music, and for 'the longest sulk in history' against the woman who took over his leadership in 1975 – Margaret Thatcher.

DAME CICELY SAUNDERS
22·6·1918–14·7·2005 (87)

Saunders developed new approaches and championed a Christian code of care for the terminally ill. In 1967 she founded St Christopher's Hospice, in Sydenham, SE London, from where the modern hospice movement grew.

PROFESSOR SIR RICHARD DOLL
28·10·1912–24·7·2005 (92)

In 1950, Doll co-authored a seminal study that first linked smoking with lung cancer. This, now familiar, insight is credited with saving as many lives as penicillin or the polio vaccine.

ROBIN COOK
28·2·1946–6·8·2005 (59)

A highly respected parliamentarian, Cook was credited with a forensic attention to detail, famously used to dissect the 2,000 page Scott Report on 'arms-to-Iraq'. As Blair's first Foreign Secretary, Cook promised policy with an 'ethical dimension' – an ambition at odds with the *realpolitik* of his sanctioning the sale of 16 Hawk fighters to Indonesia. Demoted in 2001 to Leader of the Commons, Cook resigned from the Cabinet in 2003 over the Iraq war. Widely regarded as able enough to be PM, he once said: 'I'm not good-looking enough to be party leader'.

MARJORIE 'MO' MOWLAM
18·9·1949–19·8·2005 (55)

An unusually popular politician (once described as 'a national treasure'), Mo Mowlam was an unashamedly 'touchy-feely' MP. In 1997 Mowlam became Blair's first N. Ireland Secretary, and is credited with bringing fresh hope to the talks that culminated in the Good Friday Agreement. When, at the 1998 Party Conference, Blair spoke of 'our one and only Mo' his speech was interrupted by a standing ovation. Soon after, Mowlam lost the confidence of some Unionists and was replaced by Peter Mandelson. Dogged by health problems after a brain tumour, and gossip that she was too ill for her job, Mowlam resigned as an MP in 2002.

ROBERT MOOG
23·5·1934–21·8·2005 (71)

In 1963, after childhood experimentation with electronic music, Robert Moog created his revolutionary Moog synthesiser, which has been embraced by a host of musicians from the Beatles to Fatboy Slim. Contrary to popular usage, 'Moog' rhymes with 'rogue'.

SIMON WIESENTHAL
31·12·1908–20·9·2005 (96)

Wiesenthal survived starvation and torture in eleven concentration camps to become the most tenacious and famous 'Nazi hunter'. A Jewish architect, born in Lviv, Wiesenthal suffered the murder of 89 family members, but always espoused the belief 'justice not vengeance'. He helped bring to trial *c.*1,100 war criminals; and, in insisting that guilt for crimes against humanity had no time limit, Wiesenthal played a role in establishing the modern climate of international justice whereby those, like Milosevic, are held to account.

The World

The world is not merely the world. It is our world. It is not merely
an industrial world. It is, above all things, a human world.
— AGNES E. MEYER

THE PLANETS

symbol	name	diameter	no. of moons	surface gravity	rings?	distance from Sun	mean temp	day length
		km		m/s^2		x10^6 km	°C	hours
☿	Mercury	4,878	0	3.7	N	57.9	167	4222.6
♀	Venus	12,102	0	8.9	N	108.2	462	2802.0
⊕	Earth	12,756	1	9.8	N	149.6	15	24.0
♂	Mars	6,794	2	3.7	N	227.9	-65	24.6
♃	Jupiter	142,800	63	23.1	Y	778.4	-110	9.9
♄	Saturn	120,536	46	9.0	Y	1,433.5	-148	10.7
♅	Uranus	51,118	27	8.4	Y	2,872.5	-195	17.2
♆	Neptune	49,492	13	10.7	Y	4,495.1	-200	16.1
♇	Pluto	2,302	1	0.8	N	5,906.3	-225	153.3

New moons for some planets have been discovered. For details of the possible new planet, see p.180.

PLANETARY MNEMONIC

My   Very   Eager   Monkey   Just   Sets   Up   Nine   Planets
Mercury   Venus   Earth   Mars   Jupiter   Saturn   Uranus   Neptune   Pluto

THE EARTH

From a distance, The world looks blue and green — BETTE MIDDLER

Equatorial radius............6378·1km	Distance to moon.........384,467km
Polar radius.................6356·8km	Gravity..........................9·8m/s^2
Temperature at core..........6700° C	Density...................5,515 kg/m^3
Core constituents.......nickel & iron	Earth orbits sun...........66,600mph
Core radius....................3485km	Age (approximately)....4,500m years
Axial tilt..........................23·5°	Area total..............510·072m km^2
Atmosphere.............78% Nitrogen	— *land*..................148·94m km^2
21% Oxygen · 1% trace gases	— *water*...............361·132m km^2
Planetary satellites....................1	Water/land.............70·8%/29·2%
Mass....................5·98 x 10^{24}kg	Coastline..................356,000 km

THE CONTINENTS

Continent	km^2	est. population	population density
Asia	45,036,492	3,776m	83·4
Africa	30,343,578	832m	27·4
North America	24,680,331	501m	20·3
South America	17,815,420	357m	20·0
Antarctica	12,093,000	(some scientists)	—
Europe	9,908,599	727m	73·3
Australia†	7,682,850	20m	2·6

† Australia is usually considered a continent because it is a continuous landmass, though this leaves Polynesia, New Zealand, and many other areas unclassified. Consequently, some prefer the usage of Oceania – a continental grouping that includes all the Pacific islands surrounding Australia. ❧ Geographically, there are 6 continents, but the Americas are generally split into two. Some 225 million years ago the only continent was Pangaea – a super-continent surrounded by the Panthalassa ocean. Approximately 180 million years ago Pangaea split into two continents, Laurasia and Gondwanaland, before shifting plate tectonics created the landmasses we have today. ❧ In George Orwell's dystopian novel *Ninteen Eighty-Four* (1949), three continents or super-states are locked in an ever-shifting war against each other: Oceania (Britain, America, and Australia); Eurasia (the Soviet Union, and Europe); and Eastasia (China, Japan, and Korea).

OCEANS & SEAS

Oceans are the largest bodies of water, making up more than 70% of the globe's surface. The structure of the continents demarcates the Pacific, Indian, and Atlantic Oceans, to which maritime organisations added the Arctic. In 2000, the International Hydrographic Organization, the body responsible for charting the oceans, defined the Southern (or Antarctic) Ocean, due to its unique eco-system.

Ocean	km^2	greatest known depth at	depth
Pacific	155,557,000	Mariana Trench	11,033m
Atlantic	76,763,000	Puerto Rico Trench	8,605m
Indian	68,556,000	Java Trench	7,258m
Southern	20,327,000	South Sandwich Trench	7,235m
Arctic	14,056,000	Fram Basin	4,665m

Seas are sub-divisions of oceans, or large salt-water lakes; often, they are arbitrarily defined by their geographical proximity to a landmass. Some seas of note follow:

Sea	km^2		
South China Sea	2,974,600	Sea of Okhotsk	1,580,000
Caribbean Sea	2,754,000	Gulf of Mexico	1,544,000
Mediterranean Sea	2,510,000	Sea of Japan	1,013,000
Bering Sea	2,261,000	Hudson Bay	730,000
		East China Sea	665,000

─────────── A WORLD OF SUPERLATIVES ───────────

Highest city	La Paz, Bolivia	3,636m
Highest mountain	Everest, Nepal/Tibet	8,850m
Highest volcano	Ojos del Salado, Chile	6,908m
Highest dam	Rogan, Tajikistan	335m
Highest waterfall	Angel Falls, Venezuela	979m
Biggest waterfall (volume)	Inga, Dem. Rep. of Congo	43,000m³/s
Lowest point	Dead Sea, Israel/Jordan	400m
Deepest point	Challenger Deep, Mariana Trench	11,033m
Deepest ocean	Pacific	average depth 4,300m
Deepest freshwater lake	Baikal, Russia	1,741m
Largest lake	Caspian Sea	370,848km²
Largest desert	Sahara	9,065,000km²
Largest island	Greenland	2,174,760km²
Largest country	Russia	17,068,759km²
Largest population	China	1·3bn people
Largest monolith	Uluru, Australia	345m high; 9·4km base
Largest landmass	Eurasia	54,745,500km²
Largest river (volume)	Amazon	28bn gall/min
Largest peninsula	Arabian	3,236,250km²
Largest rainforest	Amazon, South America	1·2bn acres
Largest forest	Northern Russia	1·87bn acres
Largest atoll	Kwajalein, Marshall Islands	16km²
Largest glacier	Vatnajökull, Iceland	8,540km²
Largest concrete banana	The Big Banana, Australia	13m x 5m
Largest archipelago	Indonesia	17,508 islands
Largest lake in a lake	Manitou, on an island in Lake Huron	155km²
Largest city by area	Mount Isa, Australia	40,977km²
Smallest country	Vatican City	0·52km²
Smallest population	Vatican City	770 people
Smallest republic	Republic of Nauru	21km²
Longest coastline	Canada	202,080km
Longest mountain range	Andes	8,500km
Longest suspension bridge	Akashi-Kaikyo, Japan	1,990m
Longest rail tunnel	Seikan, Japan	52km
Longest road tunnel	Laerdal, Norway	24·5km
Longest river	The Nile	6,677km
Tallest inhabited building	Taipei 101, Taiwan	508m
Tallest structure	KVLY-TV Mast, USA	629m
Most land borders	China & Russia	14 countries
Most populated urban area	Tokyo, Japan	26·5m
Most remote settlement	Tristan da Cunha	2,334km from neighbours
Least populous capital city	Torshavn, Faroe Islands	pop. 16,300
Warmest sea	Red Sea	Average temp. c.25°C
Longest bay	Bay of Bengal	1,850km
Largest banknote	Brobdingnagian bills, Philippines	14" x 8½"

Unsurprisingly, a degree of uncertainty and debate surrounds some of these entries and their specifications.

——————— WORLD BIRTH & DEATH RATES ———————

Births	time unit	deaths	change
129,908,352	*per* YEAR	56,622,744	+73,285,608
10,825,696	*per* MONTH	4,718,562	+6,107,134
355,913	*per* DAY	155,131	+200,782
14,830	*per* HOUR	6,464	+8,366
247	*per* MINUTE	108	+139
4·1	*per* SECOND	1·8	+2·13

[Source: US Census Bureau, 2005 · Figures may not add to totals because of rounding]

——————— WORLD POPULATION MILESTONES ———————

According to the US Census Bureau, it took 118 years for the world's population to grow from 1 to 2 billion (1804–1922). Since then, total population has increased dramatically, and is still increasing despite the prevalence of AIDS, a decrease in the global rate of growth, and the fall of fertility levels in many countries. Below are some estimated milestones, with the number of years taken for each billion rise:

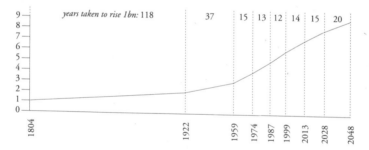

——————— THE TOP TEN MOST POPULOUS COUNTRIES ———————

rank	1950	2002	2050 (est.)	rank
1	China	China	India	1
2	India	India	China	2
3	United States	United States	United States	3
4	Russia	Indonesia	Indonesia	4
5	Japan	Brazil	Nigeria	5
6	Indonesia	Pakistan	Bangladesh	6
7	Germany	Russia	Pakistan	7
8	Brazil	Bangladesh	Brazil	8
9	United Kingdom	Nigeria	Congo	9
10	Italy	Japan	Mexico	10

[Source: US Census, Global Population Profile 2002]

———————— NOBEL PEACE PRIZE ————————

The 2004 Nobel Peace Prize was awarded to WANGARI MAATHAI (1940–)

for her contribution to sustainable development, democracy, and peace

Born in Kenya, Maathai was the first woman in East and Central Africa to earn a doctorate degree (in biological sciences, 1964), after which she pursued an academic career in veterinary anatomy. Yet, it was while chairing the National Council of Women in Kenya that Maathai pioneered a project of tree planting – encouraging women to conserve the environment and improve their quality of life. This project developed into the Green Belt Movement, whose mission is to 'mobilise community consciousness, equity, improved livelihoods, security and environmental conservation – using tree planting as an entry point'. Over the last 30 years, Maathai's movement has assisted women in planting over 20 million trees. Not only has the Green Belt Movement exported its work to other African countries, but Maathai has used its 'grass-roots' success as a platform for wider social change, campaigning on issues like debt cancellation, women's rights, and the prevention of deforestation and desertification in Africa. Maathai has won a host of other international honours and awards, including Woman of the Year, 1983. In 2002 she was elected to the Kenyan Parliament with a vote of 98%. ❦ On being awarded her laureate Maathai said: 'I know that this prize has given me a special responsibility as spokesperson, not only here in Kenya, but in the whole of Africa. And there is plenty to be done.'

Wangari Maathai

Some recent Nobel Peace Laureates:

2003	Shirin Ebadi
2002	Jimmy Carter
2001	United Nations; Kofi Annan
2000	Kim Dae-jung
1999	*Médecins Sans Frontières*
1998	John Hume; David Trimble
1997	Int. Campaign to Ban Landmines; Jody Williams
1996	Ximenes Belo; Ramos-Horta
1995	Joseph Rotblat; *Pugwash Conferences on Science & World Affairs*

———————— ROWNTREE VISIONARIES ————————

In 2005, the *Joseph Rowntree Charitable Trust* appointed 6 'Rowntree Visionaries', to be paid a salary of £40,000 for a 5-year mission to 'change the world'. They are:

Karen Chouhan ..... *black-led decision-making approach to race equality in the UK*
Roy Head .... *improve health information in the developing world*
Heather Parker, Mark Hinton.... *bridge UK communities and the developing world*
Carne Ross .... *help marginalised countries through independent diplomacy*
Clive Stafford Smith ...... *champion human rights by closing Guantanamo Bay &c.*
Geoff Tansey .... *change international law and regulation to ease food inequalities*

——— THE HIV/AIDS EPIDEMIC IN NUMBERS · 2004 ———

People living with HIV worldwide
Total..............................39·4m
Adults ....37·2m
Women.........................17·6m
Children <15 years...............2·2m

Newly infected with HIV worldwide
Total ....4·9m
Adults.............................4·3m
Children <15 years..............0·64m

AIDS deaths worldwide
Total ....3·1m
Adults.............................2·6m
Children <15 years..............0·51m

*Estimated number of people
infected with HIV by region*
Sub-Saharan Africa ....25·4m
South and South-east Asia.......7·1m
Latin America ....1·7m
E. Europe & Central Asia ....1·4m
East Asia...........................1·1m
North America 1m
Western Europe.................0·61m
N. Africa & Middle East.......0·54m
Carribean........................0·44m
Oceania.........................35,000

[See also the detailed breakdown of infection
rates by country in the Gazetteer on pp.72–9]

Global funding for AIDS response ....$6·1b
No. of people on antiretroviral drugs in Africa............................150,000
Estimated need for antiretroviral drugs in Africa 3,800,000
No. of people on antiretroviral drugs worldwide...........................440,000
Estimated need for antiretroviral drugs worldwide 5,500,000
Approximate no. of new infections each day in 2003.......................14,000

[Source: UNAIDS/WHO figures for 2004 · the numbers quoted are their best estimates]

——— GRAND CHALLENGES IN GLOBAL HEALTH ———

After two years of canvassing scientific opinion, in June 2005 the Bill and Melinda
Gates Foundation gave $436m (£245m) to be shared by 43 innovative projects
working to find solutions to these fourteen 'Grand Challenges in Global Health':

1..create effective single-dose vaccines
2...................................prepare vaccines that do not require refrigeration
3.......................................develop needle-free vaccine delivery systems
4...devise testing systems for new vaccines
5 ....design antigens for protective immunity
6 ....learn about immunological responses
7 ....develop genetic strategy to control insects (e.g. malarial mosquitoes)
8..develop chemical strategy to control insects
9 ....create nutrient-rich staple plant species
10 ....find drugs and delivery systems to limit drug resistance
11 ....create therapies that can cure latent infection
12...........................create immunological methods to cure latent infection
13.................................develop technologies to assess population health
14..develop versatile diagnostic tools

——————————————— THREE WORLDS THEORY ———————————————

Developed during the Cold War, the 'three worlds' theory asserted that the world might usefully be divided into blocs based upon economic status: the FIRST WORLD of developed capitalist economies (e.g. USA and western Europe); the SECOND WORLD of developed communist countries (e.g. the Soviet Union); and the THIRD WORLD of underdeveloped countries (e.g. Latin America and Africa). It was assumed in terms of the Cold War that much of the third world could safely be considered neutral (for reasons of poverty perhaps more than ideology). The FOURTH WORLD was a term used to describe the world's 25 poorest nations. The International Monetary Fund [IMF] employs its own tripartite world classification:

Advanced Economies .... *e.g. Australia, Norway, Sweden, UK, US*
Countries in Transition .... *e.g. Albania, Croatia, Poland, Russia*
Developing Countries .... *e.g. Afghanistan, Ethiopia, Swaziland*

A range of other groupings are employed by nation states and international organisations to categorise the (often rapid) shifts in global economic prosperity:

Developed Countries [DCs] .... *e.g. France, Canada, UK*
Former USSR & Eastern Europe [FORMER USSR/EE] ... *e.g. Armenia, Uzbekistan,*
Less Developed Countries [LDCs] .... *e.g. Egypt, Sierra Leone, Yemen*
Newly Industrialising Economies [NIEs] .... *e.g. Singapore, Taiwan, Brazil*
Heavily Indebted Poor Countries [HIPCs] .... *e.g. Burkina Faso, Zambia*

——————————————— WORLD ECONOMIC FORUM ———————————————

The 2005 World Economic Forum in Davos had the theme *Taking Responsibility for Tough Choices*. Amongst those hoping to 'improve the state of the world' were: Tony Blair, Bono, Thabo Mbeki, Sharon Stone, and Bill Gates. Debates included:

Blessed Are the (Non-Traditional) Peacemakers · The Price of Plug and Play
To Travel or Not to Travel? · Are Stem Cells Silver Bullets? · The Power of One
Putting the 'Non' Back Into Non-Proliferation · Is Cancer Unstoppable?
What Does it Mean to be Chinese? · Must We Call a Revolution for Children?
Are Zoonotic Diseases as Scary as they Sound?

——————————————— TOP TEN RECIPIENTS OF UK AID ———————————————

The top 10 UK aid beneficiaries, according to latest 2003 figures from the OECD:

India	$346m	Afghanistan	$115m
Serbia & Montenegro	$237m	Pakistan	$106m
Tanzania	$208m	Iraq	$97m
Bangladesh	$188m	Uganda	$94m
Ghana	$130m	South Africa	$87m

THE GLOBAL GENDER GAP

The World Economic Forum studied 58 countries worldwide to assess the extent of the gender gap between men and women. The study ranked each country on five areas: economic status (UK ranking: 21st); political empowerment (UK: 5th); economic opportunity (UK: 41st); educational attainment (UK: 4th); and health and well-being (UK: 26th). The overall top and bottom ten scoring countries were:

The Best		The Worst	
1 .... Sweden	6... New Zealand	58 .... Egypt	53 .... India
2 .... Norway	7 .... Canada	57 .... Turkey	52 .... Mexico
3 .... Iceland	8 .... UK	56 ...... Pakistan	51 .... Brazil
4 ...... Denmark	9 .... Germany	55 .... Jordan	50 .... Greece
5 .... Finland	10 ..... Australia	54 .... Korea	49 ..... Venezuela

GLOBAL FREEDOM

The US pressure-group Freedom House annually compiles a *Freedom in the World Survey* classifying countries by the political rights and civil liberties their citizens enjoy. Countries are judged to be: FREE, PARTLY FREE, or NOT FREE. The survey shows 26 countries became more free, and 11 regressed in 2005. The following countries have been classified by *www.freedomhouse.org* as still being NOT FREE:

Afghanistan · Algeria · Angola · Azerbaijan · Belarus · Bhutan · Brunei · Burma
Cambodia · Cameroon · Central African Republic · Chad · China · Congo
Côte d'Ivoire · Cuba · Egypt · Equatorial Guinea · Eritrea · Guinea · Haiti · Iran
Iraq · Kazakhstan · Kyrgyzstan · Laos · Lebanon · Libya · Maldives · Mauritania
North Korea · Oman · Pakistan · Qatar · Russia · Rwanda · Saudi Arabia
Somalia · Sudan · Swaziland · Syria · Tajikistan · Togo · Tunisia · Turkmenistan
United Arab Emirates · Uzbekistan · Vietnam · Zimbabwe

INTERNATIONAL DEVELOPMENT & AID

The Organisation for Economic Co-operation & Development's [OECD] annual review illustrates that development aid from the 22 major donors has increased from $58·3b to $69b. However, few donors are reaching the UN's target of giving 0·7% of their Gross National Income to Overseas Development Aid. For example:

Country	ODA $m	% GNI	Country	ODA $m	% GNI
Australia	1,219	0·25	Luxembourg	194	0·81
Canada	2,031	0·24	Netherlands	3,981	0·80
Denmark	1,748	0·84	Norway	2,042	0·92
France	7,253	0·41	Spain	1961	0·23
Germany	6,784	0·28	Sweden	2,400	0·79
Ireland	504	0·39	UK	6,282	0·34
Japan	8,880	0·20	US	16,254	0·15

[Latest released figures: 2003]

THE 'FORMER SOVIET UNION'

An informal term used for the successor nations to the Soviet Union or USSR:

Armenia · Azerbaijan · Belarus · Estonia · Georgia
Kazakhstan · Kyrgyzstan · Latvia · Lithuania · Moldova
Russia · Tajikistan · Turkmenistan · Ukraine · Uzbekistan

THE CIA'S WORLD VIEW

The US Central Intelligence Agency annually publishes its *World Factbook*, which tabulates statistical, political, geographical, and sociological data on the countries of the world. One of the entries details the 'comparative area' of each country, providing a comparison based on the entire US, or one of its individual states:

Afghanistan...slightly smaller than Texas
China..slightly smaller than the US
Denmark.........................slightly less than twice the size of Massachusetts
France ....less than twice the size of Colorado
Germany ....slightly smaller than Montana
Iran...slightly larger than Alaska
Iraq..slightly more than twice the size of Idaho
Israel...slightly smaller than New Jersey
Japan ....slightly smaller than California
Korea, North..slightly smaller than Mississippi
Lesotho ....slightly smaller than Maryland
Mexico..............................slightly less than three times the size of Texas
New Zealand...about the size of Colorado
Oman...slightly smaller than Kansas
Pakistan..................................less than twice the size of California
Russia ....slightly less than 1·8 times the size of the US
Spain..............................slightly more than twice the size of Oregon
United Kingdom ....slightly smaller than Oregon
Vietnam..slightly larger than New Mexico

LANDLOCKED COUNTRIES

Afghanistan · Andorra · Armenia · Austria · Azerbaijan · Belarus
Bhutan · Bolivia · Botswana · Burkina Faso · Burundi · Central African Rep.
Chad · Czech Republic · Ethiopia · Holy See (Vatican City) · Hungary
Kazakhstan · Kyrgyzstan · Laos · Lesotho · Liechtenstein[†] · Luxembourg
Malawi · Mali · Moldova · Mongolia · Nepal · Niger · Paraguay · Rwanda
San Marino · Slovakia · Swaziland · Switzerland · Tajikistan
The Former Yugoslav Republic of Macedonia · Turkmenistan
Uganda · Uzbekistan[†] · West Bank · Zambia · Zimbabwe
[† *'double landlocked' countries, being those surrounded by landlocked countries*]

UNIVERSAL DECLARATION OF HUMAN RIGHTS

[1] Right to equality and dignity. [2] Freedom from discrimination. [3] Right to life, liberty, personal security. [4] Freedom from slavery. [5] Freedom from torture and degradation. [6] Right to recognition before the law. [7] Equality before the law. [8] Right of appeal by competent tribunal. [9] Freedom from arbitrary arrest or exile. [10] Right to fair public hearing. [11] Presumption of innocence; freedom from retrospective law. [12] Freedom from interference with privacy, family, and correspondence. [13] Right of free movement. [14] Right to asylum from persecution. [15] Right to a nationality and freedom to change it. [16] Right to free marriage and family. [17] Right to own property. [18] Freedom of thought, belief, conscience, and worship. [19] Freedom of opinion and expression. [20] Right of peaceful assembly and association. [21] Right to participate in government; free elections under universal suffrage. [22] Right to social security. [23] Right to choose employment; join trades union; equal pay. [24] Right to rest and holidays. [25] Right to adequate living standards; protection of children. [26] Right to free elementary education. [27] Right to participate in cultural and scientific life. [28] Right to a social order that assures these rights. [29] Rights may only be limited by law to secure protection for others or the community. [30] Freedom from state or other interference in the above rights. *Condensed from the 1948 UN Universal Declaration*

ASYLUM DEFINED

According to the Refugee Council, the following definitions apply:

ASYLUM SEEKER · One who is fleeing persecution in their homeland and on arrival in another country has made themselves known to the authorities and exercised their legal right to apply for asylum.

FAILED ASYLUM SEEKER · One whose asylum application has been turned down and is awaiting return to their country.

REFUGEE · One whose asylum application was successful and who is allowed to stay in another country having proven they would have faced persecution in their homeland.

ILLEGAL IMMIGRANT · One who has arrived in another country and intentionally not made themselves known to the authorities and has no legal basis to be there.

ECONOMIC MIGRANT · One who has moved to another country to work.

COUNTRIES WITH MOST ASYLUM SEEKERS

The top ten international destinations for asylum seekers in the period 2000–04:

United States .. 411,700
UK 393,800
Germany....... 324,200
France.......... 279,200
Canada......... 175,200
Austria 144,800
Sweden......... 127,400
Belgium........ 118,400
Netherlands.... 118,300
Switzerland...... 99,400
[Source: *United Nations High Commissioner for Refugees*]

———————————————— THE DEATH PENALTY ————————————————

While five countries abolished the death penalty in 2004 (Bhutan, Greece, Samoa, Senegal, and Turkey), Amnesty International states that in the same year >3,797 were killed in 25 countries, the most for a decade. The worst offending states were:

China ....>3,400	USA.................59	Kuwait ....>9
Iran................>159	Saudi Arabia........>33	Bangladesh...........>7
Vietnam ....>64	Pakistan.............>15	Egypt.................>6

——————— WORLD TERRORISM RISK ASSESSMENT ———————

The risk insurance broker Aon creates an annual map of world terrorism risks. In 2005, even before 7/7, Britain was given an ELEVATED risk of attack – Glasgow, Belfast, Manchester, Birmingham, and London were identified as high risk targets with the same rating as Riyadh, Baghdad, and Mogadishu. Aon states that the risk in Britain stems from single-interest groups, Islamic extremists, and nationalists. Across the globe, the following were given a SEVERE risk rating: Israel, Saudi Arabia, Iraq, Somalia, Afghanistan, Pakistan, India, Nepal, and Colombia. In June 2005, it was reported that the courier DHL (who deliver to Baghdad) exercised caution in some areas of Britain because of attempts to steal parcels and vehicles.

———————————————— GENOCIDE ————————————————

According to Article 6 of the Rome Statute of the International Criminal Court:

... 'genocide' means any of the following acts committed with intent to destroy, in whole or in part, a national, ethnical, racial or religious group, as such:
(a) Killing members of the group;
(b) Causing serious bodily or mental harm to members of the group;

(c) Deliberately inflicting on the group conditions of life calculated to bring about its physical destruction in whole or in part;
(d) Imposing measures intended to prevent births within the group;
(e) Forcibly transferring children of the group to another group.

———————————— 'OUTPOSTS OF TYRANNY' ————————————

In January 2005, the newly appointed US Secretary of State, Condoleezza Rice, listed six 'outposts of tyranny' in which she claimed freedom had to be fostered:

IRAN · NORTH KOREA · CUBA · BURMA · BELARUS · ZIMBABWE

To many, this announcement seemed to hint at the future direction of US foreign policy, especially as it expanded on the 'axis of evil' (North Korea, Iran, and Iraq) that President George W. Bush defined in his 2002 State of the Union address.

──────── COUNTRIES WITH NUCLEAR WEAPONS ────────

Acknowledged: Britain, China, France, India, Pakistan, Russia, USA
Suspected: Israel, North Korea · *Seeking*: Iran · *Abandoned*: South Africa

──────── THE FBI'S MOST WANTED ────────

Fugitive [as at 14.9.2005]	*allegation*	*reward*
Osama Bin Laden	terrorism	$25,000,000†
Diego Leon Montoya Sanchez	drug running	$5,000,000
James J. Bulger	murder; racketeering	$1,000,000
Victor Manuel Gerena	armed robbery	$1,000,000
Genero Espinosa Dorantes	child murder	$100,000
Robert William Fisher	murder; arson	$100,000
Glen Stewart Godwin	murder; prison escape	$100,000
Richard Steve Goldberg	child abuse	$100,000
Jorge Alberto Lopez-Orozco	murder	$100,000
Donald Eugene Webb	murder	$100,000

† *An extra $2m is offered by the Airline Pilots Association and Air Transport Association. (Contact your local FBI office or the US Consulate with any information on the above.)*

──────── INTERPOL NOTICES ────────

Founded in 1923 and based in France, Interpol is the largest police organisation in the world, with 182 member countries. Its primary functions are to facilitate cross-border police co-operation and assist in combating international crime. Since 1946 Interpol has issued colour-coded notices across the world concerning people who are wanted by member countries or international tribunals. The coding is:

Red ... to seek arrest with a view to extradition
Yellow ... to help locate or identify missing persons, especially minors
Blue ... to collect additional information about a suspect or crime
Black ... to seek the identity of unidentified bodies
Green ... to provide warnings and intelligence about individuals
Orange ... to warn of potential threats from dangerous items or material

──────── EUROPEAN ARREST WARRANTS ────────

European Arrest Warrants [EAW] entered UK law in 2003; they provide for the swift arrest and extradition of suspects within the EU. Warrants can be made for 32 offences, ranging from terrorism to child pornography. The introduction of EAWs was opposed by some civil liberty groups who feared the erosion of basic legal rights. A 2005 report by the European Commission claims that EAWs had resulted in 104 extraditions, and had cut the process from 9 months to *c*.45 days.

——————— MILITARY SPENDING & AID ———————

According to a 2005 UN Report on Human Development, despite some increases in aid budgets and reductions in military spending (in a few European countries), the richest Western nations are allocating far more to defence budgets than to aid:

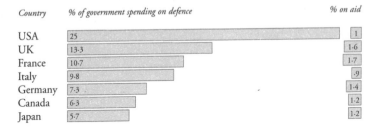

Country	% of government spending on defence	% on aid
USA	25	1
UK	13·3	1·6
France	10·7	1·7
Italy	9·8	·9
Germany	7·3	1·4
Canada	6·3	1·2
Japan	5·7	1·2

——————— SIGNIFICANT ONGOING CONFLICTS ———————

Middle East	*began*
US global war on terror & 'terrorists with global reach'	2001
Iraq interim government and allies & Iraqi and foreign resistance	2003
Israel & Hamas, Hezbollah, Islamic Jihad, &c.	1975
Israel & Palestinian Authority; Al-Aqsa Intifada	1948–94; 2000
Afghanistan: Kabul government & Al-Qaeda, Taliban and warlords	1978

Asia
India & All-Party Hurriyat Conference militants	1989
India & Assam and Manipur insurgents (ULFA & NDFB), &c.	1982; 1986
India & Pakistan	1948
Indonesia & Aceh separatists	1969–2002; 2003
Philippines & Abu Sayyaf	1999

Latin America
Colombia & National Liberation Army (ELN)	1978
Colombia & Revolutionary Armed forces of Colombia (FARC)	1978
Colombia & Autodefensas Unidas de Colombia (AUC)	1981
Haiti government & army and police factions and Aristide supporters	2004

Europe
Russia & Chechnya	1994; 1996

Africa
Algeria & Salafist Group for Preaching and Combat (GSPC)	1991
Côte d'Ivoire & Army rebels	2002
Democratic Republic of Congo & indigenous insurgents	1997
Nigeria: communal violence	1970
Somalia: Somaliland, Puntland, and other factions	1978
Sudan & Sudan Liberation and Justice and Equality Movements	1983; 2003
Uganda & Lord's Resistance Army	1986

[Source: Center for Defense Information · as of 1 January 2005 · Not all conflicts included]

———— DEPLOYMENT OF UN PEACEKEEPERS ————

There have been 60 United Nations peacekeeping missions since 1948, although the majority of these were established after 1991. The UN's peacekeeping troops are loaned voluntarily by member states, who pay troops at their own national scales but are reimbursed by the UN at a flat monthly rate *c*.$1,000 per soldier. The map below indicates ongoing UN peacekeeping missions, as of April 2005.

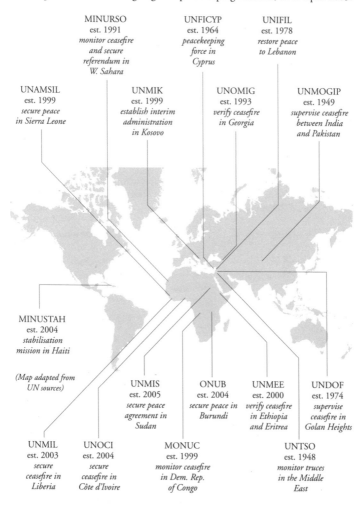

MINURSO
est. 1991
*monitor ceasefire
and secure
referendum in
W. Sahara*

UNFICYP
est. 1964
*peacekeeping
force in
Cyprus*

UNIFIL
est. 1978
*restore peace
to Lebanon*

UNAMSIL
est. 1999
*secure peace
in Sierra Leone*

UNMIK
est. 1999
*establish interim
administration
in Kosovo*

UNOMIG
est. 1993
*verify ceasefire
in Georgia*

UNMOGIP
est. 1949
*supervise ceasefire
between India
and Pakistan*

MINUSTAH
est. 2004
*stabilisation
mission in Haiti*

*(Map adapted from
UN sources)*

UNMIS
est. 2005
*secure peace
agreement in
Sudan*

ONUB
est. 2004
*secure peace in
Burundi*

UNMEE
est. 2000
*verify ceasefire
in Ethiopia
and Eritrea*

UNDOF
est. 1974
*supervise
ceasefire in
Golan Heights*

UNMIL
est. 2003
*secure
ceasefire in
Liberia*

UNOCI
est. 2004
*secure
ceasefire in
Côte d'Ivoire*

MONUC
est. 1999
*monitor ceasefire
in Dem. Rep.
of Congo*

UNTSO
est. 1948
*monitor truces
in the Middle
East*

It has been noted that the number of peacekeeping personnel (*c*.80,000) is dwarfed by the deployment of conventional forces – estimated by the World Watch Institute to be *c*.530,000 men, of which 70% are from the United States.

─────────────────── THE RED LIST ───────────────────

The World Conservation Union publishes a Red List of those species that are
under threat across the globe – from the vunerable, to those actually made extinct:

| Species | number under threat | | | extinct |
	1998	2000	2004	in 2004
Mammals	1,096	1,130	1,101	73
Birds	1,107	1,183	1,213	129
Amphibians	124	146	1,856	34
Reptiles	253	296	304	21
Fishes	734	752	800	81
Insects	537	555	559	59
Molluscs	920	938	974	291
Crustaceans	407	408	429	7
Plants	5,328	5,611	8,321	86

─────────────── ENVIRONMENTAL TIPPING POINTS ───────────────

Dr John Schellnhuber, of the Tyndall Centre for Climate Change Research, has
proposed a set of environmental 'tipping points' that, because of their sensitivity
to environmental change, would be the first to show the effects of global warming:

Region	possible effects of global warming
Sahara Desert	*wetter, greener Sahara could harm plankton in Atlantic*
Amazon forest	*death of rainforest would release dangerous amounts of CO_2*
Ozone hole	*increase in size would cause more skin cancers*
Greenland ice sheet	*temperature increase of 8° C would cause the sea to rise 7m*
Tibetan plateau	*if snow melts, temperature in Tibet will greatly increase*
Strait of Gibraltar	*acts as salinity valve; disruption could damage ecosystem*
North Atlantic current	*if stopped could cause temp. to drop by 10° C*
El Niño [see below]	*could increase incidence of flood, droughts, and storms*
West Antarctic ice sheet	*if melts, water levels would rise by 6m*
Siberian permafrost	*if melts, could release dangerous amounts of methane*
Indian monsoon	*a more severe monsoon season would damage food production*
Atlantic circumpolar current	*more rainfall would slow release of nutrients*

─────────────────────── EL NIÑO ───────────────────────

El Niño ('little boy' or 'Christ child') is a warm ocean current off the coast of Peru
that occurs every 4–12 years around Christmas. The effect of this current is to halt
the normal upwelling of cold, nutrient-rich water that supports plankton, fish,
and sea birds. Since El Niño is also associated with weakening the trade winds, its
ecological effects are widely felt. Severe El Niños (e.g. 1982–3; 1997–8) have been
linked to dramatic climate change worldwide: torrential rain across western South
America; droughts in Australia; typhoons in Japan; bush-fires in Indonesia; &c.

RECYCLING SYMBOLS

A bewildering array of recycling symbols exists across the world, and the general confusion they cause is exacerbated by a lack of international agreement. Below are some common everyday symbols and, underneath, some of those for plastics:

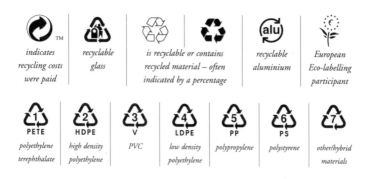

indicates recycling costs were paid	*recyclable glass*	*is recyclable or contains recycled material – often indicated by a percentage*		*recyclable aluminium*	*European Eco-labelling participant*

1 PETE	**2** HDPE	**3** V	**4** LDPE	**5** PP	**6** PS	**7**
polyethylene terephthalate	*high density polyethylene*	*PVC*	*low density polyethylene*	*polypropylene*	*polystyrene*	*other/hybrid materials*

KYOTO & CLIMATE CHANGE

The 1997 Kyoto Protocol to limit the emission of six 'greenhouse gases' came into force on 16 February 2005. Signatories to the Protocol undertook to cut their combined emissions to 5% below the 1990 levels by 2012. Each country has its own target, for example most EU countries aim for an 8% cut; Japan 5%; Canada 6%; and so on. Some countries emit such low levels that they may increase emissions, e.g. Australia by 8%, Iceland by 10%. Because countries have these varying targets, a new market in 'emissions trading' has emerged. Heavily polluting states may 'buy' credit from less polluting states, and states can earn 'credits' for projects that increase the absorption of carbon like tree planting and conservation. In Europe, over 12,000 power plants and factories are part of a carbon trading scheme where CO_2 emissions are traded like any other commodity. The current cost of 1 tonne of CO_2 is about €20. ❦ 141 countries responsible for 55% of greenhouse gases have ratified the Kyoto Protocol including, crucially, Russia. However, America (the world's most prolific emitter of greenhouse gases) and Australia have both refused. George W. Bush withdrew from Kyoto in 2001, fearing it would damage America's economy, and claiming it was 'fatally flawed' in not committing developing nations like China and India to cut emissions – only to report progress. In July 2005, the US and Australia announced a new plan to slow global warming based upon new technological solutions and voluntary reductions in gas emission. At the time of writing, details of the plan and its supporting countries are unclear – while many environmental campaigners are sceptical of the proposal, fearing a US-led pact to undermine Kyoto.

TARGETED EMISSIONS
Carbon dioxide (CO_2)
Methane (CH_4)
Hydrofluorocarbons (HFCs)
Perfluorocarbons (PFCs)
Sulphur hexafluoride (SF_6)

—SAFFIR-SIMPSON HURRICANE INTENSITY SCALE—

Category	wind (mph)	storm surge (ft)	description	example
1	74–95	3–5	Minimal	Gaston (2004)
2	96–110	6–8	Moderate	Frances (2004)
3	111–130	9–12	Extensive	Ivan (2004)
4	131–155	13–18	Extreme	Charley (2004)
5	>156	>18	Catastrophic	Katrina (2005)

The scale above is used in the USA to measure Atlantic and NE Pacific hurricanes. 'Hurricane' and 'typhoon' are regional names for strong 'tropical cyclones' – defined as 'non-frontal synoptic scale low-pressure system over tropical or sub-tropical waters with organised convection (i.e. thunderstorms) and definite cyclonic surface wind circulation'. Tropical cylcones with windspeeds >39mph are 'tropical depressions'. Those with windspeeds 39–73mph are 'tropical storms'. When tropical cyclones reach a windspeed ≥74mph, the term used depends on the Ocean they hit: 'hurricane' in N Atlantic, NE Pacific, or S Pacific; 'typhoon' in NW Pacific; 'severe tropical cyclone' in SW Pacific or SE Indian; 'severe cyclonic storm' in N Indian; and 'tropical cyclone' in SW Indian.

—DECADE VOLCANOES—

The *International Association of Volcanology and Chemistry of the Earth's Interior* has designated 16 volcanoes as *Decade Volcanoes* because of their violent histories. The *Decade Volcano* project has a number of aims – not least to encourage research and increase awareness of potential hazards. Those classified as *Decade Volcanoes* are:

Avachinsky-Koryaksky	Russia	Santa Maria/Santiaguito*	Guatemala
Colima*	Mexico	Santorini	Greece
Etna*	Italy	Taal	Philippines
Galeras*	Colombia	Teide	Spain
Mauna Loa*	Hawaii, USA	Ulawun*	Papua New Guinea
Merapi*	Indonesia	Unzen	Japan
Niragongo	Zaire	Vesuvius	Italy
Rainier*	USA		
Sakurajima*	Japan	[* denotes a volcano active in 2005]	

Below is the Volcanic Explosivity Index (VEI) used to classify volcanic eruptions:

VEI	category	plume	frequency	classification
0	Non-explosive	<100m	daily	Hawaiian
1	Gentle	100m–1km	daily	Hawaiian/Strombolian
2	Explosive	1–5km	weekly	Strombolian/Vulcanian
3	Severe	3–15km	yearly	Vulcanian
4	Cataclysmic	10–25km	10s years	Vulcanian/Plinian
5	Paroxysmal	>25km	100s years	Plinian
6	Colossal	>25km	100s years	Plinian/Ultra-Plinian
7	Super-colossal	>25km	1,000s years	Ultra-Plinian
8	Mega-colossal	>25km	10,000s years	Ultra-Plinian

BEAUFORT WIND SCALE

Beaufort Scale	sea height feet	wind knots	wind MPH	description
0	—	<1	<1	calm
1	¼	1–3	1–3	light air
2	½	4–6	4–7	light breeze
3	2	7–10	8–12	gentle breeze
4	3½	11–16	13–18	moderate breeze
5	6	17–21	19–24	fresh breeze
6	9½	22–27	25–31	strong breeze
7	13½	28–33	32–38	near gale
8	18	34–40	39–46	gale
9	23	41–47	47–54	strong gale
10	29	48–55	55–63	storm
11	37	56–63	64–72	violent storm
12	—	≥64	≥73	hurricane

EARTHQUAKE SCALES

RICHTER	MERCALLI SCALE & DESCRIPTION	SEVERITY
<4·3	i ..... *barely noticeable; doors may swing* ii .... *detected by some; slight* iii .... *traffic-like vibration*	Mild
4·3–4·8	iv .... *cars rock; pictures moved* v .... *buildings tremble; trees shake*	Moderate
4·8–6·2	vi .... *plaster cracks; hard to stand* vii .... *alarm; moderate building damage* viii .... *fright; considerable damage*	Intermediate
6·2–7·3	ix .... *panic; landslides, earth shifts* x .... *ground cracks; buildings collapse*	Severe
>7·3	xi .... *destruction; few buildings stand* xii .. *devastation; ground moves in waves*	Catastrophic

[The relationship between Richter and Mercalli scales is approximate]

FUJITA-PEARSON TORNADO INTENSITY SCALE

F-Scale	wind (mph)	damage	name
F0	40–72	*minor roof, tree, sign damage*	Gale
F1	73–112	*barns torn apart, cars thrown from road*	Moderate
F2	113–157	*weak buildings destroyed; trees uprooted*	Significant
F3	158–206	*trains overturned; most roofs torn off*	Severe
F4	207–260	*cars thrown into air; homes levelled*	Devastating
F5	261–318	*strong buildings completely blown away*	Incredible
F6	>319	*unlikely to occur on Earth*	Inconceivable

—————————— AIR POLLUTION BANDING SYSTEM ——————————

DEFRA provides a daily air pollution warning from 110 sample sites across Britain. The warning is set by the highest level of any of the following five pollutants:

sulphur dioxide [SO_2] · *nitrogen dioxide* [NO_2]
ozone [O_3]· *carbon monoxide* [CO]· *particles*

Index	band	effect on health
1–3	LOW	generally unnoticed, even by people sensitive† to pollutants
4–6	MODERATE	mild effects, unlikely to need treatment
7–9	HIGH	sensitive people may notice significant effects and should avoid spending too much time outdoors
10	VERY HIGH	worsening of effects in sensitive people

†Sensitive people are classed as those with heart or lung diseases, such as asthma; pollution may also affect the elderly more seriously · For daily forecasts specific to an area click on www.airquality.co.uk

——————————— SUN PROTECTION FACTOR ———————————

Sun Protection Factor (SPF) indicates the strength of a sunscreen lotion: the higher the SPF, the greater the protection. SPF is a measure of the time taken for skin to burn while wearing sunscreen compared to skin without protection. So, skin that would normally burn in 10 minutes, would be protected for *c.*20 minutes with a suncream SPF 2. In strong sun it is advisable to apply suncream of at least SPF 15.

————————————— THE SUN INDEX —————————————

The Sun Index, designed to protect against UV radiation, categorises 4 skin types:

[1] *white skin that burns easily and tends not to tan*
[2] *white skin that tans easily* · [3] *brown skin* · [4] *black skin*

By estimating cloud cover, forecasters can then assess the risk for each skin type:

Skin type		Sun Index									
	1	2	3	4	5	6	7	8	9	10
1·····	risk: *low*		*medium*		*high*		*very high*			
2·····	risk: *low*				*medium*		*high*			
3·····	risk: *low*					*medium*				*high*
4·····	risk: *low*						*medium*			

Low risk: sun is harmless · *Medium risk*: sun not a danger but avoid spending >2 hours in direct sun · *High risk*: you could burn within 30 minutes; cover up, stay out of the sun, and wear sunscreen ≥SPF 15 · *Very high risk*: you could burn severely in 20–30 minutes; cover up, stay out of sun, and wear sunscreen ≥SPF 15.

WEATHER RECORDS

United Kingdom [Met Office]

Max. temperature	38·5° C	Brogdale nr. Faversham	10·08·2004
Lowest temperature	-27·2° C	Braemar, Grampian	11·02·1895
Max. rainfall 24 hrs	279mm	Martinstown, Dorset	18·07·1955
Max. rainfall 60 mins	92mm	Maidenhead, Berkshire	12·07·1901
Max. rainfall 5 mins	32mm	Preston, Lancashire	10·08·1893
Max. monthly sunshine	384 hrs	Eastbourne, Sussex	July 1911
Lowest monthly sunshine	0 hrs	Westminster, London	Dec 1890
Max. gust record	150 knots	Cairngorm, Grampian	20·03·1986

The World [NOAA]

Max. annual rainfall	13,299mm	Lloro, Colombia	average
Least annual rainfall	0·762mm	Arica, Chile	average
Max. temperature	57·7° C	Al Azizia, Libya	13·09·1922
Lowest temperature	-89·4° C	Vostok, Antartica	21·07·1983

POLLEN COUNT

UK pollen counts are produced by the National Pollen and Aerobiology Research Unit that collects data from 33 monitoring sites across the country. The count measures the number of pollen grains per cubic metre of air sampled, which is then averaged out over a period of 24 hours. Below are the four bands employed:

LOW.....................<30 grains/m3 | HIGH...........................50–149
MODERATE ....30–49 | VERY HIGH.......................>150

UK HEATWAVE WARNING SYSTEM

In response to the catastrophic heatwave that hit France in 2003 and resulted in *c.*15,000 'excess deaths', the British Government introduced a *Heat-Health Watch* system to inform the public, and protect 'at risk' groups like the sick and elderly. The system operates from 1 June – 15 September and is based upon Met Office forecasts reported to the Department of Health. The four levels of response are triggered by the forecasted risk of breaking maximum 'threshold temperatures'. These thresholds vary by region; the average is 30° C by day, and 15° C at night. Each level demands a different response from local government, health and care workers, and organisations like the Health Protection Agency. The four levels are:

Level   *description*
1 – Awareness...*risk of heatwave* <50%
 – Awareness Increased Risk ....*risk of heatwave* >50%
2 – Alert..*risk of heatwave* >80%
3 – Heatwave ....*threshold temperatures will be reached in one or more regions*
4 – Emergency .....*effects of the heatwave extend outside the health and care systems*

———— SUMMITS, WORLD WONDERS, & OTHER 7s ————

7 MODERN WONDERS
(American Society of Civil Engineers)
The Empire State Building
The Itaipu Dam · The CN Tower
The Panama Canal · Channel Tunnel
The North Sea Protection Works
The Golden Gate Bridge

7 CAUSES OF GREATNESS IN CITIES
The palace of a Prince
A navigable river
The residence of the nobility
The seat of justice
Public schools of good learning
Immunities from taxes
Opinion of sanctity

7 WONDERS OF WALES
The Mountains of Snowdon
Overton Churchyard
The Bells of Gresford Church
Llangollen Bridge · Wrexham Steeple
Pystyl Rhaiadr Waterfall
St Winifrid's Well

7 PRE-MODERN WONDERS
Stonehenge · The Colosseum
The Catacombs of Kom el Shoqafa
The Great Wall of China
The Porcelain Tower of Nanjing
The Hagia Sophia
The Leaning Tower of Pisa

7 WONDERS OF THE ANCIENT WORLD
The Pyramids of Egypt
The Colossus of Rhodes
The Hanging Gardens of Babylon
The Mausoleum of Halicarnassus
The Statue of Zeus at Olympia
The Temple of Artemis at Ephesus
The Pharos of Alexandria

7 NATURAL WONDERS
(according to CNN)
The Grand Canyon
The Harbour of Rio de Janeiro
The Northern Lights
The Great Barrier Reef
Victoria Falls · Mount Everest
Paricutin Volcano

7 SORTS OF PEOPLE GREAT IN TITLE BUT POOR IN PURSE
The Dons of Spain
The Monsieurs of France
The Bishops of Italy
The Nobility of Hungary
The Lairds of Scotland
The Earls of Germany
The Knights of Naples

'No one can remember more than seven of anything.' — St Robert Bellarmine, on why his catechism omitted the eight beatitudes.

The impressive mountaineering feat of climbing the SEVEN SUMMITS, the highest peak on each of the seven continents, was first achieved by Dick Bass in 1985.

Summit	continent	country	height (ft)
Mt Everest	Asia	Nepal/Tibet	29,045
Mt Aconcagua	South America	Argentina	22,834
Mt McKinley	North America	Alaska	20,320
Mt Kilimanjaro	Africa	Tanzania	19,340
Mt Elbrus	Europe	Russia	18,510
Vinson Massif	Antarctica	Antarctic	16,066
Kosciusko[†]	Australia	Australia	7,310

† Some dispute the inclusion of this peak, proposing instead the Carstenz Pyramid (16,023ft) in Irian Jaya, Oceania. Sadly, Oceania is not officially a continent [see p.51].

——— QUALITY OF LIFE ———

The *Economist Intelligence Unit's* new 'quality of life' index is calculated using a range of variables from wealth and health to climate and security. The 2005 top 19 ranked countries are:

1 .... Ireland	11 ..... Singapore
2 ..... Switzerland	12 .... Finland
3 .... Norway	13 .... US
4 .... Luxembourg	14 .... Canada
5 .... Sweden	15 . New Zealand
6 .... Australia	16 ... Netherlands
7 .... Iceland	17 .... Japan
8 .... Italy	18 ... Hong Kong
9 .... Denmark	19 .... Portugal
10 .... Spain	(29 .... UK)

——— BRIBERY ———

Transparency International's annual Global Corruption Barometer surveys 64 countries each year. One question asked is: *'In the past twelve months have you or anyone living in your household paid a bribe in any form?'.* Below are some 'yes' results from the '04 survey:

Cameroon .. 52%		Ghana 27
Kenya 36		Romania 25
Lithuania 32		Ukraine 25
Moldova 32		Czech Rep 21
Nigeria 32		Philippines 21
Albania 30		Russia 21
Bolivia 29		Mexico 19
Ecuador 27		(UK .... 1)

——— NOTES TO THE GAZETTEER ———

The gazetteer on the following pages is designed to allow comparisons to be made between countries around the world. As might be expected, some of the data are tentative and open to debate. A range of sources has been consulted, including the CIA's *World Factbook*, Amnesty International, HM Revenue and Customs, &c.

Size km²	*sum of all land and water areas delimited by international boundaries and coastlines*
Population	*mainly July 2004 estimate; some vary*
Flying time	*approximate actual travelling time from London Heathrow to capital city; will vary depending on route and connecting flight, as well as direction travelled, &c.*
±GMT	*based on capital city; varies across some countries; varies with daylight saving*
Life expectancy at birth	*in years; mainly 2005 estimate*
Infant mortality	*deaths of infants <1, per 1,000 live births, per year; mainly 2005 estimate*
Median age	*mainly 2005 estimate*
Birth & death rates	*average per 1,000 persons in the population at mid-year; mainly 2005 estimate*
Fertility rate	*average theoretical number of children per woman; mainly 2005 estimate*
HIV rate	*percentage of adults (15–49) living with HIV/AIDS; mainly 2001 or 2003 estimate*
Literacy rate	*definition (especially of target age) varies; mainly 2005 estimate*
Exchange rate	*spot rate at 01·8·05*
GDP per capita	*($) GDP on purchasing power parity basis/population; mainly 2004*
Inflation	*annual % change in consumer prices; years vary generally from 2000*
Unemployment	*% of labour force without jobs; years vary generally from 2000*
Voting age	*voting age; (U)niversal; (C)ompulsory for at least one election; *=entitlement varies*
Death penalty	*(N) no death penalty; (N*) death penalty not used in practice (Y) death penalty for common crimes; (Y*) death penalty for exceptional crimes only;*
Military service	*age, length of service, sex and/or religion required to serve vary*
National day	*some countries have more than one; not all are universally recognised*

─── GAZETTEER · ALGERIA – SOUTH KOREA · [1/4] ───

Country	Size (km²)	Population (m)	Capital city	Phone access code	Phone country code	Flying time (h)	± GMT
United Kingdom	244,820	60·4	London	00	44	—	N/A
United States	9,631,418	295·7	Washington, DC	011	1	7h50	-5
Algeria	2,381,740	32·5	Algiers	00	213	2h45	+1
Argentina	2,766,890	39·5	Buenos Aires	00	54	15h45	-3
Australia	7,686,850	20·1	Canberra	0011	61	25h	+9½
Austria	83,870	8·2	Vienna	00	43	2h20	+1
Belarus	207,600	10·3	Minsk	810	375	4h40	+2
Belgium	30,528	10·4	Brussels	00	32	1h	+1
Brazil	8,511,965	186·1	Brasilia	0014	55	16h	-3
Bulgaria	110,910	7·5	Sofia	00	359	3h	+2
Burma/Myanmar	678,500	42·9	Rangoon/Yangon	00	95	13h	+6½
Cambodia	181,040	13·6	Phnom Penh	001	855	14h	+7
Canada	9,984,670	32·8	Ottawa	011	1	7h45	-5
Chile	756,950	16·0	Santiago	00	56	17h	-4
China	9,596,960	1·3b	Beijing	00	86	10h	+8
Colombia	1,138,910	43·0	Bogota	009	57	13h	-5
Cuba	110,860	11·3	Havana	119	53	12h	-5
Czech Republic	78,866	10·2	Prague	00	420	1h50	+1
Denmark	43,094	5·4	Copenhagen	00	45	1h50	+1
Egypt	1,001,450	77·5	Cairo	00	20	4h45	+2
Estonia	45,226	1·3	Tallinn	00	372	4h	+2
Finland	338,145	5·2	Helsinki	00	358	3h	+2
France	547,030	60·7	Paris	00	33	50m	+1
Germany	357,021	82·4	Berlin	00	49	1h40	+1
Greece	131,940	10·7	Athens	00	30	3h45m	+2
Haiti	27,750	8·1	Port-au-Prince	00	509	20h30	-5
Hong Kong	1,092	6·9	—	001	852	12h	+8
Hungary	93,030	10·0	Budapest	00	36	2h25	+1
India	3,287,590	1·1b	New Delhi	00	91	8h30	+5½
Indonesia	1,919,440	242·0	Jakarta	001	62	16h	+8
Iran	1,648,000	68·0	Tehran	00	98	6h	+3½
Iraq	437,072	26·1	Baghdad	00	964	14h30	+3
Ireland	70,280	4·0	Dublin	00	353	1h	0
Israel	20,770	6·3	Jerusalem/Tel Aviv	00	972	5h	+2
Italy	301,230	58·1	Rome	00	39	2h20	+1
Japan	377,835	127·4	Tokyo	010	81	11h30	+9
Jordan	92,300	5·8	Amman	00	962	6h	+2
Kazakhstan	2,717,300	15·2	Astana	810	7	8h15	+4
Kenya	582,650	33·8	Nairobi	000	254	8h20	+3
Korea, North	120,540	22·9	Pyongyang	00	850	13h45	+9
Korea, South	98,480	48·4	Seoul	001	82	11h	+9

———— GAZETTEER · KUWAIT – ZIMBABWE · [1/4] ————

Country	Size (km²)	Population (m)	Capital city	Phone access code	Phone country code	Flying time (h)	± GMT
United Kingdom	244,820	60·4	London	00	44	—	N/A
United States	9,631,418	295·7	Washington DC	011	1	7h50	-5
Kuwait	17,820	2·3	Kuwait City	00	965	6h	+3
Latvia	64,589	2·3	Riga	00	371	2h45	+2
Lebanon	10,400	3·8	Beirut	00	961	4h45	+2
Liberia	111,370	3·5	Monrovia	00	231	12h	0
Lithuania	65,200	3·6	Vilnius	00	370	4h	+2
Malaysia	329,750	24·0	Kuala Lumpur	00	60	12h25	+8
Mexico	1,972,550	106·2	Mexico City	00	52	11h15	-7
Monaco	195	32·4k	Monaco	00	377	2h	+1
Morocco	446,300	32·7	Rabat	00	212	5h45	0
Netherlands	41,526	16·4	Amsterdam	00	31	1h15	+1
New Zealand	268,680	4·0	Wellington	00	64	28h	+12
Nigeria	923,768	128·8	Abuja	009	234	6h15	+1
Norway	324,220	4·6	Oslo	00	47	2h	+1
Pakistan	803,940	162·4	Islamabad	00	92	10h	+5
Peru	1,285,220	27·9	Lima	00	51	15h15	-5
Philippines	300,000	87·9	Manila	00	63	15h	+8
Poland	312,685	38·6	Warsaw	00	48	2h20	+1
Portugal	92,391	10·6	Lisbon	00	351	2h30	0
Romania	237,500	22·3	Bucharest	00	40	3h15	+2
Russia	17,075,200	143·4	Moscow	810	7	4h	+3
Rwanda	26,338	8·4	Kigali	00	250	11h20	+2
Saudi Arabia	1,960,582	26·4	Riyadh	00	966	6h15	+3
Singapore	692·7	4·4	Singapore	001	65	12h45	+8
Slovakia	48,845	5·4	Bratislava	00	421	3h30	+1
Slovenia	20,273	2·0	Ljubljana	00	386	3h30	+1
Somalia	637,657	8·6	Mogadishu	00	252	12h45	+3
South Africa	1,219,912	44·3	Pretoria/Tshwane	09	27	11h	+2
Spain	504,782	40·3	Madrid	00	34	2h20	+1
Sudan	2,505,810	40·2	Khartoum	00	249	12h	+3
Sweden	449,964	9·0	Stockholm	00	46	2h30	+1
Switzerland	41,290	7·5	Bern	00	41	2h	+1
Syria	185,180	18·4	Damascus	00	963	6h30	+2
Taiwan	35,980	22·9	Taipei	002	886	14h30	+8
Thailand	514,000	65·4	Bangkok	001	66	14h20	+7
Turkey	780,580	69·7	Ankara	00	90	5h15	+2
Ukraine	603,700	47·4	Kiev	810	380	3h25	+2
Venezuela	912,050	25·4	Caracas	00	58	11h30	-4
Vietnam	329,560	83·5	Hanoi	00	84	13h45	+7
Zimbabwe	390,580	12·7	Harare	00	263	12h50	+2

——— GAZETTEER · ALGERIA – SOUTH KOREA · [2/4] ———

Country	Male life expectancy	Female life expectancy	difference	Infant mortality	Median age	Birth rate	Death rate	Fertility rate	Adult HIV rate	Literacy
United Kingdom	75·9	81·0	-5·1	5·2	39·0	10·8	10·2	1·7	0·2	99
United States	74·9	80·7	-5·8	6·5	36·3	14·1	8·3	2·1	0·6	97
Algeria	71·5	74·6	-3·1	31·0	24·4	17·1	4·6	1·9	0·1	70
Argentina	72·2	79·9	-7·7	15·2	29·4	16·9	7·6	2·2	0·7	97
Australia	77·5	83·4	-5·9	4·7	36·6	12·3	7·4	1·8	0·1	100
Austria	76·0	82·0	-6	4·7	40·4	8·8	9·7	1·4	0·3	98
Belarus	63·0	74·7	-11·7	13·4	37·0	10·8	14·2	1·4	0·3	100
Belgium	75·4	81·9	-6·5	4·7	40·6	10·5	10·2	1·6	0·2	98
Brazil	67·7	75·9	-8·2	29·6	27·8	16·8	6·2	1·9	0·7	86
Bulgaria	68·4	75·9	-7·5	20·6	40·7	9·7	14·3	1·4	0·1	99
Burma/Myanmar	54·3	58·2	-3·9	67·3	26·1	18·1	12·2	2·0	1·2	85
Cambodia	55·9	62·0	-6·1	71·5	19·9	27·1	9·0	3·4	2·6	69
Canada	76·7	83·6	-6·9	4·8	38·5	10·8	7·7	1·6	0·3	97
Chile	73·3	80·0	-6·7	8·8	30·1	15·4	5·8	2·0	0·3	96
China	70·7	74·1	-3·4	24·9	32·3	13·1	6·9	1·7	0·1	91
Colombia	67·9	75·7	-7·8	21·0	26·0	20·8	5·6	2·6	0·7	93
Cuba	74·9	79·7	-4·8	6·3	35·4	12·0	7·2	1·7	0·1	97
Czech Republic	72·7	79·5	-6·8	3·9	39·0	9·1	10·5	1·2	0·1	100
Denmark	75·3	80·0	-4·7	4·6	39·5	11·4	10·4	1·7	0·2	100
Egypt	68·5	73·6	-5·1	32·6	23·7	23·3	5·3	2·9	0·1	58
Estonia	66·3	77·6	-11·3	7·9	39·1	9·9	13·2	1·4	1·1	100
Finland	74·8	82·0	-7·2	3·6	41·0	10·5	9·8	1·7	0·1	100
France	76·0	83·4	-7·4	4·3	38·9	12·2	9·1	1·9	0·4	99
Germany	75·7	81·8	-6·1	4·2	42·2	8·3	10·6	1·4	0·1	99
Greece	76·6	81·8	-5·2	5·5	40·5	9·7	10·2	1·3	0·2	98
Haiti	51·6	54·3	-2·7	73·5	18·0	36·7	12·3	5·0	5·6	53
Hong Kong	78·7	84·3	-5·6	3·0	39·4	7·2	6·0	0·9	0·1	94
Hungary	68·2	76·9	-8·7	8·6	38·6	9·8	13·2	1·3	0·1	99
India	63·6	65·2	-1·6	56·3	24·7	22·3	8·3	2·8	0·9	60
Indonesia	67·1	72·1	-5·0	35·6	26·5	20·7	6·3	2·4	0·1	88
Iran	68·6	71·4	-2·8	41·6	24·2	16·8	5·6	1·8	0·1	79
Iraq	67·5	70·0	-2·5	50·3	19·4	32·5	5·5	4·3	0·1	40
Ireland	75·0	80·3	-5·3	5·4	33·7	14·5	7·9	1·9	0·1	98
Israel	77·2	81·6	-4·4	7·0	29·4	18·2	6·2	2·4	0·1	95
Italy	76·8	82·8	-6·0	5·9	41·8	8·9	10·3	1·3	0·5	99
Japan	77·9	84·6	-6·7	3·3	42·6	9·5	9·0	1·4	0·1	99
Jordan	75·8	80·9	-5·1	17·4	22·6	21·8	2·6	2·7	0·1	91
Kazakhstan	61·2	72·2	-11·0	29·2	28·5	15·8	9·5	1·9	0·2	98
Kenya	48·9	47·1	1·8	61·5	18·2	40·1	14·7	5·0	6·7	85
Korea, North	68·7	74·2	-5·5	24·0	31·7	16·1	7·1	2·2	—	99
Korea, South	72·2	79·8	-7·6	7·1	34·5	10·1	6·3	1·3	0·1	98

Country	Male life expectancy	Female life expectancy	difference	Infant mortality	Median age	Birth rate	Death rate	Fertility rate	Adult HIV rate	Literacy
United Kingdom	75·9	81·0	-5·1	5·2	39·0	10·8	10·2	1·7	0·2	99
United States	74·9	80·7	-5·8	6·5	36·3	14·1	8·3	2·1	0·6	97
Kuwait	76·0	78·1	-2·1	10·0	25·9	21·9	2·4	3·0	0·1	84
Latvia	65·8	76·6	-10·8	9·6	39·1	9·0	13·7	1·3	0·6	100
Lebanon	70·2	75·2	-5·0	24·5	27·3	18·9	6·2	1·9	0·1	87
Liberia	46·8	48·7	-1·9	128·9	18·1	44·2	17·9	6·1	5·9	58
Lithuania	68·9	79·3	-10·4	6·9	37·8	8·6	10·9	1·2	0·1	100
Malaysia	69·6	75·1	-5·5	17·7	23·9	23·1	5·1	3·1	0·4	89
Mexico	72·4	78·1	-5·7	20·9	24·9	21·0	4·7	2·5	0·3	92
Monaco	75·7	83·6	-7·9	5·4	45·3	9·3	12·7	1·8	—	99
Morocco	68·4	73·0	-4·6	41·6	23·6	22·3	5·6	2·7	0·1	52
Netherlands	76·3	81·5	-5·2	5·0	39·0	11·1	8·7	1·7	0·2	99
New Zealand	75·7	81·8	-6·1	5·9	33·7	13·9	7·5	1·8	0·1	99
Nigeria	46·5	47·3	-0·8	98·8	18·6	40·7	17·2	5·5	5·4	68
Norway	76·8	82·2	-5·4	3·7	38·2	11·7	9·5	1·8	0·1	100
Pakistan	62·0	64·0	-2·0	72·4	19·6	30·4	8·5	4·1	0·1	46
Peru	67·8	71·4	-3·6	31·9	25·0	20·9	6·3	2·6	0·5	91
Philippines	67·0	72·9	-5·9	23·5	22·3	25·3	5·5	3·2	0·1	93
Poland	70·3	78·8	-8·5	8·5	36·4	10·8	10·0	1·4	0·1	100
Portugal	74·3	81·0	-6·7	5·1	38·2	10·8	10·4	1·5	0·4	93
Romania	67·9	75·1	-7·2	26·4	36·4	10·7	11·7	1·4	0·1	98
Russia	60·6	74·0	-13·4	15·4	38·2	9·8	14·5	1·3	1·1	100
Rwanda	45·9	48·0	-2·1	91·2	18·5	40·6	16·3	5·5	5·1	70
Saudi Arabia	73·5	77·6	-4·1	13·2	21·3	29·6	2·6	4·1	0·1	79
Singapore	79·1	84·4	-5·3	2·3	36·8	9·5	4·2	1·1	0·2	93
Slovakia	70·5	78·7	-8·2	7·4	35·4	10·6	9·4	1·3	0·1	—
Slovenia	72·4	80·1	-7·7	4·5	40·2	9·0	10·2	1·2	0·1	100
Somalia	46·4	49·9	-3·5	116·7	17·6	45·6	17·0	6·8	1·0	38
South Africa	43·5	43·1	0·4	61·8	24·0	18·5	21·3	2·2	21·5	86
Spain	76·2	83·1	-6·9	4·4	39·5	10·1	9·6	1·3	0·7	98
Sudan	57·3	59·8	-2·5	62·5	18·1	35·2	9·2	4·9	2·3	61
Sweden	78·2	82·7	-4·5	2·8	40·6	10·4	10·4	1·7	0·1	99
Switzerland	77·6	83·4	-5·8	4·4	39·8	9·8	8·5	1·4	0·4	99
Syria	68·8	71·4	-2·6	29·5	20·4	28·3	4·9	3·5	0·1	77
Taiwan	74·5	80·3	-5·8	6·4	34·1	12·6	6·4	1·6	—	96
Thailand	69·4	73·9	-4·5	20·5	30·9	15·7	7·0	1·9	1·5	93
Turkey	69·9	74·9	-5·0	41·0	27·7	16·8	6·0	1·9	0·1	87
Ukraine	61·6	72·4	-10·8	20·3	38·2	10·5	16·4	1·4	1·4	100
Venezuela	71·3	77·6	-6·3	22·2	25·6	18·9	4·9	2·3	0·7	93
Vietnam	67·8	73·6	-5·8	26·0	25·5	17·1	6·2	1·9	0·4	90
Zimbabwe	37·2	36·1	1·1	67·7	19·3	29·7	24·7	3·5	24·6	91

Country	Currency	Currency code	£1 =	GDP per capita $	Inflation %	Unemployment %	Fiscal year end
United Kingdom	Pound=100 Pence	GPB		29,600	1·4	4·8	5 Apr
United States	Dollar=100 Cents	USD	1·7	40,100	2·5	5·5	30 Oct
Algeria	Dinar=100 Centimes	DZD	129·6	6,600	3·1	25·4	31 Dec
Argentina	Peso=10,000 Australes	ARS	4·9	12,400	6·1	14·8	31 Dec
Australia	Dollar=100 Cents	AUD	2·3	30,700	2·3	5·1	30 Jun
Austria	euro=100 cent	EUR	1·4	31,300	1·8	4·4	31 Dec
Belarus	Ruble=100 Kopecks	BYB	3771·7	6,800	17·4	2	31 Dec
Belgium	euro=100 cent	EUR	1·4	30,600	1·9	12	31 Dec
Brazil	Real=100 Centavos	BRL	4·1	8,100	7·6	11·5	31 Dec
Bulgaria	Lev=100 Stotinki	BGN	2·8	8,200	6·1	12·7	31 Dec
Burma/Myanmar	Kyat=100 Pyas	MMK	11·3	1,700	17·2	5·2	31 Mar
Cambodia	Riel=100 Sen	KHR	7188·8	2,000	3·1	2·5	31 Dec
Canada	Dollar=100 Cents	CAD	2·1	31,500	1·9	7	31 Mar
Chile	Peso=100 Centavos	CLP	1011·6	10,700	2·4	8·5	31 Dec
China	Renminbi Yuan=100 Fen	CNY	14·5	5,600	4·1	9·8	31 Dec
Colombia	Peso=100 Centavos	COP	4086·4	6,600	5·9	13·6	31 Dec
Cuba	Peso=100 Centavos	CUP/C	1·6	3,000	3·1	2·5	31 Dec
Czech Republic	Koruna=100 Haléru	CZK	44·0	16,800	3·2	10·6	31 Dec
Denmark	Krone=100 Øre	DKK	10·7	32,200	1·4	6·2	31 Dec
Egypt	Pound=100 Piastres	EGP	10·1	4,200	9·5	10·9	30 Jun
Estonia	Kroon=100 sents	EEK	22·1	14,300	3	9·6	31 Dec
Finland	euro=100 cent	EUR	1·4	29,000	0·7	8·9	31 Dec
France	euro=100 cent	EUR	1·4	28,700	2·3	10·1	31 Dec
Germany	euro=100 cent	EUR	1·4	28,700	1·6	10·6	31 Dec
Greece	euro=100 cent	EUR	1·4	21,300	2·9	10	31 Dec
Haiti	Gourde=100 Centimes	HTG	73·0	1,500	22	c·65	30 Sep
Hong Kong	HK Dollar=100 Cents	HKD	13·5	34,200	-0·3	6·7	31 Mar
Hungary	Forint=100 Fillér	HUF	358·9	14,900	7	5·9	31 Dec
India	Rupee=100 Paisa	INR	75·2	3,100	4·2	9·2	31 Mar
Indonesia	Rupiah=100 Sen	IDR	17135·6	3,500	6·1	9·2	31 Dec
Iran	Rial	IRR	15776·3	7,700	15·5	11·2	20 Mar
Iraq	New Iraqi Dinar	NID	2588·1	3,500	25·4	30	31 Dec
Ireland	euro=100 cent	EUR	1·4	31,900	2·2	4·3	31 Dec
Israel	Shekel=100 Agora	ILS	7·9	20,800	0	10·7	31 Dec
Italy	euro=100 cent	EUR	1·4	27,700	2·3	8·6	31 Dec
Japan	Yen=100 Sen	JPY	196·6	29,400	-0·1	4·7	31 Mar
Jordan	Dinar=1,000 Fils	JOD	1·2	4,500	3·2	15	31 Dec
Kazakhstan	Tenge=100 Tiyn	KZT	237·8	7,800	6·9	8	31 Dec
Kenya	Shilling=100 Cents	KES	133·9	1,100	9	40	30 Jun
Korea, North	NK Won=100 Chon	KPW	1578·5	1,400	—	—	31 Dec
Korea, South	SK Won=100 Chon	KRW	1802·9	19,200	3·6	3·6	31 Dec

———— GAZETTEER · KUWAIT – ZIMBABWE · [3/4] ————

Country	Currency	Currency code	£1 =	GDP per capita $	Inflation %	Unemployment %	Fiscal year end
United Kingdom	Pound=100 Pence	GBP		29,600	1·4	4·8	5 Apr
United States	Dollar=100 Cents	USD	1·7	40,100	2·5	5·5	30 Sep
Kuwait	Dinar=1,000 Fils	KWD	0·5	21,300	2·3	2·2	31 Mar
Latvia	Lats=100 Santims	LVL	1·0	11,500	6	8·8	31 Dec
Lebanon	Pound=100 Piastres	LBP	2640·0	5,000	2	18	31 Dec
Liberia	Dollar=100 Cents	LRD	1·7	900	15	85	31 Dec
Lithuania	Litas=100 Centas	LTL	5·0	12,500	1·1	8	31 Dec
Malaysia	Ringgit=100 Sen	MYR	6·6	9,700	1·3	3	31 Dec
Mexico	Peso=100 Centavos	MXN	18·4	9,600	5·4	3·2	31 Dec
Monaco	euro=100 cent	EUR	1·4	27,000	1·9	22	31 Dec
Morocco	Dirham=100 centimes	MAD	16·3	4,200	2·1	12·1	31 Dec
Netherlands	euro=100 cent	EUR	1·4	29,500	1·4	6	31 Dec
New Zealand	Dollar=100 Cents	NZD	2·6	23,200	2·4	4·2	30 Jun
Nigeria	Naira=100 Kobo	NGN	237·9	1,000	16·5	—	31 Dec
Norway	Krone=100 Øre	NOK	11·5	40,000	1	4·3	31 Dec
Pakistan	Rupee=100 Paisa	PKR	104·5	2,200	4·8	8·3	30 Jun
Peru	New Sol=100 Cénts	PEN	5·7	5,600	3·8	9·6	31 Dec
Philippines	Peso=100 Centavos	PHP	96·6	5,000	5·5	11·7	31 Dec
Poland	Zloty=100 Groszy	PLN	6·0	12,000	3·4	19·5	31 Dec
Portugal	euro=100 cent	EUR	1·4	17,900	2·1	6·5	31 Dec
Romania	Leu=100 Bani	ROL	5·1	7,700	9·6	6·3	31 Dec
Russia	Rouble=100 Kopecks	RUR	50·3	9,800	11·5	8·3	31 Dec
Rwanda	Franc=100 Centimes	RWF	950·9	1,300	7	—	31 Dec
Saudi Arabia	Riyal=100 Halala	SAR	6·5	12,000	0·8	25	31 Dec
Singapore	Dollar=100 Cents	SGD	2·9	27,800	1·7	3·4	31 Mar
Slovakia	Koruna=100 Halierov	SKK	56·9	14,500	7·5	13·1	31 Dec
Slovenia	Tolar=100 Stotin	SIT	348·7	19,600	3·3	6·4	31 Dec
Somalia	Shilling=100 Cents	SOS	4612·7	600	—	—	—
South Africa	Rand=100 Cents	ZAR	11·6	11,100	4·5	26·2	31 Mar
Spain	euro=100 cent	EUR	1·4	23,300	3·2	10·4	31 Dec
Sudan	Dinar= 100 Piastres	SDD	433·2	1,900	9	18·7	31 Dec
Sweden	Krona=100 Öre	SEK	13·6	28,400	0·7	5·6	31 Dec
Switzerland	Franc=100 Centimes	CHF	2·3	33,800	0·9	3·4	31 Dec
Syria	Pound=100 Piastres	SYP	91·6	3,400	2·1	20	31 Dec
Taiwan	Dollar=100 Cents	TWD	55·1	25,300	1·7	4·5	31 Dec
Thailand	Baht=100 Satang	THB	72·9	8,100	2·8	1·5	30 Sep
Turkey	Lira=100 Kurus	TRL	2·3	7,400	9·3	9·3	31 Dec
Ukraine	Hryvena=100 Kopiykas	UAH	8·8	6,300	12	3·5	31 Dec
Venezuela	Bolívar=100 Centimos	VEB	4450·5	5,800	22·4	17·1	31 Dec
Vietnam	Dong=100 Xu	VND	27839·7	2,700	9·5	1·9	31 Dec
Zimbabwe	Dollar=100 Cents	ZWD	18407·5	1,900	133	70	31 Dec

—— GAZETTEER · ALGERIA – SOUTH KOREA · [4/4] ——

Country	Voting age	Driving side	UN vehicle code	Internet country code	Military service	Death penalty	National Day
United Kingdom	18 U	L	GB	.uk	N	N	—
United States	18 U	R	USA	.us	N	Y	4 Jul
Algeria	18 U	R	DZ	.dz	Y	N*	1 Nov
Argentina	18 UC	R	RA	.ar	N	Y*	25 May
Australia	18 UC	L	AUS	.au	N	N	26 Jan
Austria	18 UC*	R	A	.at	Y	N	26 Oct
Belarus	18 U	R	BY	.by	Y	Y	3 Jul
Belgium	18 UC	R	B	.be	N	N	21 Jul
Brazil	16 U*	R	BR	.br	Y	Y*	7 Sep
Bulgaria	18 U	R	BG	.bg	Y	N	3 Mar
Burma/Myanmar	18 U	R	BUR	.mm	N	N*	4 Jan
Cambodia	18 U	R	K	.kh	Y	N	9 Nov
Canada	18 U	R	CDN	.ca	N	N	1 Jul
Chile	18 UC	R	RCH	.cl	Y	Y*	18 Sep
China	18 U	R	RC	.cn	Y	Y	1 Oct
Colombia	18 U	R	CO	.co	Y	N	20 Jul
Cuba	16 U	R	CU	.cu	N	Y	10 Dec
Czech Republic	18 U	R	CZ	.cz	N	N	28 Oct
Denmark	18 U	R	DK	.dk	Y	N	5 Jun
Egypt	18 UC	R	ET	.eg	Y	Y	23 Jul
Estonia	18 U	R	EST	.ee	Y	N	24 Feb
Finland	18 U	R	FIN	.fi	Y	N	6 Dec
France	18 U	R	F	.fr	N	N	14 Jul
Germany	18 U	R	D	.de	Y	N	3 Oct
Greece	18 UC	R	GR	.gr	Y	N	25 Mar
Haiti	18 U	R	RH	.ht	N	N	1 Jan
Hong Kong	18 U*	L	CN/HK	.hk	N	N	1 Oct
Hungary	18 U	R	H	.hu	N	N	20 Aug
India	18 U	L	IND	.in	N	Y	26 Jan
Indonesia	17 U*	L	RI	.id	Y	Y	17 Aug
Iran	15 U	R	IR	.ir	Y	Y	1 Apr
Iraq	18 U	R	IRQ	.iq	N	Y	17 Jul
Ireland	18 U	L	IRL	.ie	N	N	17 Mar
Israel	18 U	R	IL	.il	Y	Y*	14 May
Italy	18 U*	R	I	.it	N	N	2 Jun
Japan	20 U	L	J	.jp	N	Y	23 Dec
Jordan	18 U	R	HKJ	.jo	N	Y	25 May
Kazakhstan	18 U	R	KZ	.kz	Y	Y	16 Dec
Kenya	18 U	L	EAK	.ke	N	N*	12 Dec
Korea, North	17 U	R	DVRK	.kp	N	Y	9 Sep
Korea, South	20 U	R	ROK	.kr	Y	Y	15 Aug

—————— GAZETTEER · KUWAIT – ZIMBABWE · [4/4] ——————

Country	Voting age	Driving side	UN vehicle code	Internet country code	Military service	Death penalty	National Day
United Kingdom	18 U	L	GB	.uk	N	N	—
United States	18 U	R	USA	.us	N	Y	4 Jul
Kuwait	21 C	R	KWT	.kw	Y	Y	25 Feb
Latvia	18 U	R	LV	.lv	Y	Y*	18 Nov
Lebanon	21 C*	R	RL	.lb	Y	Y	22 Nov
Liberia	18 U	R	LB	.lr	N	Y	26 Jul
Lithuania	18 U	R	LT	.lt	Y	N	16 Feb
Malaysia	21 U	L	MAL	.my	N	Y	31 Aug
Mexico	18 UC	R	MEX	.mx	Y	N	16 Sep
Monaco	21 U	R	MC	.mc	N	N	19 Nov
Morocco	18 U	R	MA	.ma	Y	N	3 Mar
Netherlands	18 U	R	NL	.nl	N	N	30 Apr
New Zealand	18 U	L	NZ	.nz	N	N	6 Feb
Nigeria	18 U	R	WAN	.ng	N	Y	1 Oct
Norway	18 U	R	N	.no	Y	N	17 May
Pakistan	18 U	L	PK	.pk	N	Y	23 Mar
Peru	18 UC*	R	PE	.pe	Y	Y*	28 Jul
Philippines	18 U	R	RP	.ph	Y	Y	12 Jun
Poland	18 U	R	PL	.pl	Y	N	3 May
Portugal	18 U	R	P	.pt	N	N	10 Jun
Romania	18 U	R	RO	.ro	Y	N	1 Dec
Russia	18 U	R	RU	.ru	Y	N*	12 Jun
Rwanda	18 U	R	RWA	.rw	N	Y	1 Jul
Saudi Arabia	21 C	R	SA	.sa	N	Y	23 Sep
Singapore	21 UC	L	SGP	.sg	Y	Y	9 Aug
Slovakia	18 U	R	SK	.sk	Y	N	1 Sep
Slovenia	18 U*	R	SLO	.si	N	N	25 Jun
Somalia	18 U	L	SO	.so	N	Y	1 Jul
South Africa	18 U	L	ZA	.za	N	N	27 Apr
Spain	18 U	R	E	.es	N	N	12 Oct
Sudan	17 U	R	SUD	.sd	Y	Y	1 Jan
Sweden	18 U	R	S	.se	Y	N	6 Jun
Switzerland	18 U	R	CH	.ch	Y	N	1 Aug
Syria	18 U	R	SYR	.sy	Y	Y	17 Apr
Taiwan	20 U	R	RC	.tw	Y	Y	10 Oct
Thailand	18 UC	L	T	.th	Y	Y	5 Dec
Turkey	18 U	R	TR	.tr	Y	N	29 Oct
Ukraine	18 U	R	UA	.ua	Y	N	24 Aug
Venezuela	18 U	R	YV	.ve	Y	N	5 Jul
Vietnam	18 U	R	VN	.vn	Y	Y	2 Sep
Zimbabwe	18 U	L	ZW	.zw	N	Y	18 Apr

Society & Health

No man is an Island, entire of itself;
every man is a piece of the Continent, a part of the main.
— JOHN DONNE, *Devotions on Emergent Occasions*, 1624

RIBBONS AND WRISTBANDS

It seems that Jeremy Irons catalysed the wearing of coloured ribbons for social causes when he sported a red AIDS ribbon at the 1991 Tony Awards. (This was inspired by yellow ribbons worn for casualties of the first Iraq war, which were themselves part of a long US folk-tradition of 'tying a yellow ribbon' to welcome soldiers home.) The AIDS ribbon led to a bewildering array of other colours, from the yellow and purple 'chemical injury awareness', to the highly successful pink 'breast cancer awareness'. Recently, fashion has shifted to wristbands. An early example was the yellow *Livestrong* bracelet worn by Lance Armstrong who overcame testicular cancer to win a 6th and 7th *Tour de France* [see p.294]. Since then, the spectrum has again been plundered to raise public awareness of a variety of causes, for example:

White . . . . *Make Poverty History*
Blue . . . . *anti-bullying†; anti-George W. Bush; Tsunami relief; prostate cancer*
Yellow . . . . *Livestrong cancer awareness; Support Our [US] Troops*
Black & white . . . . *anti-racism (in football)*
Orange . . . . *pro-Ukraine Orange party; Asperger's syndrome; self-harm*
Green . . . . *leukemia awareness; organ donor*
Black . . . . *melanoma awareness; 'livewrong' anti-fashion campaign*
Red . . *British Heart Foundation; strings worn by followers of the Kabbalah* [see p.291]
Purple . . . . *cystic fibrosis; domestic violence; lupus*
Grey . . . . *brain cancer; diabetes*

During 2005, in the drought-ravaged Maradi region of Niger, wristbands showed how close a child was to death. Forced to ration their supplies, aid agencies used coloured bands to classify starving children and identify what food they would get:

Red . . . . . limb circumference <100mm . . . . *intensive 5-day feeding course*
Yellow . . . limb circumference 100–124mm . . . . *mother given flour and oil*
Blue . . . . . limb circumference >124mm . . . . *children allowed to revisit aid camp*

† These bracelets became the subject of inflated eBay bids, and some children wearing anti-bullying wristbands themselves became targets of bullying. A number of charities were embarrassed when it was revealed that some of their bracelets had been manufactured in sweatshop conditions. Research by *www.the-lab.tv* suggests that some teenagers use wristbands as a coded way of communicating sexual preference and availability. White wristbands indicate the wearer is 'currently attached'; purple or blue indicates 'gay'; black, 'recently separated'; pink and blue together, 'bisexual'; &c.

—————————— UK POPULATION FIGURES ——————————

(million)	1971	1981	1991	2001	2003	2011	2021
England	46·4	46·8	47·9	49·4	49·9	51·6	54·0
Wales	2·7	2·8	2·9	2·9	2·9	3·0	3·1
Scotland	5·2	5·2	5·1	5·1	5·1	5·0	5·0
N. Ireland	1·5	1·5	1·6	1·7	1·7	1·8	1·8
UK	55·9	56·4	57·4	59·1	59·6	61·4	63·8

[Mid-year estimates for 1971–2003; 2003-based projections for 2011 & 2021 · Source: ONS]

———————————— UK BIRTHS & DEATHS ————————————

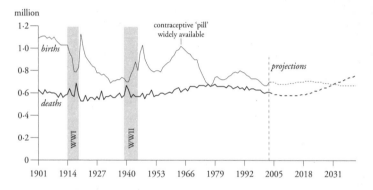

[Data for 1901–21 exclude Ireland. Data from 1981 exclude the non-residents of Northern Ireland. 2003-based projections for 2004–44. Source: Social Trends 35 · Crown ©]

———————— UK LIFE EXPECTANCY AT BIRTH ————————

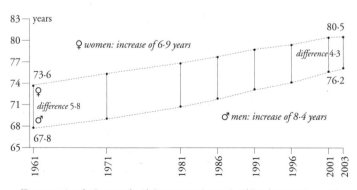

[Dates are primarily Census and mid-Census years. Source: Social Trends 2005 · Crown ©]

── UK POPULATION BY AGE & SEX ──

Below is the breakdown of UK population (in 2003) by age and sex. It illustrates the effects of the post-war boom in childbirth, and subsequent boom when that generation reached child-bearing age. It also shows how the population is ageing:

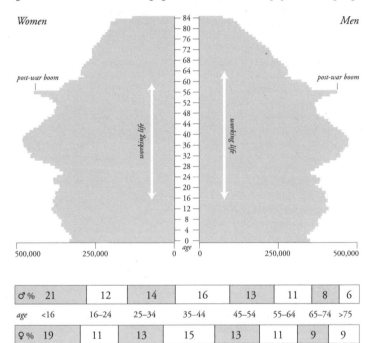

♂ %	21	12	14	16	13	11	8	6
age	<16	16–24	25–34	35–44	45–54	55–64	65–74	>75
♀ %	19	11	13	15	13	11	9	9

── GB POPULATION BY ETHNIC GROUP ──

All White .... 91·9% ⎰ White British .... 88·2%
                                       ⎱ White Irish..................... 1·2%
                                         Other White .... 2·5%

All Asian or Asian British ...... 4·1% ⎰ Indian .... 1·8%
                                       ⎱ Pakistani....................... 1·3%
                                         Bangladeshi .... 0·5%
                                         Other Asian..................... 0·4%

All Black or Black British ...... 2·0% ⎰ Black Caribbean .... 1·0%
                                       ⎱ Black African.................. 0·9%
                                         Other Black.................... 0·2%

Mixed .... 1·2%
Chinese.......................... 0·4%
Other ethnic groups............ 0·4%

[Source: Social Trends 2005 · Crown © data from 2001 Census]

BRITISH PLEDGE OF ALLEGIANCE

Under the Nationality, Immigration & Asylum Act 2002, all applicants for naturalisation to become British citizens must make the following oath and pledge:

OATH
I, [name], swear by Almighty God that, on becoming a British citizen, I will be faithful and bear true allegiance to Her Majesty Queen Elizabeth the Second, Her Heirs and Successors according to law.

PLEDGE
I will give my loyalty to the United Kingdom and respect its rights and freedoms. I will uphold its democratic values. I will observe its laws faithfully and fulfil my duties and obligations as a British citizen.

Below are some extracts from *Life in the United Kingdom: a journey to citizenship*, published by the Home Office in 2004 to help immigrants to the UK integrate. 'In the beginning of history there were no nations on these islands, only local tribes with a predominantly common culture called Celtic.' ❦ 'Spokesmen and women of all political parties put their slant on things too – known today as "spin".' ❦ 'If you spill a stranger's drink by accident, it is good manners (and prudent) to offer to buy another.' ❦ 'All dogs in public places must wear a collar showing the name and address of the owner.' ❦ 'Accents are a clear indication of regional differences in Britain.' ❦ 'Tourist guides commonly paint a view of rural Britain that is not always recognisable to those who live there.' ❦ 'The British Father Christmas is a cheerful old man with a beard, dressed in a red suit trimmed with fur.'

ILLEGAL MIGRANT POPULATION IN UK

Despite Tony Blair claiming during the 2005 election campaign that 'you cannot determine specifically how many people are here illegally', in July 2005 the Home Office published a tentative estimate of the illegal population in the UK in 2001.

2001 figures	low estimate	central estimate	high estimate
Unauthorised migrant population	310,000	430,000	570,000
Percentage of total UK population	0·5%	0·7%	1%

RECENT UK ASYLUM STATISTICS

Asylum applications by quarter	Most asylum applications by country 2005 Q2	Most asylum removals by country 2005 Q2
2003 Q2 10,670	Iran 715	Serbia & Mont. 430
2003 Q3 12,055	Somalia 455	Afghanistan.........265
2003 Q4 10,825	Afghanistan.........415	Iraq 180
2004 Q1 8,955	China...............380	Iran 135
2004 Q2 7,915	Pakistan.............300	Albania 135
2004 Q3 8,615	Eritrea 275	Pakistan.............135
2004 Q4 8,480	Nigeria..............240	Nigeria..............125
2005 Q1 7,015	India.................235	All other..........1,700
2005 Q2 6,220	All other..........2,775	[Source: Home Office]

——————— CHILDHOOD IMMUNISATION SCHEDULE ———————

Age	*vaccination*	*injections*
2m	*diphtheria, tetanus, whooping cough, polio, Hib* [DTaP/IPV/Hib]	1
	meningitis C	1
3m	[DTaP/IPV/Hib]	1
4m	[DTaP/IPV/Hib]	1
13m	*measles, mumps, rubella* [MMR]	1
3y4m–5y	*diphtheria, tetanus, whooping cough, polio* [DTaP/IPV]	1
	measles, mumps, rubella [MMR]	1
13y–18y	*diphtheria, tetanus, polio* [Td/IPV]	1

Below are the immunisation rates of UK children by their 2nd birthday, showing the worrying decline in MMR vaccinations because of public fears about its safety.

Immunisation (%)	1991–92	1994–95	1999–2000	2003–04
Tetanus	94	93	95	94
Diphtheria & polio	94	95	95	94
Whooping cough	88	95	94	94
Measles, mumps, rubella [MMR]	90	91	88	81

[From September 2005 the universal school immunisation against tuberculosis (BCG) was halted in favour of immunising high-risk groups. Sources: NHS Immunisation Service · Social Trends 2005 · Crown © · The above is a rough guide. For up-to-date information seek medical advice.]

——————— NEW FIRST NAMES OF THE YEAR ———————

Below are the most popular first names in 2004 recorded by the Office of National Statistics – and the top-five male and female names from various historic years:

Jack	*nickname for John*	1	*from the Latin Aemilia*		Emily
Joshua	*Jehova saves*	2	*shortened form of Eleanor &c.*		Ellie
Thomas	*Greek form of Aramaic for 'twin'*	3	*allegedly created by Shakespeare*		Jessica
James	*English form of Jacomus and Jacob*	4	*French form of Sophia*		Sophie
Daniel	*from Hebrew for 'God is my judge'*	5	*Greek for 'young green shoot'*		Chloe
Samuel	*from Hebrew for 'name of God'*	6	*from the Latin Lucia*		Lucy
Oliver	*? from Latin for 'olive tree'*	7	*? feminine version of Oliver*		Olivia
William	*from German for 'protector'*	8	*feminine form of Carlo/Charles*		Charlotte
Benjamin	*Hebrew for 'son of the right hand'*	9	*diminutive form of Kate*		Katie
Joseph	*from Hebrew for 'God will add'*	10	*diminutive form of Margaret*		Megan

1904	1934	1964
William & Mary	John & Margaret	David & Susan
John & Florence	Peter & Jean	Paul & Julie
George & Doris	William & Mary	Andrew & Karen
Thomas & Edith	Brian & Joan	Mark & Jacqueline
Arthur & Dorothy	David & Patricia	John & Deborah

YEARS OF AGE & THE LAW

Below are the ages at which certain activities become lawful:

5 can be given alcoholic drinks ❦ age of compulsory schooling

7 open some bank, savings, and Post Office accounts

10 work on an occasional basis in light agriculture or horticulture ❦ be held criminally responsible ❦ be cautioned ❦ be sent to a juvenile justice centre ❦ open a building society account

12 purchase 12-rated videos, computer games, and DVDs ❦ required to have a rod licence if freshwater fishing ❦ buy certain pets without parental consent

13 engage in light work (e.g. paper rounds)

14 enter a pub (which does not have a special licence) ❦ ride a horse without a helmet

15 purchase 15-rated videos, computer games, and DVDs

16 leave school ❦ buy or be bought beer or cider to drink with a meal ❦ purchase tobacco products; lottery tickets; scratchcards; knives and offensive weapons; caps; snaps; novelty matches; party poppers &c.; petrol; and liqueur chocolates ❦ consent to sex, gay sex, and buggery ❦ play the football pools ❦ choose a GP ❦ get contraceptive advice and supplies ❦ get a National Insurance number ❦ access school records ❦ enter full-time employment ❦ usual recommended minimum age for babysitting†

17 purchase air guns and pellets, and crossbows ❦ donate blood ❦ be sent to an adult prison

18 serve on a jury ❦ sign legal contracts ❦ be left in charge of a petrol station ❦ purchase alcohol; 18-rated videos, computer games and DVDs ❦ consent to a tattoo ❦ place a bet ❦ play bingo ❦ gamble in a casino ❦ Care Orders lapse ❦ enter a tenancy agreement ❦ entitled to information on one's natural parents (with restrictions) ❦ work in a betting shop

21 adopt a child ❦ be elected an MP or councillor ❦ supervise a learner driver

60 women eligible for State Pension (set to change) ❦ eligible for Winter Fuel Payment ❦ entitled to free prescriptions and sight tests

65 men eligible for State Pension (possibly set to change)

70 DVLA requires proof that no medical disability is present (thereafter a 3 year licence is issued)

75 entitled to a free TV licence

This should be treated as a guide only, since restrictions apply to certain categories, and certain differences may apply in Scotland. For a detailed listing of the ages at which certain vehicles can be driven see p.198 ❦ † Although it seems that there is no statutory minimum age for babysitters, most authorities advise that babysitters are at least sixteen. The NSPCC recommends that only registered childminders are used.

EDUCATION KEY STAGES

The chart below illustrates the basic structure of the English education system:

Stage	*age*	*year*	*test or qualification*
FOUNDATION	3–4		
	4–5	reception	*foundation stage profile*
KEY STAGE 1	5–6	year 1	
	6–7	year 2	*tests in English & maths*
KEY STAGE 2	7–8	year 3	
	8–9	year 4	
	9–10	year 5	
	10–11	year 6	*tests in English, maths, & science*
KEY STAGE 3	11–12	year 7	
	12–13	year 8	
	13–14	year 9	*tests in English, maths, & science*
KEY STAGE 4	14–15	year 10	*some take* GCSEs
	15–16	year 11	*most take* GCSEs *or other*
post compulsory education/training	16–17	year 12	AS *or* A LEVELS *or other*
	17–18	year 13	A LEVELS *or other*
	18–19		

33 THINGS TO DO BEFORE YOU'RE 10

A survey conducted by Persil, in support of their 'dirt is good' ad campaign, listed thirty-three valuable childhood experiences to be enjoyed before the age of ten:

1 .... roll down a grassy bank
2 .... make a mud pie
3 . prepare a modelling-dough mixture
4 .... collect frogspawn
5 .... make perfume from flower petals
6 .... grow cress on a window sill
7 .... make a papier mâché mask
8 .... build a sandcastle
9 .... climb a tree
10 .... make a den in the garden
11 .... paint using hands and feet
12 ...... organise a teddy bears' picnic
13 .... have a face-painting session
14 .... bury a friend in the sand
15 .... bake some bread
16 .... make snow angels†
17 .... create a clay sculpture

18 .... take part in a scavenger hunt
19 .... camp out in the garden
20 .... bake a cake
21 .... feed a farm animal
22 .... pick some strawberries
23 .... play Pooh Sticks‡
24 .... recognise five bird species
25 .... find some worms
26 ..... cycle through a muddy puddle
27 .... make and fly a kite
28 .... plant a tree
29 ... build a nest from grass and twigs
30 . find 10 different leaves in the park
31 .... grow vegetables
32 .. make breakfast in bed for parents
33 . create a garden mini assault course

[‡ See *Schott's Sporting, Gaming, & Idling Miscellany*]

† These are created by lying down in fresh snow (don't forget to wrap up warm), and waving your arms from your sides over your head. The impression left in the snow will resemble an angel's wings.

SCHOOL FOOD & JAMIE OLIVER

School food, forever the butt of popular scorn, was forced onto the political agenda in 2005 by celebrity TV chef Jamie Oliver. On 23 February, the first episode of *Jamie's School Dinners* was shown on Channel 4. Oliver signed up as a dinner lady at Kidbrooke School in Greenwich with the aim of cooking more nutritious school food within the budget of 37p per pupil per day. From the outset, many viewers were shocked by the relentless barrage of junk food served in schools, and the inability of pupils to identify (let alone eat) vegetables such as leeks.

Jamie Oliver has done more for the public health of our children than a corduroy army of health promotion workers or a £100m Saatchi & Saatchi campaign — THE LANCET

The public and media outcry caused by *Jamie's School Dinners* was dramatic, and by the end of March 271,677 had signed a petition for better school food. Stung by the furore, and mindful of an impending election, Blair pledged £280m for school dinners, and set a minimum spend on ingredients at 50p per pupil per day for primary schools; 60p for secondary schools. *Jamie's School Dinners* had two other results: public ridicule of the bizarre fast-food 'Turkey Twizzler', and public adoration of the splendidly charismatic Kidbrooke dinner lady, Nora Sands.

SOME SCHOOL STATISTICS

Average class size [primary schools · 2005 provisional figures]............................26·2
Average class size [secondary schools · 2005 provisional figures].........................21·7
Pupils per teacher [all UK state schools 2002/3]......................................17·6
Pupils per teacher [independent schools 2005] ....9·98
First language is other than English [primary schools]............................11·7%
First language is other than English [secondary schools] ....9·1%
First language is other than English, *Inner London* [primary schools]...........51·3%
First language is other than English, *Inner London* [secondary schools] ....46·6%

[Source: Annual Schools' Census 2005 (provisional) for England · DFES · Crown © · ISC]

INDEPENDENT SCHOOLS

Some 615,000 children attend *c.*2,500 independent schools in the UK, which, according to the Independent Schools' Council (ISC) 'saves' the state *c.*£2bn a year. ISC figures show that with just 7% of the school population, independents supply 38% of all candidates achieving 3 As or higher at A level. In 2004, 13·4% of state schools pupils achieved a GCSE A or A*, compared to 53% at independent schools.

Average yearly fee	£		
Boarding schools	18,828	Day fee average	8,388
Day fee at boarding schools	9,915	Overall average	9,777
Day fee at day schools	7,668	Eton College	23,688

[Sources: 2005 ISC Census; Eton College]

—————————— UK MARRIAGES & DIVORCES —————————

Despite the 1970s' decline in marriages, and the rise in divorces after the Divorce
Reform Act 1969†, *c.*50% of UK adults were in marriages in 2003. ONS data from
2001 show that in 26% of marriages the man was younger than his wife; in 48%
the man was up to 5 years older; and in 26% the man was 6 or more years older.

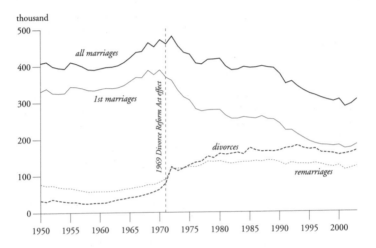

[† Act came into force in 1971 · Data are for both partners · Divorce includes annulments. 1950–70
is for GB only. Remarriage is for one or both partners. Source: Social Trends 35 · Crown ©]

————————————————— GRETNA GREEN —————————————————

A village in Dumfries and Galloway, just inside Scotland, Gretna Green became
notorious as a venue for runaway English elopers when clandestine marriages were
made illegal in England in 1753. Before a series of laws changed the rules, couples
in Scotland could be married simply by declaring their consent in front of a
witness (often the Gretna Green blacksmith). The practice was stopped in 1939.

————————— DURATION OF MARRIAGE BEFORE DIVORCE —————————

There were 166,737 decrees absolute† granted in 2003 in the UK; the following
chart illustrates how long these marriages had lasted before they ended in divorce:

years	0–4	5–9	10–14	15–19	>20
%	17·3	26·1	19·5	13·9	23·2

[2 cases unrecorded · † includes decrees of nullities · Source: Annual Abstract Stats · Crown ©]

——————————SEXUAL PARTNERS & CHASTITY——————————

Below are ONS figures for the number of sexual partners in the previous year (2003/4), reported by individuals in interviews, broken down by age and sex:

%	16–19		20–24		25–34		35–44		45–49	
	♂	♀	♂	♀	♂	♀	♂	♀	♂	♀
0 partners	34	35	16	11	7	8	6	11	7	16
1 partner	34	42	51	72	75	82	84	85	86	82
2–3 partners	21	18	19	16	11	9	7	4	5	1
>4 partners	11	5	13	2	7	2	3	1	2	0

[Source: Social Trends 2005 · Crown ©]

Increasingly, teenagers in America are being targeted by campaigns that encourage chastity. Organisations like *Silver Ring Thing* and *True Love Waits* promote 'pre-martial purity' as the best way to reduce teenage pregnancy and the prevalence of sexually transmitted diseases. For more information see www.silverringthing.com

——————————MARRIAGE TERMINOLOGY OF NOTE——————————

Adelphogamy....................................*marriage between brothers and sisters*
Ambilocal.......*a marriage where the couple may live in either partner's community*
Arranged..........*where a couple is matched by others, sometimes with their consent*
Bigamy....*having more than one husband or wife at once (a crime in most cultures)*
Coenogamy.....*group marriage between two or more men and two or more women*
Deuterogamy.....................*a second marriage after the termination of the first*
Digamy ....*a second marriage after the death of a spouse*
Endogamy ....*marriage between members of a group or lineage*
Exogamy...................*marriage between members of different groups or lineages*
Heterogamy ....*marriage between different social backgrounds*
Hierogamy....................*a sacred marriage (e.g. that between Europa and Zeus)*
Homogamy...............................*marriage within a shared social background*
Hypergamy ....*marriage into an equal or higher social group*
Lavender marriage........*of convenience or companionship where either party is gay*
Matrilocal ....*married couples living with or near the wife's parents*
Misalliance...........................*a marriage between people unsuited to each other*
Misogamy ....*antipathy towards or hatred of marriage*
Monogamy ....*having one spouse*
Morganatic ....*a marriage between high and low social rank,*
          where the lower-ranking (and any offspring) has no claim to title or property
Opsigamy...*marriage late in life*
Pantagamy.............*where members of a community are regarded as intermarried*
Patrilocal...................*married couples living with or near the husband's parents*
Polyandry ....*a woman who has a number of husbands*
Polygamy ....*having a number of spouses*
Totem exogamy.....*American Indian tradition of marrying outside one's totem-clan*
Trigamy....................*having three spouses simultaneously; or a third marriage*

—————————— GB HOUSEHOLD SIZE ——————————

The following table shows the trends in the size of British households, illustrating, for example, the dramatic 11% rise in single-occupancy households since 1971.

Occupants	1	2	3	4	5	≥6
1971	18	32	19	17	8	6
1981	22	32	17	18	7	4
1991	27	34	16	16	5	2
2001	29	35	16	14	5	2
2004	29	35	16	14	5	2

[Source: Social Trends 35 · ONS · Crown ©]

————————— FAMILIES WITH DEPENDENT CHILDREN —————————

In 2004, 13·1m dependent children were part of 7·4m families; the majority of children (66%) lived with married couples. The breakdown of UK family types is:

Children living with
Married couples 66%
Lone mothers.................................... 22%
Cohabiting couples............................. 11%
Lone fathers..................................... 2%

[Source: Labour Force Survey 2004 · ONS · Crown ©]

————————————— FAMILIES BY RELIGION —————————————

The following table shows the breakdown of families by the number of dependent children they have, and the main religion of the household. It illustrates, for example, that families headed by a Muslim are more likely to have children with them, and that 27% of Muslim families have three or more dependent children:

Religion	families with no dependent children	1–2 children	≥3
Christian %	60	33	7
Buddhist %	47	45	8
Hindu %	44	48	8
Muslim %	27	46	27
Sikh %	40	46	14
Jewish %	59	31	9
Other %	54	40	7
Not stated %	58	34	7
No religion %	46	45	9

[Source: Focus on Families · 2005 · ONS · Crown © · see their report for detailed notes]

—— LIFETIME EXPERIENCE OF STRESSFUL EVENTS ——

The percentage of those (aged 16–74) who reported experiencing these life events:

Life event	Men %	Women %
Death of close friend or other relative........	68	73
Death of a close relative†	51	53
Being sacked or made redundant.............	40	19
Serious or life-threatening illness/injury......	30	22
Separation or breakdown of relationship.....	25	29
Bullying..	19	17
Serious money problems......................	14	8
Violence at work	6	2
Running away from home....................	5	5
Violence at home..............................	4	10
Being homeless................................	4	3
Being expelled from school..................	2	1
Sexual abuse	2	5

[† Parent, spouse or partner, child, or sibling. Source: Psychiatric Morbidity Survey
& Office of National Statistics · 2000 figures · Crown ©]

—————— SOCIOLOGICAL GROUPINGS ——————

A	Upper-middle-class	*higher managerial, administrative, or professional*
B	Middle-class	*intermediate managerial, administrative, or professional*
C1	Lower-middle-class	*supervisory or clerical & junior managerial,*
		administrative, or professional
C2	Skilled working-class	*skilled manual workers*
D	Working-class	*semi and unskilled manual workers*
E	At lowest levels of subsistence	*state pensioners or widows (no other earner),*
		casual or lowest-grade workers

—————— REGISTERING BIRTHS & DEATHS ——————

Registering　　　　　　　　　　　　　　　　　　*within time period*
Birth............................42 days (England, Wales, N. Ireland); 21 days (Scotland)
Death† ....5 days (England, Wales, N. Ireland); 8 days (Scotland)
Stillbirth.......................42 days (England, Wales, N. Ireland); 21 days (Scotland)

Relevant authority
England & Wales Register.......................www.gro.gov.uk · 0151 471 4805
Scotland Register.......................www.gro-scotland.gov.uk · 0131 314 4467
Northern Ireland Register ....www.groni.gov.uk · 028 90 252000

[† May depend on involvement of a coroner. See www.gro.gov.uk for more information]

UK UNEMPLOYMENT RATES

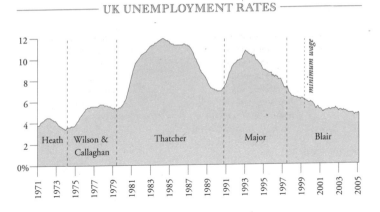

[Seasonally adjusted monthly data based on 3-month rolling averages. All persons >16.
Source: Labour Force Survey, Office for National Statistics · Crown ©]

NORWAY & IDLING

Organization for Economic Cooperation and Development (OECD) figures show that Norway is the ideal country to move to if you're idle. There, the 'average hours worked' per year per person in work is 1,337, compared to 2,390 in South Korea.

Country	hours		
South Korea	2,390	UK	1,673
Greece	1,938	Ireland	1,613
Mexico	1,857	Italy	1,591
Australia	1,814	Denmark	1,475
Japan	1,801	Germany	1,446
US	1,792	France	1,431
Canada	1,718	Netherlands	1,354
		Norway	1,337

NORWAY

Oslo

HOW EUROPEANS SPEND THEIR DAYS

Activity (hours:minutes)	UK ♂	UK ♀	France ♂	France ♀	Germany ♂	Germany ♀	Sweden ♂	Sweden ♀
Sleep	8:18	8:27	8:45	8:55	8:12	8:19	8:01	8:11
Meals; personal care	2:04	2:16	3:01	3:02	2:33	2:43	2:11	2:28
Travel	1:30	1:25	1:03	0:54	1:27	1:18	1:30	1:23
Gainful work; study	4:18	2:33	4:03	2:31	3:35	2:05	4:25	3:12
Free; unspecified	5:30	5:05	4:46	4:08	5:53	5:24	5:24	5:03
Domestic work	2:18	4:15	2:22	4:30	2:21	4:11	2:29	3:42

[Source: European Commission, *How Europeans Spend their Time*, 2004]

———————— SO, WHAT DO YOU DO? ————————

Women are most attracted to:	Men are most attracted to:
surgeons · solicitors/barristers	*journalists · TV directors*
company directors · journalists	*human resources workers*
IT professionals · management consults.	*designers/architects*
architects/designers	*property · academics*
bankers/brokers	*bankers · advertising*
TV directors · academics	*doctors · writers*

[Source: *Drawing Down the Moon* & *Only Lunch*]

——— INDUSTRIAL ACTION & UNION MEMBERSHIP ———

The number of days lost to strikes (and some key strikes); and union membership:

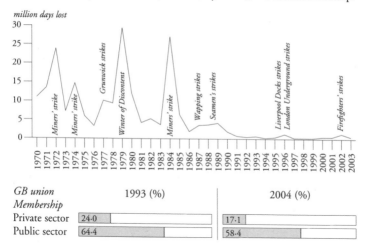

million days lost

GB union Membership	1993 (%)	2004 (%)
Private sector	24·0	17·1
Public sector	64·4	58·4

[Sources: Labour Force Survey; Social Trends 35 · ONS · Crown ©]

——————— JOB SATISFACTION ———————

% claiming to be happy in their job		
Hairdressers 40	Florists................18	Teachers................8
Clergy 24	Fitness instructors....18	Bankers 8
Chefs/cooks 23	Health professionals..17	Accountants...........7
Beauticians 22	Media.................18	Lawyers 5
Plumbers 20	Pharmacists..........15	Secretaries.............5
Electricians 18	Butchers 14	Civil servants 3
	DJs...................13	Architects 2
	Interior designers......9	[*City & Guilds* survey '04]

THE NHS

Administration is going to be the chief headache for years to come.
— ANEURIN BEVAN, 1945

NHS STAFF

There are 1,331,860 NHS employees. (For the record, the Chinese Army only has *c.*710,000 active troops and 290,000 reservists.) The breakdown of NHS staff is:

Qualified nurses	29·9%	Hotel, property, & estate staff	5·6%
Clinical support staff	22·8%	Support to ST&T† staff	4·1%
Qualified ST&T† staff	9·7%	Managers & senior managers	2·8%
Doctors	8·8%	Qualified ambulance staff	1·3%
Central administration	7·5%	Support to ambulance staff	0·7%
GP practice staff	6·8%	[†Scientific, Therapeutic, & Technical]	

WAITING TIMES

The political significance of NHS waiting means that successive governments have used reorganisation, targeting, and a host of other methods to bring times down. As a result, there is considerable scepticism surrounding waiting-time data, with suggestions that some patients wait before being allowed to join the waiting list.

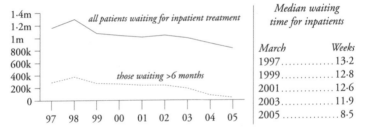

Median waiting time for inpatients

March	Weeks
1997	13·2
1999	12·8
2001	12·6
2003	11·9
2005	8·5

NHS 'PATIENT CONTACTS' PER DAY

The scale of the NHS becomes clear with the number of patient contacts per day:

GP or nurse consult	836,000	A&E attendance	49,000
All community contacts	389,000	In NHS bed (as elective)	36,000
Outpatient attendance	124,000	NHS eye test	28,000
In NHS bed (as emergency)	94,000	NHS Direct calls	18,000
NHS dental treatment	73,000	Walk-in centre	6,000

PATIENT RATING OF THE OVERALL NHS CARE THEY RECEIVED

	Excellent	Very good	Good	Fair – v. poor
A&E	34%	36%	18%	13%
Inpatients	42%	35%	14%	9%
Outpatients	37%	41%	16%	7%

[Sources: 2005 Chief Exec's Report to the NHS; Staff in the NHS 2004; Crown ©]

———————— ORGAN DONATION & TRANSPLANT ————————

At present, UK organ donation works as an 'opt in' scheme where individuals signal their consent to donate by carrying an Organ Donor Card and/or signing up to the NHS Organ Donor Register. However, by custom, the final decision resides with the deceased's next of kin who can withhold their consent – and sometimes do if the wishes of the deceased are unknown. Some organisations, including the BMA, are keen to see a system of 'presumed consent' in which individuals have to 'opt out' of donation by registering an objection while alive. A range of parts can currently be transplanted; medical advances suggest that this list may soon grow:

KIDNEYS · LIVER · HEART · LUNGS · SMALL BOWEL & PANCREAS
CORNEAS · TISSUE · HEART VALVES · BONE · SKIN

Patients who received organ transplants [2004–5]............................2,724
of which 2,241 were from cadaveric donation, 483 from a living donor
Patients who received corneal transplants [2004–5]............................2,379
Patients registered for a transplant [31·3·04]................................7,672
Patients who died waiting for a transplant [2004–5]............................460
Number on the NHS Organ Donation Register [31·3·04]....................12·1m

To enrol onto the Register call 0845 60 60 400 or visit www.uktransplant.org.uk,
and remember to inform your next of kin of your wishes. [Source: NHS UK Transplant]

———————————— BLOOD DONATIONS ————————————

'A pint? Why, that's very nearly an armful!'
— TONY HANCOCK

Donors are able to give blood roughly every 16 weeks, and the standard quantity of blood taken each time is 475ml (just under a pint). The minimum age for donation is 17 [see also p.85], and the maximum age is usually 59. A range of conditions can delay blood donations (e.g. if you have had a body piercing or tattoo within 6 months, or if you are pregnant), or prohibit the donation of blood altogether (e.g. if you have worked as a prostitute, or have ever injected yourself with drugs). Human blood is divided into four groups – A, B, AB, O – the letter refers to the kind of antigen on the surface of red blood cells. Each type is then subdivided by whether the Rhesus (Rh) antigen is present or not, which makes blood Rhesus positive or negative. Therefore, there are 8 different blood groups:

Type	%	who can receive it	Type	%	who can receive it
O+	38	O+, A+, B+, AB+	B+	8	B+, AB+
O−	7	all blood types	B−	1	B+, B−, AB+, AB−
A+	36	A+, AB+	AB+	2	AB+
A−	7	A+, A−, AB+, AB−	AB−	1	AB+, AB−

The above is a very simplified guide.

To enrol to give blood, or to find out more, contact: 0845 7711711 or www.blood.co.uk

──────────── UK MOST COMMON CAUSE OF DEATH ────────────

Male	*cause of death*	*female*
3,173	circulatory	1,988
2,373	cancers	1,655
990	respiratory	682
72	infections	51

[Rates per million population · Source: Social Trends 2002 · ONS · Crown ©]

──────────── AVIAN INFLUENZA · H5N1 ────────────

Avian influenza (or bird 'flu) is a naturally occurring bird disease caused by influenza viruses that closely resemble those affecting humans. Although bird 'flu is highly contagious and often deadly to birds, it rarely infects humans. Yet, since 1997, a number of human cases of bird 'flu have been reported, with symptoms ranging from normal 'flu [see over] to life-threatening complications. Avian 'flu is spread by secretions in saliva and faeces, and human infections are probably caused by infected animals or contaminated surfaces. The current cause for concern is the highly pathogenic strain A(H5N1), first identified in 1961. In 2003–4 tens of millions of birds in Asia died from infection by H5N1, and in the attempt to stem the outbreak by culling. In June 2004, H5N1 re-emerged in many Asian countries and human infections were reported in Cambodia, Thailand, and Vietnam. In August 2005, it transpired that H5N1 had expanded its geographical range when Russia, Kazakhstan, Mongolia, and Tibet reported bird infections presumably via migration. Although man's risk from avian 'flu is low, H5N1 has jumped the 'species barrier'. In the 1997 Hong Kong outbreak, H5N1 infected 18 humans of whom 6 died. As of 5 August 2005, the World Health Organisation reported that the latest outbreak of H5N1 had infected 112 humans resulting in 57 deaths. This low rate of infection gives some hope for the avoidance of a 'flu pandemic, though if H5N1 mutates, as some fear, it is possible that a new strain might result in potentially catastrophic human-to-human transmission. The primary drug to treat human cases of H5N1 is currently in short supply, and although intensive research is now underway, there is at present no vaccine to protect humans from infection.

──────────── SOME CURIOUS ACCIDENTS OF NOTE ────────────

The Department of Health 'Hospital Episode Statistics' (2003–4) reveal some of the curious causes behind the 13 million or so admissions to NHS hospitals each year:

Fall involving chair	7,114	*Contact with scorpions*	6
Struck by sporting equipment	2,848	*Exposure to noise*	4
Contact with hot drinks	1,481	*Exposure to vibration*	4
Contact with hornets	451	*Contact with centipedes*	2
Contact with powered lawn-mower	299	*Bitten/struck by crocodile/alligator*	1
Contact with sharp plants	207	*Prolonged stay in*	
Ignition or melting of pyjamas	22	*weightless environment*	1

———————— COLD OR 'FLU? ————————

According to the American *National Institute of Allergy and Infectious Diseases*, fundamental differences exist between colds and the 'flu (men, please take note):

Cold	symptom	'flu
rare.................................	fever.................	high fever (3–4 days)
rare	headache........................	prominent
slight...............................	aches and pains.............	usual, can be severe
mild.............................	fatigue, weakness...............	up to 2–3 weeks
never............................	extreme exhaustion...........	early and prominent
common.....................	stuffy nose, sore throat...................	sometimes

———————— DEFINING OBESITY ————————

According to the Health Survey for England (2001), 21% of men and 23% of women are obese. Obesity is measured by the Body Mass Index (BMI), derived by dividing weight (Kg) by the square of height (m). A BMI >30 defines one as obese.

CLASS	underweight	normal	overweight	obese		
				class I	class II	class III
BMI	<18.5	18.5–24.9	25–29.9	30–34.9	35–39.9	>40
RISK	varies	average	increased	moderate	severe	very severe

See *Schott's Food & Drink Miscellany* for a full chart of BMI calculations.

———————— PRESCRIPTIONS ————————

Prescriptions currently cost £6·50 per item. This payment does not reflect the cost of the item but is considered to be a general contribution towards NHS funds.

Year	prescription items	actual cost	av. cost/item	items/head
1994	456·1m	£3·4bn	£7.47	9.5
2004	686·1m	£8·1bn	£11.78	13.7

Below are the drugs most prescribed by doctors and dentists, by chemical name:

Name (typical use)	million scripts
Aspirin (heart disease, stroke, pain relief)	23·6
Bendroflumethiazide (blood pressure)	18·8
Atenolol (blood pressure)	17·3
Salbutamol (asthma)	16·2
Levothyroxine Sodium (thyroid)	14·2
Simvastatin (cholesterol)	12·7
Amoxicillin (antibiotic)	12·5
Paracetamol (pain relief)	12·4
Atorvastatin (cholesterol)	11·3
Lansoprazole (stomach ulcers)	10·2
Furosemide (diuretic)	10·0

In total 1,024,305 prescriptions for Viagra were issued in England in 2004.

[Source: Prescription Cost Analysis: England 2004; Chief Exec. Report to NHS 2005 · Crown ©]

——————— SOME HEALTH SCARES OF NOTE ———————

Some health scares that have hit the headlines, from the scientifically rigorous to the somewhat suspect:

{JAN 2005} The National Radiological Protection Board advises that children under eight should not use mobile phones. ❧ According to research published in *The Lancet,* the anti-inflammatory drug Vioxx might have contributed to *c.*140,000 cases of coronary heart disease in America since 1999; it has since been withdrawn from use. ❧ George Knox, emeritus Prof. at the University of Birmingham, claims that childhood cancers may be caused by exposure to pollutants in the womb. ❧ The Department of Health's committee on carcinogenicity calls for further research into links between pesticides and brain diseases like Parkinson's. ❧ Co-Proxamol, one of the most prescribed painkillers in Britain, may be withdrawn over fears of accidental overdoses, and its use in a high number of suicides. ❧ {FEB} Hundreds of products are withdrawn from supermarket shelves after they are found to contain Sudan I [see p.179]. ❧ Leading US nutritionist Prof. Linsey Allen claims that parents who feed their children vegan or vegetarian diets might be acting unethically, since children who don't eat meat, milk, or cheese in early life may suffer mental and physical impairment. ❧ {MAR} Japanese research quoted in *New Scientist* finds no link between MMR and autism [see p.84]. ❧ Teresa McCarney, a lecturer at N. Ireland's College of Agriculture, Food and Rural Enterprise expounds the health benefits of chocolate, claiming that 50g of dark chocolate contains the same levels of antioxidants as 2 glasses of wine or 17 glasses of orange juice. ❧ *The Lancet* publishes research warning of the risk of a new, virulent drug-resistant strain of HIV, after a man dies of full-blown AIDS in only a few months. ❧ Pregnant women are advised to avoid green tea, after claims that it might increase the risk of birth defects. ❧ {APR} Scientists at the Monell Chemical Senses Centre in Philadelphia claim that drinking even small amounts of alcohol while breast-feeding may dramatically reduce levels of milk production. ❧ Scientists at King's College Institute of Psychiatry suggest that as many as 1 in 4 may carry a gene that increases the risk of psychotic illness if they smoke cannabis as teenagers. The findings result in calls for the reversal of the re-classification of cannabis [see p.101]. ❧ The painkiller Bextra, used in the treatment of arthritis, is withdrawn amidst concern that it may cause heart and skin problems. ❧ A Danish study claims to find no link between mobile phone use and brain tumours. ❧ Researchers at the University of Minnesota claim to have found 14 cases of men suffering strokes of the eye (resulting in irreversible blindness) possibly as a consequence of taking Viagra. ❧ A paper in the *BMJ* on the effects of a Mediterranean diet (low in meat, and high in fish, olive oil, cereals and vegetables) claims that, at the age of 60, such a diet may increase life by up to a year. ❧ A study in the *Journal of the American Medical Association* reports that those who are moderately overweight have a lower relative risk of dying than those at their optimum weight. ❧ Life tables produced by the

—————— SOME HEALTH SCARES OF NOTE cont. ——————

Institute of Actuaries show that being a smoker at 30 cuts male life expectancy by 5·5 years, and female by 6·5. Up to the age of 80, the risk of dying in the next year is virtually doubled for smokers. ❧ A study in *Anaesthesia* states that more than half of air travellers suffer average falls in blood oxygen levels from a normal 97% to 93% when at altitude – a level at which many doctors would give extra oxygen. {MAY} Research in Sweden indicates that health is maximised by having a waist measurement less than 39·37 inches, or 1 metre, since fat deposited  within the abdomen secretes toxins and raises cholesterol. ❧ Research published in *Environmental Health Perspectives* suggests that some plastics chemicals used in clingfilms, toys, and cosmetics might affect the sexual development of unborn children. ❧ Scientists at Boston University Medical College suggest that the contraceptive pill could permanently lower the libido of users. ❧ {JUN} Research by the Childhood Cancer Research Group and the National Grid indicates that children living near power lines may have an increased risk of leukemia. However, the results also show that children living even 600m from power lines could be affected – a distance so great that the effect of the magnetic fields generated is insignificant. The researchers admit that their results may be due to chance. ❧ A study from Nottingham University claims that arthritis sufferers using non-steroidal anti-inflammatory drugs like ibuprofen may be significantly increasing their risk of heart attack. ❧ Researchers at St Thomas's Hospital suggest that smoking and obesity have an ageing effect. Their study indicates that the obese were 8·8 years older in biological terms than those of healthy weight; smokers were 7·4 years older than non-smokers. ❧ Research by the European Prospective Investigation into Cancer and Nutrition suggests that those eating two portions of red or processed meat a day might be at greater risk of developing bowel cancer. ❧ A Finnish-Australian review of 55 studies into the effectiveness of Vitamin C claims that even large daily doses do not reduce the risk of catching a common cold. ❧ Research by the Copenhagen Institute of Preventative Medicine suggests that overweight people who diet are at a greater risk of dying than those who don't. ❧ {JUL} A study by the Wake Forest University School of Medicine, North Carolina, claims that taking regular showers may result in brain damage because of harmful levels of manganese dissolved in water. ❧ {AUG} A 17-year study into childbirth by researchers at the University of Aberdeen suggests that Caesareans may reduce fertility. The research indicates that the average time between births was longer for those who had Caesareans compared with natural births. It was also claimed that women who had Caesareans were more likely to have complications in future pregnancies. ❧ A study into the effects of over-65-year-olds taking vitamin supplements suggests that they make little or no difference to health. Researchers at Aberdeen University claim that, after taking supplements for 12 months, patients made as many trips to the doctor and reported no improvement in their quality of life. ❧

SMOKING: SOME FIGURES

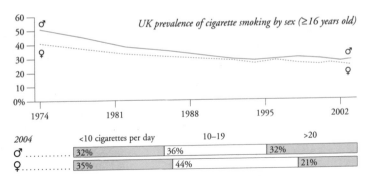

UK prevalence of cigarette smoking by sex (≥16 years old)

2004	<10 cigarettes per day	10–19	>20
♂	32%	36%	32%
♀	35%	44%	21%

Smokers who had their first cigarette within 5 minutes of waking up........11%
— 5–15 minutes of waking up 15%
Smokers who had tried to give up 74%
Smokers who would like to give up...73%
— mentioning health-related reasons..88%
— mentioning financial reasons 26%
Smokers who intended to give up within 12 months.........................55%
Non-smokers who minded people smoking near them........................60%
Smokers who did not smoke at all in a room with a child 67%
Smokers who smoked less when in a room with a child........................25%
Men who smoked ≥1 cigar per month..3%
Expectant mothers who smoked throughout pregnancy [2000]...............19%
— aged under 20 who smoked throughout pregnancy.........................39%
General public who support above-inflation tax rises on tobacco............51%
Heavy smokers who support above-inflation tax rises on tobacco.............8%
English children (11–15) who smoke ≥1 cigarette a week....................10%

Amongst the general public, the following agreed with smoking restrictions in:

workplace 88% · *restaurants* 91% · *indoor leisure centres* 93% · *pubs* 65%

According to the Tobacco Manufacturers Association, the following prices are for 20 cigarettes in the 'most popular price category' in various European countries:

UK ....£4·82	Sweden ....£3·03	Austria.....£2·33	Poland.....£0·92
Ireland.....£4·42	Germany ..£2·98	Italy........£2·12	Latvia......£0·41
France .....£3·53	Denmark..£2·85	Spain ......£1·49	[3 January 2005]

According to the TMA, each cigarette in the UK carries the following taxation:

specific duty 41%	ad valorem 22%	VAT 15%	*not tax* 22%

[Sources: ONS · 2004 *Smoking Related Behaviour & Attitudes* · Crown © · TMA]

DRUG CLASSIFICATION

CLASS A	CLASS B	CLASS C
heroin, methadone, cocaine, ecstasy, LSD, crack, magic mushrooms – when they are prepared	amphetamines (e.g. speed), barbiturates [any Class B drug prepared for injection is treated as Class A]	cannabis (inc. plants), GHB, anabolic steroids, tranquillisers (e.g. diazepam)
MAXIMUM PENALTIES *possession*: 7 years in jail and unlimited fine *supplying or dealing*: life imprisonment and unlimited fine *possession with intent to supply*: life imprisonment and unlimited fine	MAXIMUM PENALTIES *possession*: 5 years in jail and unlimited fine *supplying or dealing*: 14 years in jail and unlimited fine *possession with intent to supply*: 14 years in jail and unlimited fine	MAXIMUM PENALTIES *possession*: 2 years in jail and unlimited fine *supplying or dealing*: 14 years in jail and unlimited fine *possession with intent to supply*: 14 years in jail and unlimited fine

As of 29 January 2004, cannabis was reclassified from Class B to C since it is considered less harmful than other Class B drugs. However, the drug is still illegal and the only substantive difference in classification is that the maximum sentence for possession is 3 years less. Yet, this move also signalled a shift in the policing of cannabis possession, which is likely now to result in confiscation and a warning. There are reports that the Home Office currently has this reclassification under review. On 18 July 2005, a legal loophole that allowed the import and sale of magic mushrooms was closed.

PREVALENCE OF DRUG MISUSE

Drug	users last year
Cocaine	755,000
Crack	55,000
Ecstasy	614,000
Heroin	43,999
Tranquillisers	186,000
Cannabis	3,364,000
Amyl nitrate	418,000
Glue	30,000
All Class A	1,091,000
Any drug	3,854,000

['Best estimate' · 16–59 year-olds]

[Sources: British Crime Survey Findings 2005 · Crown ©]

DRUG PRICES & NICKNAMES

Drug	quantity	1995 prices	2004	some nicknames
Cocaine	line (1/20 g)	£2·83	£2·25	*Charlie, C, Percy, snow, toot*
Cannabis	8th	£20·21	£9·85	*dope, draw, herb, spliff, skunk*
Crack	1 rock	£21·50	£7·55	*rocks, wash, stones, base*
Heroin	1g	£83·33	£26·00	*skag, H, horse, gear, smack*
Ecstasy	1 tab	£11·65	£3·50	*E, pills, XTC*

[Source: Independent Drug Monitoring Unit, & various]

——————— ALCOHOL UNITS, CONSUMPTION, & CRIME ———————

A thumbnail guide to the units found in various forms of alcoholic beverage:

Drink	measure	typical units	typical Calories
Cider, medium	1 pint	2	200
Cider, strong	1 pint	3–4	260–400
Lager/beer, medium	1 pint	2	180
Lager/beer, strong	1 pint	3–4	280–440
Alcopops	275ml	1½–2	100–250
Spirits, port & sherry	25ml (⅙ gill)	1	40–50
Wine, 9%	125ml	1	90
Wine, 12%	125ml	1½	90
Wine, 14%	125ml	2	100

The Government's current advice is that men drink ≤3–4 units, and women ≤2–3 on any particular day. However, research shows this advice is not always heeded:

per day † (%)	16–24	25–44	45–64	≥65	all ages
♂ >4 units	51	47	41	19	40
≥4–8 units	14	17	21	14	17
>8 units	37	30	20	6	23
♀ >3 units	40	30	20	4	23
≥3–6 units	14	18	15	4	13
> 6 units	26	13	5	1	9

[† On at least one day in the previous week. Source: General Household Survey 2005 · Crown ©]

'Binge drinking' is usually defined as drinking alcohol to excess over a short period of time, and being very drunk at least once a month in the previous 12 months. As might be expected, binge drinking is much more prevalent amongst the young:

Binge drinking by age   18–24=44%   25–35=22%   36–45=12%   45–65=5%

However, while research differs on the breakdown of binge drinking by sex, girls are as – if not more – likely to drink to excess than boys. And, it seems that while binge drinkers often claimed that alcohol made them 'more friendly and outgoing' – young binge drinkers actually commit a disproportionate amount of all crimes:

% committing an offence in last year	binge drinker (18–24)			other drinker (18–24)		
	♂	♀	all	♂	♀	all
Any crime	31	21	27	16	11	13
Any violent crime	16	10	14	7	6	7
Drug dealing	10	4	7	3	1	2
Theft	14	11	13	9	5	7
Criminal damage	3	1	2	2	1	1

[Source: Findings from the 2003 Offending, Crime & Justice Survey · 2005 · Crown ©]

———— PRISON POPULATION & STATISTICS ————

The degree of civilisation in a society can be judged by entering its prisons.
— FYODOR DOSTOEVSKY [attrib.]

Prison population	total	♂	♀	capacity†
2 September 2005	76,875	72,273	4,602	78,271

† Useable operational capacity is the sum of all establishments' operational capacity less 1,700 places for 'operating margin' caused by the need for separate accommodation for various classes of prisoner i.e. by sex, age, security category, conviction status, risk assessment and geographical distribution.

Indicator	2004–5		
Public:private-sector prisons... 128:11		Minority ethnic prison staff..... 5·7%
Overcrowding (average).......... 23·7%		Average hours of purposeful activity per prisoner per week............. 25·7
— in male local prisons 53%		Average hours per day for which cells are unlocked per prisoner......... 10·3
Average cost/prisoner/year.... £26,412		Serious assaults by population... 1·5%
Escapes from escorts.................. 6		Serious assaults on fellow inmate . 710
Escapes from prisons................ 12		Serious sexual assaults 110
Positive mandatory drug tests.. 11·6%		Serious assaults on staff............ 162
Self-inflicted deaths 82		

[2004–5 figures for public sector England & Wales · Source: HMPS Annual Report · Crown ©]

———— PRISONER CATEGORIES ————

A Prisoners whose escape would be highly dangerous to the public or the police or the security of the state, no matter how unlikely that escape might be, and for whom the aim must be to make escape impossible.

B Prisoners for whom the very highest conditions of security are not necessary, but for whom escape must be made very difficult.

C Prisoners who cannot be trusted in open conditions, but who do not have the resources and will to make a determined escape attempt.

D Prisoners who can be reasonably trusted in open conditions.

———— WORLD PRISON POPULATION RATES ————

The International Centre for Prison Studies regularly surveys prison populations around the world. Below are some incarceration rates per 100,000 of population:

Rate/100,000 population			
USA 714	S. Africa 413	Canada 116	N. Ireland..... 72
Russia........532	Israel.........209	Germany......96	Denmark......70
Cuba.........487	England & Wls .. 142	Rep. Ireland...85	Japan..........58
	Scotland 132	Switzerland ...81	India 29

[The calculation of these 2003 figures is complex; readers are advised to consult the excellent report.]

—————— BRITISH CRIME SURVEY 2005 ——————

The annual British Crime Survey (BCS) measures crime in England and Wales by interviewing people about crimes they have experienced in the past year, and their fear of crime. The BCS is widely seen as a useful partner to the Police's recorded crime figures [overleaf] since, for a number of reasons, many crimes go unreported.

% change in incidents of crime · British Crime Survey · 2003/4 – 2004/5

Vandalism	+4
Burglary	-20
All vehicle thefts	-11
Bicycle theft	+9
All BCS violence	-11
Domestic violence	-10
All household crime	-5
TOTAL BCS CRIME	-7

% change in Police recorded crime · 2003/4 – 2004/5

More serious violence against the person	+3
Other offences against the person, with injury	+13
Other offences against the person, with no injury	-1
Sexual offences	+17
Robbery	-12
Domestic burglary	-20
Other burglary	-14
Thefts of and from vehicles	-17
Other thefts and handling	-7
Criminal damage	-2
TOTAL RECORDED CRIME	-6

The following chart indicates those who are 'very worried' about 3 forms of crime:

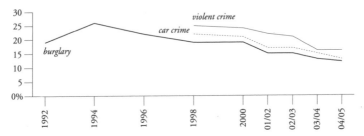

Despite BCS and Police figures indicating that levels of crime are falling, BCS data show that people perceive crime to have increased nationally and in their area:

Perception	a lot more crime	a little more crime
Whole country	34%	27%
Their own area	27%	16%

—— SOME POLICE RECORDED CRIME BY OFFENCE——

Offence or grouping of offences	1995	2003/4	2004/5	detected[†]
Homicide [murder, manslaughter, infanticide]	745	853	859	98%
Attempted murder	634	884	736	73%
Endangering railway passengers	12	7	9	78%
Endangering life at sea	N/A	2	3	100%
Child abduction	355	921	1,028	33%
Procuring illegal abortion	5	9	15	60%
Assault on a constable	N/A	21,927	23,267	95%
Total violence against the person	*212,528*	*955,752*	*1,035,046*	*53%*
Buggery	818	247	73	59%
Rape of a female	4,986	12,354	12,867	29%
Rape of a male	150	893	1,135	29%
Bigamy	86	71	105	54%
Sexual grooming	N/A	N/A	185	28%
Total sexual offences	*30,274*	*52,070*	*60,946*	*34%*
Total burglary	*1,239,484*	*818,642*	*679,973*	*13%*
Theft of and from vehicles	1,321,544	889,171	738,531	10%
Theft by an employee	14,357	17,571	17,131	56%
Abstracting electricity	2,600	1,303	1,289	70%
Theft/taking of a pedal cycle	169,476	102,520	102,680	5%
Theft from a shop	275,802	301,796	280,461	61%
Handling stolen goods	41,568	17,022	13,896	93%
Total theft & handling stolen goods	*2,452,109*	*2,268,143*	*2,027,516*	*16%*
Total fraud & forgery	*133,016*	*317,947*	*278,902*	*26%*
Arson	29,985	57,162	48,038	9%
Total criminal damage	*913,991*	*1,205,576*	*1,185,388*	*14%*
Total property crime	*4,738,600*	*4,610,308*	*4,171,779*	*16%*
Total drugs offences	*21,272*	*141,060*	*142,338*	*95%*
Going equipped for stealing, &c.	6,754	5,623	4,494	79%
Blackmail	856	1,475	1,459	26%
Kidnapping	1,247	3,125	2,790	44%
Riot	12	6	4	50%
Perjury	287	205	259	66%
Aiding suicide	10	11	6	50%
Perverting the course of justice	4,394	11,834	11,532	66%
Absconding from lawful custody	1,547	1,711	1,356	92%
Trade descriptions, &c.	N/A	510	1,326	81%
Obscene publications, &c.	N/A	2,881	2,860	71%
Adulteration of food	N/A	34	29	48%
TOTAL RECORDED CRIME	5,100,241	5,934,577	5,562,691	26%

[Italicised headings indicate a group of offences by type. 1995 figures are for calendar year; after 1997 for financial year. Some offences shown as N/A were later added to the series. † Detection figures relate to 2004/5 reported crime. The definition of detection is complex, but it broadly means that a suspect has been identified, there is sufficient evidence for a charge, and the victim has been informed that the crime is 'cleared up'. It does not necessarily mean that a suspect appeared in court, or was even charged. Figures for England & Wales. Source: 2005 British Crime Survey · Crown ©.]

Media & Celebrity

A celebrity is a person who works hard all his life to become known,
then wears dark glasses to avoid being recognised. — FRED ALLEN

HELLO! vs OK! COVER STARS

Date	*Hello!*	*OK!*
04·01·05	Michael Owen & family	Jordan & Peter Andre
11·01·05	Zara Phillips & Mike Tindall	Jade Goody
18·01·05	Brad Pitt & Jennifer Aniston	Brad & Jen
25·01·05	Victoria, Countess Spencer	Kerry Katona
01·02·05	Donald Trump & Melania Knauss	Jennifer Aniston
08·02·05	Donald Trump's wedding	Kerry Katona
15·02·05	David & Victoria Beckham	Jordan
22·02·05	Charles & Camilla	Jade Goody & new man, Ryan
01·03·05	David Beckham	Jessie Wallace
08·03·05	Cate Blanchett & Hilary Swank	Jordan & Peter Andre
15·03·05	Heather Mills-McCartney	Victoria Beckham
22·03·05	Perry Fenwick weds Angela Lonsdale	Jennifer Aniston
29·03·05	Charlotte Church & Gavin Henson	Kerry Katona
05·04·05	Duchess of York & her daughters	Jordan & Peter Andre
12·04·05	Camilla, Duchess of Cornwall	Kerry Katona
19·04·05	Charles & Camilla	Victoria Beckham
26·04·05	Camilla, Duchess of Cornwall	Jordan & son, Harvey
03·05·05	Lady Helen Taylor	David & Victoria Beckham
10·05·05	Victoria Beckham	Jennifer Aniston
17·05·05	Queen Rania of Jordan	Kerry Katona & Jordan
24·05·05	Sharon Stone & baby Laird	Jessie Wallace
31·05·05	Kylie Minogue	Jordan & Peter Andre
07·06·05	Rod Stewart & Penny Lancaster	Brad Pitt & Angelina Jolie
14·06·05	Prince William & Kate Middleton	Victoria Beckham
21·06·05	Camilla, Duchess of Cornwall	Steven Gerrard & Alex Curran
28·06·05	Tom Cruise & Katie Holmes	Kerry Katona & boyfriend, Dave
05·07·05	Michael Owen weds Louise Bonsall	Jennifer Aniston
12·07·05	Live8 participants	Jordan, Peter Andre & baby Junior
19·07·05	Penny Lancaster	Cheryl Tweedy & Ashley Cole
26·07·05	Lady Gabriella Windsor	Kerry Katona
02·08·05	Sienna Miller	Jordan & Peter Andre
09·08·05	David & Victoria Beckham	Victoria Beckham
16·08·05	Prince William	Jordan
23·08·05	Victoria Beckham	Anthony Hutton (*Big Brother* winner)
01·09·05	Madonna	Jordan
08·09·05	Ulrika Jonsson	Victoria Beckham

——— SOME HATCHED, MATCHED, & DISPATCHED ———

HATCHED

Cruz† *to*	David & Victoria Beckham
Corey *to*	Suzanne Shaw & Darren Day
Laird Vonne *adopted by*	Sharon Stone
Lola *to*	Denise Richards & Charlie Sheen
Junior *to*	Jordan & Peter Andre
Zahara Marley *adopted by*	Angelina Jolie
Gracie Ellen Mary *to*	Anna Friel & David Thewlis
Preston Michael *to*	Britney Spears & Kevin Federline
Henry Guenther Ademola Dashtu Samuel *to*	Heidi Klum & Seal

MATCHED

Donald Trump & Melania Knauss	*at* Palm Beach, Florida
Prince Charles & Camilla Parker-Bowles	Windsor Guildhall
Renee Zellweger & Kenny Chesney	US Virgin Islands
Heidi Klum & Seal	Mexico
Jack White & Karen Elson	Brazil (by a shaman, in a canoe on the Amazon)
Ben Affleck & Jennifer Garner	Turks & Caicos Islands
Peter Andre & Jordan	Highclere Castle, Berkshire

DISPATCHED

Jennifer Aniston & Brad Pitt (*married for* 4 years)	divorced
Gail Porter & Dan Hipgrave (4 years)	separated
George & Alex Best (9 years)	divorced
Mena Suvari & Robert Brinkmann (5 years)	divorced
Elle Macpherson & Arpad Busson (*together for* 9 years)	separated
Renee Zellweger & Kenny Chesney (*married for* 4 months)	separated

† It has been reported that, in Spain, Cruz is usually a girl's name. The children of other celebs may also face playground taunts: Ace to Natalie Appleton & Liam Howlett; Apple to Gwyneth Paltrow & Chris Martin; Atticus to Tony Adams; Heavenly Hirrani Tiger Lily to Paula Yates & Michael Hutchence; Rolan to Marc Bolan; Tallulah Lilac to Jessie Wallace; Banjo to Rachel Griffiths; Zowie to David Bowie; Dixie Dot and Bibi Belle to Anna Ryder Richardson; Blue Angel to The Edge; Peaches, Pixie, & Fifi Trixibelle to Bob Geldof and Paula Yates; and Pilot Inspektor to Jason Lee.

——— TATLER'S MOST INVITED LIST ———

Tatler annually charts celebrities, socialites, and aristocrats who top the guest-lists at the most exclusive parties and society events. 2005's top ten most invited were:

1	Kate Moss & Pete Doherty	6	Mick Jagger & L'Wren Scott
2	Ben & Kate Goldsmith	7	Hugh Grant & Jemima Khan
3	Peaches Geldof	8	Lady Gabriella Windsor
4	Jemma Kidd & Earl of Mornington	9	Jamie & Jools Oliver
5	Tamara Mellon	10	Prince of Wales & Camilla

——— IACGMOOH ———

The fourth series of *I'm a Celebrity ... Get Me Out of Here* was the standard formula of petulant tantrums and bug-filled trials. Twelve million viewers watched squeaky Joe Pasquale crowned *King of the Jungle*. The 'celebrities' left in the following order:

11th	Brian Harvey (quit)
10th	Natalie Appleton (quit)
9th	Nancy Sorrell
8th	*(surprise guest)* Vic Reeves
7th	Sheila Ferguson
6th	Antonio 'Huggy Bear' Fargas
5th	Sophie Anderton
4th	Janet Street-Porter
3rd	Fran Cosgrave
2nd	Paul Burrell
WINNER	JOE PASQUALE

QUOTES OF NOTE

FRAN COSGRAVE · I've had a few dangerous creatures round my shorts before! ❦ NATALIE APPLETON · Argh! I just touched a tree! ❦ BRIAN HARVEY · I need a Big Mac, fries, a bath and maybe a spray tan! ❦ JANET STREET-PORTER · I didn't get where I am today by being feeble. ❦ SOPHIE ANDERTON in a misguided rant against SHEILA FERGUSON · Yeah, you sold millions of records. Whoopy-do. I sold absolutely tons of bras and they cost twice as much! ❦

——— BIG BROTHER ———

BB6 was longer and more packed with housemates than ever before. Special new features included the 'secret garden', and the contestants 'secret missions' – most of which were carried out with aplomb by Makosi. BB's twist came when Eugene was offered half the prize money, and to the public's delight, he took it. The housemates were evicted in the following order:

16th	Mary	8th	Kemal
15th	Lesley	7th	Orlaith (quit)
14th	Sam	6th	Derek
13th	Roberto	5th	Craig
12th	Saskia	4th	Kinga
11th	Maxwell	3rd	Makosi
10th	Vanessa	2nd	Eugene
9th	Science	1st	ANTHONY

QUOTES OF NOTE

LESLEY · I've got the biggest boobs in Huddersfield, apart from me mum 'n' me nan. ❦ SCIENCE · Yes, I am from the ghetto, yes, I live with my mum. ❦ DEREK · Science is the first black man I've met who makes me want to join the BNP. ❦ KEMAL *(to Saskia and Maxwell)* · Is this ordeal ever going to end so we can get some sleep? I'm sure you've secured your magazine deal. ❦ CRAIG *(to Anthony)* · Even if you tried to stab me I'd still look after you. How can you do this to me? I love you. ❦

——— WORST-DRESSED WOMEN ———

Each year, a self-styled American fashion guru mysteriously known only as Mr Blackwell produces a list of Tinseltown's worst style offenders. The 2005 top ten:

1	Nicolette Sheridan	6	Serena Williams
2	Lindsay Lohan	7	Britney Spears
3	Jessica & Ashlee Simpson	8	Paula Abdul
4	Courtney Love	9	Meryl Streep
5	Paris Hilton	10	Anna Nicole Smith

VANITY FAIR'S HOLLYWOOD

The stars featured on the cover of the 2005 *Vanity Fair* 'Hollywood issue' were:

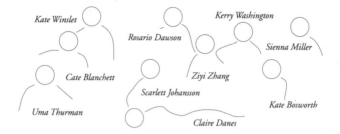

The 2004 *VF* cover-stars: Jennifer Connelly, Gwyneth Paltrow, Julianne Moore, Salma Hayek, Jennifer Aniston, Diane Lane, Naomi Watts, Kirsten Dunst, Lucy Liu, Hilary Swank, Alison Lohman, Scarlett Johansson, and Maggie Gyllenhaal.

CELEBRITY STARS IN THEIR EYES

A couple of times a year the Saturday night family favourite *Stars in their Eyes* adds an extra element to its dynamic format by inviting celebrities to impersonate other celebrities – confusing, and yet strangely pleasing. The following are some of the 'celebs' that have appeared over the years, and the singers they 'reinterpreted':

Celeb	*impersonated*		
Frank Skinner	Elvis Costello	Jarvis Cocker	Rolf Harris
Carol Vorderman	Cher	Anne Diamond	Sheena Easton
Kim Wilde	Doris Day	Boy George	David Bowie
Gabby Logan	Sharleen Spiteri	Ron Atkinson	Frank Sinatra
Esther Rantzen	Edith Piaf	Rachel Hunter	Marilyn Monroe
		Sam Fox	Dusty Springfield

SEXIEST MEN & WOMEN 2005

FHM's women		COMPANY's men
Kelly Brook	1	Brad Pitt
Cheryl Tweedy	2	Orlando Bloom
Angelina Jolie	3	Johnny Depp
Michelle Ryan	4	Jude Law
Elisha Cuthbert	5	David Beckham
Britney Spears	6	Nigel Harman
Abi Titmuss	7	Callum Best
Sarah Harding	8	Steve Jones
Beyoncé Knowles	9	Ashton Kutcher
Charlotte Church	10	Dermot O'Leary

—————————— CELEBRITY IN QUOTES ——————————

LIAM GALLAGHER · I'm a tender, loving and beautiful guy who tends to slap a photographer now and then. ❦ PAMELA ANDERSON · I always think clothes make you look fat, so I prefer to be naked. ❦ PARIS HILTON · Wal-mart … do they, like, make walls there? ❦ LINDSAY LOHAN · I am a normal person. I don't always have make-up on. Sometimes I wear sweat-pants to Starbucks. ❦ BRITNEY SPEARS · I have a new dog named Lucky and I just bought her a new dresser for her room. Yes, she has a room, which she shares with Bit Bit. For Christmas, they got a baby chandelier to go in it. It's the cutest thing in the world. ❦ EWAN McGREGOR · If movies are representative of life, then a huge part of my life is nudity and sex. I'm naked half the time, so why not in a movie? ❦ KELLY OSBOURNE · Other celebri-ties will work and work to become this huge thing – and I just sat there and got videotaped. ❦ ABI TITMUSS · I have had to embrace being sexy and being a sexual person but there is a difference between being that and being a slapper. ❦ DAVID BECKHAM · Moisturiser in the morning is a big thing. At night it's eye cream. A mani-cure is probably my favourite pamper-ing splurge. ❦ BRAD PITT · The idea that marriage has to be for all time – that I don't understand. ❦ ANGELINA JOLIE · I wouldn't be attracted to a man who would cheat on his wife. ❦ TARA PALMER TOMPKINSON [on her boyfriend Jacobi] · We could never marry, as Tara Palmer-Tomkinson-Anstruther-Gough-Calthorpe would not fit on my passport. ❦ LIZ HURLEY · I've always wanted to be a spy and, frankly, I'm a little surprised that British intelligence has never approached me. ❦ SHARON STONE · Women might be able to fake orgasms, but men can fake whole relationships. ❦ CHARLOTTE CHURCH · I am just so common – it's ridiculous. ❦ P. DIDDY · I feel safe in white because, deep down inside, I'm an angel.

—————————— FORBES CELEBRITY POWER RANKING ——————————

Power	celebrity	pay rank	web rank	press rank	TV rank
1	Oprah Winfrey	2	2	8	4
2	Tiger Woods	4	12	2	11
3	Mel Gibson	3	13	33	15
4	George Lucas	1	3	41	34
5	Shaquille O'Neal	26	26	5	12
6	Steven Spielberg	5	11	34	22
7	Johnny Depp	21	16	36	31
8	Madonna	11	5	30	19
9	Elton John	15	10	19	24
10	Tom Cruise	30	7	24	16

Forbes magazine's Power Rank combines all the other rankings. Pay Rank is from entertainment earnings June 2004–June 2005; Web Rank from number of times mentioned on Google; Press Ranking from clippings by LexisNexis plus the number of times celebs appeared on cover of 17 major magazines; and TV Ranking from Factiva.

CELEBRITY INTRIGUE

{JAN} · Jennifer Aniston and Brad Pitt announced the end of their marriage; allegations about any involvement of Angelina Jolie were firmly denied. ❦ {FEB} · Pete Doherty, heroin-addict boyfriend of Kate Moss and sometime singer with *Libertines* and *Babyshambles,* was arrested for assault. {MAR} · After much 'soul searching' Darren Day and Suzanne Shaw finally split up; tabloids raked through what they termed 'Darren's "love rat" past'. ❦ Gail Porter was rushed to hospital after an overdose of tablets; the split with husband Dan Hipgrave was blamed for her depression. {APR} · Callum Best and Elizabeth Jagger secured an injunction preventing the publication of CCTV footage showing them engaged in hanky-panky in a nightclub doorway. ❦ Wayne Rooney threatened to sue *The Sun* for libel following its report of a spat with his girlfriend, Colleen, in a nightclub, which he denied. ❦ The Beckhams' nanny alleged cracks in David and Victoria's 'perfect façade', reporting arguments, David's threats to leave, and his supposed infidelities. She later promised the High Court that she would not make any further allegations and would not dispose of the money she had received for her story until the Beckhams' claim was heard in court. {MAY} · Tom Cruise acted erratically on Oprah Winfrey's talk-show, and declared love for new girlfriend Katie Holmes who, at 26, is 16 years his junior. Cruise dismissed as laughable suggestions that the romance was a publicity stunt to promote their new

Pete Doherty

I just want to say I am deeply ashamed and upset that I've hurt Sienna and the people most close to us. – JUDE LAW

films. {JUN} · Kelly Osborne was re-admitted to rehab after 'personal issues'. ❦ George Best was pictured with two black eyes, allegedly dished out by a girlfriend after arriving drunk at her home. ❦ Russell Crowe was arrested in a New York hotel after allegedly throwing a telephone at a staff member when a 4am call to his wife would not connect. ❦ {JUL} · Sunday newspapers revealed that Jude Law had been cheating on fiancée Sienna Miller with the nanny. Law took the unusual step of issuing a public apology to Sienna stating: 'I just want to say I am deeply ashamed and upset that I've hurt Sienna and the people most close to us'. ❦ Kate Moss was reported to have ditched Pete Doherty, tiring of his unpredictable behaviour and constant partying. The on-off romance continued. ❦ Ex-*Eastender* Chris Parker admitted in an interview that his 2004 suicide bid was due to false rumours circulating that he was gay. {AUG} · Naomi Campbell attracted further unwelcome publicity when an Italian actress Yvonne Scio complained to the police that Campbell attacked her for wearing the same dress. Naomi Campbell vigorously denied the allegation. ❦ Courtney Love and Alan Partridge comic Steve Coogan both strenuously denied a *News of the World* story alleging Love was pregnant with Coogan's child. ❦ Eminem cancelled his European tour after admitting an addiction to sleeping pills. ❦ Jade Goody's estranged father was found dead in the toilets of a KFC after a heroin overdose.

—————— AND YOU ARE ... ? ——————

A ready reckoner of some of the key 'famous for being famous' C-list 'celebrities':

Jade Goody.....................*contestant on Big Brother; famous for dim comments*
Jeff Brazier............................*became tabloid fodder after dating Jade Goody*
Fran Cosgrave.......................*nightclub owner; dated Atomic Kitten's Natasha*
Kerry Katona....:.......................*ex-Atomic Kitten; ex-wife of ex-Westlife singer*
Abi Titmuss.....*shot to tabloid infamy after sex video with John Leslie posted on net*
Darren Day.....*West End performer; drug problem, and tabloids' favourite 'love-rat'*
Suzanne Shaw....*member of reality TV pop group Hearsay; dumped by Darren Day*
Paris Hilton..............*heiress to hotel fortune; sex-tape-on-net related shame/fame*
Gail Porter.............*TV presenter; lads mag favourite; arse projected onto Big Ben*
Jodie Marsh......*famous for wearing very little; spat with fellow busty babe, Jordan*
Tara Palmer-Tomkinson..........*'It' girl; friend of the Royals; reformed cocaine user*
Daniella Westbrook.....*soap-star turned coke-user; damaged septum; now recovered*
Brian Harvey........*ex-pop star; ex of Daniella Westbrook; drug-struggle/car mishap*
Rebecca Loos..*alleged affair with David Beckham; collected pig semen on reality TV*
Callum Best...................*son of football legend George; model; man about town*
Alex Best.............*ex-wife of boozer-Best; contestant on IACGMOOH; curious tan*
Penny Lancaster.......*Rod Stewart's betrothed; bra-related spat with Rachel Hunter*
Lady Isabella Hervey............*socialite; reality TV fodder; now 'face' of Playboy UK*

—————— REALITY SHOW WINNERS ——————

'Reality television' programmes continue to dominate schedules, with ever more unlikely formats competing to secure an audience. In 2005, terrestrial TV aired the following reality shows; the winners are listed below, with prizes in brackets:

Channel & show		*winner (prize)*
BBC1	*Strictly Come Dancing*	Jill Halfpenny (£850,000 raised for charity)
ITV1	*X-Factor*	Steve Brookstein (£1m record contract)
C4	*Celebrity Big Brother*	Bez (£50,000)
ITV1	*Celebrity Fit Club*	Tina Baker (lost 2st 7lb)
BBC1	*Celebrity Fame Academy*	Edith Bowman (£1·3m raised for Comic Relief)
C4	*The Games*	Philip Olivier & Kirsty Gallagher
	(a nice medal and a percentage of money raised to the celeb's favourite charity)	
FIVE	*Make Me a Supermodel*	Alice Sinclair (a years' modelling contract)
BBC2	*The Apprentice*	Tim Campbell (£100,000 job with Alan Sugar)
ITV1	*Hell's Kitchen*	Terry Miller (£250,000 to set up own restaurant)
FIVE	*The Farm*	Keith & Orville (£50,000)
ITV1	*Celebrity Wrestling* †	Annabelle Croft (a.k.a. Solitaire) (a tasteful belt)
		Iwan Thomas (a.k.a. Dragon) (a tasteful belt)
BBC1	*Strictly Dance Fever*	Sadie Flower & Joseph Hall (£50,000)
ITV1	*Celebrity Love Island*	Jayne Middlemiss & Fran Cosgrave (£50,000)

† *Celebrity Wrestling* was trounced in the ratings by *Dr Who*, and shunted into a graveyard slot.

—————— UK ADVERTISING EXPENDITURE ——————

Sector	% of expenditure
The press†	41·5%
Television	23·9%
Direct mail	14·6%
Directories	6·4%
Outdoor	5·0%
Internet	3·9%
Radio	3·8%
Cinema	0·9%

† Newspapers and magazines
[Source: Interactive Advertising Bureau, 2004]

—————— TOP TEN ADVERTISING FIRMS ——————

Agency ranked by billings — key clients
1...Abbott Mead Vickers BBDO.............. *Guinness; Gillette; Oxo; Royal Mail*
2...J. Walter Thompson......................... *Kellogg's; HSBC; Vodafone; Shell*
3...McCann-Erickson................................. *L'Oréal; Microsoft; Cadbury*
4...Publicis................................. *Renault; Asda; Müller; Hewlett-Packard*
5...M & C Saatchi........................... *Foster's; Kronenbourg; British Airways*
6...Ogilvy & Mather .... *Ford; Dove; Ocado*
7...Euro RSCG London .... *Harrods; Citroën; Danone*
8...Saatchi & Saatchi.. *Lexus; Toyota; NSPCC*
9...DDB London .... *Marmite; VW; Weetabix; Anadin*
10..Leo Burnett.............................. *Kellogg's; Heinz; Diageo; Disney; Fiat*

[Source: Ranked by Nielsen Media Research billings/*Campaign* · 2005]

—————— MOST COMPLAINED-ABOUT ADVERTS ——————

The Advertising Standards Authority (ASA) is an independent body set up to regulate the advertising industry. In their annual report (2004) they detailed the most complained about broadcast adverts, the top five of which were as follows:

AUCTIONWORLD · Shopping channel with poor customer service, misleading prices, and delays in delivering goods.
1,360 complaints · £450,000 fine
Revocation of licence to broadcast

MR KIPLING MINCE PIES · Advert portrayed a woman called Mary giving birth during a nativity play, which was deemed to mock a holy event.
806 complaints · Upheld

VIRGIN MOBILE · Commercial showed a young man urinating in a urinal with an attendant 'assisting', implying that he was holding the man's penis.
459 complaints · Not upheld

LANDROVER, FREELANDER SPORT · A woman grabs a gun from her drawer and shoots it in the air, revealing it to be a starting pistol. Complainants felt the domestic setting normalised gun culture and made light of the risks.
361 complaints · Upheld

TROJAN CONDOMS · Despite a post-9pm restriction on the advert, which showed a woman simulating orgasm, many complained that it was 'unnecessarily and overly explicit'.
317 complaints · Not Upheld

[Decisions taken by Ofcom. See p.127. Source: www.asa.org.uk]

─────────────── MEDIA CONSUMPTION ───────────────

UK households with selected goods

Goods	%
Television	99
Satellite TV	27
Cable TV	13
Digital	40
Land-line phone	92
Video recorder	89
Microwave	89
CD player	84
Mobile phone	76
Home computer	58
DVD player	50
Home access to internet	48
Dishwasher	31

[Source: ONS General House Survey 2003]

Average household spend

Media	weekly spend
Mobile (voice & text)	£6·57
Land-line phone	£5·69
TV	£5.38
Internet & broadband	£1·59
Radio	£0·55
Total spend per week	£19·78
% of total household spend	4%
other	
Newspapers	£1·90
Cinema/theatre/museums	£1·70
Books	£1·50
Magazines/periodicals	£1·10
Postal services	£0·50

[Source: Ofcom 2005; ONS 2004]

──── INTEREST IN TV PROGRAMMES BY TYPE & AGE ────

[ONS/ITC 2002]	age 16–24	25–64	≥65	all
News	83%	94%	97%	93%
Factual	69	87	84	84
Drama	75	80	87	81
Entertainment	89	76	70	77
Current affairs	57	68	79	68
Educational	45	61	52	57
Sports	51	54	53	53
Arts	30	33	43	35
Children's	41	33	17	31
Religious	11	19	51	24

──── MAIN SOURCE OF UK NEWS · OFCOM 2005 ────

% 11	15	70	4
Radio	*newspapers*	*television*	*other*

──── TRENDS IN UK NEWSPAPER READERSHIP ────

[NMA]	1999	2000	2001	2002	2003	2004
Daily	25·8m	24·9m	24·5m	25·1m	23·7m	23·7m
Sunday	27·5m	26·6m	26·1m	25·9m	25·4m	25·6m

——— WEEKLY HOUSEHOLD COMMUNICATION USE ———

TV viewing	26·1h	Dial-up internet	94m
Radio listening	43·5h	Broadband internet	c.3h
Phone – fixed line	81m	SMS texts	15 texts
Phone – mobile	27m	[Ofcom 2003 · Average for all households]	

——— SOCIAL ATTITUDES TOWARDS TV CONTENT ———

[Ofcom 2004]	*sex*	*violence*	*swearing*	*intrusion*
Too much	42%	59%	57%	59%
About right	48	36	39	31
Too little	3	1	1	2

——— ONLINE ACTIVITY: CHILDREN & PARENTS ———

In 2004, the *Economic & Social Research Council* surveyed 9–15 year olds and their parents to see how children's online activities differed from parental perceptions:

children	have you/has your child done these things on the internet?	parents
72%	visited a chat room	30%
47	seen pornography	15
33	given out information that they shouldn't	5
31	made new friends	15
27	been bullied	4
26	seen violent or gruesome material	7
23	been sent unsolicited sexual material	9
19	received sexual comments	8
9	seen racial or hateful material	4
9	met someone face to face that you first met online	3

——— MISCELLANEOUS MEDIA FACTS & OPINIONS ———

If you could only have one TV channel?.................... BBC1 43%; ITV1 26%
Opinions on the 9pm 'watershed' .... *too early* 32%; *about right* 57%; *too late* 7%
Standards on TV .... *improved* 10%; *stayed the same* 46%; *got worse* 42%
Households with digital .... *paid satellite (Sky)* 29%; *Freeview* 18%
Average weekly radio listening hours..................... 22·3h (or c.191 min/day)
Average daily time spent watching TV, video, DVD .... ♂ 175m; ♀ 161m
News source considered impartial..... TV 94%; *radio* 91%; *papers* 84%; *net* 69%
% BBC channels with subtitles .... BBC1 87·4%; BBC2 88·5%
% BBC channels with signing................................. BBC1 3%; BBC2 3%
% who have encountered offensive material............. *on radio* 14%; *on* TV 32%

[Sources: Ofcom, *The Communications Market 2005* · BBC Annual Report 2004/5]

——————————————— THE BBC ———————————————

Director General: Mark Thompson · address: Television Centre, Wood Lane,
London, W12 7RJ · 020 8743 8000 · www.bbc.co.uk

THE BBC GOVERNORS

Michael Grade CBE (Chairman)	Professor Merfyn Jones
Anthony Salz (Vice-Chairman)	Professor Fabian Monds
Deborah Bull CBE	Jeremy Peat
Sir Andrew Burns	Angela Sarkis CBE
Dame Ruth Deech	Ranjit Sondhi CBE
Dermot Gleeson	Richard Tait

——————————————— THE LICENCE FEE ———————————————

The licence fee is currently £121 *(colour)* and £40·50 *(b&w)*; there is no radio licence.

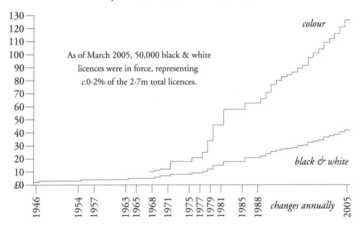

As of March 2005, 50,000 black & white licences were in force, representing *c.*0·2% of the 2·7m total licences.

——————————— COST PER HOUR OF BBC PROGRAMMES ———————————

Television channel	cost/hour £000	Radio station	cost/hour £000
BBC1	174·4	BBC Radio 1	3·1
BBC2	97·7	BBC Radio 2	3·9
BBC3	157·5	BBC Radio 3	4·3
BBC4	62·6	BBC Radio 4	11·4
CBBC	42·2	BBC Radio Five Live	7·3
CBeebies	63·3	BBC 6 Music	0·5
BBC News 24	5·3	BBC 7	3·8
BBC Parliament	0·5	BBC Asian Network	0·8

[Source: BBC Annual Report 2004/5]

———— HOURS OF TV PROGRAMMING BY GENRE————

Genre	hours/week				
Factual	134	Films	102	Education	46
Entertainment	112	Children	96	Current affairs	21
News	108	Drama	94	Arts	10
		Sport	91	Religious	7

[Source: Ofcom 2004 · Programmes from all five terrestrial channels]

———————— CHANGING TV AUDIENCE SHARE————————

	BBC1	BBC2	ITV	C4	5	other
1997	31%	12	33	11	2	12
1998	30%	11	32	10	4	13
1999	28%	11	31	10	5	14
2000	27%	11	29	11	6	17
2001	27%	11	27	10	6	20
2002	26%	11	24	10	6	22
2003	26%	11	24	10	7	24
2004	25%	10	23	10	7	26

[Source: BARB 2004]

———————————— REPEATS————————————

Over the next few years, I hope we can make BBC1 and BBC2 repeat-free zones.
I think the licence-fee payers would like to see that. — MICHAEL GRADE, 2005

The following shows the percentage of repeats on the main TV channels in 2004:

BBC1.....26%   BBC2.....34%   ITV 1....28%   C4.......38%   FIVE.....41%

———————— TELEVISION VIEWING FIGURES————————

The Broadcasters' Audience Research Board (BARB) collates audience viewing figures for television in the United Kingdom. The figures are extrapolated from a panel of 5,100 homes across the UK, designed to represent a broad cross-section of the British public. The BARB panel reflects about 11,500 viewers and their habits. Analogue, digital, satellite, and cable are all measured; video recordings are taken into account if they are viewed within seven days of transmission. Viewing information is automatically processed by an electronic meter attached to every television in the house. Each household member registers their presence in a room by pressing a button specifically allocated to them. The figures from each home are downloaded every night between 2am–6am to provide an up-to-date snapshot of the UK's television viewing habits. For more information see www.barb.co.uk.

———————THE TV BAFTAS · 2005———————

Award	winner
Best actor	Rhys Ifans · *Not Only But Always* [C4]
Best actress	Anamaria Marinca · *Sex Traffic* [C4]
Entertainment performance	Paul O'Grady · *Paul O'Grady Show* [ITV1]
Comedy performance	Matt Lucas & David Walliams · *Little Britain* [BBC3]
Single drama	*Omagh* [C4]
Drama series	*Shameless* [C4]
Drama serial	*Sex Traffic* [C4]
Continuing drama	*Coronation Street* [ITV1]
Feature	*Ramsay's Kitchen Nightmares* [C4]
Factual series or strand	*The Power of Nightmares* [BBC2]
Huw Wheldon award for specialist factual	*Dunkirk* [BBC2]
Flaherty award for single documentary	*Orphans of Nkandla* [BBC4]
Sport	*Olympics 2004 (Matthew Pinsent rowing for gold)* [BBC1]
News	*BBC Ten O'clock News: Madrid bombing* [BBC1]
Current affairs	*Death in Gaza* [C4]
Lew Grade for entertainment	*I'm A Celebrity...* [ITV1]
Sitcom	*Black Books* [C4]
Comedy programme or series	*Little Britain* [BBC3]
Pioneer audience award	*Green Wing* [C4]
Special award	Michael Palin
Richard Dimbleby award	Jon Snow
Alan Clarke award	Paul Greengrass
Dennis Potter award	Alan Plater

BAFTA IN QUOTES

❧ DAVID WALLIAMS · We are really lucky Ricky Gervais wasn't eligible this year ... We'd really like to thank the BBC who have believed in us for many years, even when we were rubbish. ❧ MATT LUCAS · We were really mediocre. Now we're brilliant. ❧ RHYS IFANS · Winning is a relief, being nominated is the award. ❧ MICHAEL PALIN · When you get awards like this at my age there's always a touch of the valedictory about them. This is the gold watch of the television industry. ❧

———————CHANNEL 4's TOP 100s———————

Channel 4 likes nothing better than listing top 100s on Saturday nights, such as:

Greatest	winner		
Album	Radiohead *OK Computer*	Movie Star	Al Pacino
Car	McLaren F1	Musical	*Grease*
Cartoon	*The Simpsons*	Pop Video	Michael Jackson *Thriller*
Tear jerker	*E.T. The Extra Terrestrial*	Scary moment	*The Shining*
Christmas moment	Band Aid	Sexy moment	Ursula Andress *Dr No*
Film	*Star Wars*	Sporting moment	Redgrave's 5th gold
Kids' TV Show	*The Simpsons*	TV character	Homer Simpson
		Sketch	Lou & Andy swimming

─────────────── 'EXTRAS' ───────────────

Celebrities who featured in *Extras*, Ricky Gervais' 2005 follow-up to *The Office*:

Samuel L. Jackson, Kate Winslet, Ben Stiller, Ross Kemp,
Vinnie Jones, Les Dennis, Patrick Stewart

─────────── OTHER TV AWARDS OF NOTE · 2005 ───────────

Awards	*category*	*winner*
	Most popular actress	Suranne Jones
	Most popular actor	David Jason
National TV Awards [2004]	Most popular factual	*Wife Swap*
	Most popular drama	*The Bill*
	Most popular serial drama	*Coronation Street*
TV Quick Awards	Best soap actress	Emma Atkinson · *Emmerdale*
	Best soap actor	Shane Richie · *Eastenders*
	Best actor	Shane Richie · *Eastenders*
British Soap Awards	Best actress	Suranne Jones · *Coronation Street*
	Best soap	*Coronation Street*
	Best villain	Sasha Behar · *Coronation Street*
	Actress in drama	Patricia Arquette · *Medium*
	Actress in comedy	Felicity Huffman · *Desp. H.wives*
Primetime Emmys	Actor in drama	James Spader · *Boston Legal*
	Actor in comedy	Tony Shalhoub · *Monk*
	Outstanding drama	*Lost*
	Outstanding comedy	*Everybody Loves Raymond*
	Sit-com and comedy drama	*Nighty Night*
Royal Television Society	Entertainment	*Strictly Come Dancing*
	Soap	*Coronation Street*
	Drama Series	*Shameless*

─────────── DOCTOR WHO ───────────

In March 2005, *Doctor Who* triumphantly regenerated onto BBC1, written by
Russell T. Davies, with Christopher Eccleston as the Doctor and Billie Piper as his
assistant, Rose. The first episode attracted 9·9m viewers, comfortably beating the
7·2m viewers of ITV's *Ant and Dec's Saturday Night Takeaway*. Despite continued
viewing success, critical acclaim, and even appreciation from the Queen, Eccleston
resigned after the first series, fearing typecasting, to be replaced by David Tennant.

1963–66	William Hartnell	1984–86	Colin Baker
1966–69	Patrick Troughton	1987–1989	Sylvester McCoy
1970–74	Jon Pertwee	1996	Paul McGann
1974–81	Tom Baker	2005	Christopher Eccleston
1981–84	Peter Davison	2005–	David Tennant

──────── SOME RADIO STATIONS OF NOTE ────────

Station name	frequency	share %	controller/editor
BBC Radio 1	97–99 FM	9·2	Andy Parfitt
BBC Radio 2	88–91 FM	16	Lesley Douglas
BBC Radio 3	90–93 FM	1·1	Roger Wright
BBC Radio 4	92–95 FM · 198 LW	11·2	Mark Damazer
BBC Five Live	909 & 693 AM	4·4	Bob Shennan
BBC 6 music	DAB	0·1	Lesley Douglas
BBC 1Xtra	DAB	0·1	Andy Parfitt
BBC 7	DAB	0·2	Mark Damazer
BBC World Service	648 MW	0·5	Nigel Chapman
BBC Asian Network	DAB	0·2	Bob Shennan
Talksport	1053/1089 AM	1·8	Mike Franklin
Virgin	1215 AM	1·5	Paul Jackson
Classic FM	99·9–101·9 FM	4·3	Darren Henley

[Source: Rajar – period Q2 2005 · All radio stations above are available on DAB and the internet]

──────── RADIO STYLE & CONSUMPTION ────────

Analogue radio stations by style

Style	%
Adult mainstream	52
Chart led	19
35+/Gold	16
Adult mainstream 'n' chat	3
Ethnic	3
Other	8
youth music	5
other music	1
news and speech	1

[Source: Ofcom 2005]

Location of radio listening

Home	70%
Car	16%
Work	12%
Other	2%

Commercial listening by platform

FM	78%
AM	14%
DAB	8%

[Source: Ofcom/Rajar 2004]

──────── NUMBER OF UK RADIO STATIONS ────────

Band	MW/AM	VHF/FM	DAB
Frequency	522–1611 kHz	88–108 MHz	217·5–230 MHz
Local commercial	59	213	164
UK commercial	2	1	8
BBC UK networks	1	4	11
BBC local	36	46	32
TOTAL	98	264	215

[Source: Ofcom 2005]

NOTABLE DESERT ISLAND DISCS · 2005

Castaway	luxury	favourite Desert Island Disc
Carlos Acosta	a case of Havana rum	Bacalao Con Pan (Irakere)
Andy McNab	a gollock (type of machete)	Sweet Thing (David Bowie)
Sam Taylor-Wood	a karaoke machine	Tiny Dancer (Elton John)
Jonathan Miller	his dissecting kit	Glenn Gould, Aria from Goldberg Variations (Bach)
Peter Maxwell Davies	a copper-plate engraving of Dürer's Passion	Victimae Paschali Laudes (Eustache du Caurroy)
David Starkey	hot and cold running water, a bath and bath oil	Dove Sono (Mozart)
Ursula Fanthorpe	a bird-identification book	Come Away, Fellow Sailors (Purcell)
Geoffrey Palmer	a fly-fishing rod	Benny Goodman, One O'Clock Jump (E. Durham, B. Smith & O. Page)
Stephen Poliakoff	a box of plastic straws to fiddle with	Quintet for Clarinet and Strings in A Major (Mozart)
Raymond Briggs	a full-size billiard table with Radio 4 in each leg	Parce Mihi Domine (Christobel de Morales)
Yvonne Brewster	some olive oil	Many Rivers to Cross (Jimmy Cliff)
Lorin Maazel	The Music Lesson by Vermeer	Quartet 14, Death and the Maiden (Schubert)
Philippe Petit	his father's 'Mysterious Object' which none can identify	Sonatine for Violin and Piano (Dvorak)
Patrick Stewart	a billiard table and a shed in which to keep it	Serenade for Tenor, Horn & Strings (Benjamin Britten)
Jarvis Cocker	a bed with a mosquito net	Sailing By (Ronald Binge)
Katharine Whitehorn	a machine to distil whatever is available	Double Violin Concerto (Bach)
Josephine Cox	her family photo album	Imagine (John Lennon)
Imelda Staunton	modelling clay and tools	I'll Know (Frank Loesser)
Prof. Sir David King	canvas with oils and brushes	I Don't Know Why (Norah Jones)
Satish Kumar	a spade	Ma Solitude (Moustaki)
Nigel Slater	Learning About Russian Music by Howard Hodgkin	Teddy Bears' Picnic (Jimmy Kennedy and John W. Bratton)
Betsy Blair	an ice cream maker	There's a Boat Dat's Leavin' Soon for New York (George Gershwin)
Alexander McCall Smith	a pair of handmade shoes	Soave Sia Il Vento (Mozart)
Ruby Wax	a huge bed	A Day in the Life (The Beatles)
Paulo Coelho	a trip round his island on Concorde	Ode to Joy (Beethoven)
Ronald Searle	the best possible Champagne	The Champagne Song (Strauss)

RADIO'S MOST POWERFUL

In a *Radio Times* survey (June 2005) a panel of 70 industry experts from both BBC and commercial radio chose the following top ten most powerful people in radio:

1 ... Jonathan Ross .... Radio 2	6 ... Peter Allen............... Five Live
2 ... Terry Wogan.............. Radio 2	7 ... Chris Moyles .... Radio 1
3 ... John Humphrys.......... Radio 4	8 ... Zane Lowe................ Radio 1
4 ... Christian O'Connell........ Xfm	9 ... Jane Garvey .... Five Live
5 ... Eddie Mair .... Radio 4	10.. Chris Evans.................... n/a

THE SONY AWARDS

The Sony Radio Academy Awards have, for over twenty years, been rewarding excellence in British radio. The judges present either bronze, silver, or gold awards depending on the level attained. Some of the gold award winners in 2005 were:

Daily music show	Drivetime with Lucio [Kerrang! 105.2]
Weekly music show..	The Selector [FCUK FM]
Breakfast show	Christian O'Connell's Breakfast Show [XFM]
DJ of the year..	Danny Baker [BBC London]
Entertainment award	Christian O'Connell's Breakfast Show [XFM]
Special award...	UK Radio Aid · Chris Evans
Speech broadcaster	Jeremy Vine [BBC Radio 2]
News journalist..	Eddie Mair [BBC Radio 4]
Drama award	Laughter in The Dark [BBC Radio 3]
Station of the year UK..	BBC Radio 2
The Gold award	Steve Wright

ACCENTS

In 2005, the BBC carried out a survey to discover the British public's attitude to regional accents. As part of the project the 5,000 people questioned were asked to identify the celebrity voices they found most and least pleasant. The results were:

MOST PLEASANT VOICES		LEAST PLEASANT VOICES
Sean Connery..............................	1	...............................Ian Paisley
Trevor McDonald	2	...........................Billy Connolly
Terry Wogan...............................	3	...............................Cilla Black
Hugh Grant................................	4	.... Paul O'Grady – Lily Savage
Moira Stuart...............................	5	............................Jasper Carrott
The Queen.................................	6	.......................Janet Street-Porter
Billy Connolly.............................	7	..........................David Beckham
Ewan McGregor...........................	8	...............................The Queen
Joanna Lumley.............................	9	...........................Frank Skinner
Pierce Brosnan	10	...............................Tony Blair

SUDOKU

Sudoku is the Japanese term for an American adaptation of a puzzle devised by a Swiss mathematician. In 1783, Leonhard Euler (the man who gave us 'i' for the square root of -1) created a new kind of magic square he called 'Latin Squares'. These were grids of equal dimension in which every symbol or number appeared once in each row or column. In the 1970s a variant of Latin Squares was introduced into the US magazine *Math Puzzles & Logic Problems*, under the title 'Number Place'. Grids are solved by placing a number (1–9) in each blank cell so that each row and column of 9 cells, and every internal 3x3 block, contains a digit from 1–9. In 1984, Japanese publisher Nikoli ran the puzzle under the name *Suuji wa dokushin ni kagiru* ('the numbers must be unmarried'). This was swiftly abbreviated to *Su* [number] *doku* [single].

It seems that the man responsible for importing Sudoku into Britain was retired judge, Wayne Gould. He saw the puzzles when in Tokyo and approached *The Times* which published them from November 2004. The popularity of Sudoku quickly blossomed and soon other papers realised the potential of a number puzzle that requires no mathematical ability, costs nothing to produce, and boosts circulation without the need for prizes. By June 2005 Sudoku was running in most newspapers (the *Sun* had introduced *Sundoku*); books of Sudoku puzzles were in the bestseller lists; Sudoku magazines were published; and Carol Vorderman was fronting 'Sudoku Live' on SKY. It remains to be seen whether Sudoku ('broadsheet bingo' and the 'C21st Rubik's Cube) will have the staying power of the crossword [started in 1913].

BRITISH PRESS AWARDS 2005

National paper	*The News of the World*
Political journalist	Simon Walters · *The Mail on Sunday*
Show business	Debbie Manley · *The People*
Columnist	Peter Hitchens · *The Mail on Sunday*
Feature writer	A.A. Gill · *The Sunday Times*
Interviewer	Robert Chalmers · *The Independent on Sunday*
Sports reporter	Jeff Powell · *The Daily Mail*
Reporter	Trevor Kavanagh · *The Sun*
Scoop	Beckham's secret affair · *The News of the World*
Front page	leak of the Hutton Report · *The Sun*
Team	illegal abortions · *The Sunday Telegraph*

The British Press Awards have often been improved by drunken behaviour, such as when Jeremy Clarkson punched the then *Mirror* editor, Piers Morgan, whom he claimed had insulted his wife. In 2005, eleven editors withdrew from the awards after Bob Geldof condemned them (except *The Sun*) for failing to support Africa. With only the support of News International titles, the future of the Awards is currently uncertain.

———————— THE PULITZER PRIZE ————————

In his 1904 will, Joseph Pulitzer made provision for the establishment of the
Pulitzer Prizes as an incentive to excellence. The prizes are awarded in journalism,
letters and drama, and education. The journalism prizes in 2005 were awarded to:

PUBLIC SERVICE AWARD · *Los Angeles
Times* for its *'courageous, exhaustively
researched series exposing deadly medical
problems and racial injustice at a major
public hospital'.*

BREAKING NEWS REPORTING · Staff
of *The Star-Ledger* for its *'clear-headed
coverage of the resignation of New Jersey's
Governor after he announced he was gay
and confessed to adultery with a male
lover'.*

INVESTIGATIVE REPORTING · Nigel
Jaquiss of *Willamette Week* for *'exposing
a former Governor's concealed sexual
misconduct with a 14-year-old girl'.*

INTERNATIONAL REPORTING · Kim
Murphy of the *Los Angeles Times* for
her *'eloquent, wide ranging coverage of
Russia's struggle to cope with terrorism,
improve the economy and make democracy work.'* And Dele Olojede,
Newsday, for his *'haunting look at
Rwanda a decade after rape and genoci-
dal slaughter had ravaged the Tutsi tribe'.*

BREAKING NEWS PHOTOGRAPHY ·
Associated Press staff for their *'stunning
series of photographs of bloody year-long
combat inside Iraqi cities'.*

For a full list of all the Pulitzer Prizes
see www.pulitzer.org

———— WORLD'S LARGEST NEWSPAPER MARKETS ————

China	India	Japan	USA	Germany
93·5m	78·8m	70·4m	55·6m	22·1m

[Source: World Association of Newspapers · Figures represent the number of copies sold daily]

———————— NEWSPAPER SIZES ————————

According to the World Association of Newspapers the trend for shrinking papers
from broadsheet to compact continues apace, with 56 newspapers around the
world becoming compact during 2004. 36% of all world papers are now compact.

Format	*size* (mm)	example
Compact	295 x 370	*The Sun; The Times; The Independent*
Berliner†	315 x 470	*Le Monde; The Guardian* [from 12·9·2005]
Broadsheet	375 x 600	*The Daily Telegraph; Wall Street Journal*

† Despite Berliner's German-themed name, most German newspapers are broadsheet.
Some have puzzled over *The Guardian*'s decision to switch to Berliner at a cost of
£100m, when they could move to tabloid with ease, utilising their G2 printing presses.
It is thought that with all its supplements, a compact *Guardian* would be too unwieldy.

MAJOR BRITISH NEWSPAPERS

Title	editorial address	phone	editor	circulation	readership	cost	owner	founded
Sun	1 Virginia St, Wapping, London E1 9XJ	020 7782 4000	Rebekah Wade	3,343,486	8,093,000	30p	N	1911
Daily Mail	Northcliffe Ho, 2 Derry St, London W8 5TT	020 7938 6000	Paul Dacre	2,420,601	5,861,000	40p	A	1896
Daily Mirror	1 Canada Sq, Canary Wharf, London E14 5AP	020 7293 3000	Richard Wallace	1,752,948	4,491,000	35p	T	1903
Daily Telegraph	1 Canada Sq, Canary Wharf, London E14 5DT	020 7538 5000	Martin Newland	912,319	2,358,000	60p	H	1855
Daily Express	10 Lower Thames St, London EC3R 6HB	0871 434 1010	Peter Hill	835,937	2,140,000	40p	S	1900
Daily Star	10 Lower Thames St, London EC3R 6HB	0871 434 1010	Dawn Neesom	889,860	1,980,000	35p	S	1888
Times	1 Virginia St, London E98 1PL	020 7782 7000	Robert Thomson	698,043	1,644,000	60p	N	1785
Financial Times	1 Southwark Bridge London SE1 9HL	020 7873 3000	Andrew Gowers	377,930	485,000	100p	P	1888
Evening Standard	Northcliffe Ho, 2 Derry St, London W8 5TT	020 7938 6000	Veronica Wadley	372,955	960,000	40p	A	1827
Guardian	119 Farringdon Rd, London EC1R 3ER	020 7278 2332	Alan Rusbridger	358,345	1,287,000	60p	G	1821
Independent	191 Marsh Wall, London E14 9RS	020 7005 2000	Simon Kelner	255,603	673,000	65p	I	1986
News of the World	Virginia St, Wapping, London E1 9XJ	020 7782 4550	Andy Coulson	3,701,988	8,568,000	80p	N	1843
Mail on Sunday	Northcliffe Ho, 2 Derry St, London W8 5TT	020 7938 6000	Peter Wright	2,261,511	6,468,000	130p	A	1982
Sunday Mirror	1 Canada Sq, Canary Wharf, London E14 5AP	020 7293 3000	Tina Weaver	1,548,851	4,899,000	85p	T	1915
Sunday Times	1 Virginia St, London E98 1PL	020 7782 7000	John Witherow	1,339,063	3,853,000	150p	N	1821
Sunday People	1 Canada Sq, Canary Wharf, London E14 5AP	020 7293 3000	Mark Thomas	976,194	1,920,000	80p	T	1881
Sunday Express	10 Lower Thames St, London EC3R 6HB	0871 434 1010	Martin Townsend	887,401	2,388,000	110p	S	1918
Sunday Telegraph	1 Canada Sq, Canary Wharf, London E14 5DT	020 7538 5000	Sarah Sands	682,900	2,196,000	140p	H	1961
Observer	119 Farringdon Rd, London EC1R 3ER	020 7278 2332	Roger Alton	445,738	1,321,000	150p	G	1791
Independent on Sun.	191 Marsh Wall, London E14 9RS	020 7005 2000	Tristan Davies	206,689	887,000	150p	I	1990
Sunday Star	10 Lower Thames St, London EC3R 6HB	0871 434 1010	Gareth Morgan	432,600	1,028,000	70p	S	2002
(Sunday) Business	292 Vauxhall Br. Rd, London SW1V 1AE	020 7961 0000	Ian Watson	18,030	N/A	100p	H	1996

Ownership: [N]ews Corporation · Northern & [S]hell Media · [P]earson · Press [H]oldings Ltd · [A]ssociated Newspapers · [G]uardian Media Group · [I]ndependent News & Media · [T]rinity Mirror · Circulation: ABC [07-05] Readership: NRS [03-05] · Founded dates relate for the paper's earliest incarnation.

FREESHEETS

In 1999, *Metro* was launched in London by Associated Press; it is now distributed across eight major UK cities. With a combined daily circulation of over a million, *Metro* is the world's largest free newspaper, and the fourth most popular paper in Britain. The success of *Metro*, combined with a general decline in newspaper circulation figures, unnerved the newspaper industry, and encouraged both *The Evening Standard* (*Standard Lite*) and *The Financial Times* (*FTpm*) to produce afternoon freesheets in an attempt to bolster their market share. In 2005 the Office of Fair trading ruled that *Metro's* monopoly on Tube distribution was unfair. Consequently, the Mayor of London has opened bids for a rival to be distributed in the afternoons. The successful bidder is likely to be announced in early 2006.

NEWSPAPER READERSHIP & VOTING INTENTION

%	Labour	Conservative	Lib Dem
The Sun	44	35	10
The Daily Mail	24	57	14
The Daily Mirror	66	13	15
The Daily Express	29	44	20
The Daily Telegraph	14	64	18
The Daily Star	53	17	13
The Times	27	44	24
The Guardian	48	7	34
The Independent	38	11	43
The Financial Times	34	36	23

[Source: MORI Jan–Mar '05, certain to vote, base: 11,786 adults (8,982 giving voting intention)]

DEEP THROAT

The identity of *Deep Throat*†, the most famous informer in journalistic history, was revealed in the July 2005 *Vanity Fair*. *Deep Throat* assisted Bob Woodward and Carl Bernstein's *Washington Post* investigation into the Watergate break-in that catalysed President Nixon's resignation in 1974. For decades speculation has hovered over a host of names, including George Bush senior, but Woodward and Bernstein confirmed the confession by Mark Felt, Nixon's number two at the FBI.

†This somewhat indelicate pseudonym derives from the 1972 porn film of the same name. The film, which lasts an hour, was made in Florida over just six days for around £10,000. By taking porn into mainstream US cinema, it is suggested that the film has grossed over £300m. The 'star' of the film, Linda Lovelace (Linda Boreman) alleged that she was forced to make the film, and campaigned against pornography until she died in a car crash in 2002. In May 2005 the British Board of Film Classification gave *Deep Throat* an R18 certificate, allowing it to be shown in 'adult' cinemas [see p.145].

2005 GUARDIAN MEDIA 100

The top 20 from *The Guardian's* 2005 list of the top 100 powerful media players:

1= .. Mark Thompson; Michael Grade .... *BBC Director General; Chairman*
3.... Rupert Murdoch........................ *Chairman & Chief Exec. News Corp.*
4.... Charles Allen .... *Chief Executive ITV*
5.... Tessa Jowell .... *Sec. State Culture, Media, & Sport*
6.... Steve Jobs .... *Chief Exec. Apple Computers & Pixar Animation*
7.... Kevin Lygo.. *Director of TV, Channel 4*
8.... Martin Sorrell .... *Chief Exec. WPP (e.g. J. Walter Thompson; Grey)*
9.... Sergey Brin & Larry Page .... *Directors, Google*
10 .. Paul Dacre.............. *Editor-in-Chief Associated News (e.g. The Daily Mail)*
11 .. James Murdoch.. *Chief Executive BSkyB*
12 .. Peter Fincham .... *Controller BBC1*
13 .. Rebekah Wade.. *Editor, The Sun*
14 .. Russell T. Davies .... *Writer (e.g. Queer as Folk, Doctor Who)*
15 .. Andy Coulson.. *Editor, News of the World*
16 .. Tom Moloney.......... *Chief Exec. Emap (e.g. Kiss FM; Heat; FHM; Grazia)*
17 .. Stephen Carter.. *Chief Exec. Ofcom*
18 .. David & Frederick Barclay ..... *owners of Telegraph Group, The Scotsman, &c*
19 .. Andy Duncan.. *Chief Exec. Channel 4*
20 .. Helen Boaden .... *Director BBC News*

HOW TO COMPLAIN

Television and Radio Programmes
Ofcom · www.ofcom.org.uk · 0845 456 3000 or 020 7981 3040
Ofcom advises complainants initially to contact the programme makers directly, and then, if the response is unsatisfactory, to contact them. Ofcom considers complaints in the following areas: whether an item is biased, inaccurate, harmful, offensive or if it breaches someone's privacy. To complain, call Ofcom's contact centre which will record, assess, and adjudicate the complaint using the Programme Code. For details of the Code and to read recent rulings see the Ofcom website.

Press Complaints Commission
www.pcc.org.uk · 020 7353 3732
If a newspaper or magazine article is in breach of the press Code of Practice (details of which can be found on PCC's website) then complain to the editor of the publication. Should their response be unsatisfactory, refer the case to the PCC by summarising the complaint in a letter. Complaints should be made within 2 months of publication of the article.

Advertising Standards Authority
www.asa.org.uk · 020 7492 2222
The ASA presides over adverts, direct marketing and sales promotions. Complain to them: if something is wrong with an advert, if experiencing difficulty in getting goods or refunds for items purchased by mail order or through TV shopping channels, or to halt direct mail sent by post, fax, text message, or e-mail. Complaints can be completed online or by letter.

Music & Cinema

*When people hear good music, it makes them homesick for
something they never had, and never will have.*
— EDGAR WATSON HOWE

UK NUMBER ONES · 2005

W/ending	weeks	artist	song
01·01·05	1	Band Aid 20	*Do They Know It's Christmas?*
08·01·05	1	Steve Brookstein	*Against All Odds*
15·01·05	1	Elvis Presley	*Jailhouse Rock*
22·01·05	1	Elvis Presley	*I Got Stung & One Night*
29·01·05	1	Ciara featuring Petey Pablo	*Goodies*
05·02·05	1	Elvis Presley	*It's Now Or Never*
12·02·05	1	Eminem	*Like Toy Soldiers*
19·02·05	1	U2	*Sometimes You Can't Make It on Your Own*
26·02·05	1	Jennifer Lopez	*Get Right*
05·03·05	1	Nelly featuring Tim McGraw	*Over and Over*
12·03·05	1	Stereophonics	*Dakota*
19·03·05	1	McFly	*All About You & You've Got a Friend*
26·03·05	7	Tony Christie & Peter Kay	*(Is This the Way to) Amarillo*
14·05·05	1	Akon	*Lonely*
28·05·05	1	Oasis	*Lyla*
04·06·05	4	Crazy Frog	*Axel F*
02·07·05	3	2Pac featuring Elton John	*Ghetto Gospel*
23·07·05	5	James Blunt	*You're Beautiful*
27·08·05	1	McFly	*I'll be OK*
03·09·05	1	Oasis	*The Importance of Being Idle*
10·09·05	1	Gorillaz	*Dare*

THE BILL CLINTON COLLECTION

Bill Clinton, famed for his love of jazz, released a compilation album featuring his
favourite tracks. Proceeds from the sale will go towards the ex-President's charity
projects. Clinton's album, released in September 2005, includes the following:

My One and Only Love – John Coltrane · *Harlem Nocturne* – David Sanborn
My Funny Valentine – Miles Davis · *The Town I Loved So Well* – Phil Coulter
There Will Never Be Another You – Art Tatum · *Summertime* – Zoot Sims
In The Presence of Jehovah – Mickey Mangun · *Nostalgie* – Igor Butman
I Wish I Knew How It Would Feel to Be Free – Nina Simone · *Take My Hand,
Precious Lord* – Mahalia Jackson · *Chelsea Morning* – Judy Collins

---
SINGLES SALES

Sales of CD singles continue to decline in 2005 – tempered by the growth in singles downloaded from the internet and the resurgence of fashionable 7" vinyl.

Year	downloads	CDs	vinyl	other	TOTAL
2004	659,377	5,721,873	154,216	710,745	7,246,211
2005	5,562,638	4,408,453	288,780	780,204	11,040,075
% change	+ 743%	-23%	+87%	+10%	+52%

[Source: The Official UK Chart Company · Figures from April–June 2004 and 2005]

RECORD SALES AWARDS

SINGLES	British Phonographic Industry	ALBUMS
200,000	Silver	60,000
400,000	Gold	100,000
600,000	Platinum	300,000

SINGLES	Recording Industry Association of America	ALBUMS
500,000	Gold	500,000
1,000,000	Platinum	1,000,000
10,000,000	Diamond	10,000,000

MUSIC DOWNLOADS & THE CHARTS

The growth in the sale of legally downloaded music files has provided a welcome boost to a music industry in decline. According to the *International Federation of Phonographic Industry*, UK single-track downloads in the first half of 2005 grew ten-fold compared with the same period in 2004, with over 10m tracks legally downloaded. This dramatic rise meant that by April 2005 the *Official UK Chart Company* had decided to include legally downloaded tracks in their calculations. Previously, the singles' chart had been the preserve of teenage girls purchasing boy-bands and dubious dance tracks. Nowadays, as downloading has developed and is increasingly popular among adult males, the composition of sales has become more balanced, with indie and rock bands creeping up the charts. The following illustrates the differing tastes of the download markets and the CD singles market:

Download singles	position	purchased CD singles
Dakota · Stereophonics	1	*Amarillo* · Tony Christie
Galvanize · Chemical Brothers	2	*All About You* · McFly
Get Right · Jennifer Lopez	3	*Get Right* · Jennifer Lopez
Over and Over · Nelly	4	*Over and Over* · Nelly
What You Waiting For · Gwen Stefani	5	*Like Toy Soldiers* · Eminem

[Source: BPI · Singles sales from the period Jan–Mar 2005]

—————————— THE BRIT AWARDS · 2005 ——————————

Hosted by a resurgent Chris Evans, the 25th annual Brit Awards opened in high camp style, with the Scissor Sisters performing *Take Your Mama* alongside a troupe of Muppet melons and a 20-foot pink ostrich. The award winners were as follows:

British male . . . . The Streets
British female . . . . Joss Stone
British group . . . . Franz Ferdinand
MasterCard British album . . . . Keane · *Hopes and Fears*
British single [1] . . . . Will Young · *Your Game*
British rock act [2] . . . . Franz Ferdinand
British urban act [3] [presumably, Devon is urban] . . . . Joss Stone
British live act [4] . . . . Muse
British breakthrough act [5] . . . . Keane
Pop act . . . . McFly
International male . . . . Eminem
International female . . . . Gwen Stefani
International album . . . . Scissor Sisters · *Scissor Sisters*
International group . . . . Scissor Sisters
International breakthrough artist . . . . Scissor Sisters
Outstanding contribution to music . . . . Bob Geldof
Brits25 – best song in the last 25 years [6] . . . . Robbie Williams · *Angels*

[1] Voted by commercial radio listeners. [2] Voted by Kerrang! TV viewers.
[3] Voted by MTV Base viewers. [4] Replaced the old 'dance act' category as the trend for dance
music waned. [5] Voted by Radio 1 listeners. [6] Voted by Radio 2 listeners.

THE BRIT AWARDS IN QUOTES

❦ JOSS STONE · I don't even know what to do right now. Thank you all you guys for voting for me, I feel sick right now. ❦ ANA MATRONIC – SCISSOR SISTERS · If you told us a year ago we would be getting these awards today we would have called you crazy. You guys made our dream come true. ❦ ROBBIE WILLIAMS [speaking for everyone, it would seem] · I'm just amazed that my career keeps going. ❦ ALEX KAPRANOS – FRANZ FERDINAND · It's a long way from Glasgow to The Brits, but we would walk 500 miles, and we would walk 500 more to pick up our Brit award. ❦ CHRIS EVANS [to his recently estranged wife BILLIE PIPER] · You look nice. D'you fancy a drink later? · BILLIE PIPER · No, sorry. I'm busy. ❦

—————————— GEORGE W. BUSH & 'iPOD ONE' ——————————

It has been revealed by Presidential media adviser Mark McKinnon that, while mountain-biking around his Texas ranch, George W. Bush likes nothing better than to listen to his iPod (dubbed 'iPod One'). His favourite songs are said to be: *(You're So Square) Baby, I Don't Care* by Joni Mitchell; *Brown Eyed Girl* by Van Morrison; *Say it Ain't So* by The Thrills; *Centerfield* by John Fogerty; *Circle Back* by John Hiatt; and *My Sharona* by The Knack. McKinnon stressed that 'no one should psychoanalyse the song selection – it's music to get over the next hill'.

─────── FUNERAL MUSIC ───────

Digital channel Music Choice polled 20,000 British people to discover which song they would most like to be played at their funeral; the top ten were as follows:

1 .. Robbie Williams............. *Angels*
2 .. Frank Sinatra .... *My Way*
3 .. Eric Idle........... *Always Look on the Bright Side of Life*
4 .. Led Zeppelin .. *Stairway to Heaven*
5 .. Queen.. *Who Wants to Live Forever*
6 .. Green Day.......... *Good Riddance*
7 .. R.E.M. .... *Everybody Hurts*
8 .. Oasis.................... *Live Forever*
9 .. Bette Midler......... *Wind Beneath My Wings*
10. Royal Scots......... *Amazing Grace*

─────── CHRISTMAS NUMBER ONE ───────

Charity single *Do They Know It's Christmas?* by Band Aid 20 held the top spot in 2004, outselling its rivals five-to-one – shifting >600,000 units. Ronan Keating & Yusuf Islam came in at number 2 with their version of *Father and Son*, while Kylie Minogue claimed number 3 with her un-festive offering of *I Believe in You*.

─────── ROCK 'N' ROLL HALL OF FAME ───────

The following were inducted into the American *Rock & Roll Hall of Fame* in 2005:

Buddy Guy · Percy Sledge
The Pretenders (Martin Chambers, Pete Farndon, James Honeyman-Scott, Chrissie Hynde)
U2 (Bono, Adam Clayton, The Edge, Larry Mullen Jr.)

Artists become eligible for induction 25 years after their first record release.

─────── SOME MUSICAL SOBRIQUETS ───────

Louis Armstrong.............. *Satchmo*
David Bowie.... *The Thin White Duke*
Eric Clapton .... *Slowhand; God*
John Entwistle .... *The Ox*
Michael Jackson ...... *The King of Pop*
Mick 'n' Keith .... *The Glimmer Twins*
Bob Marley.................. *Tuff Gong*
Jim Morrison .... *The Lizard King*
Van Morrison .... *The Man*
Ozzy Osborne .... *The Blizzard of Ozz*
Charlie Parker .... *Bird*
Elvis Presley .... *The King*
Cliff Richard..... *The Peter Pan of Pop*
Frank Sinatra .. *Chairman of the Board*
Bruce Springsteen............. *The Boss*
Mel Tormé .... *The Velvet Fog*
Paul Weller .... *The Modfather*
Barry White........ *The Walrus of Love*

James Brown is — *The Hardest Working Man In Showbusiness · Mr Dynamite The Godfather of Soul · Soul Brother Number One · The Original Disco Man The Funky President · Papa · The Minister Of The New New Super Heavy Funk*

———————— THE EUROVISION SONG CONTEST · 2005 ————————

On 5 March 2005 the *Making Your Mind Up* final was held, with the following acts battling it out to represent Great Britain at the Eurovision song contest final:

Tricolore – *Brand New Day* · Gina G – *Flashback* · Javine – *Touch My Fire*
Andy Scott-Lee – *Guardian Angel* · Jordan [Katie Price] – *Not Just Anybody*

All eyes were on Jordan who, had she won, would have been 8 months pregnant by the finals. However, it was Javine who inadvertently flashed a boob, and won.

Ladbroke's predictions

Greece 7/4 · Norway 4/1 · Hungary 7/1 · UK 20/1 · Javine flashing a boob 14/1

THE FINAL · 21·05·05 · KIEV, UKRAINE

The 50th anniversary Eurovision was characterised by the usual fare of Euro-pop, tortured ballads, novelty songs, and generous use of oversized drums, most notably in Moldova's epic number, *Grandma Beats the Drum-a*. The top 5 countries were:

Country	artist	song	score
Greece	Helena Paparizou	*My Number One*	230
Malta	Chiara	*Angel*	192
Romania	Luminita & Sistem	*Let Me Try*	158
Israel	Shiri Maimon	*Hasheket Shenishar*	154
Latvia	Walters & Kazha	*The War is Not Over*	153

WOGANISMS OF NOTE

'Usually I'm the worse for drink by about song seven. Mind you, looking at this line-up I think we'll start drinking by song three.' ❦ 'Trust me, this year's cornucopia overflows even more with the banal, the bizarre and the downright barking.' ❦ 'Now I know it's early days in the contest, but if I never heard another drum beat between now and Christmas I'd be a happy man.' ❦ 'I'm just worried about Moldova. I'm not sure where it is. If they win, grannies all over Europe will be unbearable.' ❦ 'All the usual bizarre voting but we're used to that now.' ❦

SONG LYRICS OF MERIT

GREECE · *You're delicious, So capricious, If I find out you don't want me I'll be vicious* ❦ MOLDOVA · *She's flying into trance like an Indian shaman!* ❦ UKRAINE · *Revolution is on! Because lies be the weapon of mass destruction* ❦ BOSNIA & HERZ · *Singer after singer, remembered, Different flags, but nations gathered* ❦ NORWAY · *Baby let's get into the groove, Show me all your dirty moves* ❦ LATVIA · *I'm so helpless in this angry world, If only I could change it for one day* ❦ UNITED KINGDOM · *Touch my fire can you feel the heat, My crazy rhythm's gonna knock you off your feet* ❦

RECENT UK EUROVISION PLACINGS

Year	artist	song	points	position
2005	Javine	*Touch My Fire*	18	22nd
2004	James Fox	*Hold On to Your Love*	29	16th
2003	Jemini	*Cry Baby*	0	26th

OTHER NOTABLE MUSIC AWARDS · 2005

Awards	*prize*	*winner*
	Best UK band	McFly
Smash Hits ['04]	Most fanciable male	Danny from McFly
	Most fanciable female	Rachel Stevens
	Top pop mop	Mattie from Busted
Kerrang!	Icon award	Marilyn Manson
	Best band on the planet	Green Day
NME	Best British band	The Libertines
	God-like genius award	New Order
Digital Music ['04]	Best artist download	Coldplay · *2000 miles*
	Best music website	www.madonnalicious.com
	Best video	Green Day · *Boulevard of Broken Dreams*
MTV	Best female video	Kelly Clarkson · *Since U Been Gone*
	Best male video	Kanye West · *Jesus Walks*
	Best group video	Green Day · *Boulevard of Broken Dreams*
	Record of the year	Ray Charles & Norah Jones · *Here We Go Again*
Grammys	Album of the year	Ray Charles · *Genius Loves Company*
	Song of the year	John Mayer · *Daughters*
	Best polka album	Brave Combo · *Let's Kiss*
	Best song	Franz Ferdinand · *Take Me Out*
Ivor Novello	Songwriters of the year	Keane
	Most performed work	Britney Spears · *Toxic*
	Best album	Snow Patrol · *Final Straw*
	Best R&B act	John Legend
MOBO	Best hip-hop	Sway
	Best single	Lethal B · *Pow (Forward)*
	Best album	Lemar · *Time to Grow*
Naomi	Worst British male	Jamie Cullum
	Worst British female	Rachel Stevens
	Icon award	Siouxsie Sioux
Mojo	Hall of fame	Madness
	Best new act	The Magic Numbers

TOP TEN MUSIC ACTS OF ALL TIME

In a list compiled for the new *Guinness Book of British Hits Singles and Albums*, the following reveals the most popular music acts of all time, judged on the number of weeks they spent in the UK singles and album charts from 1952 to the present:

Elvis Presley	*total weeks* 2,463	Elton John	1,615
Cliff Richard	1,972	The Shadows	1,578
The Beatles	1,749	Michael Jackson	1,477
Queen	1,725	David Bowie	1,459
Madonna	1,653	U2	1,402

——— PRS & ROYALTIES ———

The Performing Rights Society (PRS) is a not-for-profit organisation that tracks, collects, and polices royalty payments on behalf of member composers, lyricists, and music publishers. The PRS was established in 1914, as a consequence of the 1911 Copyright Act, by a group of music publishers who were keen to see a return when their music was performed commercially. Nowadays, the PRS represents *c.*42,000 members, and licences the commercial play of music in a myriad of environments, including: pubs, clubs, and concert venues; cable, terrestrial, and satellite broadcasters; the internet; factories, offices, zoos, and aircraft. In 2004, the PRS distributed *c.*£256m to its members, with the following income breakdown:

Income received	% of members
<£250	57%
£250–£1,000	17%
£1,000–£5,000	15%
£5,000–£10,000	4%
>£10,000	7%

The PRS issues 'blanket licences' to all national TV and radio stations (calculated on audience size). Broadcasters then provide the PRS with detailed information on each piece of music performed and the duration of its performance; the PRS then divides and distributes royalties to its members accordingly. Below are sums that copyright holders can expect to earn in royalties from some major broadcasters:

Station	£ per minute				
BBC Radio 1	18·44	BBC 5 Live	20·49	BBC 1	45·85
BBC Radio 2	18·09	Virgin Radio	1·52	BBC 2	43·33
BBC Radio 3	17·18	Classic FM	1·42	ITV 1	68·97
BBC Radio 4	20·34	Capital FM	2·32	Channel 4	18·12
		Talksport	0·71	Channel 5	8·53

——— THE MERCURY MUSIC PRIZE · 2005 ———

The 2005 (£20,000) Mercury Music Prize was awarded to Antony Hegarty for his album *I Am a Bird Now*. Hegarty (who records with the group 'Antony and The Johnsons') was seen as an unlikely winner, both because the Kaiser Chiefs were so hotly favoured, and because, while a British national, Hegarty has lived in America since a child. The judges were won over by his unique and haunting musical style.

> *There must have been a mistake. I am completely overwhelmed. I think it's insane, this is like a crazy contest between a spaceship, a potted plant, and a spoon as to which you like better* — ANTONY (AND THE JOHNSONS) HEGARTY

The 2005 Mercury nominees:

Bloc Party	*Silent Alarm*
Coldplay	*X&Y*
Hard-Fi	*Stars of CCTV*
The Go! Team	*Thunder, Lightning, Strike*
Kaiser Chiefs	*Employment*
K.T. Tunstall	*Eye to the Telescope*
Maximo Park	*A Certain Trigger*
The Magic Numbers	*The Magic Numbers*
M.I.A.	*Arular*
Polar Bear	*Held on The Tips of Fingers*
Seth Lakeman	*Kitty Jay*

MUSIC OUT OF ©

A quirk in European copyright law means that over the next few years many classic rock 'n' roll recordings will go out of copyright. Consequently, anyone will be able to release the songs without paying a penny in royalties to the owners of the master tapes or the performers of the songs. This presents a problem for music companies and artists who rely on their back catalogues to make money. Presently the law across Europe means that copyright runs out on the 1 January fifty years after any recording is first released. Campaigners are attempting to get the law changed so it falls in line with the American system, where copyright lasts 95 years. The following songs will become free of copyright within the next ten years:

2006 .... Bo Diddley – *Bo Diddley* · Fats Domino – *Ain't That a Shame*
2007 .... Chuck Berry – *Roll Over Beethoven* · Little Richard – *Tutti Frutti*
2008 .... Cliff Richard – *Move It* · Buddy Holly – *That'll Be the Day*
2009 .... Eddie Cochran – *Summertime Blues*
2010 .... Ben E. King – *Stand By Me*
2013 .... The Beatles – *Love Me Do* · Bob Dylan – *Blowin' in the Wind*
2014 .... The Rolling Stones – *Come On* · The Beach Boys – *Surfin' USA*
2016 .... The Who – *My Generation* · The Beatles – *Yesterday*

POP'S TOP EARNERS

Prince topped *Rolling Stone* magazine's 2004 top moneymakers' poll, having earned over £30 million from touring across America. The top ten were as follows:

Artist	$m				
Prince	56·5	Elton John	42·9	Phil Collins	33·2
Madonna	54·9	Jimmy Buffett†	36·5	Linkin Park	33·1
Metallica	43·1	Rod Stewart	34·6	Simon & Garf.	31·3
		Shania Twain	33·2	† *US country musician*	

SOME FESTIVALS OF NOTE

Festival	when	where	more information
Cambridge Folk	Jul	Cambridge	cambridgefolkfestival.co.uk
Download	Jun	Donnington	downloadfestival.co.uk
Glastonbury	Jun†	Somerset	glastonburyfestivals.co.uk
Isle of Wight	Jun	Isle of Wight	isleofwightfestival.org
Leeds	Aug	Leeds	leedsfestival.com
Reading	Aug	Reading	readingfestival.com
T in the Park	Jul	Strathclyde	tinthepark.com
V Festival	Aug	Chelmsford & Stafford	vfestival.com
Womad	Jul	Reading	womad.org
Wireless	Jun	Hyde Park, London	wirelessfestival.co.uk

† In 2006 Glastonbury will be having a well-deserved year off.

THE CLASSICAL BRITS · 2005

Best album . . . . Katherine Jenkins · *Second Nature*
Best artist · Male/Female. . . . . Bryn Terfel/ Marin Alsop
Contemporary music award. . . . John Adams · *On the Transmigration of Souls,* &c.
Young British classical composer . . . . Natalie Clein
Ensemble/orchestral album . . . . Harry Christopher and the Sixteens
Soundtrack composer. . . . . John Williams
Critics' award. . . . Stephen Hough, Dallas Symphony Orchestra & Andrew Litton
Outstanding contribution. . . . . James Galway

RICH COMPOSERS

A 2005 Classic FM rank of composers by the fortunes they made while alive:

1 . . . . George Gershwin (1898–1937)
2 . . . . Johann Strauss II (1825–99)
3. . . . . Giuseppe Verdi (1813–1901)
4 . . . . . Gioacchino Rossini (1792–1868)
5 . . . . George F. Handel (1685–1759)
6 . . . . Franz Josef Haydn (1732–1809)
7 . . . . . Sergei Rachmaninov (1873–1943)
8. . . . . Giacomo Puccini (1858–1924)
9. . . . . Niccolò Paganini (1782–1840)
10 . . . . Pyotr Tchaikovsky (1840–93)

NEW BACH ARIA

A previously unknown composition by J.S. Bach for soprano and harpsichord was discovered in June 2005 in a shoebox of papers taken from the Anna Amalia Library, Weimar, just months before it burnt down. The piece is an accompaniment to 12-stanza poem written for the Duke of Saxony in 1713. Christoph Wolff of the Bach Foundation called it 'an occasional piece of exceptional quality'. The new aria *'Alles mit Gott und nichts ohn' ihn'* is catalogued BWV1127 [see p.139].

ORCHESTRAS & PRINCIPAL CONDUCTORS

BBC Concert Orchestra. . . . . Barry Wordsworth
BBC National Orchestra of Wales. . . . . Richard Hickox
BBC Philharmonic. . . . . Gianandrea Noseda
BBC Scottish Symphony Orchestra. . . . . Ilan Volkov
BBC Symphony Orchestra . . . . Jiří Belohlávek
London Philharmonic . . . . Kurt Masur
London Symphony . . . . Sir Colin Davis
Philharmonia Orchestra . . . . Christoph von Dohnányi
Royal Liverpool Philharmonic Orchestra . . . . Libor Pesek
Royal Philharmonic. . . . . Yuri Temirkanov
Royal Scottish National Orchestra . . . . Alexander Lazarev

YOUNG MUSICIAN OF THE YEAR · 2004

16 year old violinist Nicola Benedetti won the competition, performing the first violin concerto by Karol Szymanowski at the Wigmore Hall on 19 October 2004.

TRADITIONAL ORCHESTRA SCHEMATIC

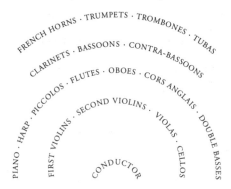

SOME CLASSICAL MUSIC IN ADVERTS

Levi's Jeans	*Sarabande in D minor* · Handel
Hamlet cigars	*Air on a G-string* · Bach
British Airways; Jif (Cif)	*Flower Duet* from *Lakmé* · Delibes
Hovis	*Symphony No. 9, 'From the New World'* · Dvorák
Cheltenham & Gloucester	*Adiemus/Cantilena* · Jenkins
Woolworths; Chanel No. 19	*Arrival of the Queen of Sheba* · Handel
Old Spice	*O Fortuna* from *Carmina Burana* · Orff
Lea & Perrins Worcestershire sauce	*The Sorcerer's Apprentice* · Dukas
Harrods	*Lascia ch'io Pianga* from *Rinaldo* · Handel
Smirnoff	*1492: Conquest of Paradise* · Vangelis
Lloyds Bank	*Sleepers Awake* · Bach
Hellmann's mayonnaise	*Waltz of the Flowers* · Tchaikovsky
Orange picture messaging	*The Lamb* · Tavener
De Beer's diamonds	*Palladio: Allegretto* · Jenkins
Maynards wine-gums	*Hoots Mon* · Lord Rockingham's XI
Adidas	*Sabre Dance* from *Gayane* · Khachaturian
Lurpak butter	*Flight of the Bumblebee* · Rimsky-Korsakov
Nescafé	*Morning* from *Peer Gynt* · Grieg

QUEEN'S MEDAL FOR MUSIC

In March 2005 it was announced that the Queen had approved a new award, the Queen's Medal for Music. The medal will be awarded annually on St Cecilia's Day (22 November, so chosen because Cecilia is Patron Saint of music). The award will recognise an individual of any nationality who has had a positive effect on the musical life of the British nation and contributed to raising the profile of music.

——————— CLASSIC FM HALL OF FAME · 2005 ———————

Each year the radio station *Classic FM* compiles its 'Hall of Fame', reflecting its listeners' 300 favourite classical tunes. With 21, Mozart has the most entries in the chart. The top ten in 2005 were as follows (the 2004 results are in brackets):

1 ... Sergei Rachmaninov .... *Piano Concerto No. 2 in C minor* .. [1]
2 ... Ralph Vaughan Williams .... *The Lark Ascending* .. [4]
3 ... Wolfgang Amadeus Mozart .... *Clarinet Concerto in A* .. [2]
4 ... Ludwig van Beethoven ..... *Piano Concerto No. 5 in E flat (The Emperor)* .. [6]
5 ... Max Bruch .... *Violin Concerto No. 1 in G minor* .. [3]
6 ... Ludwig van Beethoven .... *Symphony No. 6 (Pastoral)*. [10]
7 ... Edward Elgar .... *Cello Concerto in E minor* .. [9]
8 ... Edward Elgar .... *Enigma Variations* .. [7]
9 ... Karl Jenkins .... *The Armed Man (A Mass for Peace)* .. [8]
10 . Edvard Grieg .... *Piano Concerto in A minor* .. [5]

——————— DOWNLOADING BEETHOVEN ———————

For two weeks in June 2005, the BBC took the unprecedented step of making the nine Beethoven symphonies available to download for free. The vast popularity of the symphonies surprised many, when Beethoven downloads surpassed sales for the entire legal download chart in the same week. The numbers downloaded were:

Symphony No. 6 (Pastoral) .. 220,461   Symphony No. 8 148,553
Symphony No. 7 185,718   Symphony No. 5 139,905
Symphony No. 1 164,662   Symphony No. 4 108,958
Symphony No. 9 (Choral) ... 157,822   Symphony No. 3 (Eroica) 89,318
Symphony No. 2 154,496   TOTAL 1,369,893

——————— ROYAL PHILHARMONIC SOCIETY AWARDS · 2005 ———————

The *Royal Philharmonic Society Awards* celebrate the best of the UK's live classical music. In 2005, some of the many awards presented included the following:

BBC Radio 3 audience award .... Sir Charles Mackerras
Chamber-scale composition .... *Tendrils* · Howard Skempton
Concert series and festivals .... *Omaggio* · A Celebration of Luciano Berio
Conductor .... Antonio Pappano
Education .... Operation Hackney · On London Fields Ensemble
Ensemble .... The Hallé
Instrumentalist .... Pierre-Laurent Aimard
Large-scale composition .... *The Tempest* · Thomas Adès
Opera .... *Eight Little Greats* · Opera North
Singer .... Ben Heppner
Young artist .... Edward Gardner

───────SOME CLASSICAL ANNIVERSARIES IN 2006───────

2006 marks two major classical music anniversaries: the 250th anniversary of the
birth of WOLFGANG AMADEUS MOZART† in Salzburg (27·1·1756); and the 100th
anniversary of the birth of Russian composer DMITRI SHOSTAKOVICH (5·9·1906).
Other classical music anniversaries of note during 2006 include the following:

d. 1706	Johann Pachelbel	*b.* 1906	Klaus Egge
b. 1706	Giovanni Martini	*b.* 1926	György Kurtág
d. 1806	Michael Haydn	*b.* 1936	Steve Reich
d. 1856	Robert Schumann	*d.* 1956	Alexander Gretchaninov
b. 1906	Elisabeth Lutyens	*b.* 1956	Daniel Dorff

† *Oddly, while Cockney rhyming slang for 'pissed' is 'Brahms-n-Liszt', in Australia it is 'Mozart-n-Liszt'.*
'Mozart ear' is a congenital fusion of the crura of the anthelix and the helix, from which Mozart suffered.

───────────────THEMATIC CATALOGUES───────────────

The work of some composers, especially those prolific in the C18–19th, has been
organised and catalogued – often by a dedicated scholar – to aid the identification
of each piece. To take a famous example, the work of Mozart was chronologically
ordered by the Austrian naturalist Ludwig von Köchel (1800–77) who gave each
piece a number prefixed with his initial 'K'. So, Mozart's *Eine Kleine Nachtmusik*
(1787) is generally referred to as K525. Some other thematic catalogues include:

Code	*composer*	*cataloguer*
BWV	Johann Sebastian Bach	Wolfgang Schmieder
BB	Béla Bartók	Laszlo Somfai
BuxWV	Dietrich Buxtehude	Georg Karstadt
HWV	George Frederick Handel	Bernd Bäselt
H(ob)	Franz Joseph Haydn	Anthony van Hoboken
S	Franz Liszt	Humphrey Searle
D	Franz Schubert	Otto Erich Deutsch
TFV	Richard Strauss	Franz Trenner
RV	Antonio Vivaldi	Peter Ryom
WWV	Richard Wagner	Deathridge, Geck, & Voss

────────────OPERA COMPANIES OF NOTE────────────

ENGLISH NATIONAL OPERA · London Coliseum, WC2 .... 020 78360111 · eno.org
ROYAL OPERA HOUSE · London, WC2 · .... 020 73044000 · royaloperahouse.org
GLYNDEBOURNE · Lewes, East Sussex.................. 01273 813813 · glyndebourne.com
WELSH NATIONAL OPERA · John Street, Cardiff .... 029 20464666 · wno.org.uk
OPERA NORTH · Grand Theatre, Leeds................... 0113 2226222 · operanorth.co.uk
SCOTTISH OPERA · Elmbank Cres., Glasgow .... 0141 2484567 · scottishopera.org.uk
GARSINGTON OPERA · Oxford .... 01865 361636 · garsingtonopera.org

———————————— THE BBC PROMS · 2005 ————————————

Each year the BBC Proms explore different themes. In 2005, the first theme was 'the sea' – to coincide with the Year of the Sea celebrations 200 years after Trafalgar. Pieces included: Berlioz, *Overture, Le Corsaire*; Gilbert & Sullivan, *HMS Pinafore*; Haydn, *'Nelson' Mass*; Vaughan Williams, *A Sea Symphony*; Britten, *Four Sea Interludes* from *Peter Grimes*; Debussy, *La Mer*; and some 'Last Night' pieces. To mark the 200th birthday of Hans Christian Andersen, the second theme of 2005 was 'fairy tales'. Pieces included: Purcell, *The Fairy Queen*; Wagner, *Die Walküre*; Ravel, *Mother Goose Suite*; Tchaikovsky, *The Snow Maiden*; and Mendelssohn, *A Midsummer Night's Dream*. To celebrate some major musical anniversaries, a number of composers were honoured, including: Tallis, Berg, Berio, and Lambert. Michael Tippett's 100th birthday was marked with his *A Child of Our Time*. Some of the new works premièred during 2005 included: Fraser Trainer, *Violin Concerto*; Mark-Anthony Turnage, *From the Wreckage*; Michael Berkeley, *Orchestra Concerto*; Detlev Glanert, *Theatrum Bestiarum*; and Bent Sørensen, *The Little Mermaid*.

PROM 74 · THE LAST NIGHT OF THE PROMS · 10·9·2005

William Walton .... *Overture, Portsmouth Point*
Handel ...... *Xerxes, Ombra mai fu; Rodelinda, Dove sei; Giustino, Se parla nel mio cor*
Joaquín Rodrigo .... *Concierto de Aranjuez*
Constant Lambert .... *The Rio Grande*
Erich Korngold .... *Suite from music for 'Sea Hawk'*
Simon Bainbridge .... *Scherzi*
Traditional (arr. Crawford Young) .... *Down by the Salley Gardens*
Henry Purcell .... *King Arthur, Fairest Isle*
Edward Elgar .... *Pomp and Circumstance March No.1*
Henry Wood .... *Fantasia on British Sea Songs*
Hubert Parry (orch. Edward Elgar) .... *Jerusalem*
Traditional (arr. Henry Wood) .... *The National Anthem*
Traditional .... *Auld Lang Syne*

PAUL DANIEL *conducted*	Andreas Scholl (counter-tenor)
BBC Symphony Orchestra	John Williams (guitar)
BBC Symphony Chorus	Paul Lewis (piano)
BBC Singers	Karen Cargill (mezzo-soprano)

———————————— CLASSICAL RING-TONES ————————————

In 2005, the London Symphony Orchestra (LSO) became the first orchestra to record and sell ring-tones. In July 2005, the LSO's most popular ring-tones were:

1 .. Williams .... *Star Wars theme*	6 .. Goodwin .... *633 Squadron*
2 .. Tchaikovsky... *Nutcracker Suite 03*	7 .. Tchaikovsky... *Nutcracker Suite 02*
3 .. Gray .... *Thunderbirds theme*	8 .. Beethoven .... *9th Symphony*
4 .. Verdi .... *Aida Grand March*	9 .. Norman .... *James Bond theme*
5 .. Beethoven... *5th Symphony, Allegro*	10. Barry .... *Goldfinger*

UK TOP-GROSSING FILMS · 2004

Film	UK box-office gross (£m)	Director
*Shrek 2**	48·1	Andrew Adamson
*Harry Potter: The Prisoner of Azkaban**	46·1	Alfonso Cuaron
*Bridget Jones: The Edge of Reason**	36·0	Beeban Kidron
The Incredibles	32·3	Brad Bird
*Spider-Man 2**	26·7	Sam Raimi
The Day After Tomorrow	25·2	Roland Emmerich
Shark Tale	22·8	Bibo Bergeron
Troy	18·0	Wolfgang Petersen
I, Robot	18·0	Alex Proyas
*Scooby-Doo Too**	16·5	Raja Gosnell
Van Helsing	15·2	Stephen Sommers
Lemony Snicket	13·3	Brad Silberling
Starsky & Hutch	12·6	Todd Phillips
The Last Samurai	11·9	Edward Zwick
*The Bourne Supremacy**	11·6	Paul Greengrass

[Source: UK Film Council/Nielsen EDI · * indicates a sequel]

UK CINEMA ADMISSIONS BY MONTH

Below are the cinema admissions by month (in millions), comparing '03 and '04.

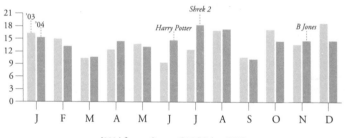

[2004 figures. Source: CAA/Nielsen EDI]

UK CINEMA ADMISSIONS BY AGE

Viewing habits by age	7–14	15–24	25–34	35+
See at least 1 film per year[†]	92%	90%	84%	61%
Visit cinema at least once a month[†]	39	53	34	16
Saw top-20 film*	20	26	22	32
Saw top-UK film*	12	27	23	39

[Source: UK Film Council · 2004 · †Proportion of population · *Proportion of audience]

THE BRITISH FILM INDUSTRY

British Film Institute
21 Stephen Street
London W1T 1LN · 020 7957 4787
www.bfi.org.uk

The UK Film Council
10 Little Portland Street,
London W1W 7JG · 020 7861 7861
www.ukfilmcouncil.org.uk

TOP UK-MADE FILMS 2004 · BOX OFFICE GROSS

Harry Potter Prisoner of Az.	...£46·1m	*King Arthur*	£7·1
Bridget Jones Edge Reason	£36	*Sean of the Dead*	£6·7
Troy	£18	*Thunderbirds*	£5·4
Phantom of the Opera	£9·0	*Bride & Prejudice*	£5·2
Wimbledon	£7·2	*Alien* vs *Predator*	£5·2

UK SCREEN ADMISSIONS

1997 .... 138·9m	2000 .... 142·5	2003 .... 167·3
1998 .... 135·2	2001 .... 155·9	2004 .... 171·3
1999 .... 139·1	2002 .... 175·9	[CAA/Nielsen EDI]

UK OSCAR NOMINATIONS 2005

Mike Leigh	*director & orig. screenplay*	Sandy Powell*	*costume design*
Imelda Staunton	*actress*	Alexandra Byrne	*costume design*
Kate Winslet	*actress*	Andrew Lloyd-Webber	*song*
Sophie Okonedo	*supporting actress*	John Mathieson	*cinematographer*
Clive Owen	*supporting actor*	Gemma Jackson	*art direction*
Andrea Arnold*	*short film*	Harry Potter	*special effects*
Gary McKendry	*short film*	Vera Drake	*screenplay*
Ashvin Kumar	*short film*	[* indicates a winner, see p.146]	

UNUSUAL FILM CREDIT GLOSSARY

Gaffer .... *senior electrician who sets up lighting*
Best Boy .... *head electrician responsible for set power; reports to gaffer*
Electrician .... *member of the electrical crew; reports to the Best Boy*
Grip .... *stagehand responsible for moving and setting up equipment*
Key Grip .... *the head of the Grips*
Best Boy Grip .... *assistant to the Key Grip*
Dolly† Grip .... *prepares and operates the camera dolly*
Craft Services‡ .... *provide refreshment for cast and crew*
Foley Artist .... *sound-effects artist who matches sounds to visuals*
Wrangler .... *handles any animals used in the film*

† The 'dolly' is a moving platform on which the camera is mounted for tracking shots.
‡ Some craft services vie for the most inventive name. The best is 'Cecil B. deMeals'.

MOVIE AWARDS OF NOTE

BAFTAs 2005 · *bafta.com*

Best film .... *The Aviator*
Best British film .... *My Summer of Love*
Best actor in a leading role .... Jamie Foxx · *Ray*
Best actress in a leading role .... Imelda Staunton · *Vera Drake*
Best actor in a supporting role .... Clive Owen · *Closer*
Best actress in a supporting role .... Cate Blanchett · *The Aviator*
Orange film of the year .... *Harry Potter: The Prisoner of Azkaban*

MTV MOVIE AWARDS 2005 · *www.mtv.com*

Best male performance .... Leonardo DiCaprio · *The Aviator*
Best female performance .... Lindsay Lohan · *Mean Girls*
Best villain .... Ben Stiller · *Dodgeball*
Best kiss .... Rachel McAdams & Ryan Gosling · *The Notebook*

GOLDEN GLOBES 2005 · *hfpa.org*

Best dramatic film .... *The Aviator*
Best dramatic actress .... Hilary Swank · *Million Dollar Baby*
Best dramatic actor .... Leonardo DiCaprio · *The Aviator*
Best director .... Clint Eastwood · *Million Dollar Baby*
Best supporting actress .... Natalie Portman · *Closer*
Best supporting actor .... Clive Owen · *Closer*

BRITISH INDEPENDENT FILM AWARDS 2004 · *bifa.org.uk*

Best British film .... *Vera Drake*
Best actor .... Phil Davis · *Vera Drake*
Best actress .... Imelda Staunton · *Vera Drake*

GOLDEN RASPBERRIES 2005 · *razzies.com*

Worst picture .... *Catwoman*
Worst actor .... George Bush · *Fahrenheit 9/11*
Worst actress .... Halle Berry[†] · *Catwoman*

EMPIRE AWARDS 2005 · *empireonline.co.uk*

Best British actress .... Kate Winslet · *Eternal Sunshine of the Spotless Mind*
Best British actor .... Paddy Considine · *Dead Man's Shoes*
Best British director .... Matthew Vaughn · *Layer Cake*
Best British film .... *Shaun of the Dead*

EVENING STANDARD BRITISH FILM AWARDS 2005

Best film .... *Vera Drake*
Best actress .... Imelda Staunton · *Vera Drake*
Best actor .... Paddy Considine · *Dead Man's Shoes*

[†] Halle Berry sportingly went to the ceremony to collect her 'prize', recreating her emotional Oscar speech from 2002 and adding 'I want to thank Warner Brothers for casting me in this piece of shit'.

——————————— GRAUMAN'S CHINESE THEATRE ———————————

A curious fusion of oriental and Art Deco, Grauman's Chinese Theatre (6925 Hollywood Boulevard) is famed for its collection of filmstars' concrete foot- and hand-prints, and for hosting Hollywood film premières. Since its construction in 1927, when it opened Cecil B. de Mille's silent film *King of Kings*, the theatre has hosted a wealth of glittering premières, including: *King Kong* (1933); *The Wizard of Oz* (1939); *Gentlemen Prefer Blondes* (1953); *Mary Poppins* (1964); and *Star Wars* (1977). Some of the films that premièred at the Chinese Theatre in 2005 included:

> *Charlie and the Chocolate Factory* · *War of the Worlds* · *Batman Begins*
> *Constantine* · *Racing Stripes* · *Coach Carter* · *Be Cool* · *Guess Who*
> *The Helix* · *Sahara* · *Longest Yard* · *Lords of Dogtown*
> *Sisterhood of the Travelling Pants* · *Honeymooners*

In 2005 there was consternation when the final *Star Wars* film, *Revenge of the Sith*, was not premièred at the Chinese Theatre like its five predecessors, but at the new Arclight Cinema instead. Many hardcore fans refused to believe the news and insisted on queuing regardless at Grauman's for days to get tickets, but to no avail.

——————————— HOLLYWOOD WALK OF FAME ———————————

In 1960, the Hollywood Chamber of Commerce created the *Hollywood Walk of Fame* by placing some 2,500 blank stars along (and around) Hollywood Boulevard. To date, approximately 2,130 of these stars have been occupied. Each year, the Hollywood Walk of Fame Committee considers the nominations for this honour. The stars are divided into five categories, each with its own symbol:

Symbol	*for*		
Record	singers & songwriters	Television set	television stars
Film camera	film stars & directors	Microphone	radio stars
		Theatrical masks	stage performers

In 2005, the following celebrities were presented with a star – at a cost of $15,000:

> Tim Allen · Antonio Banderas · Donald Duck · Kevin Kline
> Julianne Moore · Dennis Quaid · Ben Stiller · Keanu Reeves
> Rod Stewart · Carly Simon · The Righteous Brothers · Al Green

——————————— THE NEXT BOND ———————————

It was announced in February 2005 that Martin Campbell will direct the 21st Bond film: a new version of Ian Fleming's *Casino Royale* (1953), that was parodied in John Huston's 1967 film starring David Niven as James Bond. Speculation has surrounded the casting of the 7th (including Niven) Bond, after Pierce Brosnan was axed from the part by phone. Dougray Scott, Hugh Jackman, Colin Farrell, Goran Visnjic, Chris Feeney, and Clive Owen are some of the touted successors.

BRITISH FILM CLASSIFICATIONS

The British Board of Film Classification [BBFC] is an independent, non-governmental body responsible for viewing and classifying all films before they are released for public screening. In February 2005, the BBFC published new classification guidelines reflecting a nationwide survey of 11,000 people. The research indicated that audiences were increasingly relaxed about casual swearing and mild violence, but were concerned about incitement to racial hatred, suicide, self-harm, and sexual violence. The new classifications can be summarised thus:

Uc 'particularly suitable for pre-school children'.

U Universal, for audiences aged 4 and over. 'Films should be set within a positive moral framework and offer reassuring counterbalances to any violence, threat or horror.' Infequent use of mild bad language, occasional natural nudity, and mild violence.

PG Parental Guidance; children of any age may watch. 'A PG film should not disturb a child aged 8 or older'. Mild bad language, infrequent implied sexual activity. Realistic weapons should not be glamourised. References to drugs should be innocuous and carry an anti-drugs message.

12A Not suitable for those under the age of 12. Mature themes acceptable but must be suitable for young teen viewers. Infrequent strong swearing, nudity shown only in context. Violence should not dwell on details. May be occasional gory moments.

15 Not suitable for those under the age of 15. 'No themes are prohibited, provided the treatment is appropriate to 15-year-olds.' Frequent use of strong language, nudity allowed in a sexual context but no overt detail. Violence may be strong but should not dwell on the infliction of pain. Strong threat and menace are allowed.

18 Not suitable for those under the age of 18. 'No constraints at this level on theme, language, nudity or horror. The Board may cut or reject detailed portrayal of violent or dangerous acts which are likely to promote the activity, or the more explicit images of sex.'

R18 To be supplied only in licensed sex shops or shown in specially licensed cinemas to adults over 18. The following themes are unacceptable: any breach of the Obscene Publications Act (1959), material likely to encourage sexual abuse, infliction of pain in a sexual context, sexual threats, or sexual humiliation.

The two signatures which appear on the certification of each film are those of Quentin Thomas (President) and David Cooke (Director). See www.bbfc.co.uk.

Recently, the BBFC has started adding content advisory statements to films, e.g.: *Finding Nemo* – Contains mild peril · *Team America: World Police* – Strong language, violence and sex, all involving puppets · *War of the Worlds* – Contains sustained menace, threat and moderate horror · *Cinderella Man* – Contains moderate boxing violence · *Sideways* – Contains strong language and moderate sex.

—————————— 77TH ACADEMY AWARD WINNERS ——————————

Comedian Chris Rock was the controversial choice to host the 2005 Oscars, though he received a standing ovation before speaking a word. None of the British actors nominated won Oscars; neither did Martin Scorsese who, for the fifth time in his career, was unsuccessful in the Best Director category. And the winners were:

Leading actor ....Jamie Foxx · *Ray*
Leading actress ....Hilary Swank · *Million Dollar Baby*
Supporting actor ....Morgan Freeman · *Million Dollar Baby*
Supporting actress ....Cate Blanchett · *The Aviator*
Best picture...*Million Dollar Baby*
Directing.....................................Clint Eastwood · *Million Dollar Baby*
Animated feature...Brad Bird · *The Incredibles*
Art direction...Dante Ferretti · *The Aviator*
Cinematography...................................Robert Richardson · *The Aviator*
Costume design...Sandy Powell · *The Aviator*
Doc. feature ....Ross Kauffman & Zana Briski · *Born into Brothels*
Doc. short subject ....Robert Hudson & Bobby Houston · *Mighty Times*
Film editing......................................Thelma Schoonmaker · *The Aviator*
Foreign language film.........................Alejandro Amenábar · *The Sea Inside*
Make-up..............................Valli O'Reilly & Bill Corso · *Lemony Snicket*
Music (score) ....Jan A.P. Kaczmarek · *Finding Neverland*
Music (song) .... Jorge Drexler *Al Otro Lado Del Río* · *Motorcycle Diaries*
Short film (animated) ....Chris Landreth · *Ryan*
Short film (live) ....Andrea Arnold · *Wasp*
Sound..................................Millan, Orloff, Beemer, & Cantamessa · *Ray*
Sound editing....................Michael Silvers & Randy Thom · *The Incredibles*
Visual effects.............Dykstra, Stokdyk, LaMolinara, & Frazier · *Spiderman 2*
Screenplay (adapted).....................Alexander Payne & Jim Taylor · *Sideways*
Screenplay (original) .... Charlie Kaufman · *Eternal Sunshine of the Spotless Mind*
Honorary award.....................................Roger Mayer & Sidney Lumet

SOME OSCAR NIGHT QUOTES

❦ CHRIS ROCK · Welcome to the 77th and last Oscars. ❦ HILARY SWANK · I'm just a girl from a trailer park who had a dream. ❦ BRAD BIRD · Animation is about creating the illusion of life. And you can't create it if you don't have one. ❦ MORGAN FREEMAN · Getting a standing ovation was kind of humbling. ❦ CATE BLANCHETT · Thank you to Martin Scorsese – I hope my son will marry your daughter. ❦ GWYNETH PALTROW · I wanted to introduce each of the foreign language films in the appropriate language but unfortunately there just isn't time. ❦ CHARLIE KAUFMAN [under pressure from the clock] · Thanks to the Academy … 29 seconds … 27 seconds … that's really intimidating. I'll try and look somewhere else. ❦ CHRIS ROCK · You won't be able to take your eyes off the next four presenters: Salma Hayek and Penelope Cruz. ❦ JAMIE FOXX · Give it up for Ray Charles and his beautiful legacy. And thank you Ray Charles, for living. ❦ ANDREA ARNOLD · I said dog's bollocks during the ceremony – was it beeped? ❦

OSCAR NIGHT FASHION · 2005

Actor	dress	designer
Hilary Swank	*midnight blue, high neck, backless*	Guy Laroche
Gwyneth Paltrow	*pale-pink silk, strapless, corseted*	Stella McCartney
Renée Zellweger	*red strapless, silk, fishtail gown*	Carolina Herrara
Charlize Theron	*pale-blue strapless, layered net skirt*	Christian Dior
Scarlett Johansson	*black, taffeta, fishtail, boat neck*	Roland Mouret
Kate Winslet	*low-cut, sky-blue, jewel detail*	Badgeley Mischka
Cate Blanchett	*lemon yellow, single strap, belted*	Valentino
Halle Berry	*oyster grey, single strap, satin*	Versace
Kirsten Dunst	*black, sweetheart neck with lace overlay*	Chanel
Gisele Bundchen	*white, empire-line, strapless dress*	Christian Dior
Natalie Portman	*Grecian style, low-cut, bronze frock*	Lanvin

OSCAR MISCELLANY

First held .... 16 May 1929 (tickets cost $10; 250 attended)
First televised .... 1953 (25th Academy Awards, hosted by Bob Hope)
Most nominations: film .... (14) *All about Eve* (1940); *Titanic* (1997)
Most wins: film .... (11) *Ben-Hur* (1959); *Titanic* (1997);
                          The Lord of the Rings – The Return of the King (2003)
Most nominations: actress .... (13) Meryl Streep
Most nominations: actor .... (12) Jack Nicholson
Most nominations: director .... (12) William Wyler
Most awards .... (4) Katharine Hepburn
Films that have won the Best Picture, Director, Actor, Actress, and Writer Oscars:
          It Happened One Night (1934); *One Flew over the Cuckoo's Nest* (1975);
                          The Silence of the Lambs (1991)
Oldest winner: actor .... (76y 317d) Henry Fonda · *On Golden Pond* (1981)
Youngest winner: actor .... (29y 343d) Adrien Brody · *The Pianist* (2002)
Oldest winner: actress .... (80y 293d) Jessica Tandy · *Driving Miss Daisy* (1989)
Youngest winner: actress ...... (21y 218d) Marlee Matlin · *Childr. Lesser God* (1986)

OSCAR STATUETTE

Each Oscar stands 13½ inches high, weighs 8½ pounds, and is made from bronze coated with 24-carat gold. It was designed by MGM's chief art-director Cedric Gibbons and depicts a knight with a crusader's sword. The figure stands on a reel of film with five spokes, representing the original branches of the Academy: actors, writers, directors, producers, and technicians. From 1949, the statuettes began to be numbered starting, arbitrarily, at 501. During WWII, as part of the war-effort to save metal, the statues were made from plaster; these were swapped for golden models after the conflict ended. No one really knows why the awards were nicknamed Oscar – one suggestion is that the Academy's librarian, Margaret Herrick, noted that the statuette looked like her uncle Oscar, and the name stuck.

FILM FESTIVAL PRIZES · 2005

Sundance · World Dramatic Grand Jury Prize [JAN] ..... *The Hero* · Zeze Gamboa
Berlin · Golden Bear [FEB] .... *U-Carmen e Khayelitsha* · M. Dornford-May
Tribeca · Best Narrative Feature Film [APR] .... *Stolen Life* · Li Shaohong
Cannes · Palme d'Or [MAY] .... *L'Enfant* · Jean-Pierre & Luc Dardenne
Moscow · Golden St George [JUN] .... *Dreaming of Space* · Alexei Uchitel
Edinburgh · Audience Award [AUG] .... *Tsotsi* · Gavin Hood
Montreal · Grand Prix Award [AUG] .... *Off Screen* · P. Kuijpers
Venice · Golden Lion [SEP] .... *Brokeback Mountain* · Ang Lee
Toronto · People's Choice Award [SEP] .... *Tsotsi* · Gavin Hood
London · The Sutherland Trophy [OCT '04] .... *Tarnation* · Jonathan Caouette

MUST-SEE CHILDREN'S FILMS

In 2005 the British Film Institute, with the help of the public, compiled a list of films that children should watch before the age of 14 [see p.145]. The top ten were:

1.. *Bicycle Thieves* .... Italy, 1948
2.. *E.T.* .... USA, 1982
3.. *Kes* .... UK, 1969
4.. *Quatre Cents Coups* ... France, 1959
5.. *Night of the Hunter* ...... USA, 1955

6.. *Show Me Love* ..... Swe/Den, 1998
7.. *Spirited Away* .... Japan, 2001
8.. *Toy Story* .... USA, 1995
9.. *Where Is the Friend's House?* ... Iran, 1987
10 *The Wizard of Oz* .... USA, 1939

SOME MOVIE TAGLINES OF NOTE

In search of wine. In search of women. In search of themselves .... *Sideways*
There is no justice without sin .... *Sin City*
Just when you thought it was safe to go back in the water .... *Jaws 2*
In space no one can hear you scream .... *Alien*
Some men dream the future. He built it .... *The Aviator*
Would you erase me? .... *Eternal Sunshine of the Spotless Mind*
Someone's got a zoo loose .... *Madagascar*
No gut, no glory .... *The Incredibles*
Mysteries will unfold, Darkness will descend .... *Harry Potter & the Pris. of Az.*
His story will touch you, even though he can't .... *Edward Scissorhands*
Willy Wonka is semi-sweet and nuts ...... *Charlie & the Chocolate Factory (2005)*
A romantic comedy. With zombies .... *Shaun of the Dead*
They had a date with fate in Casablanca! .... *Casablanca*
They're already here .... *War of the Worlds (2005)*
Murderers come with smiles .... *Goodfellas*
If you believe in love at first sight, you never stop looking .... *Closer*
Wife. Mother. Criminal .... *Vera Drake*
Same Bridget. Brand new diary .... *Bridget Jones: The Edge of Reason*
One man's struggle to take it easy .... *Ferris Bueller's Day Off*
Hide your bridesmaids .... *Wedding Crashers*

─────── EMPIRE BEST DIRECTORS ───────

In June 2005 Steven Spielberg was named as the greatest film director in a poll of 10,000 *Empire* magazine readers. The top twenty directors were as follows:

1 .... Steven Spielberg	11 .... Clint Eastwood
2 .... Alfred Hitchcock	12 .... David Lean
3 .... Martin Scorsese	13 .... The Coen brothers
4 .... Stanley Kubrick	14 .... James Cameron
5 .... Ridley Scott	15 .... Francis Ford Coppola
6 .... Akira Kurosawa	16 .... Oliver Stone
7 .... Peter Jackson	17 .... Sergio Leone
8 .... Quentin Tarantino	18 .... John Ford
9 .... Orson Welles	19 .... Billy Wilder
10 .... Woody Allen	20 .... Sam Peckinpah

─────── ALAN SMITHEE ───────

Alan Smithee is responsible for some of the worst Hollywood films, and yet Alan does not exist. The name Alan Smithee was the sole pseudonym sanctioned by the Directors Guild of America [DGA] for use when directors feel the need to distance themselves from a film. However, the DGA will not grant the use of a Smithee to hide a director's shame about a terrible film. Smithees are granted only where creative differences have destroyed a director's 'vision'. Those allowed to hide behind a Smithee are required to keep their reasons secret. *Death of a Gunfighter* (1969) was the first film to credit Alan Smithee, after director Robert Totten fell out with the star, Richard Widmark, and was replaced by Don Siegel. At the end of filming neither director wanted to be credited. Since the DGA demands that all films list a director, Alan Smithee was created to take their place. In 1997, a comedy entitled *An Alan Smithee Film: Burn Hollywood, Burn* was released, which told the story of a director actually called Alan Smithee who wanted his name removed from a film. Bizarrely (or for reasons of publicity) the director of the film, Arthur Hiller, was himself granted an Alan Smithee for the film. After that, the DGA retired Alan Smithee and now grants each director a new pseudonym.

Some Alan Smithee films

Hellraiser: Bloodline
The Barking Dog
Putz
I Love N.Y.
Appointment with Fear
The Shrimp on the Barbie
Ghost Fever
Solar Crisis

George and Georgina Spelvin were pseudonyms traditionally used by actors in American theatres when they were playing more than one part. Georgina Spelvin lost favour when it was adopted as a screen name by porn-star Dorothy May. ❦ Walter Plinge was similarly used in London theatres. ❦ In the 1970s, the BBC used the pseudonym David Agnew when a writer's name could not be used for contractual reasons. ❦ The DGA only allows one director to be listed on the credits of a film, even if more were actually involved. The only exception to this is if there is a death mid-production.

Books & Arts

It's all very well to be able to write books, but can you waggle your ears?
— J.M. BARRIE

NOBEL PRIZE IN LITERATURE

The 2004 Nobel prize was awarded to the Austrian ELFRIEDE JELINEK (1946–),

for her musical flow of voices and counter-voices in novels
and plays that with extraordinary linguistic zeal reveal the
absurdity of society's clichés and their subjugating power

Jelinek's literary career spans poetry, literature, radio-drama, and theatre – though she is probably best known for her autobiographical novel *The Piano Teacher*, which was adapted for film by Michael Haneke and won the 2001 Cannes Grand Jury prize. Despite some commercial and critical success, Jelinek's work has proved controversial in both subject and style. A longstanding member of the Austrian Communist movement, Jelinek has used her work to explore the darker side of the state, the entertainment industry, and gender relations. According to the Nobel judges, she 'builds on a lengthy Austrian tradition of linguistically sophisticated social criticism'. The effect of this criticism is intensified by her blurring of traditional styles, combining the forms of prose, poetry, incantation, theatre, and film, to challenge cultural stereotypes. Elfriede Jelinek is only the ninth woman to win the prize, now valued at £760,000. Past Nobel Laureates of note include:

2003	J.M. Coetzee	1959	Salvatore Quasimodo
1997	Dario Fo	1958	Boris Pasternak
1995	Seamus Heaney	1957	Albert Camus
1993	Toni Morrison	1954	Ernest Hemingway
1983	William Golding	1953	Winston Churchill
1982	Gabriel García Márquez	1948	T.S. Eliot
1969	Samuel Beckett	1947	André Gide

MOST POPULAR AUTHORS

The top-selling authors in Britain, as calculated by Nielsen BookScan from 1998:

1	J.K. 'Harry Potter' Rowling	6	Terry 'Discworld' Pratchett
2	Ordnance 'You Are Here' Survey	7	John 'legal thriller' Grisham
3	Jacqueline 'Tracy Beaker' Wilson	8	Danielle 'Answered Prayers' Steele
4	Roger 'Mr Men' Hargreaves	9	Bill 'Small Island' Bryson
5	Dan 'Da Vinci' Brown	10	Richard 'textbooks' Parsons

──────── TOP 10 BESTSELLING UK BOOKS · 2004–5 ────────

Author	title
J.K. Rowling	*Harry Potter and the Half-Blood Prince* [children's edition]
Dan Brown	*The Da Vinci Code*
Dan Brown	*Angels and Demons*
Dan Brown	*Deception Point*
Dan Brown	*Digital Fortress*
J.K. Rowling	*Harry Potter and the Half-Blood Prince* [adult edition]
Bill Bryson	*A Short History of Nearly Everything*
Jamie Oliver	*Jamie's Dinners*
Gillian McKeith	*You are What you Eat: the plan that will change your life*
Michael Palin	*Himalaya*

[Period: 4·9·2004–3·9·2005 · Source: Nielsen BookScan TCM panel ©]

──────── LONG-LASTING BEST-SELLERS ────────

The following are some of the 23 titles that have appeared in Nielsen BookScan's top 5000 every week since it was first established in December 1998 (509 weeks):

The Very Hungry Caterpillar (Eric Carle) · *Birdsong* (Sebastian Faulks)
Complete Cookery Course (Delia Smith) · *The Hobbit* (J.R.R. Tolkein)
The Wasp Factory (Iain Banks) · *A Brief History of Time* (Stephen Hawking)

──────── TOP BOOKSELLERS ────────

UK bookseller	sales 2002/3	UK internet bookseller	market share
Waterstones	£406·2m	amazon.co.uk	30·63%
WHSmith	£354·2m	booksdirect.co.uk	9·63%
amazon.co.uk	£166·3m	whsmith.co.uk	3·91%
Borders	£152·2m	abebooks.co.uk	1·93%
Ottakar's	£114·8m	tesco.com/books	1·76%

[Source: *The Bookseller*]   [Source: Hitwise 2005]

──────── STRIKEOUT NUMBER ────────

It is common for books to have *strikeout numbers* printed on their copyright page:

1 2 3 4 5 6 7 8 9 10

The purpose of these numbers is to indicate the impression, or 'run', from which the book came. The lowest number visible indicates the book's impression. (The term 'strikeout' comes from the practice of literally scratching the numbers from the printing plate as the impression changed.) The numbers are sometimes printed in a different order – with even numbers preceding odd – or as a series of letters.

—————————— MAN BOOKER PRIZES ——————————

The 2004 (£50,000) Man Booker prize for best novel was awarded to ALAN HOLLINGHURST for *The Line of Beauty* (Picador). The 2005 shortlist includes:

John Banville .... *The Sea* .... Picador
Julian Barnes............. *Arthur & George*........................... Jonathan Cape
Sebastian Barry .... *A Long Long Way* .... Faber & Faber
Kazuo Ishiguro .... *Never Let Me Go*........................... Faber & Faber
Ali Smith .... *The Accidental*........................ Hamish Hamilton
Zadie Smith .... *On Beauty* .... Hamish Hamilton

> *It's very amazing to me that the long, solitary process of writing a novel should lead to a moment like this. My whole psychological technique for dealing with this evening was to convince myself I wasn't going to win it.* — ALAN HOLLINGHURST

The inaugural *International Man Booker* was presented in June 2005 to Albanian dissident writer ISMAIL KADARÉ. The award will be presented every two years to a writer from any country, to reward that author's body of work. Kadaré beat off stiff competition from Gabriel García Márquez, Ian McEwan, and Margaret Atwood – amongst others – to claim the £60,000 prize. Many of Kadaré's books were banned in his native Albania due to his satirical criticism of the repressive regime. Ismail Kadaré's best-known work is perhaps the novel *Broken April* (1990).

—————————— NOMS DE ... ——————————

Nom de plume .... a pseudonymous name assumed by authors, for example

George Eliot............ *Mary Ann Evans*	Barbara Vine .... *Ruth Rendell*
George Orwell .... *Eric Arthur Blair*	Dr Seuss .... *Theodor Seuss Geisel*
John le Carré............ *David Cornwell*	Richard Bachman .... *Stephen King*
Lewis Carroll . *Charles Lutwidge Dodgson*	Voltaire .... *François-Marie Arouet*
O. Henry .... *William Sydney Porter*	Mary Westmacott........ *Agatha Christie*
James Herriot .... *James Alfred Wight*	Hergé .... *Georges Rémi*
P.D. James... *Phyllis Dorothy James White*	Mark Twain............. *Samuel Clemens*

Nom de Dieu .... a French oath of exasperation (literally, 'name of God')
Nom de guerre* .... a fictitious name assumed during war or espionage
Nom de théâtre† .... a stage name assumed by actors
Nom de vente .... an assumed name under which one bids at an auction

*At one time it was customary for all those who entered the French army to assume a *nom de guerre*; indeed, during the time of chivalry, Knights were often known only by the devices on their shields. Perhaps the most famous contemporary *nom de guerre* is 'P. O'Neill', the name which usually signs statements issued by the Irish Republican Army (IRA). There are some suggestions that Osama Bin Laden fought (and perhaps still does) under the nom de guerre 'Abu Abdullah'. † See also Alan Smithee on p.149.

──────── ODDEST BOOK TITLE OF THE YEAR ────────

The Diagram Group's prize for the *Oddest Book Title of the Year* has been contested annually since 1978. It is run by *The Bookseller* and voted for eagerly by publishers and booksellers. Previous winners have included such splendid classics as these: *Living with Crazy Buttocks*; *Proceedings of the Second International Workshop on Nude Mice*; *How to Avoid Huge Ships*; and *The Big Book of Lesbian Horse Stories*. The 2004 winning title (which took 46% of the vote) and the runners-up were:

BOMBPROOF YOUR HORSE...................Rick Pelicano and Lauren Tjaden
The Aesthetics of the Japanese Lunchbox..............................Kenji Ekuan
Detecting Foreign Bodies in Food..............................Mike Edwards (ed.)
Equids in Time and Space..................................Marjan Mashkour (ed.)
Sexual Health at Your Fingertips..............Dr Philip Kell and Vanessa Griffiths
Applications of High Tech Squids..John Clarke

──────────── CHILDREN'S LAUREATE ────────────

In May 2005, Jacqueline Wilson was announced as the latest Children's Laureate, a two-year post rewarding an outstanding children's writer or illustrator. Previous holders of the title include Quentin Blake, Anne Fine, and Michael Morpurgo.

─────── SOME LITERARY FESTIVALS OF NOTE ───────

BATH · bathlitfest.org.uk ....Feb/Mar
ESSEX · essexcc.gov.uk ....Mar
OXFORD · sundaytimes-oxfordliteraryfestival.co.uk..............................Mar/Apr
CAMBRIDGE CONF. OF CONTEMPORARY POETRY · cccp-online.org............Apr
BELFAST LITERARY FESTIVAL · crescentarts.org....................................Apr
BRIGHTON FESTIVAL · brighton-festival.org.uk....................................May
HAY-ON-WYE · hayfestival.com ....May/Jun/Dec
LOWDHAM · lowdhambookfestival.co.uk..Jun/Jul
BROADSTAIRS DICKENS' FESTIVAL · broadstairsdickensfestival.co.uk ....Jun
EDINBURGH INTERNATIONAL · edbookfest.co.uk................................Aug
FOLKESTONE LITERARY FESTIVAL · folkestonelitfest.co.uk ....Sep
ILKLEY LITERATURE FESTIVAL · ilkleyliteraturefestival.co.uk ....Sep/Oct
CHELTENHAM · cheltenhamfestivals.co.uk..Oct
MANCHESTER POETRY FESTIVAL · manchesterpoetryfestival.co.uk................Oct

───────────────── ISBN 13 ─────────────────

Due to growth in publishing, the International Standard Book Number [ISBN] is to change. The existing 10-digit system, introduced in the 1960s, is set to run out of numbers. So, the International Organization for Standardization [ISO] has ruled that ISBNs will grow from 10 digits to 13 digits, as from 1 January 2007.

——————— OTHER BOOK PRIZES OF NOTE · 2005 ———————

Carnegie Medal	Frank Cottrell Boyce · *Millions*
Kate Greenaway Medal	Chris Riddell · *Jonathan Swift's Gulliver*
Commonwealth Writer's Prize	Andrea Levy · *Small Island*
Forward Prize: best poetry collection [2004]	Kathleen Jamie · *The Tree House*
Guardian Children's fiction [2004]	Meg Rosoff · *How I Live Now*
first book award	Armand Marie Leroi · *Mutants*
Orange Prize	Lionel Shriver · *We Need to Talk about Kevin*
Samuel Johnson Prize for non-fiction	Jonathan Coe
	Like a Fiery Elephant: The Story of B.S. Johnson
T.S. Eliot Prize for poetry	George Szirtes · *Reel*
Whitbread First novel	Susan Fletcher · *Eve Green*
Children's prize	Geraldine McCaughrean · *Not the End of the World*
Poetry	Michael Symmons Roberts · *Corpus*
Overall Whitbread & novel winner	Andrea Levy · *Small Island*
Smarties Prize [2004]: 5 and under	Mini Grey · *Biscuit Bear*
6–8	Paul Stewart & Chris Riddell · *Fergus Crane*
9–11	Sally Grindley · *Spilled Water*
Pulitzer Prize: Fiction	Marilynne Robinson · *Gilead*
Drama	John Patrick Shanley · *Doubt, a Parable*
Poetry	Ted Kooser · *Delights & Shadows*
British Book Awards: Author of the year	Sheila Hancock · *The Two of Us*
Book of the year	Dan Brown · *The Da Vinci Code*
Newcomer of the year	Susanna Clarke · *Jonathan Strange and Mr Norrell*
Sports book of the year	Paul Gascoigne · *Gazza: My Story*
Somerset Maugham Award	Justin Hill · *Passing Under Heaven*
	Maggie O'Farrell · *The Distance Between Us*
Bollinger Everyman Wodehouse Prize	Marina Lewycka
	A Short History of Tractors in Ukrainian
Impac	Edward P. Jones · *The Known World*
James Tait Black Memorial Prize	David Peace · *GB84*

——————— BAD SEX IN FICTION PRIZE ———————

Each year the *Literary Review* awards its 'Bad Sex in Fiction' prize to the novel featuring the most 'inept, embarrassing and unnecessary' sex scene. The 2004 'prize' winner was TOM WOLFE, for his splendid novel *I am Charlotte Simmons*.

> *Slither slither slither slither went the tongue. But the hand, that was what she tried to concentrate on, the hand, since it has the entire terrain of her torso to explore and not just the otorhinolaryngological caverns – oh God, it was not just at the border where the flesh of the breast joins the pectoral sheath of the chest – no, the hand was cupping her entire right – Now!*

Tom Wolfe responded to this dubious honour with the elegant line: – 'In this case, you can lead an English literary wannabe to irony but you can't make him get it.'

COPYRIGHT DURATION

The duration of copyright depends on a number of variable factors, including the type of material and the country in which it originated. The various durations of copyright for works originating in the United Kingdom or Europe are as follows:

Literary, dramatic, musical, or artistic work · lasts the lifetime of the author + 70 years from the end of the year in which they died.

Film · expires 70 years after the end of the year in which the death occurs of the last to survive of: the principal director, the authors of the screenplay and dialogue, and the composer of music specially created for the film.

Sound recording · expires 50 years from the end of the year it was made or, if published in this time, 50 years from the end of the year of publication.

Broadcast · expires 50 years from the end of the year of production.

Different rules may apply to works created before 1·1·96 – and for photographs, for which the copyright rules are complicated.

SOME OPENING LINES OF NOTE

Two years after my mother died, my father fell in love with a glamourous blonde Ukrainian divorcée.
A Short History of Tractors in Ukrainian
Marina Lweycka

It was a dark and stormy night; the rain fell in torrents.
Paul Clifford · E.G.E. Bulwer-Lytton

Renowned curator Jacques Sauniere staggered through the vaulted archway of the museum's Grand Gallery.
The Da Vinci Code · Dan Brown

It brought it all back to me. Celia Langley. Celia Langley standing in front of me, her hands on her hips and her head in a cloud.
Small Island · Andrea Levy

It is a truth universally acknowledged, that a single man in possession of a good fortune must be in want of a wife.
Pride and Prejudice · Jane Austen

We've been working on a potentially big story for weeks, involving photographs of British troops apparently abusing Iraqi civilians in Basra.
The Insider: Diaries · Piers Morgan

It was nearing midnight and the Prime Minister was sitting alone in his office, reading a long memo that was slipping through his brain without leaving the slightest trace of meaning behind.
Harry Potter and the Half-Blood Prince
J.K. Rowling

At twenty-four the ambassador's daughter slept badly through the warm, unsurprising nights.
Shalimar the Clown · Salman Rushdie

Anyone living in the United States in the early 1990s and paying even a whisper of attention to the nightly news or a daily paper could be forgiven for having been scared out of his skin.
Freakonomics · Levitt & Dubner

———————— BULWER-LYTTON FICTION CONTEST ————————

In 1982, the English Dept. of San José State University created a literary contest in honour of E.G.E. Bulwer-Lytton (1803–73) who infamously opened his book *Paul Clifford* with 'It was a dark and stormy night.' The contest rewards the best 'bad' opening line to an imaginary novel. The 2005 prize went to Dan McKay, for:

> *As he stared at her ample bosom, he daydreamed of the dual Stromberg carburetors in his vintage Triumph Spitfire, highly functional yet pleasingly formed, perched prominently on top of the intake manifold, aching for experienced hands, the small knurled caps of the oil dampeners begging to be inspected and adjusted as described in chapter seven of the shop manual.*

———————————— LIBRARY LENDING ————————————

The Public Lending Right (PLR) pays authors 'royalties' when their books are borrowed from public libraries; it is funded by the taxpayer via the Department for Culture, Media & Sport. Payments are calculated using an annually reviewed Rate per Loan which, in 2005, was 5·26p per loan (4·85p in 2004) – although the maximum that any one author can receive per year is £6,000. The top ten 'most borrowed' authors from public libraries in 2003–4 were the following:

1 ..... Jacqueline Wilson	5 ... Catherine Cookson	9 .... Ian Rankin
2 .... Danielle Steel	6 .... James Patterson	10 .... Roald Dahl
3 .... Josephine Cox	7 Janet & Allan Ahlberg	
4 .... Mick Inkpen	8 .... Agatha Christie	[Source: PLR]

———————————— LIBRARIES OF NOTE ————————————

THE BRITISH LIBRARY[†] .... Euston Rd, London · 0870 444 1500 · bl.uk
BRITISH LIBRARY NEWSPAPERS .... Colindale Ave, London · 0207 412 7353
BRITISH LIBRARY, BOSTON SPA .... Wetherby · 0870 444 1500
NATIONAL LIBRARY OF SCOTLAND[†] .... Edinburgh · 0131 226 4531 · nls.uk
NATIONAL LIBRARY OF WALES[†] .... Aberystwyth · 01970 632 800 · llgc.org.uk
BODLEIAN[†] .... Broad Street, Oxford · 01865 277 180 · bodley.ox.ac.uk
CAMBRIDGE UNI. LIBRARY[†] .... West Rd, Cambridge · 01223 333 000 · lib.cam.ac.uk
TRINITY COLLEGE LIBRARY[†] .... Dublin, +353 1 608 1661 · www2.tcd.ie/Library
NATURAL HISTORY MUSEUM LIBRARY .... London · 020 7942 5507 · nhm.ac.uk
SCIENCE MUSEUM LIBRARY .... London · 020 794 24242 · sciencemuseum.org.uk
NATIONAL ART LIBRARY .... London · 020 7942 2400 · vam.ac.uk/nal/index.html
WELLCOME LIBRARY.................... London · 020 7611 8722 · library.wellcome.ac.uk
THE WOMEN'S LIBRARY.............. London · 020 7320 2222 · thewomenslibrary.ac.uk

† Denotes a legal deposit library. All printed publications in Great Britain and Ireland must be deposited with each of the deposit libraries. Since the Legal Deposit Libraries Act 2003 was passed, this requirement now includes offline and electronic publications.

──────────── THE TURNER PRIZE ────────────

Founded in 1984, the Turner Prize is awarded each year to a British artist, under 50, for an outstanding exhibition or other presentation in the twelve months prior to each May. The winner receives £25,000 – and three runners-up receive £5,000.

In terms of confirming the public's prejudices, JEREMY DELLER was the ideal candidate to win the 2004 Turner Prize. He was discouraged from taking Art O-level at Dulwich College school (his teachers didn't think he was up to the task), he was the bookies' favourite, and he admitted, apparently, that he couldn't draw or paint. Deller regards himself as a 'party planner' and his works of art as 'social interactions' and 'events'. To this end, Deller's previous works include re-enacting a pitched battle between strik-ing miners and the police (which was filmed by Mike Figgis), and persuading the Williams Fairey Brass Band to play acid-house anthems. His Turner Prize entry included photographs of curious memorials he had erected across Britain to his own personal heroes; a bench he installed near Brian Epstein's old home; and a film shot in Texas in which he interviewed a woman who

Jeremy Deller

had once sold George W. Bush a burger. The most widely reproduced of Deller's images from the competition was a scribbled wall-sized flow-chart which tenuously linked acid-house and brass bands, titled *The History of the World 1997–2004*. The Turner judges claimed to have awarded 'substance over shock', and praised Deller's 'generosity of spirit across a succession of projects which engage with social and cultural contacts and celebrate the creativity of individuals'. Sir Nicholas Serota, Director of Tate, said of Deller 'he is able to release creativity in others in a way that makes memorable events or memorable images'. By contrast, and very much in the spirit of the annual Turner Prize headline hunt, Brian Sewell of *The Evening Standard* called the event 'a show entirely for video nerds', and the art collector Charles Saatchi denounced the Turner Prize as 'pseudo-intellectual rehashed claptrap'.

Year	previous winner
'84	Malcolm Morley
'85	Howard Hodgkin
'86	Gilbert & George
'87	Richard Deacon
'88	Tony Cragg
'89	Richard Long
'91	Anish Kapoor
'92	Grenville Davey
'93	Rachel Whiteread
'94	Antony Gormley
'95	Damien Hirst
'96	Douglas Gordon
'97	Gillian Wearing
'98	Chris Ofili
'99	Steve McQueen
'00	Wolfgang Tillmans
'01	Martin Creed
'02	Keith Tyson
'03	Grayson Perry

2005 NOMINATIONS

It was announced in June 2005 that the following four artists are shortlisted for the 2005 Turner Prize, the winner of which will be announced on 5 December:

Traditional oil painter, Gillian Carnegie; Darren Almond, who utilises both video and photography; and the installation artists Simon Starling and Jim Lambie.

———————— THE GULBENKIAN PRIZE ————————

The £100,000 *Gulbenkian Prize for Museum of the Year* is UK's largest museum prize, celebrating innovative and challenging British museums and galleries. In 2005 the prize went to the *Big Pit* in Blaenafon, South Wales. The judges praised the coal-mining museum for the insight given into life in a pit-community, and for the exciting underground tour into the heart of a coalmine. The other finalists were: *Coventry Transport Museum; Time and Tide, Museum of Great Yarmouth Life*; and *Locomotion: The National Railway Museum* at Shildon, County Durham.

———————— TOP EXHIBITIONS · 2004 ————————

The Art Newspaper's figures for the most popular art exhibitions in the world during 2004 illustrate that gallery visits are flourishing, with 241 exhibitions receiving more than 1,000 visitors a day. Below are the most popular exhibitions from 2004, around the world and in London, by the number of daily visitors:

GLOBAL TOP TEN

Exhibition	museum	daily attendance
Treasures of a Sacred Mountain	Tokyo National	7,638
El Greco	Metropolitan Museum of Art, NY	6,897
MoMA	Neue Nationalgalerie, Berlin	6,568
Manet	Prado, Madrid	5,832
Gauguin-Tahiti	Grand Palais, Paris	5,812
Pre-Raphaelites in Florence	Galleria degli Uffizi, Florence	5,507
Matisse: Process/Variation	Museum of Western Art, Tokyo	5,389
Treasures of Chinese Art	Tokyo National Museum	4,997
Joan Miró 1917–34	Pompidou Centre, Paris	4,742
Art in the age of Dante	Accademia, Florence	4,343

LONDON TOP TEN

Edward Hopper	Tate Modern	4,215
El Greco	National Gallery	2,126
Turner Prize 2003	Tate Britain	2,066
BP Portrait Award 2004	National Portrait Gallery	1,916
Vuillard	Royal Academy of Arts	1,796
Dürer	National Gallery	1,719
Vivienne Westwood	Victoria & Albert	1,567
Cy Twombly	Serpentine Gallery	1,539
Gabriel Orozco	Serpentine Gallery	1,448
Schweppes Prize 2003	National Portrait Gallery	1,402

———————— BECK'S FUTURES PRIZE ————————

Beck's Futures is Britain's most valuable art prize. In 2005 Christina Mackie received the £26,666 award for her sculptural installations on spatial relationships.

SOME MUSEUMS & GALLERIES OF NOTE

[key exhibits]

ASHMOLEAN MUSEUM · Oxford · 01865 278000 · ashmol.ox.ac.uk — *The Metrological Relief · The Parian Marble*

BIRMINGHAM MUSEUM & GALLERY · 0121 303 2834 · bmag.org.uk — *Ford Madox Brown, Pretty Baa Lambs · Lely, Sir Oliver Cromwell*

BOWES MUSEUM · Durham · 01833 690606 · bowesmuseum.org.uk — *Warwick Cabinet · Silver Swan · Canaletto, Regatta on the Grand Canal*

BRITISH MUSEUM · London · 020 7323 8000 · thebritishmuseum.ac.uk — *Rosetta stone · 'Queen of the Night' relief · Lindow Man*

CABINET WAR ROOMS & CHURCHILL MUSEUM · London · 020 7930 6961 · cwr.iwm.org.uk — *chronological lifeline of Winston Churchill*

DESIGN MUSEUM · London · 0870 8339955 · designmuseum.org — *changing displays of the best in design*

DULWICH PICTURE GALLERY · London · 020 8693 525 · dulwichpicturegallery.org.uk — *Rembrandt, Girl at a Window · Gainsborough, Linley Sisters*

FITZWILLIAM · Cambridge · 01223 332900 · fitzmuseum.cam.ac.uk — *Veneziano, The Annunciation · Titian, Tarquin & Lucretia · Degas, At the Café*

HORNIMAN MUSEUM · London · 020 8699 1872 · horniman.ac.uk — *eclectic collection of objects from around the world*

IMPERIAL WAR MUSEUM · London · 020 7 416 5000 · iwm.org.uk — *Holocaust exhibition · Orpen, The Signing of the Peace in the Hall of Mirrors*

LOWRY MUSEUM · Salford · 0870 111 2000 · thelowry.com 0161 876 2066 — *Lowry, Going to the Match; Portrait of Anne; Man with Red Eyes*

MERSEYSIDE MARITIME MUSEUM · Liverpool · 0151 478 4499 · merseysidemaritimemuseum.org.uk — *Edmund Gardner, Pilot Cutter · Titanic display*

MUSEUM OF CHILDHOOD · London · 20 8980 2415 · museumofchildhood.org.uk — *Tate Baby House · Princess Daisy doll · Cattley family teddy bears*

MUSEUM OF SCOTLAND · Edinburgh · 0131 247 4422 · nms.ac.uk — *Lewis chess pieces · Paolozzi figures · The Monymusk Reliquary*

NATIONAL GALLERY · London · 020 7942 2000 · nationalgallery.org.uk — *da Vinci, Virgin of the Rocks · Stubbs, Whistlejacket · Van Gogh, Sunflowers*

NATURAL HISTORY MUSEUM · London · 020 7942 5011 · nhm.ac.uk — *the Whale Hall · Dippy the diplodocus · Darwin's zoology specimens*

NATIONAL MARITIME MUSEUM · London · 020 8312 6565 · nmm.ac.uk — *Nelson's undress coat worn at Trafalgar · Harrison's timekeepers H1–4*

NATIONAL MUSEUM & GALLERY · Cardiff · 0122 2397951 · nmgw.ac.uk — *Unknown, Portrait of William Herbert · Reynolds, Charlotte Grenville*

NATIONAL PORTRAIT GALLERY · London · 020 7306 0055 · npg.org.uk — *Royal portraits · pre-Raphaelite portraits · modern portraits*

SCIENCE MUSEUM · London · 0870 870 4868 · sciencemuseum.org.uk — *Charles Babbage, Difference Engine No. 2 · Stephenson, Rocket*

SOANE MUSEUM · London · 020 7405 2107 · soane.org — *The Sarcophagus of Seti I · Hogarth, A Rake's Progress; An Election*

TATE BRITAIN · London · 020 7887 8000 · tate.org.uk — *Pre-Raphaelite collection · Francis Bacon · Tracy Emin*

TATE MODERN · London · 020 7887 8000 · tate.org — *thematically-arranged exhibitions from the collection · special and commissioned exhibitions*

ULSTER MUSEUM · Belfast · 028 9038 3000 · ulstermuseum.org.uk — *artefacts from the Armada shipwreck, Girona · Irish archaeology collection*

VICTORIA & ALBERT MUSEUM · London · 020 7747 2885 · vam.ac.uk — *Great Bed of Ware · Chihuly chandelier · Tippu's Tiger*

WALLACE COLLECTION · London · 020 7563 9500 · wallacecollection.org — *collection of paintings, armour, furniture, sculpture*

WORLD MUSEUM LIVERPOOL · 0151 478 4393 · liverpoolmuseums.org.uk — *The Codex Fejérváry-Mayer · Head of Iyoba, Queen Mother*

ARTS COUNCIL

The Arts Council is a QUANGO [see p.253] responsible for developing the arts in England. Up until 2008 they will be funding more than 1,100 arts projects. The following lists some of the many grants the Arts Council will make in 2005–06:

Organisation	*grant (£)*
Royal Opera House	24,866,154
English National Opera	16,556,220
English National Ballet	6,029,838
Sadler's Wells	1,950,000
Almeida Theatre	925,000
Asian Music Circuit	449,407
Film London	327,251
Hackney Empire	259,638
National Youth Theatre	200,000
Cambridge Arts Theatre	166,762
Dance UK	165,794
Luton Carnival Arts	154,519
Folk Arts England	140,000
Norwich Puppet Theatre	55,106
Buxton Festival	54,991
Poems on the Underground	50,000
The Poetry Trust	48,545
British Youth Opera	40,000
Art Monthly	29,595

LOTTERY SPEND BY ART-FORM

The breakdown of Arts Council lottery funding 1994–2004 (total of £1,755m):

Form	Music	Literature	Visual arts	Combined arts	Dance	Theatre/drama
%	26	1	24	15	9	25

CULTURAL PLEASURES

A national survey undertaken by the Arts Council demonstrates the percentage of English people taking part in various cultural and social activities during 2003:

Cinema	59%
Park or gardens	48
Library	44
Stately home	42
Museum; gallery	37
Live music	29
Musical	26
Play	25
Art, sculpture, &c	22
Carnival	19
Pantomime	14
Classical music	10

ART FAIRS OF NOTE

London Art Fair	Jan	020 7288 6427	londonartfair.co.uk
Affordable Art London	Mar/Oct	020 7371 8787	affordableartfair.co.uk
Glasgow Art Fair	Apr/May	0141 204 4400	glasgowartfair.com
Affordable Art Bristol	May	020 7371 8787	affordableartfair.co.uk
Art London	Jun	020 7259 0700	artlondon.net
Frieze Art Fair	Oct	020 7025 3970	friezeartfair.com

———WHERE TO SEE MAJOR WORKS OF ART———

On the Balcony	Blake	Tate Gallery, London
Garden of Earthly Delights	Bosch	Prado, Madrid
The Birth of Venus	Botticelli	Galleria degli Uffizi, Florence
Massacre of the Innocents	Bruegel (Elder)	Hampton Court, Middlesex
Venice: Regatta on Grand Canal	Canaletto	National Gallery, London
I and the Village	Chagall	Museum of Modern Art, NY
The Hay Wain	Constable	National Gallery, London
Persistence of Memory	Dali	Museum of Modern Art, NY
The Last Supper	da Vinci	Santa Maria delle Grazie, Milan
Mona Lisa	da Vinci	Louvre, Paris
The Dancing Lesson	Degas	Musée National d'Orsay, Paris
The Swing	Fragonard	Wallace Collection, London
Girl With a White Dog	Freud	Tate Britain, London
The Blue Boy	Gainsborough	Huntington Library, CA
Merry-Go-Round	Gertler	Tate Britain, London
Turin Shroud	God	Cathedral of St John the Baptist, Turin
Saturn Devouring His Children	Goya	Prado, Madrid
Single Form	Hepworth	United Nations HQ, NY
A Bigger Splash	Hockney	Tate, London
Nighthawks	Hopper	The Art Institute of Chicago
Composition VIII	Kandinsky	Guggenheim, NY
Magic Garden	Klee	Guggenheim, NY
The Kiss	Klimt	Belvedere, Vienna
Coming from the Mill	Lowry	Salford Museum and Art Gallery
Le Double Secret	Magritte	Centre Pompidou, Paris
Creation of Adam	Michelangelo	Sistine Chapel, Rome
David	Michelangelo	Accademia, Florence
Broadway Boogie Woogie	Mondrian	Museum of Modern Art, NY
Nympheas	Monet	Orangerie, Paris
UNESCO Reclining Figure	Moore	UNESCO HQ, Paris
Guernica	Picasso	Reina Sofía Museum, Madrid
Self-Portrait (1661)	Rembrandt	Kenwood House, London
Luncheon of the Boating Party	Renoir	Phillips Collection, Washington
The Thinker	Rodin	Musée Rodin, Paris
Bacchus	Rubens	Hermitage, St Petersburg
At the Moulin Rouge	Toulouse-Lautrec	Art Institute, Chicago
Ulysses defending Polyphemus	Turner	National Gallery, London
Elgin Marbles	unknown	British Museum, London
Rosetta Stone	unknown	British Museum, London
Tutankhamun's gold mask	unknown	Egyptian Museum, Cairo
The Arnolfini Marriage	Van Eyck	National Gallery, London
Starry Night	Van Gogh	Museum of Modern Art, NY
Girl with a Pearl Earring	Vermeer	Mauritshuis, The Hague
100 Soup Cans	Warhol	Albright-Knox Gallery, Buffalo
Marilyn Monroe print	Warhol	The Warhol Museum, Pittsburgh

Because of sales, restoration, loans, multiple copies, and other factors, the location of some works may vary.

————————— TOP TEN ARTISTS BY REVENUE · 2004 —————————

Artprice annually publishes a ranking of artists based on sales generated by their works at auction. In 2004, revenue from the top ten artists reached $662 million:

Artist	sales in 2004 ($)		
Pablo Picasso	241·0m	Henri Matisse	38·6m
Claude Monet	80·5m	Paul Gauguin	38·2m
Andy Warhol	77·5m	John Singer Sargent	37·6m
Auguste Renoir	44·6m	Edgar Degas	31·4m
Amedeo Modigliani	42·6m	Joan Miró	30·2m
		[www.artprice.com]	

————————— SOME AUCTION HOUSES OF NOTE —————————

Bonham's	101 New Bond Street, London, W1S	020 7447 7447
Christie's	8 King Street, London, SW1	020 7839 9060
Coys	Queen's Gate Mews, London, SW7	020 7584 7444
Phillips	101 New Bond Street, London, W1Y	020 7629 6602
Sotheby's	34-35 New Bond Street, London, W1A	020 7293 5000
Spink	69 Southampton Row, London, WC1	020 7563 4000

————————— AUCTIONS & ROCK, PAPER, SCISSORS —————————

In May 2005, the Maspro Denkoh Corporation of Japan (manufacturers of TV and satellite equipment) resolved to sell off part of its impressive art collection. The firm's president, Takashi Hashiyama, was unable to decide whether to let Sotheby's or Christie's conduct the sale, and asked them to settle the question by playing rock, paper, scissors. 'I sometimes use such methods when I cannot make a decision,' Hashiyama told the *New York Times,* 'As both companies were equally good and I just could not choose one, I asked them to please decide between themselves and suggested to use such methods as rock, paper, scissors'. Sadly, rather than have the two auctioneers face each other in battle, each firm recorded its choice on paper. It is claimed that while Sotheby's accepted Hashiyama's challenge as a simple 50/50 draw, Christie's decided to analyse the psychology of the game. Naturally, they asked Flora and Alice, the 11-year-old daughters of their Director of Impressionist and Modern Art. The girls' strategy was thus: STONE is the weapon that feels the strongest, therefore a novice will expect their opponent to go for STONE, and will themselves choose PAPER to beat it. Given this, the canny player will choose SCISSORS to beat PAPER. Splendidly, Flora and Alice proved to be correct: Sotheby's chose PAPER – which was defeated by the SCISSORS of Christie's, who undertook the sale of the following major paintings:

Paul Cézanne · *Les grands arbres au Jas de Bouffan*		$11·8m
Vincent van Gogh · *Vue de la chambre de l'artiste, rue Lepic*		$2·7m
Alfred Sisley · *La manufacture de Sèvres*		$1·6m
Pablo Picasso · *Boulevard de Clichy*		$1·7m

——————————— PRINCIPAL LONDON THEATRES ———————

ADELPHI · Strand, WC2 · [*Tube station* · Charing Cross] 08704 030 303
ALBERY · St Martin's Lane, WC2 · [Leicester Square] 08700 606 621
ALDWYCH · 49 Aldwych, WC2 · [Covent Garden] 08704 000 805
ALMEIDA · Almeida St, N1 · [Angel] 020 7359 4404
APOLLO · Shaftesbury Ave, W1 · [Piccadilly Circus] 020 7494 5070
APOLLO VICTORIA · Wilton Rd, SW1 · [Victoria] 0870 161 1977
ARTS THEATRE · Great Newport St, WC2 · [Leicester Square] 020 7836 3334
BARBICAN CENTRE · Silk St, EC2 · [Barbican] 020 7638 8891
CAMBRIDGE · Earlham St, WC2 · [Covent Garden] 020 7494 5080
COMEDY · Panton St, SW1 · [Leicester Square] 0870 060 6637
CRITERION · Piccadilly Circus, W1 · [Piccadilly Circus] 08705 344 444
DOMINION · Tottenham Crt Rd, W1 · [Tottenham Court Rd] 08705 344 444
DONMAR · Earlham St, WC2 · [Covent Garden] 08700 606 624
DRURY LANE, THTR. ROYAL · Catherine St, WC2 · [Covent Garden] . 08708 901 109
DUCHESS · Catherine St, WC2 · [Covent Garden] 020 7494 5075
DUKE OF YORK'S · St Martin's Lane, WC2 · [Leicester Square] 08700 606 623
FORTUNE · Russell St, WC2 · [Covent Garden] 08700 606 626
GARRICK · Charing Cross Rd, WC2 · [Tottenham Court Rd] 020 7494 5085
GIELGUD · Shaftesbury Ave, W1 · [Piccadilly Circus] 020 7494 5065
GLOBE · Bankside, SE1 · [London Bridge] 020 7401 9919
HAYMARKET · Haymarket, SW1 · [Piccadilly Circus] 020 7930 8800
HER MAJESTY'S · Haymarket, SW1 · [Piccadilly Circus] 020 7494 5400
LONDON APOLLO HAM'SMITH · Queen Caroline St, W6 [H'smith]. 08706 063 400
LONDON PALLADIUM · Argyll St, W1 · [Oxford Circus] 08708 901 108
LYCEUM · Wellington St, WC2 · [Covent Garden] 08702 439 000
LYRIC · Shaftesbury Ave, W1 · [Piccadilly Circus] 020 7494 5045
NATIONAL THEATRE · South Bank, SE1 · [Waterloo] 020 7452 3000
NEW AMBASSADORS · West St, WC2 · [Leicester Square] 08700 606 627
NEW LONDON · Drury Lane, WC2 · [Covent Garden] 08708 900 141
OLD VIC · Waterloo Rd, SE1 · [Waterloo] 08700 606 628
PALACE · Shaftesbury Ave, W1 · [Leicester Square] 08708 955 579
PEACOCK · Portugal St, WC2 · [Holborn] 08707 370 337
PHOENIX · Charing Cross Rd, WC2 · [Tottenham Court Rd] 08700 606 629
PICCADILLY · Denman St, W1 · [Piccadilly Circus] 08700 606 630
PLAYHOUSE · Northumberland Ave, WC2 · [Charing Cross] 08700 606 631
PRINCE EDWARD · Old Compton St, W1 · [Leicester Square] 020 7447 5400
PRINCE OF WALES · Coventry St, W1 · [Piccadilly Circus] 08708 500 393
QUEEN'S · Shaftesbury Ave, W1 · [Piccadilly Circus] 020 7494 5040
ROYAL COURT · Sloane Sq, SW1 · [Sloane Square] 020 7565 5000
SAVOY · Strand, WC2 · [Charing Cross] 020 7836 8888
SHAFTESBURY · Shaftesbury Ave, WC2 · [Covent Garden] 020 7379 5399
ST MARTIN'S · West St, WC2 · [Leicester Square] 020 7836 1443
STRAND · Aldwych, WC2 · [Charing Cross] 08708 509 170
VICTORIA PALACE · Victoria St, SW1 · [Victoria] 08708 955 577
WYNDHAM'S · Charing Cross Rd, WC2 · [Tottenham Court Rd] 08700 606 633
YOUNG VIC · The Cut, SE1 · [Waterloo] 020 7928 6363

LAURENCE OLIVIER AWARDS · 2005

Best actress	Clare Higgins · *Hecuba*
Best actor	Richard Griffiths · *The History Boys*
Best performance in a supporting role	Amanda Harris · *Othello*
Best new play	*The History Boys* · Alan Bennett
Best new musical	*The Producers* · Mel Brooks & Thomas Meehan
Best actress in a musical	Laura Michelle Kelly · *Mary Poppins*
Best actor in a musical	Nathan Lane · *The Producers*
Best director	Nicholas Hytner · *The History Boys*
Best new opera	*Lady Macbeth of Mtsensk* · Royal Opera House
Best new dance	*SWAMP* · Rambert Dance Company
Special award	Alan Bennett

STAGE DIRECTIONS & LAYOUT

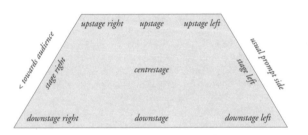

CRITICS' CIRCLE AWARDS · 2004

Best new play	*The History Boys* · Alan Bennett
Best musical	*The Producers* · Mel Brooks & Thomas Meehan
Best actor	Richard Griffiths · *The History Boys*
Best actress	Victoria Hamilton · *Suddenly Last Summer*
Best Shakespearean performance	Paul Rhys · *Measure for Measure*
Best director	Rufus Norris · *Festen*

EQUITY MEMBERSHIP

Subscription to Equity, the British actors' union, is calculated at 1% of gross earnings (in the previous tax year) from professional work, including royalties, repeats, and residuals. For example, if an actor earned £20,000 in the previous year then their subscription would be £200. The minimum annual subscription is £80, the maximum £1,750. To enrol, actors must be working professionally in the field of entertainment, and must pay a joining fee of £25. In return, Equity strives to negotiate reasonable minimum terms and conditions for those employed in the entertainment business, and will provide free legal advice in professional disputes.

PRINCIPAL REGIONAL THEATRES

BATH THEATRE ROYAL · Sawclose, BA1 .... 01225 448 844
BELFAST LYRIC THEATRE · Ridgeway St, BT9....................... 02890 381 081
BIRMINGHAM REP · Broad St, B1....................................... 01212 364 455
BOLTON OCTAGON THEATRE · Howell Croft South, BL1 .... 01204 520 661
BRIGHTON THEATRE ROYAL · New Rd, BN1....................... 08700 606 650
BRISTOL OLD VIC · King St, BS1...................................... 01179 877 877
CANTERBURY MARLOWE THEATRE · The Friars, CT1 .... 01227 787 787
CARDIFF NEW THEATRE · Park Place, CF10 .... 02920 878 889
CLWYD THEATRE CYMRU · Civic Centre, Mold, CH7 .... 08453 303 565
COLCHESTER MERCURY THEATRE · Balkerne Gate, CO1 .... 01206 573 948
COVENTRY BELGRADE THEATRE · Belgrade Sq, CV1 .... 02476 553 055
EDINBURGH ROYAL LYCEUM THEATRE · Grindlay St, EH3 .... 01312 484 848
EDINBURGH TRAVERSE THEATRE · Cambridge St, EH1 .... 01312 281 404
GLASGOW KING'S THEATRE · Bath St, G2 .... 01412 401 111
LIVERPOOL PLAYHOUSE · Williamson Sq, L1 .... 01517 094 776
MANCHESTER ROYAL EXCHANGE · St Ann's Sq, M2............... 01618 339 833
MILTON KEYNES THEATRE · Marlborough Gate, MK9............. 01908 606 090
NORWICH THEATRE ROYAL · Theatre St, NR2 .... 01603 630 000
OXFORD PLAYHOUSE · Beaumont St, OX1........................... 01865 305 305
PLYMOUTH THEATRE ROYAL · Royal Parade, PL1 .... 01752 267 222
ROYAL SHAKESPEARE · Waterside, Stratford-upon-Avon, CV37..... 08706 091 110
SOUTHAMPTON NUFFIELD THEATRE · University Rd, SO17 ...... 02380 671 771
YORK THEATRE ROYAL · St Leonard's Place, YO1................... 01904 623 568

SOME CAUSES OF THEATRICAL BAD LUCK

❦ Actors and stage-hands alike believe WHISTLING or CLAPPING backstage to be bad luck. This may derive from the time when sailors operated the scenery, since they were handy with knots. The sailors communicated with one another by a system of whistles and claps that, if inadvertently used by an actor, might result in scenery falling on his bonce. ❦ Wishing an actor GOOD LUCK is unlucky, since folklore tells that to fool evil spirits, actors should request the very opposite of what they want – hence the phrase BREAK A LEG. ❦ Never say MACBETH in a theatre; instead use THE SCOTTISH PLAY, since the play is associated with many tragedies and mishaps. If you do happen to utter *Macbeth* in a theatre, there are several ways to counteract the curse: turn around three times; spit over your left shoulder; say the rudest word you can imagine (yes, that one); or speak a line from *A Midsummer Night's Dream*. ❦ WEARING GREEN is considered unwise in any theatre since green is the fairies' favourite colour, and to wear it will provoke their jealousy and ire. ❦ Using a MIRROR on stage is considered taboo – possibly due to the technical difficulty of lighting mirrors, but also because of the age-old belief that mirrors can open one's soul to the devil. ❦ Some theatre-hands believe in leaving a GHOST LIGHT lit when the stage is not in use. It is said that such lights keep alive the spirit of theatres. ❦

PERRIER COMEDY AWARD · 2005

Founded in 1981, the *Perrier* Comedy Award is given for the best revue at the Edinburgh Festival Fringe. Winners receive £7,500, and a West End performance. In 2005 Laura Solon won the *Perrier* Award; Tim Minchin won best newcomer.

WINNER & NOMINEES 2005	PREVIOUS WINNERS	
LAURA SOLON ... *Kopfrapers Syndrome*	2000	Rich Hall
Chris Addison ... *Atomicity*	2001	Garth Merenghi
Dutch Elm Conservatoire .. *Conspiracy*	2002	Daniel Kitson
Jason Manford ... *Urban Legend*	2003	Demetri Martin
Jeremy Lion .. *What's the time, Mr Lion*	2004	Will Adamsdale

CATCHPHRASES OF NOTE

In January 2005, the digital channel UKTV Gold conducted a survey to discover the nation's favourite catchphrases. The results reveal the extent and speed with which *Little Britain* characters have entered the nation's consciousness; three of their many catchphrases appear in the top twenty. The top ten catchphrases were:

I'm the only gay in the village	Dafydd · *Little Britain*
Just like that	Tommy Cooper
Doh!	Homer Simpson · *The Simpsons*
Lovely jubbly	Del Boy · *Only Fools and Horses*
Yeah, but no, but yeah	Vicky Pollard · *Little Britain*
Suits you, Sir!	*The Fast Show*
Drink, feck, arse	Father Jack · *Father Ted*
I don't belieeeeeve it	Victor Meldrew · *One Foot in the Grave*
Garlic bread, I've tasted it, it's the future	Peter Kay · *Phoenix Nights*
I have a cunning plan	Baldrick · *Blackadder*

BRITISH COMEDY AWARDS · 2004

Best TV comedy actor	Matt Lucas & David Walliams
Best TV comedy actress	Caroline Quentin
Best comedy entertainment personality	Ant & Dec
Best comedy newcomer	Catherine Tate
Best new TV comedy	*Nighty Night*
Best TV comedy	*Little Britain*

FUNNIEST WOMEN

In August 2005, *Reader's Digest* asked over 4,000 of its readers to nominate their favourite comediennes. Victoria Wood was the winner, with Dawn French second, and Jo Brand third. Jennifer Saunders and Julie Walters made up the top five.

――――――― SOME DANCE COMPANIES OF NOTE ―――――――

THE ROYAL BALLET
Royal Opera House
Covent Garden WC2
020 7304 4000
Director: Monica Mason OBE
Some principals of note:
Darcey Bussell · Alina Cojocaru
Carlos Acosta · Federico Bonelli

BIRMINGHAM ROYAL BALLET
Thorp Street
Birmingham B5 4AU
0121 245 3500
Director: David Bintley CBE
Some principals of note: Chi Cao ·
Ambra Vallo · Dominic Antonucci

RAMBERT DANCE COMPANY
94 Chiswick High Road
London W4 1SH
020 8630 0600
Artistic director: Mark Baldwin
Some principals of note:
Lucila Alves · Simon Cooper
Thomasin Gülgec · Angela Towler
Clara Barberá

ENGLISH NATIONAL BALLET
Markova House, 39 Jay Mews
London SW7 2ES
020 7581 1245
Artistic director: Matz Skoog
Some principals of note: Agnes Oaks
Dmitri Gruzdyev · Sarah McIlroy
Thomas Edur

――― GENÉE INTERNATIONAL BALLET COMPETITION ―――

The Genée International Ballet Competition is the Royal Academy of Dance's most prestigious contest for young dancers aged 14–19 years. In 2005, the gold medal and £5,000 were awarded to 17-year-old Canadian dancer Céline Gittens.

――――――― NATIONAL DANCE AWARDS · 2004 ―――――――

The Critics' Circle National Dance Awards are judged and presented by the critics and journalists responsible for reviewing dance productions, and aim to celebrate the diversity of dance in Great Britain. Some of the winners in 2004 included:

Outstanding achievement............Sir Peter Wright · *Birmingham Royal Ballet*
Best male dancer................................Jonathan Cope · *The Royal Ballet*
Best female dancer............................Leanne Benjamin · *The Royal Ballet*
Audience award...Northern Ballet Theatre
Dance UK industry award ....Dick Matchett
Best choreography: classical.........................Christopher Wheeldon · *Rush*
— modern...........................Javier de Frutos · *Elsa Canasta and Milagros*
— musical theatre ....Matthew Bourne · *Play Without Words*
Outstanding female artist (modern)...............Amy Hollingsworth · *Rambert*
Outstanding male artist (modern)..........................Paul Liburd · *Rambert*
Outstanding female artist (classical) ....Lauren Cuthbertson · *Royal Ballet*
Outstanding male artist (classical) ....Thiago Soares · *Royal Ballet*
Company prize for outstanding repertoire (modern)......................Rambert
Company prize for outstanding repertoire (classical).............The Royal Ballet

THE CRITICAL YEAR · 2005

{JAN} The Old Vic's brave decision to stage the panto *Aladdin* with Sir Ian McKellen as Widow Twankey was greeted with mixed reviews: Sarah Hemming in the *FT* gushed 'McKellen has waited for 40 years to play this part and his utter glee is infectious … His performance has a warmth that is irresistible'. Kate Bassett in the *Independent on Sunday* disagreed, calling *Aladdin* 'an absolute turkey'. ❧ The Royal Opera House resurrected the original 1895 choreography of *Swan Lake* which, according to Ismene Brown of *The Telegraph,* 'gives the ballet the tragic scope that Tchaikovsky intended'. ❧ *Faces in the Crowd* at the Whitechapel Gallery aimed to represent modern life from Manet to the present. The exhibition featured such works as Manet, *Masked Ball at the Opera*; Carlo Carra, *Leaving the Theatre*; and very modern work like Gillian Wearing's video *Dancing in Peckham.* ❧ {FEB} *Don Carlos* at the Gielgud Theatre starred Derek Jacobi and was universally praised: Michael Billington in *The Guardian* noted 'the spellbound audience and the loud huzzas bore testament not only to the grip of this great romantic tragedy: they paid tribute to the brilliance of Michael Grandage's Sheffield Crucible production'. ❧ Mozart's *La Clemenza di Tito* performed by the ENO was, according to Anna Picard in *The Independent on Sunday*, 'beautifully sung, compellingly acted, cleverly framed, expertly paced and conducted with style'. ❧ Victoria Wood's eagerly awaited musical version of *Acorn Antiques* was criticised for being absurdly long: 'tedious beyond

Bryn Terfel

endurance' said Georgina Brown in *The Mail on Sunday.* However Paul Taylor in *The Independent* stated 'Trevor Nunn pushes the ingredients of this pedigree dog's dinner around the plate with sass and flair. The show gets away with it, gloriously'. ❧ Tate Britain hosted *Turner, Whistler, Monet* – an exhibition giving three impressions of the Thames. The show was a critical hit: 'it is rare for me to say that every single picture in the show is ravishing, but that is the simple truth', waxed Richard Dorment in *The Telegraph.* ❧ {MAR} The National Gallery's show *Caravaggio: The Final Years* was widely praised: 'utterly compelling', said Andrew Graham-Dixon in *The Sunday Telegraph.* ❧ It was generally agreed that Wagner's *Die Walküre* (the second of the Ring cycle) at the Royal Opera House suffered from cluttered staging, but had impressive performances from some – like Bryn Terfel, who, according to Andrew Clements in *The Guardian*, 'was in glorious form, and his rapt account of the Farewell, every word glowing and intense, was enough almost to erase memories of the ludicrous, infantile way in which his first scene with his daughter is directed'. ❧ The Manchester Palace Theatre hosted the bizarre ballet *Diana, The Princess.* Lyndsey Winship in *The Independent* concluded: 'you can't help wondering if we have here the makings of a future camp-classic, *Rocky Horror* style. Until then it's one for die-hard Di fans only'. ❧ {APR} The RSC's production of *Hecuba* at the Albery was called a 'monumental fiasco' by Charles Spencer in *The Telegraph.* He heaped

THE CRITICAL YEAR · 2005 cont.

criticism on Vanessa Redgrave: 'wild haired and tottering arthritically around the stage, [she] exudes all the passion of an eccentric old dear who has mislaid her pension book'. ❦ The musical *The Far Pavilions* opened at the Shaftesbury. Lyn Gardner declared in *The Guardian* 'No, it's not high art, but it is not kitsch rubbish either, and to tell the truth I've had far more painful and unpleasant nights out watching Pinter plays'. ❦ At the new Wales Millennium Centre, the Kirov Ballet's *Don Quixote* was 'hugely enjoyable' according to Jann Parry in *The Observer*. {MAY} Stephen Daldry's *Billy Elliot* jumped from screen to stage at the Victoria Palace Theatre – a move greeted with high

Ewan McGregor

praise. Susannah Clapp wrote in *The Observer* 'Stephen Daldry's fierce and gorgeous improvement on his own movie, is that it never says anything if it can dance it.' ❦ At the National, Jim Broadbent starred in *Theatre of Blood* – a camp horror where an actor takes revenge on his critics. Paul Taylor of the *Indy* called it 'an intelligent, larky evening, that is, in more senses than one, a bloody good show'. {JUN} Ewan McGregor starred in *Guys and Dolls* at the Piccadilly Theatre; the verdict on McGregor, according to Benedict Nightingale of *The Times*: 'what surprised me was his ability to not just talk his songs, but to sing them, and sing them smoothly and tunefully'.❦ Tate Liverpool hosted the Art exhibition *Summer of Love: Art of the Psychedelic Era*, featuring works by Andy Warhol, Allen Ginsberg and Gustav Metzger. Richard Dorment of *The Telegraph* summed it up: '*Summer of Love* at Tate Liverpool is that rare

thing, a good show about bad art'. ❦ Holland Park Opera staged *Macbeth* by Verdi, with Miriam Murphy playing Lady Macbeth to much praise. Tim Ashley of *The Guardian* described the bloodsoaked sets, and concluded that the performance 'is at once supremely intelligent and nerve shredding. See it, if you think your stomach can take it'. {JUL} *Stubbs and the Horse* opened at the National Gallery with 70 of George Stubbs' major works. Andrew Graham-Dixon of *The Telegraph* echoed the praise of many: 'this enthralling show should, once and for all, put paid to the foolish misconception that Stubbs was no more than an animalier in the service of the Georgian aristocracy'. ❦ Chichester Festival Theatre hosted a production of Gogol's comedy *The Government Inspector*, starring Alistair McGowan. His performance did not impress Michael Billington of *The Guardian* 'while McGowan is a dazzling TV impressionist, he fails to build a convincing character'. {AUG} Adam Cooper's new ballet adaptation of *Les Liaisons Dangereuses* at Sadler's Wells was reported to be a somewhat confusing affair. Jann Parry in *The Observer* bemoaned 'Cooper can't quite bring it off. The cast is limited to nine, but the intrigues are bewildering unless you know the story already'. ❦ *The Odd Couple* at the Edinburgh Festival starred Alan Davies, who according to Kate Bassett in the *Indy* 'permanently looks as if he's about to corpse'. Alongside Davies was Bill Bailey, whom Bassett called 'a delight'. However, she summed up the production as a whole as 'watchable'.

READY-TO-WEAR FASHION WEEKS

NEW YORK
February & September
Contact: 7th on Sixth/IMG
+212 253 2692
www.olympusfashionweek.com
Who shows: *Ralph Lauren, Vera Wang,*
Marc Jacobs, Calvin Klein, Zac Posen,
Oscar de la Renta, Tommy Hilfiger,
Donna Karan

MILAN
February & September/October
Contact: Camera Nazionale della
Moda Italiana, +39 02 777 10 81
www.cameramoda.it
Who shows: *Gucci, Armani, Prada,*
Dolce & Gabbana, Moschino, Versace,
Roberto Cavalli, Miu Miu,
Missoni, Burberry

LONDON
February & September
Contact: British Fashion Council
020 7636 7788
www.londonfashionweek.co.uk
Who shows: *Ben de Lisi,*
Paul Smith women, Nicole Farhi,
Clements Ribeiro, Betty Jackson,
Margaret Howell, Aquascutum, Ghost

PARIS
February/March & October. Contact:
Fédération Française de la Couture,
du Prêt-à-Porter des Couturiers &c.
+33 1 42 66 64 44
www.modeaparis.com
Who shows: *Louis Vuitton, Chanel,*
Vivienne Westwood, Jean Paul Gaultier,
John Galliano, Christian Dior, Chloé

FUR & FASHION

As the wearing of fur became more controversial in the late 1980s and early 1990s, a number of supermodels declared an anti-fur stance including: Naomi Campbell, Christy Turlington, Claudia Schiffer, Amber Valletta, Cindy Crawford, and Elle Macpherson. Since then, fur has returned to the catwalks, and Naomi Campbell, Elle Macpherson, and Cindy Crawford have subsequently performed about-turns to model the material. The American fur company Blackglama has employed both Macpherson and Crawford to advertise their exclusive mink coats, and celebrities such as Jennifer Lopez are frequently pictured sporting fur. Despite the resurgence of fur on many catwalks, protesters continue to denounce its use – for example storming Julien Macdonald's London Fashion Week show in September 2005.

THE FACE OF...

Celeb	face of...
Christina Aguilera	*Skechers*
David Beckham	*Gillette*
Halle Berry	*Revlon*
Penelope Cruz	*Ralph Lauren*
Sarah Michelle Gellar	*Maybelline*
Enrique Iglesias	*Tommy Hilfiger*
Scarlett Johansson	*Calvin Klein*
Nicole Kidman	*Chanel No.5*
Beyonce Knowles	*L'Oréal*
Demi Moore	*Versace*
Tamzin Outhwaite	*Avon*
Gwyneth Paltrow	*Estée Lauder*
Michael Schumacher	*L'Oréal*
Joss Stone	*Gap*
Charlize Theron	*Dior*
Uma Thurman	*Louis Vuitton*
Jonny Wilkinson	*Hackett*

FASHION HOUSES & THEIR DESIGNERS

Aquascutum	Michael Hertz	*Gucci*	Frida Giannini
Burberry	Christopher Bailey	*Lanvin*	Alber Elbaz
Chanel	Karl Lagerfeld	*Louis Vuitton*	Marc Jacobs
Chloé	Phoebe Philo	*Marni*	Consuelo Castiglioni
Christian Dior	John Galliano	*Missoni*	Angela Missoni
Ghost	Tanya Sarne	*Prada*	Miuccia Prada
Givenchy	Riccardo Tisci	*Yves Saint Laurent*	Stefano Pilati

BRITISH FASHION AWARDS · 2004

Designer of the year ...... Phoebe Philo for Chloé
Best menswear designer ...... Alexander McQueen
Best accessories designer ...... Mulberry
Best new designer ...... Giles Deacon
Best model ...... Lily Cole
Outstanding achievement in fashion ...... David Bailey

ELLE STYLE AWARDS · 2005

Most stylish	*winner*	*Woman of the year*	Cate Blanchett
Actress	Cate Blanchett	*Individual style*	Cat Deeley
Actor	Daniel Craig	*Style icon*	Helena Christensen
TV stars	Matt Lucas & David Walliams	*Lifetime achievement*	Kylie Minogue
		Brit designer	Matthew Williamson
Male musician	Will Young	*Young designer*	Giles Deacon
Female musician	Jamelia	*International designer*	Phoebe Philo

FASHION ICONS

The May 2005 issue of *Harpers and Queen* listed their top 100 Most Stylish Women. *Gwen Stefani* was named the best dressed of 2005, followed by burlesque performer and fiancée of Marilyn Manson, *Dita Von Teese*. Enduring fashion-waif *Kate Moss* came third, beating 'boho' pretender *Sienna Miller* into fourth place. Russian model *Natalia Vodianova* was fifth, with *Cate Blanchett*, *Jacquetta Wheeler*, *Jasmine Guinness*, *Daphne Guinness*, and *Zadie Smith* finishing off the top ten.

SCENTS OF THE FAMOUS

Jennifer Lopez	*Glow*	Beyonce Knowles	*True Star*
Britney Spears	*Curious*	Jessica Simpson	*Taste*
Elizabeth Taylor	*White Diamonds*	Paris Hilton	*Paris Hilton*
Donald Trump	*The Fragrance*	Celine Dion	*Celine*

THE STIRLING PRIZE · 2004

The 9th annual Royal Institute of British Architects [RIBA] Stirling Prize was awarded in 2004 to Foster and Partners for their design of 30 St Mary Axe, affectionately known as the 'Gherkin'. Judges praised the building's iconic nature and, for the first time, came to a unanimous decision. The Gherkin's specs are:

Client	Swiss Re Insurance	Exterior	$c.$5,500 glass panels
Structural engineer	Arup	Widest point	17th floor (56·5m)
Completion	2004	Diameter at base	49·3m
Area	76,400m²	Diameter at top	26·5m
Height	179·8m	Steel frame	$c.$10,000 tonnes
Storeys	41	Passenger lifts	16

The other buildings and architects shortlisted for the £20,000 prize were:

Kunsthaus, Graz .... Peter Cook, Colin Fournier
The Spire, Dublin .... Ian Ritchie Architects
Imperial War Museum North, Manchester .... Studio Daniel Libeskind
Phoenix Initiative, Coventry .... MacCormac Jamieson Prichard
Business Academy, Bexley .... Foster and Partners

LONDON'S BEST & WORST BUILDINGS

In 2005, *Time Out* magazine polled their readers to discover Londoners' attitudes to the capital's landmarks. The following were rated the best and worst buildings:

BEST			WORST
Tate Modern	1		Elephant & Castle Centre
Houses of Parliament	2		Tower Thistle Hotel
Battersea Power Station	3		Centre Point
30 St Mary-Axe (Gherkin)	4		Buckingham Palace
St Pancras Hotel	5		No. 1 Poultry

PRITZKER ARCHITECTURE PRIZE

The international *Pritzker Architecture Prize,* founded by the Hyatt Foundation in 1979, aims to honour living architects who have created buildings that have significantly contributed to the beauty and functionality of the built environment. In 2005 the prize was awarded to the American Thom Mayne, whose recent work includes: Caltrans District 7 HQ, Los Angeles; and the Sun Tower, in Seoul, South Korea. The winner receives a $100,000 cash prize, and a tasteful bronze medallion.

Previous Pritzker winners		1998	Renzo Piano [ITA]
1990	Aldo Rossi [ITA]	1999	Sir Norman Foster [UK]
1991	Robert Venturi [USA]	2004	Zaha Hadid [UK]

Sci, Tech, Net

Technology, sufficiently advanced, is indistinguishable from magic.
— ARTHUR C. CLARKE

———— 2006 SCI, TECH, NET ANNIVERSARIES ————

10 *years since* . . . . British scientists cloned a sheep called Dolly (1996)
20 . . . . the Soviet space station Mir was launched (1986)
30 . . . . Concorde entered commercial service (1976)
30 . . unmanned Viking II landed on Mars and took first pictures of surface (1976)
45 . . . . Yuri Gagarin became the first man in space (1961)
45 . . . . the chimpanzee Ham survived space flight up to 155 miles (1961)
50 . . . . the oral polio vaccine was developed by Dr Albert Sabin (1956)
50 . . the atomic clock Atomicron was unveiled at Overseas Press Club, NY (1956)
60 . . . . . . the discovery of 'PAS', the first effective treatment for tuberculosis (1946)
60 . . . . TV licences were first issued in UK, costing £2 (1946)
75 . . . . a rocket was first used to transport post in Austria (1931)
80 . . . . the first TV pictures were demonstrated by John Logie Baird (1926)
90 . . . . the tank entered modern warfare at the Somme (1916)
90 . . . . Einstein's General Theory of Relativity was published (1916)
100 . . . . Frederick Hopkins suggested a lack of vitamins caused scurvy (1906)
100 . . . . 'SOS' was recognised internationally as a distress signal (1906)
105 . . . . Meccano was patented by Frank Hornby (1901)
105 . . . . the first Nobel prizes were awarded (1901)
105 . . . . the loop-the-loop rollercoaster was patented by Edwin Prescott (1901)
110 . . . . Whitcomb Judson patented the zip (1896)
110 . . . . Wilhelm Röntgen announced his discovery of X-Rays (1896)
110 . . . . Guglielmo Marconi was issued a patent for the first radio (1896)
125 . . . . Sir Alexander Fleming, discoverer of penicillin, was born (1881)
125 . . . . Louis Pasteur discovered a vaccine against anthrax (1881)
130 . . . . Alexander Graham Bell sent the first telephone message (1876)
130 . . . . a direct England–New Zealand telegraph link was set up (1876)
155 . . . . the Great Exhibition opened in Hyde Park (1851)
160 . . . . Neptune was discovered by Johann Gottfried Galle (1846)
175 . . the induction of electric currents was discovered by Michael Faraday (1831)
190 . . . . Humphrey Davy's safety lamp was first used down a mine (1816)
195 . . . . the Luddite riots began in Nottingham (1811)
200 . . . . Ralph Wedgewood patented carbon paper (1806)
205 . . . . Guiseppe Piazzi sighted and named the first asteroid, Ceres (1801)
210 . . . . Edward Jenner gave the first vaccination against smallpox (1796)
225 . . . . Sir William Herschel discovered Uranus (1781)
390 . . . . Galileo was forced to renounce his beliefs on the Earth's motion (1616)
555 . . . . Nicholas of Cusa invented concave lenses for myopia (1451)

——————— NOBEL PRIZES IN SCIENCE · 2004 ———————

THE NOBEL PRIZE IN PHYSICS

David J. Gross
Kavli Institute for Theoretical Physics,
University of California
H. David Politzer
California Institute of Technology
Frank Wilczek
Massachusetts Inst. of Technology

'for the discovery of asymptotic
freedom in the theory of the
strong interaction'

The research by Gross, Politzer and
Wilczek, first published in 1973,
describes the force which holds
together quarks – the elementary
particles which build electrons and
protons. Their theory states that the
closer quarks are to one another, the
weaker the connection or *colour charge*
between them; and the further apart
they move, the stronger the charge
becomes. This research lead to development of the influential theory of
Quantum ChromoDynamics [QCD].

THE NOBEL PRIZE IN CHEMISTRY

Aaron Ciechanover
Technion – Israel Inst. of Tech.
Avram Hershko
Technion – Israel Inst. of Tech.
Irwin Rose
University of California

'for the discovery of Ubiquitin-
mediated protein degradation'

Ciechanover, Hershko & Rose studied
the breaking-down of proteins in cells,
discovering the molecule *Ubiquitin*,
which labels the proteins that are to be
destroyed. This has led to a greater
grasp of how cells control key
processes by breaking down certain
proteins and not others; when protein
degradation goes wrong it can lead to
disease. It is hoped that this research
may help in the search for treatments.

THE NOBEL PRIZE IN
PHYSIOLOGY OR MEDICINE

Richard Axel
Columbia University, USA
Linda B. Buck
Hutchinson Cancer Research Center

'for their discoveries of odorant
receptors and the organization of
the olfactory system'

Axel and Buck received the Nobel
prize in honour of their work on the
sense of smell. Their research uncov-
ered a family of over 1,000 genes that
control the production of specialised
protein receptors that allow us to identify odours. They also mapped the
biological pathways that link the nose
to the brain. The mapping of a
complete human sense in this way is
unique in the history of science.

It is an oft-repeated myth that no Nobel Prize in maths exists because Alfred Nobel's wife had an
affair with a mathematician. However, Nobel was unmarried and there seems to be no evidence of
any similar scandal. Nobel may have been discouraged by the existence of a maths prize created by
Oscar II, King of Sweden and Norway, or simply by the fact that he wasn't over-fond of the subject.

——————— AVENTIS PRIZE FOR SCIENCE BOOKS · 2005 ———————

Phillip Ball · *Critical Mass: How One Thing Leads to Another.*

─────── ABEL PRIZE ───────

A maths prize created in memory of Norwegian Niels Henrik Abel (1802 –29). In 2005 the prize was awarded to Peter D. Lax of New York University for his '*groundbreaking contributions to the theory and application of partial differential equations and to the computation of their solutions*'.

─────── FIELDS MEDAL ───────

Awarded at the *International Congress of Mathematicians* every four years to recognise past achievements in maths and future promise. In 2002 the medal was awarded to Laurent Lafforgue, *Institut des Hautes Études Scientifiques, France* and Vladimir Voevodsky, *Institute for Advanced Study, Princeton*.

─────── THE LEMELSON-MIT AWARDS ───────

Dubbed the 'Oscars for inventors', the prestigious Lemelson-MIT Award honours inventors for their creative endeavour and ingenuity – and awards a $500,000 cash prize. The award is open only to US citizens who have at least two patents, one of which must be of some benefit to society as a whole. In 2005, the prize was awarded to Elwood Norris, holder of numerous patents of which the most notable is his HyperSonic Sound (HSS) creation that cleverly allows sounds to be targeted to individual listeners. Applications of HSS technology include targeted sound in cars, shops, airports, museums, and the like. In 2005, the $100,000 Lemelson-MIT Lifetime Achievement award went to Robet Dennard who, while working for IBM, developed DRAM – the one-transistor dynamic random access memory.

─────── IG NOBEL PRIZE ───────

Ig Nobel prizes are awarded for scientific 'achievements that cannot or should not be reproduced.' In 2004 the prestigious honours were presented to the following:

MEDICINE · Steven Stack (Wayne State University) and James Gundlach (Auburn University) *for their published report into 'The Effect of Country Music on Suicide'.*

PHYSICS · R. Balasubramaniam (University of Ottawa) and Michael Turvey (University of Connecticut & Haskins Laboratory) *for their research into the dynamics of hula-hooping.*

PUBLIC HEALTH · Jillian Clarke (Howard University) *for her research into the scientific validity of the Five-Second Rule – whether it is safe to eat food that has been dropped on the floor.*

CHEMISTRY · The Coca-Cola Company of Great Britain, *for converting water from the River Thames into Dasani bottled water, which for some reason is not available in shops.*

BIOLOGY · Ben Wilson (University of British Columbia), Lawrence Dill (Simon Fraser University), Robert Batty (Scottish Association for Marine Science), Hakan Westerberg (Sweden's National Board of Fisheries), Magnus Whalberg (University of Aarhus) *for research showing that herrings might communicate through farts.*

[Source: www.improb.com/ig/ig-top.html]

———SOME NOTABLE SCIENTIFIC RESEARCH · 2005———

{JAN} Research by Till Roenneberg in *Current Biology* suggested that the end of adolescence is marked by a peak of late nights at the age of 20. ❦ Mouse studies by G. Padmanaban suggested that curcumin, the chemical that makes turmeric yellow, might help treat malaria. ❦ Researchers at Cincinnati Children's Hospital suggested that passive smoking can impede ability at school. ❦ Paul Bach-y-Rita at the Uni. of Wisconsin Medical School has developed a device that allows blind people to 'see' through their tongue. A camera attached to the head and tongue allows signals to be sent to the brain via the sense of taste. ❦ {FEB} A study by David Barker at Southampton Uni. charting the correlation between birthweight and adult health suggested that heavier babies may have a greater risk of developing cancer in later life. ❦ Macaque monkeys will make sacrifices to gain socially important information. A study by neurobiologists in North Carolina published in *Current Biology* found that the monkeys would 'pay' with fruit juice to look at pictures of the bottoms of socially dominant male or female monkeys. ❦ Research by Adriano Chio at Turin University suggested a higher incidence of the motor neuron disease ALS among professional footballers. ❦ {MAR} Claims emerged of the first patient 'cured' of diabetes by a revolutionary treatment where islets cells are transplanted into the liver. ❦ Michael Miller, at the Uni. of Maryland Medical Center, claimed that laughing relaxes the arteries and boosts bloodflow, making it almost as beneficial for the heart as a workout. ❦ Canadian neurologist Dr Helen Mayberg conducted research in which 6 severely depressed volunteers had electrodes implanted into their brain to stimulate the area associated with sadness; all reported significant improvements in mood. ❦ A paralysed man had an electrode implanted into his brain allowing him to control objects through thought alone. The project, led by Prof. John Donoghue at Brown University, is still in its infancy, but it is hoped that the technology may one day allow disabled people to control their limbs. ❦ {APR} *The Lancet Oncology* reported that trials of a vaccine for cervical cancer provides protection against the virus that may cause 70% of cases. ❦ Researchers at Russia's Novosibirsk Institute of Medicine claimed that addictions and depression can be treated by beating the buttocks. They advised a course of 30 sessions of 60 strokes of the cane to release endorphins and improve mood. ❦ A 7-year trial in the UK and US suggested that insulin inhalers could replace injections, making self-treatment for diabetics less invasive and easier to control. ❦ Research into IQ deterioration, led by Dr Glenn Wilson at the University of London, claimed that e-mailing and texting lower the IQ more than twice as much as smoking cannabis. ❦ Mark Roth's team at the Fred Hutchinson Cancer Research Center, Seattle, managed to drug mice so that they enter a period of suspended animation with no ill effects. It is hoped this may have applications for human anaesthetics. ❦ Research by the American Academy of Microbiology suggests that some serious illnesses like diabetes and schizo-

——SOME NOTABLE SCIENTIFIC RESEARCH · 2005 cont.——

phrenia may be caused by infections. ❦ {MAY} South Korean scientists employed therapeutic cloning techniques to create human Embryonic Stem Cells [ESC] that may be genetically matched to specific individuals. ❦ The Reproductive Genetics Institute, Chicago, claimed to have made patient-matched ESC without using cloning. Their system used existing ESC rather than human eggs, making it not only cheaper and simpler, but also ethically problematic. ❦ {JUN} Research published in *Science* claimed that a fungus similar to cheese mould can effectively kill mosquitoes, thus reducing malarial transmission by *c.*98%. ❦ A team at Sangamo BioSciences in California claimed to have developed a method of making blood stem cells immune to HIV. It is hoped that these cells could gradually re-populate the immune system, thereby relieving the need for anti-retroviral drugs. ❦ {JUL} GDNF (Glial Cell Line-derived Neurotrophic Factor) has been shown to reverse the effects of Parkinson's disease. Neuroscientists at Bristol's Frenchay Hospital undertook trials that indicate GDNF may improve movement control by 50–80%. ❦ A study by the University of Otago, New Zealand, suggested that watching too much TV as a child makes you stupid. The study monitored the viewing habits and academic records of 1,000 children aged 5–15. The results implied that those who watched most TV at 13–15 were most likely to drop out of school. ❦ Mitchell Krucoff of the Duke Clinical Research Institute, North Carolina, undertook research into the medical benefits of praying. He studied 4 groups of 700

patients undergoing heart surgery: one group was prayed for by a number of believers of a multitude of faiths; another group listened to soothing music; the third had music and prayer; and the fourth, nothing. The research suggested that praying made no difference to survival rates, but those who listened to soothing music were slightly more likely to survive after 6 months. ❦ {AUG} Research into breast cancer survival published in *The Lancet* indicated that those taking anastrozole after switching from tamoxifen after 2 years had 40% fewer recurrences of cancer than those who remained on tamoxifen. ❦ Scientists at Seoul National University successfully cloned a dog – an Afghan puppy called Snuppy. ❦ Research led by Bertran Auvert at the French National Institute of Health and Medical Research suggested that circumcision can protect men from HIV. 3,273 South African heterosexual males aged 18–24 who wanted to be circumcised were divided into two groups. The first group was circumcised straight away; the other was asked to wait. After 21 months, 51 of the uncircumcised men were HIV positive, compared to just 15 of circumcised men. So dramatic were these results, the study was suspended to allow all the participants to undergo surgery. ❦ The genetic code of rice was mapped: 37,544 genes make-up the genome. It is hoped this research will improve the yield of a vital food crop. ❦ A Medical Research Council study suggested that redheads may be less susceptible to pain than either blondes or brunettes, but other research seemed to cast doubt on this finding.

INTELLIGENT DESIGN

In October 2004, the school-board of Dover, Pennsylvania, decreed that Intelligent Design (ID) must be taught alongside evolution in biology classes. ❦ ID asserts that some biological structures and other aspects of the natural world are so complex and have components so intricate and interdependent that they could not have developed through evolution. ID's advocates claim that some 'higher' power or intelligence is responsible for creating or guiding creation. ID is usually distinguished from traditional Creationism: the belief that the Book of Genesis accurately describes the forming of the world, and that, calculated from Adam and Eve, the Earth is just 6,000 years old. However, central to the idea of Intelligent Design is an Intelligent Designer – an assertion that causes many to see ID not as an alternative *scientific theory* to Darwinism, but as an unprovable *theological belief.* ID points to gaps in the fossil-record, and unexplained complex structures (like the flagella of bacteria) to show

Part of education is to expose people to different schools of thought ...
— GEORGE W. BUSH

that evolution is an incomplete theory. In turn, evolutionists argue that ID presents no scientific evidence for its claims, has yet to disprove any step of the evolutionary process, and is merely a dilute form of Creationism. ❦ The ID debate has particular significance in America where the Constitution ensures the separation of Church and State. After decades of legal scuffles, the US Supreme Court finally ruled in 1987 that Creationism could not be taught alongside evolution in science classes. In August 2005, President Bush fuelled the controversy when he said that ID should be taught to children 'because part of education is to expose people to different schools of thought'. Coming from a President, and one with strong Christian beliefs, this seemingly innocuous statement has sparked fears that the separation of Church and State may be undermined, and that Creationist theory could be reintroduced into the biology lessons of America's schools under the subtle camouflage of Intelligent Design.

BIG QUESTIONS OF SCIENCE

Below are some of the 125 'big questions that face scientific inquiry over the next quarter-century', according to the magazine *Science* [see also www.sciencemag.org]:

1 .... What is the universe made of?
2 .... What is the biological basis of consciousness?
3 .... Why do humans have so few genes?
4 .... To what extent are genetic variation and personal health linked?
5 .... Can the laws of physics be unified?
6 .... How much can human life span be extended?
7 .... What controls organ regeneration?
8 .... How can a skin cell become a nerve cell?
9 .... How does a single somatic cell become a whole plant?
10 .... How does Earth's interior work?

SUDAN I

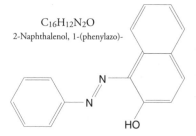

$C_{16}H_{12}N_2O$

2-Naphthalenol, 1-(phenylazo)-

Sudan I is a red dye used to colour solvents, oils, waxes, petrol, and floor polishes. Because Sudan I is linked with cancer, EU regulations prevent it from being used in food. Yet, it was discovered in 2005 that Sudan I had contaminated a chilli powder used in a brand of Worcestershire sauce. Hundreds of products were swiftly withdrawn from sale. Further concerns were raised in April 2005 after the discovery that another carcinogenic dye, Para Red ($C_{16}H_{11}N_3O_3$), had contaminated some foodstuffs. [www.food.gov.uk]

NEW PRIME NUMBER

Primes are whole numbers larger than 1 that are divisible only by 1 and themselves; for example: 2, 3, 5, 7, …, 101, …, 1093, &c. If a prime number divides a product then it must divide at least one of the factors, and every natural number larger than 1 is either prime or can be written as a product of primes. Euclid proved that there is no limit on the size of primes, though mathematicians have long sought longer and longer numbers. In March 2005, Dr Martin Nowak, a German eye specialist and dedicated amateur mathematician, discovered the latest largest prime 7,816,230 digits long: it can be expressed as $2^{25964951}-1$. The opening digits of this new prime are:

122164630061277948107753964031288439267361424223075246409537660469964558090568615690774851269040418246405468474387100505374926300211252045527909017984359393665081567696785664085904567474142036039542961590569448711318888351794115962015465903185155397082456231615502762936698561384633189068087289957391854109461063493056475770392295973664139001149317147405933072311724315844795482574100395338055771008822309093991892891224803513453742174356852572197336322786942236687061362779969653318593875917406303303079721182179510021152520657878311067921010372542343758787294837337740219485354282052106668503362251782860068296034372040608031210978832809195174894612405976846040738766834603583746465015830928623035893998235316468884023310815239239967857941317424998572335197193597441901460180781009395595090495411278707269551007935354869287382433704737589548759406521423192622098523337432490200929428513469622790065114497564295713375954860313954979647716837859394180630421397409629456570819079391187474834463231482572029687620767800666093680464505575629350745826731196343869208164591645913432425564189042922018053061723687789506280231348055365921396231699830295812788860038243116818176281883694084386984995254412138627728781957222632634588852481934619560958456993754939462111452135242655434528307039298393836585671786003708815957086428736753043214809215745028067529070641997297144142779578119933067282830628331323917632415106319765047965112875083817802339315518716...

TRIACETONE TRIPEROXIDE · 'MOTHER OF SATAN'

Nicknamed the 'Mother of Satan' by Palestinian terrorists, *triacetone triperoxide* (TATP) is thought to be the explosive used in the London bombs of 7/7 and the failed attacks on 21/7. (It was also the substance used by the failed 'shoe-bomber' Richard Reid.) TATP [$C_9H_{18}O_6$] is favoured by terrorists for a number of reasons: it is simple and cheap to make from common household substances; it is relatively difficult to detect; and it is powerfully destructive, having roughly 80% of the explosivity of TNT. However, TATP is very unstable, and is highly sensitive to heat, shock, and friction. As a consequence many have died attempting its manufacture.

─────────────── 2003 UB313 · 'XENA' ───────────────

In January 2005, Mike Brown of the California Institute of Technology discovered '2003 UB313' – an object 14·5bn km from the Sun that he believed to be the tenth planet in our Solar System. 2003 UB313 (nicknamed Xena) is the most distant 'planet' yet to be seen in our Solar System, though the status of Brown's discovery has been contested. Some embrace the possibility of a new planet, while others refuse to recognise 'Xena' as such, claiming that its remote position and small size make it more akin to an asteroid. The specifications of 2003 UB313 are:

Orbital period .... 560 years	Min distance from sun 36AU
Est. surface temperature .... -250°C	Colour .... greyish
Diameter ... *c.*2860 km (*c.*1·5 x Pluto)	Composition.............. rock and ice
Max distance from sun 97AU	1 AU (Astronomical Unit) = 156,000,000 km

─────────────── PLANETARY EVENTS 2006 ───────────────

4 January............... Perihelion: when Earth is at orbital position closest to Sun
13 January .... Venus will appear at an inferior conjunction near the Sun
24 February................................ elongation of Mercury · 18° East of Sun
14 March... penumbral Lunar eclipse†
25 March.. elongation of Venus · 47° West of Sun
29 March.......... total eclipse of the sun, visible across Africa, Turkey, and Asia
8 April..................................... elongation of Mercury · 28° West of Sun
20 June...................................... elongation of Mercury · 25° East of Sun
3 July............... Aphelion: when Earth is at orbital position farthest from Sun
7 August................................... elongation of Mercury · 19° West of Sun
7 September... partial Lunar eclipse
22 September... annular Solar eclipse*
17 October................................ elongation of Mercury · 25° East of Sun
8 November .... transit of Mercury over the Sun
25 November .... elongation of Mercury · 20° West of Sun
10 December .... occultation of Saturn by the Moon

† Penumbral refers to an eclipse when the Moon enters the Earth's penumbra, the lighter portion of the Earth's shadow. * Annular eclipses occur when the Moon passes directly in front of the Sun but does not block out the whole, leaving a ring of sunlight.

─────────────── A DARK GALAXY · VIRGOH121 ───────────────

In February 2005, a team of astronomers at Cardiff University discovered a galaxy 50m light-years away that contains no stars. The dark galaxy consists of a large cloud of hydrogen gas and 'dark matter'; it contains enough material to create millions of stars, and yet contains none. Astronomers have long suspected the existence of such dark galaxies, hypothesising that they may outnumber ordinary galaxies by up to a hundred to one, yet VIRGOH121 is the first to be identified.

———————— KEY SPACE MISSIONS OF 2005 ————————

MARS EXPRESS · A European Space Agency [ESA] mission that has orbited Mars since December 2003, looking for subsurface water. In 2005 the Mars Express detected a sea of ice near Mars' equator, which might indicate the correct conditions for the presence of primitive microbes, the best indicator yet for life on the Red Planet.

CASSINI-HUYGENS · A joint ESA and NASA effort to study Saturn and its moons. The mission consists of the Cassini orbiter (which entered Saturn's orbit in July 2004) and Huygens – a small robotic probe which landed on Titan (a moon of Saturn) in January 2005. On entering Titan's atmosphere Huygens was able to send pictures and samples of the surface. Early results indicate a windy moon with gusts of 300mph, and an ice-sand surface, with probable methane rain.

COSMOS-1 · A privately funded space mission to launch the world's first solar sail – a developing technology that might allow shuttles to travel infinite distances without fuel. Cosmos-1 aimed to use vast reflective sails propelled by light particles bouncing off them. Sadly, although Cosmos-1 was launched in June 2005, the ship did not reach orbit when its launch rockets failed. However, Japanese, European, Russian, and American space agencies are all pursuing solar sail missions.

DEEP IMPACT · On 4 July 2005 NASA's Deep Impact probe was deliberately steered into the path of comet Tempel 1. The aim was to study the structure of comets that are thought to contain matter unchanged since the birth of the solar system. Deep Impact hit the comet at 37,000 km/h, creating a vast plume of debris that provided vital images and material for analysis.

DISCOVERY · The first of NASA's space shuttles to launch since the loss of Columbia in 2003. The mission, to carry supplies to the International Space Station, was relatively simple – yet failure might well have resulted in the permanent grounding of NASA's fleet. Although Discovery successfully launched in July 2005, debris fell away from the shuttle on take-off – the same fault that had destroyed Columbia. Three spacewalks to fashion makeshift repairs were successful and Discovery returned to Earth on 9 August.

——————— NASA'S CENTENNIAL CHALLENGES ———————

NASA has created a series of Centennial Challenges to be announced over the coming years. The cash prizes have been established in order to encourage innovation into areas of technical development which would be of benefit to both space exploration and to NASA. The first 4 Centennial Challenges to be issued are:

Challenge	*prize*
Design a powerful tether for a space elevator	$50,000
Create a robot that can climb a cable in space while carrying a load	$50,000
Extract breathable oxygen from lunar soil	$250,000
Develop space gloves to maximise movement but maintain protection	$25,000

—————— SOME INVENTIONS OF NOTE · 2005 ——————

{JAN} David Chroman of Florida is issued a patent (WO 200/092463) for self-hardening rope, that has an inflatable plastic tube within its weave. Once inflated, the rope is hard enough to hold its own weight, and can easily be passed up a rock face or from a boat to a jetty. ❦ {FEB} Chef Homaru Cantu develops a method of printing sheets of food. Inkjet cartridges are filled with fruit and vegetable extracts, and these flavours are printed onto edible sheets of starch. ❦ Haptics, the technology of recreating touch via artificial stimuli, is introduced in mobiles. Samsung hopes to use vibrating motors to send tickles or slaps. ❦ {MAR} Philips develop electronic paper that can be peeled off electronic displays, such as mobile phones or in-car 'sat-nav' screens. ❦ Gashbam Enterprises, Israel, patents a self-lighting cigarette (WO 2005/018349). The fag is tipped with sulphur and phosphorus, and ignites when struck against a rough surface. ❦ A clever alarm clock (Clocky) has been invented. When the snooze button is pressed, Clocky rolls off to hide somewhere in the room, forcing the sleepyhead to search for it. Clocky is sneaky enough to find a different hiding place every day, thwarting even the most ardent Rip van Winkle. ❦ {APR} A new typeface called Read Regular is issued to aid dyslexics. Each letter is uniquely designed so that it cannot be inverted or mirrored to resemble another. ❦ In Africa, some playground roundabouts have been connected to borehole pumps, so that as local children play on them they pump clean water from depths of 100m. ❦ {MAY} A Spanish inventor has used fingerprint recognition to create a washing machine that

encourages men to do more housework. The machine scans fingerprints and prevents the same person using the machine twice in a row. ❦ A children's shoe named Square Eyes has been developed with a special in-sole that records the amount of exercise its wearer takes. The shoe calculates how much TV-time the child has 'earned' in exercise; once that time is up, the shoe transmits a signal to switch the TV off. ❦ {JUN} A Japanese phone company, NTT, proposes a system to allow people to send smells over the internet. Users will send a 'make this smell' signal to a chemical generator attached to the recipient's computer, which will then blend chemicals to create the desired aroma. ❦ Engineering student Katie Williams designs intelligent swimming goggles that display a lap count and time elapsed on the goggles' lenses. The Inview Goggles use an in-built compass to establish when a swimmer has completed a length. ❦ {JUL} Prof. Terry Cosgrove of Bristol University invents a new polymer called 'revolymer' that, when used in chewing-gum, causes it to be non-stick – potentially saving our pavements and shoes. ❦ Sharp develops a new TV, named DualView, that allows viewers to watch two separate images on the same screen, depending on where in the room they are sitting. ❦ {AUG} E-San proposes technology to allow sufferers of respiratory diseases such as cystic fibrosis to predict with a mobile phone when they will get an infection. Plugged into the phone, the device (a spirometer) measures the strength of a patient's breathing, which can then be sent via the mobile direct to their doctor's computer.

—— SOME LAWS, THEOREMS, PARADOXES, &c. ——

GAIA HYPOTHESIS · devised by James Ephraim Lovelock, the theory that the Earth is a 'living' self-regulating and self-sustaining single system.

PETER PRINCIPLE · originated by Dr Laurence J. Peter, 'in a hierarchy every employee tends to rise to his level of incompetence'.

MOORE'S LAW · assertion by Gordon Moore that the number of transistors that can be fitted onto a chip (or semi-conductor) will double every eighteen months. Generally, this has proved prescient for the expanding power, speed, and capacity of technology.

EINSTEIN'S LAW · that mass (m) and energy (E) are related by the equation:

$$E = mc^2$$

where (c) is the speed of light in a vacuum. Therefore a quantity of energy (E) has a mass (m), and a mass (m) has intrinsic energy (E).

HAWTHORN EFFECT · any change (even a negative one) to an environment (e.g. a workplace) will create a short-term improvement in mood, productivity, &c.

THEORY OF SIGNATURES · Paracelsus stated 'by the outward shapes and qualities of things we may know their inward Vertues, which God hath put in them for the good of man'. Thus, St John's Wort was said to be good for wounds as its leaves resemble skin.

BURIDAN'S ASS · C14th philosophical model showing the dilemma of competing desires, illustrated by the ass which starves when unable to choose between two equal loads of hay.

OCCAM'S RAZOR · In C14th William of Occam is said to have written *entia non sunt multiplicanda praeter necessitatem* (entities are not to be multiplied beyond necessity) – meaning that the hypothesis requiring the fewest assumptions should be preferred.

ALVAREZ' HYPOTHESIS · that the mass extinction of the dinosaurs was caused by the impact of a large asteroid on the Earth sixty-five million years ago.

GAUSE'S LAW · that no two species with identical ecology can co-exist in the same environment.

FERMAT'S LAST THEOREM · proposed by Pierre Fermat, that there are no natural numbers x, y, z, and n such that $xn + yn = zn$ when n is greater than 2. Fermat claimed to have proved it, but no record has been found. It was finally proved by British mathematician Andrew Wiles in 1993.

EPIMENIDES' PARADOX · (also known sometimes as the Liar Paradox) is best illustrated by imagining an individual saying the phrase 'I am lying'.

PARKINSON'S LAW · Cyril Northcote Parkinson's notion that work expands to fill the time available for its completion. It applies in a host of fields like office life, traffic flow, and economics.

CLEOPATRA'S NOSE EFFECT · theory that unpredictable and unlikely forces can have effects on human action and, therefore, history (e.g. the effect of Cleopatra's lovely nose upon Antony).

PALEY'S WATCHMAKER · Rev William Paley's theory that God must exist because of the complexity of nature.

—————————— TECH & NET GLOSSARY ——————————

CYBERSQUATTING · acquiring an internet domain that should rightfully belong to someone else (e.g. a well-known company) with the intention of forcing them to buy it from you. Similar to TYPOSQUATTING · registering domains that are only a few keystrokes from a popular website to draw traffic after typing errors.

SNAIL MAIL · real-life mail delivered by real-life postmen. V MAIL · email containing a virus. KNEE MAIL · a Christian euphemism for prayer.

POTS · Plain Old Telephone System.

BRICKS & MORTAR · a business that has an actual physical presence (e.g. a shop), as opposed to one that exists only online. CLICKS & MORTAR are traditional businesses that have developed an online presence.

MEATSPACE · real-life, as opposed to cyber-space.

PODCASTING · a portmanteau word from iPod + broadcasting, describing how radio stations make programmes available for download onto digital music players. The BBC has recently expanded its podcasting output.

BANDWIDTH · the amount of data that can be transferred along a digital connection in a given time period – usually measured in bytes per second.

RSS · Really Simple Syndication system that allows internet users to select data from a wide range of websites and have it delivered automatically to their computer, allowing for the customisation and personalisation of regularly updated web-content.

PHISHING *or* SPOOFING · the attempt to fraudulently acquire information like credit card details and passwords, by masquerading online as a reputable business or organisation. Emails that ask for such sensitive data should be treated with scepticism.

BIOMETRICS · considered by some to be the Holy Grail of modern security, biometrics allows personal biological information (fingerprint, iris scan, &c) to confirm an identity. (It derives from Greek *bios*, life and *metron*, measure.) Many laptop computers are now fitted with fingerprint scanners to confirm the identity of users, and increasingly ID cards and passports will contain chips holding biometric data.

BETA · a version of software or hardware that is not fully finished, but is good enough to be issued to the public for testing and feedback.

SPAMISH · the new language created by spammers [see p.188] where letters are substituted with punctuation to try and fool email filters, e.g. 'V!agra'.

WYSIWYG (*wizzy-wig*) · What You See Is What You Get · where what is shown on screen matches the output.

COOKIES · data that is sent by a website and stored on computers browsing that site. Cookies allow websites to identify and monitor information about users, for example recording all visits or what has been purchased.

VOIP · Voice Over Internet Protocol allows the transmission of voice telephony over the internet. In theory, VOIP could cut the cost of phone calls.

—————————— TECH & NET GLOSSARY cont. ——————————

MICKEY · supposedly a unit of mouse movement equal to ½ooth inch.

BLUETOOTH · short-range radio technology that allows computing and telecommunications devices to communicate with each other and with the internet wirelessly. The name alludes to Harald I of Denmark (*c.*910–85), nicknamed Blåtand or 'bluetooth', who is credited with unifying his kingdom in the way that Bluetooth seeks to unify communications devices.

BANGALORED · losing your job to cheaper labour outsourced to another country (e.g. India).

AMAZONED · losing one's job, or share of business, because of online competition.

BETAMAXED · when superior technology (e.g. Betamax videos) loses out to an inferior version (e.g. VHS).

FIREWALL · a combination of hardware and software that protects computers from outside attack by allowing only certain internet traffic in and out.

DATA MINING · trawling large databases to discover previously unknown information and, often, customers.

V2V · Voice to Voice, achieved either using the POTS or via any combination of VIOP, mobile, conference call, or MEATSPACE interaction.

TIPPING POINT · the moment when something (e.g. an infectious disease or social phenomenon) reaches a critical point and spreads suddenly from the few to the many.

3G · the third-generation of mobile phone technology that allows the transfer of non-voice data (such as music, video, and email data).

PDA · Personal Digital Assistants · hand-held 'palm-top' computers like the Blackberry or Palm Pilot.

GPS · Global Positioning System (developed and run by the US Dept of Defense), that uses a constellation of orbiting satellites to give instantaneous, real-time geographic positions to within *c.*10m. Anyone on Earth can access GPS data, and it is widely used for car 'sat-nav'igational systems.

—————————— SOME SOFTWARE TYPES ——————————

Freeware .... *distributed for free, but often with catches (like those below)*
Spyware .... *maliciously designed to monitor or control a computer*
Malware................................... *designed to harm a computer (e.g. a virus)*
Shareware........................... *asks for (or later requires) registration or payment*
Adware .... *obliges users to view adverts before or while using*
Demoware, Crippleware ...... *works for a limited time, or with only some functions*
Postcardware.................... *requests you to send the author a thank-you postcard*
Vaporware .... *hyped software (often a 'new version') that fails to materialise*
Abandonware .... *'old' software seemingly no longer supported by its creators*
Beggarware, Guiltware, Nagware... *asks or shames you to send payment or donation*

———————— GOOGLE ————————

In June 2005, just 10 months after floating on the NY stock exchange, Google became the world's largest media company, worth more than $81bn (compared to Time Warner's value of *c.*$78bn). This achievement is all the more astonishing (and, some say, worrying) since Google's sales in 2004 were only $3·2bn (Time Warner's were $42bn). The financial success of Google mirrors the effect the search engine has had on the world. Not only is Google now a commonplace verb (*'I Googled his name'*), but the search engine has entered into the culture in a myriad of other ways. Below are some Google-related terms, and their meaning:

GOOGLEWHACK · the curious pursuit of finding a pair of query words which when entered into Google produces just one result. As with *Googlebombs* their unique quality is transient as the word pair becomes widely known. Examples of successful *Googlewhacks* include: 'episcopal brachiosaur' and 'primp schadenfreude'.

GOOGLEPROOF · people who share a famous name (e.g. Harry Potter) are *Googleproof* (and thus safe from *Googlestalkers*), since any Google search for their name will be swamped with hits for their celebrity namesake.

GOOGLEFAN · a supposed fan of a writer, musician, artist, or other whose knowledge extends no further than what they can glean from Google.

GOOGLESTALK · using Google to find information on a friend, employer, or (most often) potential lover.

GOOGLEBOMB · the practice of creating multiple links to a website in order to force that site to the top of Google's ranking. So, for example, in June 2005 *Googling* 'miserable failure' brought up the official White House page for the biography of George W. Bush. By their very nature, *Googlebombs* are fated to be transient. As more people discuss a *Googlebomb* on websites or Blogs, that discussion is likely to force the target site off the top slot.

[A 'googol' is the number 10^{100} (i.e. 1 with 100 noughts after it). It is claimed that the word was invented by the nine-year-old nephew of American mathematician Edward Kasner.]

———————— COMPUTER STORAGE CAPACITY ————————

Memory				approximate storage capacity
Bit				single binary digit (1 or 0)
Byte		8 bits		a single character
Kilobyte	kB	1,024 bytes		half a page of typed text
Megabyte	MB	1,024 kB	10^6 bytes	novella of text
Gigabyte	GB	1,024 MB	10^9 bytes	500,000 pages of text
Terabyte	TB	1,024 GB	10^{12} bytes	1 million books
Petabyte	PB	1,024 TB	10^{15} bytes	200 British Libraries
Exabyte	EB	1,024 PB	10^{18} bytes	200,000 British Libraries
Zetabyte	ZB	1,024 EB	10^{24} bytes	incomprehensibly large

A CD-ROM can hold 650–700 MB, which roughly equates to *c.*75 minutes of recorded music.

TOP-LEVEL DOMAIN CODES

Original domains   *restricted to*
.com .... general use
.edu .... post-secondary institutions
.gov........ United States Government
.int........... organisations established
                by international treaties
.mil.............. United States Military
.net .... general use
.org .... non-commercial activities
New domains
.aero............. air-transport industry
.biz........................... businesses
.coop......... cooperative associations
.info........................ general use
.museum .... museums
.name...................... individuals
.pro .... credentialed professionals

Proposed new domains   *intended for*
.asia.............. Pan-Asia community
.cat................ Catalan community
.jobs .... human resources
.mail.................. 'spam-free' email
.mobi .... mobile phones
.post ..... post office and organisations
.tel .... VOIP telephony [see p.184]
.travel .... travel industry & agents
.xxx ...... pornography; adult content

Some of the proposed domains above have been approved, but are not yet in operation. It is claimed that the .xxx domain will allow for adult content to be walled-off from the public. For a listing of country codes, see pp.72–79. For additional information see www.icann.org

GAMES BAFTAS · 2005

The BAFTA Games Awards, now in their third year, recognise the success of a British computer games industry that creates £220m of net exports – compared to the negative export value of British film and television. Some 2005 winners were:

Best racing game .... Burnout 3: Takedown [EA Games]
Best sports game .... Pro Evolution Soccer 4 [Konami]
Best action/adventure... Half-Life 2 [Sierra]
Best children's .... Donkey Konga [Nintendo]
Best animation... Half-Life 2 [Sierra]
Best art direction... Half-Life 2 [Sierra]
Best PC game... Half-Life 2 [Sierra]
Best Gamecube game.................. Prince of Persia: Warrior Within [UBI Soft]
Best PS2 game .... Burnout 3: Takedown [EA games]
Best Xbox game... Halo 2 [Microsoft]
Best game .... Half-Life 2 [Sierra]

ONLINE SPELLING MISTAKES

Below are words most frequently misspelled or mistyped into Yell.com searches:

Errors in February 2005		
Restaurant.......76,515	Jewellers...........7,069	Chiropodist.........976
Accommodation 20,390	Electricians........3,016	Cinema..............706
Solicitors..........8,767	Florist..............2,716	Theatre..............535
	Optician 1,006	[Source: Yell.com]

SPAM & UCE

SPAM is the proprietory name of a brand of tinned meat, mainly pork, that was first marketed by George A. Hormel & Co. in 1937. The word, a blend of 'spiced' and 'ham', was apparently the brainchild of actor Kenneth Daigneau. It seems that the use of the word in association with junk email derives from the 1971 *Monty Python* sketch where – at The Green Midget Café, Bromley – Mr and Mrs Bun (Eric Idle and Graham Chapman) attempt to order a meal without SPAM from the waitress (Terry Jones). Their attempts are drowned out by a horde of SPAM-loving Vikings whose chanting of the word SPAM crescendoes into the now famous 'SPAM song'. Some 20 years later, the relentless Viking chanting became forever linked with the equally relent-

less bombardment of junk-email. Hormel & Co are, quite understandably, keen to protect their trademark from association with junk emails, and prefer the term UCE (unsolicited commercial email). However, like Hoover, Biro, and others, the pressure on proprietory names is intense once they become used generically. This seems especially so with the word spam, since close to 90% of all email is thought to be unsolicited and unwanted. (John Paul II's death led to an avalanche of 'Papal' spam offering books on the Papacy and fraudulently asking for donations to build a cathedral in his name.) Research by Email Systems showed that on Sunday 10 April 2005, 98·2% of all email was spam. Research by Microsoft indicates the contents of this UCE barrage:

spam type   2004

Porn/sex non-graphic *('enhancers', links with sexual connotation)*......34%
Financial *(refinancing, debt, and financial advice, &c)*.................13%
Rx/herbal *(cheap drugs or herbal supplements, &c)*.....................10%
Dubious products *(pirated software, diplomas, &c)* 10%
Other spam *(everything else that appears to be spam)*....................8%
Porn/sex graphic *(anything that contains pornographic images)* 7%
Scams *(get rich quick, phisher scams, &c)*...............................6%
Newsletters *(any newsletter that isn't selling something)* 6%
Insurance *(health, dental, life, home, auto, &c)* 4%
Travel/casino *(selling airline tickets, hotel reservations, &c)*..............3%

Some tips for reducing spam: NEVER RESPOND to spam emails: any response confirms an active account. Set up KEY-WORD FILTERS to delete emails with certain words (e.g. 'home loans', 'penis'). Set up DECOY accounts for newsgroups or auctions. Do not sign-up to ANTI-SPAM lists, since these can be fraudulent or hijacked by spammers. Do not believe the 'from' ADDRESS on emails. Set your account to initially BLOCK IMAGES LOADING: some spam contains tiny images to alert the sender to an active account. Delete spam before opening. Use specialist anti-spam SOFTWARE. CONCEAL your email address either by displaying it as a graphic or by using complete text, such as '*name at emailaccount dot com*'. Do not forward CHAIN EMAILS, no matter how worthy or charitable they might appear.

TOP TEN UK E-TAILERS

e-tailer	monthly visitors		
eBay	10,474m	Comet	1,020m
Amazon	5,859m	John Lewis	818m
Tesco	3,240m	dabs.com	798m
Argos	1,194m	CD wow	753m
B&Q	1,220m	Next	708m

[Source: Nielsen/NetRatings, Mar 2005]

THE WEBBY AWARDS

Awarded by the International Academy of Digital Arts and Sciences, the Webby Awards reward excellence in web design, innovation and functionality. The following represents a selection of the 2005 winners. See www.webbyawards.com:

Activism	*worldcitizenguide.com*	Lifestyle	*epicurious.com*
Best writing	*mcsweeneys.net*	Magazine	*alternet.org*
Best homepage	*wordsatplay.com*	Movies	*postvisual.com/theuninvited*
Blog	*boingboing.net*	Music	*bbc.co.uk/radio1/onemusic*
Celebrity/fan	*jamieoliver.com*	News	*bbc.co.uk/news*
Humour	*rathergood.com*	Newspaper	*guardian.co.uk*

TOP GIFTS BOUGHT ONLINE

Films (DVD or VHS)	61%	Digital camera/video camera	19%
Music	59%	Sports & leisure goods	18%
Books	57%	Cosmetics & perfumes	18%
Clothes	35%	Jewellery	17%
Video games	30%	Mobile phones	15%
Children's toys	30%		
Household/garden gifts	22%		

[Figures for Christmas 2004 Source: Nielsen/NetRatings]

THE BLOGGIES

The fifth annual Weblog Awards are independent, non-commercially sponsored awards, nominated and voted for by the public. Some of the 2005 awards were:

Best...	Blog		
Meme	*flickr.com*	American	*dooce.com*
Oz or NZ	*shauny.org/pussycat*	Latin American	*overcaffeinated.net*
Asian blog	*xiaxue.blogspot.com*	Entertainment	*defamer.com*
Africa/M.East	*dear_raed.blogspot.com*	Food	*cookingforengineers.com*
British/Irish	*plasticbag.org*	Politics	*wonkette.com*
European	*myboyfriendisatwat.com*	Topical	*bookslut.com/blog*
Canadian	*photojunkie.ca*	Humourous	*dooce.com*
		Weblog of the year	*boingboing.net*

—————————— SOME WEBSITES OF THE YEAR ——————————

the-shipman-inquiry.org.uk........................ *astonishing insight into the inquiry*
dec.org.uk .... *Disasters Emergency Committee* [see p.12]
nethouseprices.com .... *snoop on what your neighbours paid*
mediabistro.com/fishbowldc/................. *bloggers at White House press briefings*
vatican.va .... *the website of the Holy See*
defamer.com .... *American show-biz gossip and tittle-tattle*
uncyclopedia.org .... *parody of wikipedia*
theyworkforyou.com .... *info on what your MP has been up to in Parliament*
https://implicit.harvard.edu/implicit/demo .... *test your prejudices*
number-10.gov.uk/output/Page7445.asp ....
          Attorney-General's advice on the legality of the Iraq war, 7 March 2003
postsecret.blogspot.com .... *share your secrets through art*
huffingtonpost.com .... *American news, opinion and high-profile blog*
improveverywhere.com................................. *curious American pranksters*
futureforests.com.. *carbon-neutralise your world*
http://subvic.blogspot.com/.. *that nanny blog*
wheresgeorge.com .... *track the history of your US$ bill*
starnow.co.uk.......... *apply to be on reality TV and preview upcoming TV horrors*
advicenow.org.uk .... *financial advice for co-habiting couples who split up*
mi5.gov.uk... *official MI5 website*
campaignforcivilobedience.co.uk .... *celebrating good manners*
werenotafraid.com .... *defiance from London after 7/7*
findsounds.com .... *find sounds online*
phlog.net.. *share your digital photos online*
http://watchingamerica.com/ .... *what the world thinks about the USA*
bbc.co.uk/radio/downloadtrial/subscribe.shtml .... *BBC podcasting* [see p.184]
couchsurfing.com......................... *travel the world staying on people's couches*
cs.hut.fi/~demi/cloth_folding.mpeg .... *fold shirts like the Japanese*

—————————————— GOOGLE ZEITGEIST ——————————————

Ubiquitous search engine Google [see p.186] regularly publishes its *Zeitgeist* list, detailing
for what people are searching. Below are the top 5 UK searches for some recent months:

2005	1st	2nd	3rd	4th	5th
Aug					
Jul	*Big Brother*	*Harry Potter*	*Crazy Frog*	*Eminem*	*Jessica Alba*
Jun	*Big Brother*	*Crazy Frog*	*50 Cent*	*Paris Hilton*	*Wimbledon*
May	*Star Wars*	*Abi Titmuss*	*dog*	*Paris Hilton*	*Simpsons*
Apr	*BBC*	*easyjet*	*Britney Spears*	*Ryanair*	*face party*
Mar	*BBC*	*Argos*	*easyjet*	*paintball*	*Tesco*
Feb	*Green Day*	*Girls Aloud*	*Playboy*	*Jennifer Ellison*	*ebay.co.uk*
Jan	*tsunami*	*Little Britain*	*games*	*cars*	*Multimap*

Zeitgeist is a German word for 'spirit of the age' (*Zeit* time + *Geist* spirit). Presumably, these lists have been 'cleaned'.

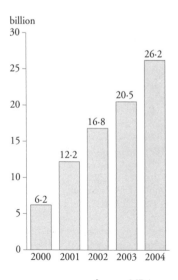

2006 SCI, TECH, NET

THE CRAZY FROG

In 2005 the Crazy Frog became the world's best-selling ring-tone, with sales of over 11 million. Uniquely, the Crazy Frog successfully crossed over into the mainstream music charts, beating *Coldplay* to number one after selling roughly 200,000 singles during one week in June [see p.129]. The Frog was born in 1997 when Daniel Malmedahl, a 17-year-old Swede, recorded an imitation of his friend's souped-up moped. This recording was posted on the internet, and in 2002 was spotted by animator Erik Wernquist, who created a froggy character to go with the sound, presciently dubbing his creation 'The Annoying Thing'. In 2004, The Annoying Thing's popularity on the web caught the attention of ring-tone company *Jamster* which bought the rights from Malmedahl and Wernquist. *Jamster* employed a strategy of blanket media promotion, and Crazy Frog adverts appeared 36,382 times in the first three weeks of May 2005 alone. (The Advertising Standards Authority received more than 1,000 complaints.) The success of the Crazy Frog is testament to synergy between all facets of modern media, as well as the popularity of ring-tones among teenagers. However, the questions over which most are losing sleep are: why does the Crazy Frog sport a crash helmet (in due deference to road safety), but neglect to wear underpants? Indeed, why does the frog have a penis?

YEARLY TEXTS · UK

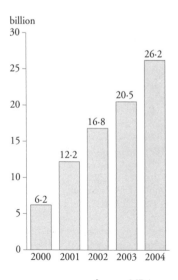

billion: 2000 6·2, 2001 12·2, 2002 16·8, 2003 20·5, 2004 26·2

TOP TEXTING DAYS

New Year's Day 2005 · *133 million texts sent – the highest ever daily total.*
New Year's Day 2003 · *The number of texts sent in one day exceeded 100 million for the first time.*
14 February 2005 · *92 million texts sent: seven times more than traditional Valentine's cards.*
19 August 2004 · *81 million text messages sent on the day that A-level results were announced.*
26 August 2004 · *On GCSE result day 79 million texts were sent.*
22 November 2003 · *76 million texts sent on the day England won the Rugby World Cup.*
11 May 2003 · *65 million texts sent on the last day of the 2002/3 Premiership season.*

[source: MDA · www.mda-mobiledata.org]

– 191 –

UK TELEPHONE NUMBERING SYSTEM

Numbers beginning	*designation*
01 · 02	geographic numbers
055	corporate numbers
070	personal numbering / 'follow me'
077 · 078 · 079	mobile services
080	freephone†

0845	provider's local rate
0844	5p/min or up to 5p/call
0870	provider's national rate
0871	5p/min or up to 5p/call
09	premium rate services
	† *Some mobile providers may charge.*

EMERGENCY TELEPHONE CONTROL

During emergencies, the police and Cabinet Office can restrict all or parts of the telephone system, rationing calls to certain users. The mobile network is governed by ACCess OverLoad Control (ACCOLC). At the request of a Police Incident Commander, specific areas of the network can be set to allow access only to users with special SIM cards in their phones (e.g. the police, security forces, emergency services, local authorities &c). Other users inside the restricted area will hear 'busy' or 'not available' tones if they try to make calls. A similar system, the Government Telephone Preference Scheme (GTPS), operates for land-lines. Under the GTPS, all telephones are able to receive incoming calls, but only authorised users can make outgoing calls. Because of the disruption caused and concern that some useful calls may not get through, call rationing is rarely used, and is not always made public. It is known that the ACCOLC was implemented after the 7/7 London bombings.

UK TELEPHONE SHORT CODES

Short code	*action*
100	operator assistance*
155	international operator assistance
999 *and* 112†	emergency services*
118xxx	directory enquiry*
195	directory enquiry for disabled
123	speaking clock

141	withhold calling line identity
1470	release calling line identity
1471	last call info & call return
1475	erase 1471 memory
1477	automatic call trace
1478	activate call screener
1479	de-activate call screener

Not all providers offer all these services, although all are obliged to offer those marked thus*; some providers may offer additional short code services. † The 112 emergency number is the European standard, and it is widely used by countries across the world as well as by mobiles. [Source: Ofcom]

ICE · IN CASE OF EMERGENCY

In 2005, British paramedic Bob Brotchie suggested a system to aid the emergency services contact the nexts-of-kin of those injured in accidents. Brotchie proposed that people save a list of essential contact numbers to their mobile phones, adding the prefix ICE ('In Case of Emergency'). After the 7/7 London bombings, ICE gained national coverage, despite a false rumour that it would help phone viruses.

─────────── SI PREFIXES ───────────   ── °C – °F ──

Below are the SI prefixes and symbols for the decimal multiples and submultiples of SI Units from 10^{24} to 10^{-24}:

10^{24}	yotta	Y	1 000 000 000 000 000 000 000 000
10^{21}	zetta	Z	1 000 000 000 000 000 000 000
10^{18}	exa	E	1 000 000 000 000 000 000
10^{15}	peta	P	1 000 000 000 000 000
10^{12}	tera	T	1 000 000 000 000
10^{9}	giga	G	1 000 000 000
10^{6}	mega	M	1 000 000
10^{3}	kilo	k	1 000
10^{2}	hecto	h	100
10	deca	da	10
1			1
10^{-1}	deci	d	0.1
10^{-2}	centi	c	0.01
10^{-3}	milli	m	0.001
10^{-6}	micro	μ	0.000 001
10^{-9}	nano	n	0.000 000 001
10^{-12}	pico	p	0.000 000 000 001
10^{-15}	femto	f	0.000 000 000 000 001
10^{-18}	atto	a	0.000 000 000 000 000 001
10^{-21}	zepto	z	0.000 000 000 000 000 000 001
10^{-24}	yocto	y	0.000 000 000 000 000 000 000 001

──────── SOME USEFUL CONVERSIONS ────────

A	A *to* B *multiply by*	B *to* A *multiply by*	B
inches	25.4	0.0397	millimetres
inches	2.54	0.3937	centimetres
feet	0.3048	3.2808	metres
yards	0.9144	1.0936	metres
miles	1.6093	0.6214	kilometres
acres	0.4047	2.471	hectares
square feet	0.0929	10.76	square metres
square miles	2.5899	0.3861	square kilometres
UK pints	0.5682	1.7598	litres
UK gallons	4.546	0.2199	litres
cubic inches	16.39	0.0610	cubic centimetres
ounces	28.35	0.0353	grams
pounds	0.4536	2.2046	kilograms
stones	6.35	0.157	kilograms
miles/gallon	0.3539	2.825	kilometres/litre
miles/US gallon	0.4250	2.353	kilometres/litre
miles/hour	1.609	0.6117	kilometres/hour

°C	°F		
100	212	49	120.2
99	210.2	48	118.4
98	208.4	47	116.6
97	206.6	46	114.8
96	204.8	45	113
95	203	44	111.2
94	201.2	43	109.4
93	199.4	42	107.6
92	197.6	41	105.8
91	195.8	40	104
90	194	39	102.2
89	192.2	38	100.4
88	190.4	37	98.6
87	188.6	36	96.8
86	186.8	35	95
85	185	34	93.2
84	183.2	33	91.4
83	181.4	32	89.6
82	179.6	31	87.8
81	177.8	30	86
80	176	29	84.2
79	174.2	28	82.4
78	172.4	27	80.6
77	170.6	26	78.8
76	168.8	25	77
75	167	24	75.2
74	165.2	23	73.4
73	163.4	22	71.6
72	161.6	21	69.8
71	159.8	20	68
70	158	19	66.2
69	156.2	18	64.4
68	154.4	17	62.6
67	152.6	16	60.8
66	150.8	15	59
65	149	14	57.2
64	147.2	13	55.4
63	145.4	12	53.6
62	143.6	11	51.8
61	141.8	10	50
60	140	9	48.2
59	138.2	8	46.4
58	136.4	7	44.6
57	134.6	6	42.8
56	132.8	5	41
55	131	4	39.2
54	129.2	3	37.4
53	127.4	2	35.6
52	125.6	1	33.8
51	123.8	0	32
50	122	-1	30.2
		-2	28.4

Normal body temp.
= 37° C (98.6° F)
range 36.1–37.2° C
(97.7°–98.9° F)

—————————————— SI UNITS ——————————————

In 1960, the *Système International d'Unités* SI Units were created to unify world measurements. Below are the technical specifications of the seven SI Base Units:

Length · METRE (m) · the length of the path travelled by light in vacuum during a time interval of 1/299,792,458 of a second.

Mass · KILOGRAM (kg) · is equal to the mass of the international prototype of the kilogram.

Amount of substance · MOLE (mol) · the amount of substance of a system which contains as many elementary entities as there are atoms in 0·012 kilogram of carbon 12.

Time · SECOND (s) · the duration of 9, 192,631,770 periods of the radiation corresponding to the transition between the two hyperfine levels of the ground state of the caesium 133 atom.

Electric current · AMPERE (A) · a constant current which, if maintained in two straight parallel conductors of infinite length, of negligible circular cross-section, and placed 1m apart in vacuum, would produce between these conductors a force equal to 2×10^{-7} newton per m of length.

Thermodynamic temperature · KELVIN (K) · 1/273·16 of the thermodynamic temperature of the triple point of water.

Luminous intensity · CANDELA (cd) · intensity, in a given direction, of a source that emits monochromatic radiation of frequency 540×10^{12} hertz and that has a radiant intensity in that direction of 1/683 watt per steradian.

————————— HACKER, CRACKER, & GEEK SPEAK —————————

HACKER . . . . *an expert computer programmer*
CRACKER . . . . *a* HACKER *who uses their skill for malicious/illegal purposes*
WHITE HAT . . . . *one who breaks into computer systems to identify security flaws*
BLACK HAT . . . . *a* CRACKER
SNEAKER . . . . *a* WHITE HAT
PHREAKER . . . . *one who tampers with telephone systems (e.g. to avoid paying)*
GEEK . . . . *one fascinated by technology; not necessarily a pejorative term*
NERD . . . . . . *above average* IQ; *below average social-skills and, often, personal hygiene*
DWEEB . . . . *a clueless though inoffensive* NERD
DORK . . . . *an offensive* DWEEB
SPOD . . . . *a* NERD/GEEK *without the interest or skill in computing*
PROPELLER HEAD . . . . *an expert in any field of technology*
NEWBIE . . . . *a newcomer to a technology or environment (e.g. chatrooms)*
LUSER . . . . *an annoying, incompetent computer user*
LAMER . . . . *one who downloads but seldom uploads; also a* LUSER
TREKKIE . . . . *obsessive fan of Star Trek[†] in its myriad incarnations*
ANORAK . . . . *one obsessed with an unfashionable interest or technology (e.g. trains)*

[†]Other sci-fi fan nicknames are: X-PHILES, *The X Files*; SCAPERS, *Farscape*; DWARFERS, *Red Dwarf.*

Travel & Leisure

I have recently been all round the world
and have formed a very poor opinion of it.
— SIR THOMAS BEECHAM

CAR STOPPING DISTANCES

Speed (mph)	Thinking distance (m)	Stopping distance (m)	Overall Stopping Distance (m)	(car lengths)	(ft)
20	6	6	12	3	40
30	9	14	23	6	75
40	12	24	36	9	120
50	15	38	53	13	175
60	18	55	73	18	240
70	21	75	96	24	315

Stopping distances should be increased on wet or icy roads or in poor visibility.

RUNNING OVER ANIMALS

According to the provisions of sub-paragraph 8, §170 of the 1988 Road Traffic Act, drivers are legally obliged to 'stop, report accident and give information or documents' if they kill or cause damage to any of the following types of animal:

Horses · Cattle · Asses · Mules · Sheep · Pigs · Goats · Dogs

---

GB PASSENGER DEATH RATES

Mode of transport	1981	1991	1996	2001	2002
Motorcycle	115·8	94·7	97·0	122·7	111·0
Walking	76·9	75·6	55·3	46·9	44·1
Bicycle	56·9	46·5	47·2	34·5	29·4
Car	6·1	3·7	3·1	2·9	2·7
Van	3·8	2·1	1·0	0·9	1·0
Bus or coach	0·3	0·6	0·2	0·2	0·4
Rail	1·0	0·8	0·4	0·1	0·3
Water	0·4	0·0	0·8	0·5	0·0
Air	0·2	0·0	0·0	0·0	0·0

[Rate per billion passenger kilometres · Source: Department for Transport]

—————————— BRITISH ROAD LENGTHS ——————————

Road classification [O.S. 2001] *km*
Motorways 4,353
A-roads 48,164

B-roads 30,216
Minor public roads 314,392
Pedestrianised streets.............. 278

—————————— UK MOTORWAYS ——————————

M1[†] .... London – Yorkshire
M2.............. London – Faversham
M3 .... London – Southampton
M4............. London – South Wales
M5 .... Birmingham – Exeter
M6............... Catthorpe – Carlisle
M8 .... Edinburgh – nr. Greenock
M9 .... Edinburgh – Dunblane
M10.................... St Albans spur
M11............. London – Cambridge
M18.............. Rotherham – Goole
M20 .... London – Folkestone
M23................ London – Gatwick
M25 .... London orbital
M26 .... M20 – M25 spur
M27............. Southampton bypass
M32 .... M4 – Bristol spur
M40 .... London – Birmingham
M41............. London – West Cross
M42 .... Birmingham – Measham
M45 .... Dunchurch spur
M50 .... Ross spur
M53............ Chester – Birkenhead
M54 .... M6 – Telford
M55.............. Preston – Blackpool

M56............. Manchester – Chester
M57 .... Liverpool outer ring
M58................ Liverpool – Wigan
M60 .... Manchester ring road
M61............. Manchester – Preston
M62 .... Liverpool – Hull
M65 .... Calder Valley
M67...... Manchester Hyde – Denton
M69 .... Coventry – Leicester
M73.......... Maryville – Mollinsburn
M74................ Glasgow – Gretna
M77.................... Ayr Road route
M80.................... Stirling – Haggs
M90 .... Inverkeithing – Perth
M180 .... South Humberside
M876 .... M80 – Kincardine Bridge

NORTHERN IRELAND

M1 .... Belfast – Dungannon
M2[†] ...... Belfast – Antrim/Ballymena
M3..... Belfast Cross-Harbour Bridge
M5................... M2 – Greencastle
M12................... M1 – Craigavon
M22 .... Antrim – Randalstown
† The M2 is incomplete, and is in two sections

† According to a 2005 RAC poll, the M1 is Britain's most liked motorway; the M25 is the least.

—————————— MOST DANGEROUS ROADS ——————————

In 2005, the AA Motoring Trust revealed that *c.*60% of all road deaths in Britain occur on country A-roads. These picturesque routes are commonly frequented by motorcyclists and speed-freaks. The most perilous roads were found to be:

A682 – *J13 on M65 to Long Preston, North Yorkshire*
A54 – *Congleton, Cheshire to Buxton, Derbyshire*
A84 – *near Lochearnhead, Scotland* · A59 – *Skipton to Harrogate, Yorkshire*
A53 – *Leek, Staffordshire to Buxton, Derbyshire*

—————————— SPEED LIMITS & SPEEDING ——————————

Type of vehicle	built-up areas	single carriageway	dual carriageway	motor way
Car or motorcycle	30mph	60mph	70mph	70mph
Cars towing caravans	30	50	60	60
Buses and coaches	30	50	60	70
Goods vehicles ≤ 7·5t	30	50	60	70
Goods vehicles ≥ 7·5t	30	40	50	60

2003 Department of Transport figures indicate the following levels of speeding:

Type of road · % who speed	cars	motorbikes	LGVs	buses
Single carriageway	9%	22%	10%	23%
Dual carriageway	50	50	43	39
Motorway	57	59	51	4

—————————— DRIVING PENALTY POINTS ——————————

Drivers who accrue twelve or more points over a three-year period face automatic disqualification. Endorsements for drinking, drugs, or causing death by careless driving remain on the licence for eleven years from the date of conviction. Those involving dangerous driving resulting in disqualification remain for 4 years from the date of conviction. Below are some offences and the penalty points they incur:

Code	offence	points
CD40	causing death by careless driving when unfit through drink	3–11
CU40	using a vehicle with defective steering	3
DD60	manslaughter or culpable homicide while driving	3–11
DD80	causing death by dangerous driving	3–11
DR70	failing to provide specimen for breath test	4
LC50	driving after a licence has been revoked on medical grounds	3–6
MS10	leaving a vehicle in a dangerous position	3
MS50	motor racing on the highway	3–11
UT50	aggravated taking of a vehicle	3–11

—————————— CAR COLOUR AND SAFETY ——————————

Research published in the *British Medical Journal* [BMJ 2003;327:1455–56] proposed a correlation between the colour of your car and your likelihood of being involved in a car accident. Sue Furness, from Auckland University, led the research team analysing car accidents in New Zealand over a 15-month period in 1998–99. The research indicated that SILVER cars were the safest, being involved in 50% fewer accidents than WHITE cars. BROWN, BLACK and GREEN cars showed an increased risk of accident, whereas the risk of serious injury arising from driving a YELLOW, RED, or BLUE car was not significantly higher than that of driving a WHITE car.

DRIVING AGES

In 1930 the minimum driving age was set at 17. The current age regulations are:

<14 years.............................. must wear a seat-belt in the back of a car
14 .... can drive electrically assisted pedal cycles
16 ....can drive mopeds; small agricultural tractors; small mowing machines
16........can apply for a provisional licence (up to 3 mths before 17th birthday)
17 ....can learn to drive; take driving test
17 ....can drive motorbikes up to 125cc; cars; large agricultural tractors
17 ....can drive small road rollers; motor tricycles and quadricycles
18..can drive lorries ≤7500kg
21.....can drive large road-roller; mini-bus; bus; any motorbike; tracked vehicles
21 ....can supervise a learner driver if a full licence holder for min. of 3 years
70........................provisional or full licence lasts until your 70th birthday†

† At 70 you must apply to renew your driving licence, declaring any medical problems which may hamper the ability to drive safely (this is currently under review and, in future, a medical exam may be required). If approved, the licence will be renewed for three years. Please note: in Northern Ireland, an 18-year-old may drive a minibus with 9–16 passenger seats, towing a trailer of up to 750kg, but *only* if they are a member of the armed forces. [For further age-related data see p.85.]

PETROL PRICES

The cost of petrol rose dramatically in 2005, catalysed initially by the security situation in the Middle East and then, in September, by Hurricane Katrina [see p.21]. In August 2005 the average UK price for unleaded petrol hit 90p/l for the first time; in mid-September some charged >£1/l. At the time of writing, pressure was mounting on the Treasury to cut the taxes that make-up *c.*70% of petrol's cost.

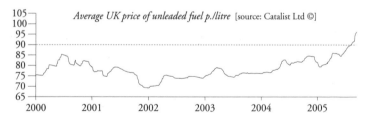

Average UK price of unleaded fuel p./litre [source: Catalyst Ltd ©]

DRIVING TEST PASS RATE

[Source: DSA]	1999–2000	2000–01	2001–02	2002–03
Tests conducted	1,130,000	1,015,000	1,216,000	1,344,000
Male passes	256,000	229,000	273,000	300,000
Female passes	240,000	214,000	254,000	283,000
Total passes	496,000	443,000	527,000	583,000

——————— NUMBER PLATES ———————

Since the 1903 Motor Car Act, all UK vehicles must be registered, and display number plates. Plates fitted since September 2001 must comply with the 2001 Road Vehicles Regulations which state that: number plates must have black lettering on a white plate at the front, and a yellow plate at the rear; the background of the plate must be 'reflex reflecting', but the lettering should not; and the lettering must be of the mandatory font to make the plate easier to read and remember. The character dimensions of modern British number plates are:

Character height 79mm	Space between groups 33mm
Width (except figure 1 or letter l)... 50mm	Top, bottom & side margins... 11mm
Stroke 14mm	Space between vertical lines.... 19mm
Space between characters....... 11mm	[Source: DVLA]

The first two letters of a number plate indicate where the vehicle was registered (e.g. OA–OY for Oxford); the following two numbers indicate the age of the car. Plate numbering is changed twice a year: March-registered plates display the last two digits of the year (e.g. 06 for 2006); those registered in September add fifty (e.g. 2006 would be 56). The final three letters are generated randomly to make each plate unique. (Letters I and Q are excluded, as are letter combinations which might be offensive). Vehicles constructed prior to 1973 may display traditional 'black and white' style plates and are exempted from using the mandatory font, as long as the characters are easy to read. Since September 2001, vehicles registered in the UK may carry 'Euro-plates' showing the EU flag and the GB country code.

——————— TIME TAKEN TO TRAVEL TO WORK ———————

The table below shows the average time taken to travel to work in different areas:

| Area | % of journeys to work by journey length | | | | average time |
	<20min	<40min	<60min	<90min	mins
North East	49	87	95	99	21
Greater Manchester	41	80	91	98	25
Merseyside	46	84	94	99	23
Yorkshire	46	84	93	98	23
East Midlands	50	86	94	98	22
West Midlands	48	83	93	98	23
Eastern	52	85	93	98	22
London	21	50	69	90	42
South East	49	83	92	97	24
South West	54	86	94	98	21
England	45	79	89	97	26
Wales	54	88	95	98	21
Scotland	49	82	92	98	24

[Source: Labour Force Survey, ONS · Crown © · 2003]

———————— HISTORY OF SPEED ON THE ROADS ————————

1861 ...... Locomotive Act 1861 imposed a 12mph speed limit on steam vehicles
1865 ...... speed limit of 2mph introduced in cities and villages; 4mph elsewhere
1865 ... pedestrian required to carry a red warning flag 60yds in front of vehicles
1878 .... red flag became optional, and distance reduced to 20 yds
1894 .... first motor car driven on a public highway
1895 .... speed limit raised to 14mph
1896 .... 1st speeding ticket issued to W. Arnold for going 8mph in a 2mph zone
1903 .... speed limit raised to 20mph; fines for reckless driving and speeding
1930 ...... 20mph speed limit scrapped; new limits dependent on class of vehicle
1930 .... no speed limit for vehicles carrying fewer than 7 passengers
1935 .... 30mph limit re-introduced in urban areas
1940 .. night-time 40mph limit imposed to counteract large number of accidents
1965 .... 70mph limit imposed on unrestricted roads, including motorways
1973 .. temporary speed limit of 50mph to conserve fuel during Egypt/Israel war
1978 .... national speed limit set at 60mph; motorways at 70mph
1988 .... all coaches to have 70mph speed limiters fitted by 1992
1991 .... in busy urban areas 20mph zones introduced to reduce accidents
1992 .... speed cameras introduced at permanent sites
1994 .... 65mph speed limit for buses and coaches; 56mph for HGVs

———————————— DRINK-DRIVING ————————————

The blood-alcohol limit for driving varies widely across the European Union:

mg/100ml blood	Cyprus 90	France 50	Italy 50
Austria 50	Denmark 50	Germany 50	Poland 20
Belgium 50	Estonia 20	Ireland 80	Spain 50

The UK legal blood-alcohol limit for driving is 80mg of alcohol/100ml blood.

Number of breath tests [2002] 570,000
Convictions for drink-driving [2002] .... ♂ 72,444 · ♀ 8,989
Total drink-drive accidents per 100,000 licence holders 34
Total casualties in accidents involving illegal alcohol levels [2003] 19,010
Total deaths in accidents involving illegal alcohol levels [2003] 560
Percentage of all road deaths resulting from drink-driving 16%
Percentage of convicted drink-drivers who are male 90%
Percentage of drink-drivers with blood-alcohol >150mg 50%
Percentage of drink-drivers with previous convictions for other offences 40%
Peak age for drink-driving 27
Percentage of convicted drink-drivers under age of 33 .... 52%
Hour in which most breath tests failed 23:00
Day of the week most breath tests failed .... Sunday (8·1% tests failed)

[Source: Institute of Alcohol Studies 2005, Home Office; ROSPA; DfT · see also p.102]

PEDESTRIAN CROSSINGS

There are five types of pedestrian crossing in use across Great Britain – they are:

ZEBRA CROSSINGS · marked by black and white stripes across the road, and with amber flashing 'Belisha'[†] beacons. The Highway Code states that drivers must give way when a pedestrian has moved onto a ZEBRA crossing.

PELICAN CROSSINGS (PEdestrian LIght CONtrolled) · traffic lights that have a red/green man showing when it is safe to cross. Pedestrians press a button to indicate their desire to cross: when it is safe to do so the green man illuminates and a beeping sound is emitted. When the green man flashes, pedestrians are warned that there is not enough time for them to reach the other side safely.

PUFFIN CROSSINGS (Pedestrian User-Friendly INtelligent) · similar to the PELICAN crossing, but without the flashing green man and with sensors to cancel unnecessary crossing demands.

TOUCAN CROSSINGS · designed to be used by pedestrians and cyclists, and thus generally found on cycle-paths. When it is safe to cross, a green bicycle lights up next to the green man.

PEGASUS CROSSINGS · TOUCAN crossings for horse-riders, with a red/green horse light and buttons set higher up to enable riders to access them without having to dismount.

South Australia has developed new crossings primarily designed to help children. They too have employed an animal theme, and their crossings are called: EMU, KOALA, and WOMBAT.

† Belisha-beacons were named after the Minister for Transport, Leslie Hore-Belisha who introduced them in 1934, and forever became associated with their gently flashing golden orbs.

TRANSPORT INFLATION

CAR *cost of medium-size car and a litre of petrol*	TRAIN *standard open return, London–Manchester*	BUS *cost of a single fare in London*
1975.....£11,970 · 85p	1975.................£30	1975................45p
2005.....£10,895 · 86p	2005..............£187	2005..............£1·20

[Prices have been adjusted to today's values · Source: DfT]

YELLOW LINES

A DOUBLE YELLOW LINE means no parking or waiting at any time. A SINGLE YELLOW LINE means that there is no parking or waiting at the times indicated by nearby signage. A DOUBLE YELLOW STRIPE on the kerb means no loading at any time. A SINGLE YELLOW STRIPE on the kerb means no loading at the times shown. RED LINES indicate areas where no stopping or loading is permitted. In Conservation Areas yellow lines may be substituted with a subtle shade of cream.

——————— CAR OWNERSHIP BY NAME ———————

An analysis by Churchill Insurance of their database in March 2005 indicated the likelihood of driving certain makes and models of car by various first names:

Those driving a	*are most likely to be called*
Ford Fiesta	Anthony, Gareth, Dennis · Audrey, Kate, Laura
Ford Escort	Justin, Wayne, Darren · Tanya, Tracey, Mandy
Nissan Micra	Dorothy, Joyce, Doreen
Peugeot 206	Rebecca, Samantha, Kerry
Renault Megane	Gavin, Nigel, Douglas · Mandy, Fiona, Kathryn
Vauxhall Astra	Carl, Lee, Gary · Jackie, Janine, Maxine
Vauxhall Corsa	Scott, Craig, Jason · Leanne, Rachel, Sheila
VW Golf	Jonathan, Daniel, Nicholas
VW Polo	Katherine, Emma, Hayley

——————— WORLDWIDE ROAD RISKS ———————

Country	population	no. of cars	pedestrian deaths	car deaths
France	60m	29·2m	626	3,709
Germany	83m	44·7m	812	3,774
Ireland	4m	1·5m	64	172
Japan	128m	54·5m	2,739	2,230
Netherlands	16m	6·9m	97	483
Spain	42m	18·7m	787	3,211
UK	60m	27m	802	1,861
USA	291m	131m	4,749	19,460

[Source: International Road Traffic and Accident Database · figures for 2003]

——— LONDON CONGESTION CHARGE & TOLL ROADS ———

GENERAL INFORMATION	HOW TO PAY
Current price .... £8 per day	Online .... www.cclondon.com
Operating times .... 7am – 6:30pm	Phone.................. 0845 900 1234
Days of operation........... Mon – Fri	Text message (SMS) 81099
The £8 charge must be paid by 10pm	*or* in shops and petrol stations
on the day of travel; if paid from	displaying the CC logo. You can
10pm–midnight, it rises by £2.	pay up to 90 days in advance.

Consultation is currently taking place on a westward extension of the charging zone. In February 2005, 74% of Edinburgh residents voted against a proposed £2 rush-hour congestion charge. Throughout Britain 15 bridges or tunnels charge a toll, ranging from 50p at the Clifton Suspension Bridge to £4·80 for the Severn Bridge. Since 2003 a toll has been in place on part of the M6 (Junction 3a–11a). In daytime it costs £2·50 for a motorbike, £3·50 for a car, and £7 for a van/coach/HGV; at night it is £1 cheaper.

MAJOR UK AIRPORTS

Airport	phone	website	passengers (m)	code
Birmingham	08707 335 511	bhx.co.uk	8·8	BHX
Bristol	0870 1212 747	bristolairport.co.uk	4·6	BRS
Cardiff	01446 711 111	cardiffairportonline.com	1·9	CWL
East Midlands	0871 919 9000	eastmidlandsairport.com	4·4	EMA
Edinburgh	0870 040 0007	baa.co.uk	8·0	EDI
Gatwick	0870 000 2468	baa.co.uk	31·4	LGW
Glasgow	0870 040 0008	baa.co.uk	8·6	GLA
Heathrow	0870 000 0123	baa.co.uk	67·1	LHR
Liverpool	0870 750 8484	liverpooljohnlennonairport.com	3·4	LPL
London City	020 7646 0088	londoncityairport.com	1·7	LCY
Luton	01582 405 100	london-luton.co.uk	7·5	LTN
Manchester	0161 489 3000	manchesterairport.co.uk	21·0	MAN
Stanstead	0870 000 0303	baa.co.uk	21·0	STN

[Source: Civil Aviation Authority · Passenger figures 2004]

CUSTOMS ALLOWANCES

WITHIN THE EU

Passengers may bring back unlimited amounts of EU duty-paid tobacco and alcohol, so long as they can prove it is for their own consumption or a gift for family or friends. They cannot bring back goods for commercial purposes. Bringing back more than the following large quantities may cause questions to be asked at customs:

3,200 .... cigarettes
400 .... cigarillos
200 .... cigars
3kg .... smoking tobacco
110 litres .... beer
10 litres .... spirits
90 litres .... wine
20 litres .... fortified wine

The above are just guidelines based on EU regulations; no absolute limits exist.

OUTSIDE THE EU

Passengers may bring the following into the UK for their own use without paying UK tax or duty; if over the allowances then goods must be declared and tax paid. It is against the law to fail to declare excess goods:

200 .... cigarettes
or 100 .... cigarillos
or 50 .... cigars
or 250g .... tobacco
60cc .... perfume
2 litres .... still table-wine
250cc .... *eau de toilette*
1 litre .... spirits/liqueurs >22%
or 2 litres ...... fortified/sparkling wine
£145 worth* .... all other goods

*Items >£145: duty must be paid on full value, not just the difference. This figure is under review. <17 cannot bring in tobacco or alcohol.

According to HM Revenue & Customs, in 2000–1 cigarette smuggling cost the British taxpayer over £2,800m in lost taxes. In the same year over 2·8b black-market cigarettes, and more than 10,000 cars, lorries, and vans used by illegal smugglers were impounded.

──────────── AIRLINES ────────────

Airline	contact	phone	code†	callsign
Aer Lingus	aerlingus.com	0845 084 4444	EIN	Shamrock
Aeroflot	aeroflot.com	0207 355 2233	AFL	Aeroflot
Air Canada	aircanada.com	0871 220 1111	ACA	Air Canada
Air France	airfrance.com	0870 142 4343	AFR	Airfrans
Air India	airindia.com	020 8745 1000	AIC	Air India
Alitalia	alitalia.co.uk	0870 544 8259	AZA	Alitalia
American	aa.com	0845 7789 789	AAL	American
BA	britishairways.com	0870 850 9850	BAW	Speedbird
bmi	flybmi.com	0870 6070 555	BMA	Midland
Cathay Pacific	cathaypacific.com	020 8834 8888	CPA	Cathay
Continental	continental.com	0845 607 6760	COA	Continental
Delta	delta.com	0800 414 767	DAL	Delta
Easyjet	easyjet.com	0905 821 0905	EZY	Easy
El Al	elal.co.il	020 7957 4100	ELY	El Al
Emirates	emirates.com	0870 243 2222	UAE	Emirates
Iberia	iberiaairlines.co.uk	0870 609 0500	IBE	Iberia
KLM	klm.com	0870 243 0541	KLM	KLM
Lufthansa	lufthansa.co.uk	0870 8377 747	DLH	Lufthansa
Qantas	qantas.com.au	0845 7747 767	QFA	Qantas
Ryanair	ryanair.com	0871 246 0000	RYR	Ryanair
SAS	scandinavian.net	0870 60727727	SAS	Scandinavian
Singapore	singaporeair.co.uk	0870 6088886	SIA	Singapore
United	unitedairlines.co.uk	0845 8444777	UAL	United
Virgin	virgin-atlantic.com	0870 3802007	VIR	Virgin

† Assigned by the International Civil Aviation Organisation (ICAO).

──────────── BAGGAGE ALLOWANCES & HAZARDS ────────────

Most airlines for transatlantic flights will permit two pieces of luggage, each weighing <32kg and with total dimensions ≤158cm in Economy Class. For European flights, 1 bag ≤20kg is the norm. No airline allows any one piece of luggage to weigh >32kgs. Hand-baggage is generally acceptable at ≤10kg but should not exceed 115cm in total dimension. Since these regulations are subject to change – and will often be more generous for business and First Class travellers – passengers are advised to check before packing. The following items cannot be carried in your hand-baggage: toy or replica guns; catapults; household cutlery; knives; razor blades; tradesmen's tools; darts; scissors; knitting needles; corkscrews; large sporting bats, such as snooker or pool cues; hypodermic syringes (unless a genuine medical need can be proven). The following dangerous articles are NOT ALLOWED WHATSOEVER: compressed gas cylinders; flammable material; poisons; radioactive material; oxidising materials; organic peroxides; briefcases with installed alarm devices; firearms; explosives; fireworks; flares; infectious substances; 'strike anywhere' matches; disposable lighters; acids; alkalis; and corrosives.

EUROPEAN AIRLINES & LOSING LUGGAGE

Airline	missing bags/1000 passengers
KLM	22·3
Austrian	18·8
Lufthansa	18·6
British Airways	18·3
TAP Portugal	16·0
Luxair	15·8
bmi	15·1
Air France	14·9
Cyprus Airways	13·8
Alitalia	12·9
Polish Airlines	12·5
Croatia Airlines	12·0
Czech Airlines	11·9
Finnair	11·9

On average 85% of missing bags are returned
to passengers within 48 hours.

[Assoc. European Airlines Jan–Mar 2005]

EU AIRLINE COMPENSATION

In February 2005, the European Union introduced compensation rules for airline passengers affected by cancellations, overbooking, or delays. The rules apply to all European airlines, and any flight leaving from a European airport. Airlines are exempt if flights are blighted by 'extraordinary circumstances', though what exactly these might be remains unclear. It is feared that the added expense of compensation payments, as tabulated below, may cause the cost of tickets to rise:

Length of journey	example from UK	delay	compensation
up to 1,500km	Paris; Amsterdam	≥2 hours	€250
1,500km–3,500km	Lisbon; Moscow	≤3 hours	€200
1,500km–3,500km	Tangiers; Reykjavik	≥3 hours	€400
>3,500km	New York; Tel Aviv	≤4 hours	€300
>3,500km	Doha; Hobart	≥4 hours	€600

THE MONTREAL CONVENTION

The Montreal Convention, which came into force within the European Union [EU] on 28 June 2004, replaced the Warsaw Convention (1929). The Montreal Convention establishes the liability of airlines for passengers and their luggage. The previous Warsaw Convention was criticised for derisory lost-luggage payments that were calculated according to the weight of luggage rather than the value of contents. Yet for many years a new international agreement could not be reached. The Montreal Convention has thus far been ratified by 37 countries, including the USA, and will apply on UK flights where the destination country is a signatory. The Convention sets a maximum payment of *c.*£850 per passenger for lost, damaged, or delayed baggage. In line with rules applicable to all EU airlines, the Convention allows for unlimited airline liability for death or bodily injury in the event of an accident; however, the maximum compensation payment has been established at *c.*£85,000 irrespective of an airline's culpability. A limit of £3,525 per passenger exists for travellers who have incurred costs resulting from airline delays. [See also: www.caa.co.uk]

——————— UNDERGROUND, LIGHT-RAIL, & TRAM ———————

Location	type	opened	lines	stations	passengers (m)	volts DC
London	U	1863	12	275	7,367	630
Blackpool	TL	1885	1	124	11	550
Glasgow	U	1896	1	15	43	600
Tyne & Wear	LR	1980	2	58	284	1,500
Docklands	LR	1987	1	34	235	750
Manchester	LR	1992	3	37	169	750
Sheffield	TL	1994	3	48	42	750
West Midlands	LR	1999	1	23	54	750
Croydon	TL	2000	3	38	105	750
Nottingham	TL	2004	1	23	2	750

Underground · Light Rail · Tram Link · [Passengers numbers per passenger km · DfT]

——————— RAILWAY TRACK LENGTH ———————

The National UK Rail Network is 16,652km long, almost half of what it was in 1928 when the network was at its peak of 32,565km. At present, 5,167km of the network is electrified, and 15,042km of track is currently open to passenger traffic.

——————— THOMAS THE TANK ENGINE ———————

Thomas the Tank Engine was created by the Reverend W. Awdry in 1945. He wrote twenty-six volumes about the charismatic engine before his son Christopher took over and added forty more books to the series. Below are tabulated the names of some of the trains and carriages – along with their characteristic colours:

Thomas............blue	Percy...............green	Diesel..............black
Henry..............green	James.................red	Edward ....blue
Donald & Douglas ..... black	Gordon ....blue	Bill & Ben ....orange
	Toby...............brown	Daisy ....green
Duck (Montague) ... green	Mavis ....black	Duncan...........yellow

——————— TRACK GAUGE ———————

Railway track gauge is the distance between two rails. In 1825, George Stephenson pioneered the Stockton & Darlington Railway, arbitrarily choosing a gauge of 4'8½". Isambard Brunel argued for a wider gauge, and used what became known as BROAD GAUGE (7') on the Great Western Railway. In search of standardisation, Parliament introduced the 1846 Gauge Act which enshrined Stephenson's 4'8½" gauge as STANDARD GAUGE (1,435mm). STANDARD GAUGE is now used across 64% of the world, including Great Britain, North America and all of Western Europe except Ireland (1,600mm), Spain (1,674mm) and Portugal (1,665mm).

—————— TRAIN PUNCTUALITY ——————

Regional	% trains on time
Island Line	97·5
Merseyrail	94·2
Wessex Trains	85·4
Gatwick Express	84·7
First ScotRail	83·1
Arriva Trains Wales	80·8
TPE	74·6
Central Trains	73·1
Northern Rail	n/a

Long-distance	% trains on time
ONE (InterCity)	84·3
First Great Western	79·6
GNER	77·5
Midland Mainline	88·3
Virgin Cross Country	77·8
Virgin West Coast	72·1

London & SE	% trains on time
c2c	93·2
Chiltern Railways	92·5
ONE	89·0
Silverlink	84·2
Southern	81·8
South Eastern Trains	84·2
South West Trains	81·4
First Great Western Link	82·9
Thameslink	83·9
WAGN	89·2

Long-distance trains are deemed to be 'on time' if they arrive within ten minutes of timetabled arrival time; London & regional trains are 'on time' if they arrive within five minutes of their timetable. [Source: SRA Jan–Mar 2005]

—————— EUROSTAR JOURNEY TIMES ——————

From Ashford	destination	from Waterloo
1h 55m	PARIS	2h 35m
1h 40m	BRUSSELS	2h 20m
57m	LILLE	1h 40m
2h	DISNEYLAND PARIS	2h 50m
5h 20m	AVIGNON	6h 10m

eurostar.com · 08705 186 186

—————— LONDON STATION DESTINATION GUIDE ——————

Charing Cross	*serves* South & South-east
Euston	Midlands, North-east of England & Scotland
King's Cross	Midlands, North of England & Scotland
Liverpool Street	East of England & East Anglia · Stanstead Express
Paddington	West of England & Wales · Heathrow Express
Marylebone	the Chilterns
Victoria	South & South-east · Gatwick Express
Waterloo	South of England · Eurostar

www.nationalrail.co.uk/planmyjourney · According to the British Transport Police, Victoria Station had the worst crime rate in 2004, with 141 incidents of violent crime: Waterloo had 93; London Bridge, 80; Liverpool Street, 68; and King's Cross had 57.

———————————————VACCINATION ADVICE———————————————

Wherever the destination, it is usually prudent to seek advice from a doctor or travel clinic on which vaccinations to obtain. Some general vaccination guidance follows. For all areas it is advisable to have these basic vaccinations: Polio, Tetanus, and Diphtheria. For areas where the standards of cleanliness and hygiene may be low: Hepatitis A and Typhoid. For infected areas: anti-Malarial tablets and Yellow Fever jab (a certificate proving this vaccination may be needed to enter some countries). Other vaccinations that may be required before visiting certain areas include: Meningococcal Meningitis, Rabies, Tick-borne or Japanese Encephalitis, Hepatitis B, Tuberculosis, and Measles/MMR. More information: www.dh.gov.uk.

———————————————TOURISM FIGURES———————————————

British abroad	to or from	visiting Britain
4·1m	North America	4·0m
45·1m	EU Europe	14·8m
5·6m	non-EU Europe	2·4m
6·6m	other countries	3·5m
61·4m	TOTAL WORLD	24·7m

[Source: Travel Trends, ONS · figures are for annual visits 2003]

———————————————UK HOLIDAYS SPENT ABROAD———————————————

Where Brits go (%)	1971	1981	1991	2001	2003
Spain	34	22	21	28	30
France	16	27	26	18	18
Greece	5	7	8	8	7
USA	1	6	7	6	5
Italy	9	6	4	4	5
Portugal	3	3	5	4	4

[Source: International Passenger Survey, ONS · Crown © · only most popular countries listed]

———————————————E111 & EHIC———————————————

If a UK citizen falls ill or has an accident while abroad, carrying an E111 form guarantees medical treatment for free or at a reduced cost. Only state-provided treatment is covered (up to a similar level received by residents). The E111 is only valid in the 25 states of the European Union [see p.264], Iceland, Liechtenstein, Norway and Switzerland. E111s are being phased out from 1 January 2006 and will be replaced by the European Health Insurance Card (EHIC), which will be issued from September 2005. Those who applied for an E111 form in 2005 will automatically be sent an EHIC when their form expires on 31 December 2005.

PASSENGER-FERRY DESTINATIONS

Port	destinations
Dover	Boulogne; Calais; Dunkirk
Harwich	Cuxhaven; Esbjerg; Hook of Holland
Holyhead	Dun Laoghaire; Dublin
Hull	Zeebrugge; Rotterdam
Liverpool	Dublin
Newcastle	Amsterdam; Gothenburg; Kristiansand
Newhaven	Dieppe
Plymouth	Santander
Portsmouth	Bilbao; Cherbourg; Isle of Wight; Le Havre

THE RNLI

The *Royal National Lifeboat Institution* [RNLI] is a charity whose boats are manned by volunteer crews. They have 232 lifeboat stations and provide lifeguard services on 57 beaches. In 2004 the RNLI's activities included:

Launches	7,656
No. people rescued	7,507
People saved by RNLI lifeguards	53
Number of volunteer crew	4,500
Cost of launching each boat	£5,800
Busiest launch	Tower Pier, Thames

MARINE DISTRESS SIGNALS

Some of the internationally recognised marine distress signals:

Continuous sounding of any fog-signalling apparatus
Gun or other explosive device fired at intervals of a minute
Rockets or shells with red stars fired singly at short intervals
The spoken word 'MAYDAY' repeated where possible
Signalling SOS (··· ――― ···) in Morse code by any method
Displaying 'N C' (November, Charlie) in flags
Square flag with ball (or anything similar) above or below it
Flames on a vessel including a burning tar or oil barrel
Rocket parachute or hand flare showing a red light
Smoke signal giving off orange smoke
Raising and lowering arms outstretched to each side
Radiotelegraphy alarm · Dye marker
Orange-coloured canvas with black square and circle

LONGEST RIVERS IN BRITAIN

Country	river	length (miles)
England	THAMES	215
Wales	TOWY	64
Scotland	TAY	117
GB	SEVERN	220

[Source: Ordnance Survey · Crown ©]

————— UK'S UNESCO WORLD HERITAGE SITES —————

The *United Nations Educational, Scientific, and Cultural Organization* (UNESCO) seeks to encourage the worldwide identification, protection, and preservation of cultural and natural heritage considered to be of outstanding value to humanity. To this end, UNESCO has granted World Heritage Status to 788 sites across the globe. The following 23 are the World Heritage Sites in the United Kingdom:

Giant's Causeway† and Causeway coast (*added in* 1986)
Durham Castle and Cathedral (1986) · Ironbridge Gorge (1986)
Studley Royal Park inc. the ruins of Fountains Abbey (1986)
Stonehenge, Avebury and associated sites (1986)
Castles and town walls of King Edward in Gwynedd (1986)
St Kilda (1986, 2004) · Blenheim Palace (1987)
Westminster Palace, Westminster Abbey and St Margaret's Church (1987)
City of Bath (1987) · Hadrian's Wall (1987) · Tower of London (1988)
Canterbury Cathedral, St Augustine's Abbey and St Mary's Church (1988)
Old and new towns of Edinburgh (1995)
Maritime Greenwich (1997) · Heart of neolithic Orkney (1999)
Blaenavon industrial landscape (2000)
Saltaire (2001) · Dorset and East Devon coast (2001)
Derwent Valley mills (2001) · New Lanark (2001)
Royal Botanic Gardens, Kew (2003)
Liverpool's maritime mercantile city (2004)

† When Samuel Johnson was asked whether Giant's Causeway was worth seeing,
he is reported by James Boswell to have replied: 'Worth seeing? Yes. Worth going to see? No.'

————— WORLD HERITAGE SITES IN DANGER —————

War, natural disaster, pollution, unchecked urban sprawl and unregulated tourism all pose significant threats to some World Heritage Sites. Consequently, UNESCO classifies a number of World Heritage Sites in Danger to highlight their plight and encourage dialogue with host nations to find ways of protecting the sites. At present, 35 of 788 World Heritage sites are considered to be 'in danger', including:

Minaret and archaeological remains of Jam .... Afghanistan
Butrint .... Albania
Royal palaces of Abomey.. Benin
Okapi wildlife reserve.............................. Democratic Republic of Congo
Cologne Cathedral .... Germany
Bam and its cultural landscape .... Iran
Ashur (Qal'at Sherqat) .... Iraq
Timbuktu .... Mali
Kathmandu valley... Nepal
Rice terraces of the Philippine Cordilleras .... Philippines
Everglades National Park... USA

──────── NATIONAL TRAILS ────────

The Countryside Agency has designated 15 national trails that run *c.*2,500 miles across England and Wales. The routes are managed and maintained, and meander through some of the most beautiful natural landscapes in the British countryside:

Trail	location	average duration	miles
Cleveland Way	North Yorkshire	9 days	110
Cotswold Way	South-west England	7	102
Glyndwr's Way	Mid-Wales	9	132
Hadrian's Wall Path	North England	7	84
North Downs Way	South-east England	14	151
Offa's Dyke Path	England/Wales border	12	177
Peddars Way	Eastern England	8	93
Pembrokeshire Coast	South-west Wales	15	186
Pennine Bridleway†	Northern England	21–28	347
Ridgeway	Southern England	6	85
South Downs Way	Southern England	8	165
South West Coast	South-west England	56	630
Thames Path	Central England	14	184
Yorkshire Wolds Way	Yorkshire	5	127

† Only 120 miles of the route currently open, the rest should be available from 2006.

──────── THE COUNTRYSIDE CODE ────────

Sadly, the traditional *Countryside Code* was revised in 2004 in an attempt to reflect the introduction of new open-access rights brought about by the *Countryside and Rights of Way Act* (2000), and a perceived change in how the countryside is utilised. The absurdly banal 'improved' version of the traditional 12-point code reads thus:

Be safe – plan ahead and follow any signs
Leave gates and property as you find them
Protect plants and animals, and take your litter home
Keep dogs under close control
Consider other people

──────── CLEAN BEACHES ────────

The Blue Flag is awarded to beaches across Europe that are safe, clean, well looked after, and have water quality that meets European legislation. Below is listed the number of Blue Flags awarded in each region of the United Kingdom in 2005:

Wales 38	North East 5	Yorkshire 5
Scotland 6	South West 25	East of England 14
N. Ireland 8	South East 12	East Midlands 3

—————————— TOP BRITISH ATTRACTIONS ——————————

Free admission	*visits*	*Charged admission*	*visits*
Blackpool Pleasure Beach	6·2m	London Eye	3·7m
National Gallery, London	4·9m	Tower of London	2·1m
British Museum, London	4·8m	Legoland, Windsor	1·3m
Tate Modern, London	4·4m	Edinburgh Castle	1·2m
Natural History Museum	3·2m	Eden Project	1·2m
Science Museum	2·1m	Chester Zoo	1·0m
V&A Museum	2·0m	Kew Gardens	1·0m

[Source: Association of Leading Visitor Attractions · 2004]

————— VISITS TO BRITISH ATTRACTIONS BY MONTH —————

Jan	Feb	Mar	Apr	May	Jun	Jul	Aug	Sep	Oct	Nov	Dec
7%	7%	7%	9%	9%	8%	10%	12%	8%	8%	6%	8%

[Figures do not total due to rounding · Source: UK Tourism Survey]

————— WORLD'S TOP TOURIST DESTINATIONS —————

Country visited	*worldwide visitors (m)*		
France	75·0	United Kingdom	24·8
Spain	52·5	Austria	19·1
United States	40·0	Mexico	18·7
Italy	39·6	Germany	18·4
China	33·0	Canada	17·5

[World Tourism Organisation · 2003]

————————— TOURISM AWARDS —————————

Organised annually by *Visit Britain,* the *Enjoy England Excellence Awards* recognise the best tourist attractions across the country. The winners in 2005 included:

B&B	Holly Lodge, Norfolk
Business tourism	Costwold conference & training centre
Caravan holiday park	Shardaroba, Nottinghamshire
Hotel	The Samling, Cumbria
Large visitor attraction	Portsmouth Historic Dockyard & Beamish North of England Open Air Museum, County Durham
Outstanding customer service	Ann Stamper, National Maritime Museum
Small visitor attraction	Holkham Hall, Norfolk
Tourism website	lythhillhouse.com
Outstanding contribution to tourism	Duchess of Northumberland

WHEN IN ROME...

Some elementary etiquette for the world traveller:

SOUTH-EAST ASIA · outside of tourist resorts it is polite to dress modestly, especially when visiting holy sites or important buildings ❧ remove shoes before entering temples, mosques, pagodas, and private homes ❧ Buddhist monks are not allowed to have close contact with women, so do not stand or sit too close ❧ in most South-east Asian cultures the head is considered sacred, therefore it is very rude to touch another person's head ❧ feet are

offensive in Brazil

considered unclean, so avoid pointing them at any person or religious image ❧ as the left hand is used for personal hygiene it is impolite to shake hands or eat with it ❧ THAILAND · visitors are advised not to criticise the much-revered Thai royal family. The National Anthem is played daily in public spaces, like stations, and visitors should stand for its duration ❧ LAOS · it is considered taboo for women to sit on a roof (e.g. of a bus or boat) – Laotians believe that boats possess magical spirits who take offence at women sitting on their roofs; it is thought to portend bad luck for all aboard ❧ JAPAN · it is polite to remove your shoes on entering a home or restaurant ❧ bowing is the traditional Japanese greeting, though in a business context handshakes are common ❧ if giving a present in Japan do not use black, white, or blue wrapping paper as these colours are associated with funerals; present any gift with both hands ❧ INDIA · apart from shaking hands, strangers should avoid touching one another, especially with their feet

❧ a side-to-side sway of the head means 'yes' ❧ THE MIDDLE EAST · respect the area's religious practices; keep dress modest and remove your shoes when entering a home or mosque ❧ it is rude to show the soles of your shoes, and never place your feet on a chair or table ❧ a raised thumb is an insulting gesture ❧ SAUDI ARABIA · do not expect to be introduced to any veiled women ❧ men often hold hands in friendship ❧ when inviting Saudis to dine, ask a number of times, since it is considered polite to decline at least once before accepting ❧ OCEANIA ❧ FIJI · be cautious about admiring an object in someone's home, since they may feel obliged to give it to you ❧ LATIN AMERICA · personal body space is not as well defined as in Europe and people like to stand close ❧ it is considered aggressive to stand with your hands on your hips ❧ COLOMBIA · it is rude to yawn in public ❧ BRAZIL · forming an 'O' with finger and thumb is considered offensive ❧ squeezing one's earlobe between the thumb and index finger demonstrates approval. ❧ ARGENTINA · it is rude to point with a finger; indicate instead with your whole hand ❧ CHILE · hitting the open palm of the left hand with the clenched right fist is an obscene gesture ❧ AFRICA · remove your shoes before entering any mosque ❧ it is rude to point the sole of your shoe at another ❧ items should not be passed nor food consumed with the left hand, as it is the hand used for personal hygiene ❧ people may try to attract your attention by snapping their fingers or hissing ❧ RUSSIA · it is offensive to drop anything in the street.

—————— THE CHELSEA FLOWER SHOW ——————

The following gardens were awarded top prizes at the 2005 Chelsea Flower Show:

Best show garden..Royal Hospital Chelsea
Best chic garden................................... Marcus Barnett & Philip Nixon
Best city garden .... The Sunday Mirror/Domoney Ltd
Best courtyard garden............................... Kim Wilde & Richard Lucas
President's Award..Hillier Nurseries Ltd

—————— BRITAIN IN BLOOM ——————

The Royal Horticultural Society's (RHS) Britain in Bloom competition rewards entrants not only for their horticultural skill, but also for: the environmental sustainability of their entry, the regeneration of the local environment, and the community's involvement. The category winners of Britain in Bloom 2004 were:

Category	winner		
Large city	Stockport	Large village	Broughshane
City	Derby	Village	Appleton Wiske
Large town/small city (12–35K)	Perth	Small village	Sorn
Large town/small city (35–100K)	Bath	Urban regeneration	Coventry City
Town	Ilkley	Urban community	Dyce
Small town	Alness	Coastal resort A	St Ives & Carbis
		Coastal resort B	Bridlington

—————— LISTED BUILDINGS ——————

The Department of Culture, Media & Sport has a responsibility under the Planning Act (1990) to provide protection for buildings or areas of historical or architectural interest. Part of this responsibility involves listing buildings, which affords them some protection. England has *c.*500,000 listed buildings, 17,700 scheduled monuments, and 8,500 conservation areas. There are 3 grades of listing:

Grade I ....*buildings of exceptional interest*
Grade II* ....*particularly important buildings of more than special interest*
Grade II...................*of special interest, warranting every effort to preserve them*

The owners of listed buildings must apply for permission before they make any alterations to their property. There is a presumption in favour of preserving listed properties, especially Grade I. For further information see: www.culture.gov.uk

—————— GARDEN OF THE YEAR ——————

In 2004, the *Historic Houses Association – Christie's Garden of the Year Award*, which was established in 1984, was awarded to BORDE HILL GARDEN, Sussex.

SOME HOMES & GARDENS OF MERIT

ALNWICK CASTLE · Northumberland · 01665 510 777 · alnwickcastle.com — *second largest inhabited castle in England; lavish Renaissance interior*

ALTHORP · Northampton · 01604 770 107 · althorp.com — *owned by the Spencer family; the grounds enclose the grave of Princess Diana*

CASTLE HOWARD ARBORETUM · York · 01653 648 160 · kewatch.co.uk — *over 6,000 exotic and native plants in 150 acres of woodland*

BELVOIR CASTLE · Leicestershire · 01476 871 002 · belvoircastle.com — *epic vistas; spring, rose and statue gardens; fine furniture and paintings*

BLENHEIM PALACE · Oxfordshire · 08700 602 080 · blenheimpalace.com — *birthplace of Winston Churchill; pleasure garden and butterfly house*

BODNANT GARDEN · Conwy, Wales · 01492 650 460 · bodnantgarden.co.uk — *Italianate terraces; formal lawns; wooded valley; and wild garden*

CHATSWORTH · Derbyshire · 01246 582 240 · chatsworth.org — *spectacular waterworks; yew maze; displays of sculpture, tapestries and porcelain*

DRUMLANRIG CASTLE · Dumfries · 01848 331 555 · buccleuch.com — *collection of antique furniture; rose garden; arboretum; salmon & trout fishing*

EDEN PROJECT · Cornwall · 01726 811 911 · edenproject.com — *project to explore the relationship between people and plants, in giant conservatories*

HAMPTON COURT PALACE · Surrey · 0870 752 7777 · hrp.org.uk — *beautiful State apartments; formal gardens and maze; Tudor kitchens*

HATFIELD HOUSE · Hertfordshire · 01707 217 010 · hatfield-house.co.uk — *armour, paintings, tapestries and an antique dutch organ*

HERGEST CROFT GARDENS · Herefordshire · 01544 230 160 · hergest.co.uk — *ancient apple orchard; azalea garden; a fine Edwardian house*

HOLKER HALL & GARDENS · Cumbria · 015395 58328 — *part woodland, part formal; essentially Victorian in character; Lakeland Motor Museum*

HOUGHTON HALL · Norfolk · 01485 528 569 · houghtonhall.com — *home to Robert Walpole; museum of model soldiers; white deer park and peacocks*

INVEREWE GARDENS · Poolewe, Scotland · 01445 781 200 · nts.org.uk — *plants from around the world in situation overlooking Loch Ewe*

KENWOOD HOUSE · London · 020 7973 3893 — *beautiful neo-Classical house set in Hampstead Heath; fine collection of art and sculpture*

KEW ROYAL BOTANICAL GARDENS · Surrey · 020 8332 5655 · rbgkew.org.uk — *extensive gardens with plants from all over the world; glasshouses*

KINGSTON LACY HOUSE · Dorset · 01202 883 402 · nationaltrust.org.uk — *Old Masters including Titian and Brueghel; parkland walks; Iron-age hill-fort*

KNEBWORTH HOUSE · Hertfordshire 01438 812 661 · knebworthhouse.com — *Jacobean banqueting hall; Edwardian drawing-room; Gothic griffins*

LEEDS CASTLE · Kent · 01622 765 400 · leeds-castle.com — *banqueting halls; maze and underground grotto; open-air concerts in early summer*

LONGLEAT HOUSE · Wiltshire · 01985 844 400 · longleat.co.uk — *high-Elizabethan house set within parkland; formal gardens; safari park and mazes*

PENSHURST PLACE · Kent · 01892 870 307 · penshurstplace.com — *once home to Sir Philip Sidney; collection of porcelain and tapestries; walled garden*

SISSINGHURST CASTLE GARDEN · Kent · 01580 710 700 · nationaltrust.org.uk — *planted by Vita Sackville-West and Harold Nicolson*

SYON PARK · Middlesex · 020 8560 0881 · syonpark.co.uk — *gardens with ice house, 100 varieties of roses, and glass-domed conservatory*

WARWICK CASTLE · 0870 442 2000 · warwick-castle.co.uk — *first stones laid by William the Conqueror; includes public gardens and waxworks*

WILTON HOUSE · Wiltshire · 01722 746 722 · wiltonhouse.co.uk — *collections of Van Dyck and Reynolds; rose garden; boathouse; C19th Italian loggia*

WOBURN ABBEY · Bedfordshire · 01525 290 333 · woburnabbey.co.uk — *stately home set in a 3,000 acre deer park, with antiques centre*

——————— THE WORLD'S TOP TABLES ———————

Restaurant Magazine's 2005 survey of the world's finest tables listed the following:

The Fat Duck	Bray, UK	*Pierre Gagnaire*	Paris
El Bulli	Girona, Spain	*Per Se*	New York
French Laundry	California	*Tom Aikens*	London
Tetsuya's	Sydney	*Jean Georges*	New York
Gordon Ramsay	London	*St John*	London

——————— NEW UK MICHELIN STARS 2005 ———————

The *Michelin Guide* was first published in 1900 by the Michelin Tyre Company. A three-star rating system is employed on a deceptively simple set of criteria: [*] 'A very good restaurant in its category'; [**] 'Excellent cooking, worth a detour'; [***] 'Exceptional cuisine, worth a special trip'. In reality, the award of one Michelin star confers instant recognition; two stars confer fame; and three stars are the culinary equivalent of a Nobel prize. The following gained UK stars in 2005:

**	*Midsummer House*	Cambridge	01223 369 299
*	*Assaggi*	Chepstow Place, London, W2	020 7792 5501
*	*Bohemia*	St Helier, Jersey	01534 880 588
*	*Box Tree*	Ilkley, West Yorkshire	01943 608 484
*	*Drakes*	Ripley, Surrey	01483 224 777
*	*L'Enclume*	Cartmel, Cumbria	015395 36 362
*	*The Goose*	Britwell Salome, Oxfordshire	01491 612 304
*	*Jessica's*	Birmingham	0121 4550 999
*	*The Lygon Arms*	Broadway, Cotswolds	01386 852 255
*	*The New Angel*	Dartmouth, Devon	01803 839 425
*	*Rhodes Twenty Four*	Tower 42, London EC2	0207 8777 703
*	*The Samling*	Windermere, Cumbria	01539 431 922
*	*Sawyards*	Storrington, West Sussex	01903 742 331
*	*Simpson's*	Birmingham	0121 4543 434
*	*Sketch*	Conduit St., London, W1	0870 7774 488
*	*Umu*	Bruton Place, London, W1	020 74998 881
*	*Whatley Manor*	Malmesbury, Cotswolds	01666 822 888
*	*Yauatcha*	Broadwick St., London, W1	020 74948 888

Anybody can make you enjoy the first bite of a dish, but only a real chef can make you enjoy the last. — FRANÇOIS MINOT, Editor, *Michelin Guide*

——————— UK WINE IMPORTS ———————

Country	sales (£m)				
Australia	850·6	USA	483·4	Chile	213
France	686	Italy	355·9	[Source: AC Neilsen	
		South Africa	353·4	ScanTrack UK, 2004]	

──────── SCANIA'S EUROPEAN TRUCK STOP GUIDE ────────

The British roadside cafés that have made it into Scania's *Truck Stop* guide (2004):

Whitwood Truck Stop [nr J31 M62] .... *'well cooked food at competitive prices'*
Cabin Transport cafe [Faygate W.Sussex] .... *'charming Swiss alpine chalet'*
Stibbington Diner [nr A47 exit A1] .... *'jam roly-poly with custard'*
Night Owl [Alconbury A1/A14] .... *'classic real English breakfast'*

──────── EU PROTECTED FOOD NAME SCHEMES ────────

The EU *Protected Food Name Schemes* protect certain speciality foods from competition from inauthentic rivals. The three types of protection are as follows:

Protected Designation of Origin [PDO]	Protected Geographical Indication [PGI]	Traditional Speciality Guaranteed [TSG]
protects names used to describe foods which are prepared, produced and processed in a given area using traditional knowledge, e.g. Parma ham	*foods must be processed, prepared or produced in a specific geographical area, and may have merited a good reputation, e.g. Brioche Vendéenne*	*not geographically specific but based upon the traditional character of the food in its composition or production, e.g. Serrano ham*

Below are the UK protected food names from each of the categories:

Traditional farmfresh turkey [TSG]
Beacon Fell Lancs. cheese [PDO]
Bonchester cheese [PDO]
Buxton Blue cheese [PDO]
Dorset Blue cheese [PGI]
Dovedale cheese [PDO]
Exmoor Blue cheese [PGI]
Single Gloucester [PDO]
Swaledale (and ewes') cheese [PDO]
Teviotdale cheese [PGI]
West Country cheddar [PDO]
White Stilton, Blue Stilton [PDO]
Jersey Royal potatoes [PDO]

Orkney lamb and beef [PDO]
Scotch beef and lamb [PGI]
Shetland lamb [PDO]
Welsh beef and lamb [PGI]
Arbroath smokies [PGI]
Whitstable oysters [PGI]
Kentish (and strong) ale [PGI]
Newcastle brown ale [PGI]
Rutland bitter [PGI]
Cornish clotted cream [PDO]
Gloucestershire cider/perry [PGI]
Herefordshire cider/perry [PGI]
Worcestershire cider/perry [PGI]

──────── HARDEN'S TOP LONDON RESTAURANTS ────────

Harden's London Restaurant Guide is compiled from a survey of 8,000 diners who visited 92,000 establishments across the capital. The top tables in the 2005 were:

Chez Bruce	*J. Sheekey*	*La Trompette*
The Ivy	*Le Caprice*	*Hakkasan*
The Wolseley	*Gordon Ramsay*	*Nobu*

—————————— TOY OF THE YEAR ——————————

The Toy of the Year Award is presented every January by the Toy Retailers Association. The award is decided by strong high street sales and the 'star quality' of a toy. The prize generally reflects the trend for the most popular Christmas toy.

2004	Robosapien	1984	Masters of the Universe
2003	Beyblades	1983	Star Wars
2002	Beyblades	1982	Star Wars
2001	Bionicles	1981	Rubik's Cube
2000	Teksta	1980	Rubik's Cube
1999	Furby Babies	1979	Legoland Space kits
1998	Furby	1978	Combine Harvester
1997	Teletubbies	1977	Playmobil Playpeople
1996	Barbie	1976	Peter Powell kites
1995	POGS	1975	Lego Basic set
1994	Power Rangers	1974	Lego Family set
1993	Thunderbird's Tracey Island	1973	Mastermind board game
1992	WWF Wrestlers	1972	Plasticraft modelling kits
1991	Nintendo Game Boy	1971	Katie Kopykat writing doll
1990	Teenage Mutant Turtles	1970	Sindy
1989	Sylvanian Families	1969	Hot Wheels cars
1988	Sylvanian Families	1968	Sindy
1987	Sylvanian Families	1967	Spirograph
1986	Transformers	1966	Action Man
1985	Transformers	1965	James Bond die-cast car

—————————— MOST POPULAR SWEETS ——————————

1966	1988	2004
Mars Bar	Mars Bar	Dairy Milk
Dairy Milk	Kit Kat	Wrigley's Extra
Wrigley's Gum	Dairy Milk	Maltesers
Milky Way	Twix	Galaxy
Polos	Yorkie	Mars Bar

[Source: The Guardian Weekend Magazine]

—————————— SCOUBIDOU ——————————

Scoubidou are 3ft-long garish coloured plastic cords from which children fashion bracelets and key-rings. They proved the low-fi toy craze of 2005, selling over a million packs a week. The strings have been sold on the Continent for many years and are said to be named after the fruit-related song *Scoubidou* by Sacha Distel. (Distel's fans created bracelets out of wire insulators). Scoubidou were brought to the UK by Amanda Miles who imported 100,000 packs from Holland after her sisters fell in love with the toys abroad and were unable to buy them at home.

CRUFTS BEST IN SHOW 2005

The 2005 Best In Show was won by Norfolk terrier *Cracknor Cause Celebre* (or *Coco* to her friends) handled by Peter Green. She won an impressive prize of £100.

PREVIOUS BEST IN SHOW WINNING BREEDS

'04............ *Whippet*	'01 .... *Basenji*	'98 .... *Welsh terrier*
'03............ *Pekingese*	'00 .... *Kerry blue terrier*	'97 ...... *Yorkshire terrier*
'02.............. *Poodle*	'99............ *Irish setter*	'96 .... *Cocker spaniel*

MOST POPULAR PEDIGREE DOG BREEDS

Breed	No. registered	
Labrador Retriever 35,978	English Springer Spaniel 12,741
German Shepherd..............20,953	Cavalier King Charles..........12,702
West Highland Terrier 15,131	Boxer...........................9,612
Golden Retriever 14,803	Yorkshire Terrier 8,818
Cocker Spaniel 14,117	Staffordshire Bull Terrier 8,563

[Source: The Kennel Club]

LABRADOODLES

The Labradoodle is a relatively new breed of dog that has become popular among those seeking an 'allergy-friendly' pet. As might be guessed, Labradoodles are a Labrador/Poodle cross and, as such, do not have a breed standard recognised by the Kennel Club. The dogs were first bred in Australia as assistance dogs for people with asthma or severe allergies, since their coats do not moult. At present, breeding programmes are still in development, and Labradoodle appearance can be slightly unpredictable. However, the dogs generally have woolly or curly coats, and come in a range of colours and sizes. Not to be outdone, Americans have begun to breed Golden Retrievers with Poodles – creating the splendidly named Goldendoodle.

PET OWNERSHIP

Pet	% own				
Dog................23·4	Goldfish..............3·9	Tropical fish ....2·4
Cat.................21·4	Budgerigar ....3·6	Guinea pig...........1·6
Rabbit...............9·3	Hamster..............3·2	Canary...............0·8
	Other bird ....2·6	[Source: petplanet.co.uk]

MOST POPULAR PET NAMES

DOGS.................*Sam; Spot; Pip; Duke; Piper; Max; Charlie; Rocky; Zak; Tiny*
BITCHES...............*Trixie; Polly; Jessie; Lucy; Bonnie; Cassie; Daisy; Heidi; Susie*
CATS............*Sooty; Tigger; Lucy; Smokey; Charlie; Smudge; Thomas; Sam; Misty*
[Source: petplanet.co.uk]

Money

For the love of money is the root of all evil: which while some coveted after,
they have erred from the faith, and pierced themselves through with many sorrows.
— I TIMOTHY 6:10

————— MONEY IN CIRCULATION —————

Note	featured personality	notes issued in 2005	size mm	circulation value 2005
£5	Elizabeth Fry	107m	135x70	£1,054m
£10	Charles Darwin	298m	142x75	£5,670m
£20	Sir Edward Elgar	318m	149x80	£21,649m
£50	Sir John Houblon†	12m	156x85	£6,082m
Others‡	—	—	—	£960m
Total	—	735m	—	£35,416m

† The first Governor of the Bank of England (1694–7); also Lord Mayor of London (1695).
‡ Includes higher-value notes used for internal transactions. [Source: Bank of England]

Coin	issued in 2004	
GOLD · Sovereign	28,821	
Half Sovereign	32,479	
SILVER · 4p Maundy	1,611	
3p Maundy	1,611	
2p Maundy	1,611	
1p Maundy	1,611	
NICKEL BRASS · £2†	13,904,500	
£1	37,286,000	
CUPRO-NICKEL · £5	1,205,158	
50p†	38,478,000	
20p	96,551,250	
10p	77,601,000	
5p	222,606,000	
BRONZE · 2p†	265,571,000	
1p	530,110,000	

† Includes special editions
[Source: Royal Mint]

————— LEGAL TENDER —————

Notes ... any sum [England & Wales only]	20p	any sum ≤ £10
£2	any sum	10p	any sum ≤ £5
£1	any sum	5p	any sum ≤ £5
50p	any sum ≤ £10	2p	any sum ≤ 20p
25p (Crown)	any sum ≤ £10	1p	any sum ≤ 20p

The meaning of 'legal tender' is somewhat complex. It is defined as a method of payment that may not legally be refused by a creditor in settlement of a *debt* already incurred. And, technically, it must be paid in exact money since no change can be demanded. It is not a means of payment that must be accepted by all the parties to a transaction, who are free to use whatever means of payment they like.

────────── FINANCIAL SNAP-SCHOTT · 2005 ──────────

Item	September 2005
Church of England · marriage service (excluding certificate)	198·00
– funeral service (excluding burial and certificate)	84·00
Season ticket · Arsenal FC (2005/6; centre, East & West upper tiers)	1,825·00
– Grimsby Football Club (2005/6; Upper Smith)	325·00
Annual membership · MCC (full London member)	334·00
– Stringfellows, London	600·00
– Groucho Club, London (+35; London member)	550·00
– Trimdon Colliery & Deaf Hill Workmen's Club	3·00
– The Conservative Party (>22)	15·00
– The Labour Party (those in work)	24·00
– The Liberal Democrats (minimum required)	5·00
– UK Independence Party	20·00
– Royal Society for the Protection of Birds (adult)	30·00
Annual television licence† · colour	121·00
– black & white	40·50
Subscription, annual · *Private Eye*	21·00
– *Vogue*	28·50
– *Saga Magazine*	22·80
New British Telecom line installation	74·99
Entrance fee · Thorpe Park (12+ 'thrill seeker' purchased on the day)	30·00
– Buckingham Palace State Rooms (adult)	13·50
– Eden Project, Cornwall (adult, day)	12·50
'Pint of best bitter' · Railway Inn, Yelverton, Devon	1·90
– Railway Inn, Juniper Green, Edinburgh	2·35
– Railway Inn, Trafford, Manchester	1·65
– Railway Inn, Coleshill, Birmingham	2·25
– Railway Tavern, Liverpool St, London	2·55
Fishing licence · Salmon and Sea Trout (full season)	63·75
List price of the cheapest new Ford (Ford Ka 1·3i 'on the road')	7,095·00
British Naturalisation (includes ceremony fee)	268·00
Manchester United Home Shirt (2004/06 season)	39·99
Tea at the Ritz, London (afternoon, per person)	34·00
Kissing the Blarney Stone (admission to Blarney Castle) [€7]	4·78
Hampton Court Maze (adult)	3·50
Ordinary London adult single bus ticket	1·20
Mersey Ferry (adult return)	2·10
Passport · new, renewal, or amendment (3 week postal service)	42·00
Driving test (practical + theory; cars, weekday)	66·50
Driving licence (first · car, motorcycle, moped)	38·00
NHS dental examination (standard)	5·84
NHS prescription charge (per item) [see p.97]	6·50
Moss Bros three-piece mourning suit hire (weekend, basic 'Lombard')	45·00
FedEx Envelope (≤0·5kg) UK–USA	27·00

† The blind concession is 50%. Those ≥75 may apply for a free licence.

––––––––––––––– BUDGET 2005 KEY POINTS –––––––––––––––

Gordon Brown's 9th budget (16 March 2005) was widely seen as a pre-election attempt to woo middle-England families and the 'grey vote'. Some of the key measures are tabulated below (and others are detailed elsewhere in this section):

Income tax	rates frozen; allowances raised with inflation
National Insurance	rates frozen; allowances raised with inflation
Corporation tax	frozen
Capital Gains tax	frozen
Airline Passenger tax	frozen
Insurance Premium tax	frozen
Climate-change levy	frozen
Company car tax	frozen
Fuel tax	raised to 1·22p/litre; delayed until September 2005
Stamp duty	threshold raised to £120,000; rates frozen
Public spending	police +3·5bn; transport +2·4bn; defence +3·7bn; &c.
Pensioners	one-off £200 Council Tax rebate
Pension credit	rise by 13% to £119/w by 2008
NHS charges	abolished for >65s
Local bus travel	to be made free for pensioners
Same-sex couples	to receive the same tax status as married couples
Road tax	increased by £5 for all but the smallest of cars
Statue of Queen Mother	to be erected on The Mall, funded by new £5 coin
VAT	rates frozen; thresholds for (de)registration increased
Regulatory bodies	to be cut and streamlined
Inheritance tax	threshold raised to £275,000 in April 2005; to £285,000 in 2006; and to £300,000 in 2007
ISAs	annual limit of £7,000 maintained until 2010
Euro	no further assessment of 'five tests' in the Budget [see p.267] (although borrowing meets the 'Maastricht criteria')
Duty free	plans to raise duty free tax allowance from £145 to £1,000
Child tax credits	to rise 13% over three years
Stem cell research	funding of £300m, and new centres for research
Tax avoidance	new regulations planned [see p.234]
Arts Council &c.	to receive an extra £12m over the next two years [see p.160]
Primary schools	£9·4b plan to rebuild and refurbish
Islamic investors	rule changes to help investments that adhere to Sharia law

––––––––––––––– BUDGET 2005 BOOZE 'n' FAGS –––––––––––––––

Typical unit	*budget ±*		
Pack 20 cigarettes	+7p	175ml glass wine	+1p
Pack 5 cigars	+3p	75cl bottle wine	+4p
25g rolling tobacco	+8p	Sparkling wine	*no change*
25g pipe tobacco	+5p	Spirits	*no change*
Pint beer	+1p	Cider	*no change*
		Sparkling cider	*no change*

——————— BUDGET 2005 REACTION & MISC ———————

Michael Howard *'a vote now, pay later Budget'* · Charles Kennedy *'the Chancellor has tinkered an awful lot but he has failed to tackle fundamental unfairness in the system'* · FT *'Brown unveils Budget package aimed at wooing crucial voters'* · Times *'Brown courts grey vote in his memorial Budget'* · Sun *'Beware the Bribes of March'*.

Brown's 2005 speech lasted 48 minutes, the shortest of his 9 budgets since 1997.

Word Count	Growth 15	NHS 4	Iraq 1
Tax(es) 54	Pensioner(s)... 12	Hard working.. 3	Prudent (-ence) 1
Child(ren) 32	Stability....... 13	Public services.. 3	Opportunity ... 1
Inflation 17	Tax cut(s) 7	Reform(ing).... 2	Africa............ 1
Family(-ies) ... 16	Young people .. 5	Euro 2	Prime Minister. 0

COMPUTERISED CONDENSATION

When Brown's speech (6880 words) is entered into the Auto Summarize feature of *Microsoft Word* and reduced to *c.*1% of the original (19 sentences), the result is:

I have examined rates of corporation tax and capital gains tax.
94% of estates will pay no inheritance tax. Education £12 billions higher.
Affordable tax cuts and essential spending increases.
A £200 winter allowance free of tax. And a £200 council tax refund.
Investment not cuts. A Budget for Britain's hard working families and pensioners.

By custom and precedent, the only time alcohol is permitted in the Chamber is during the Budget speech. Disraeli (who spoke for 5 hours in 1852) took brandy and water; Gladstone apparently consumed sherry with a beaten egg; Heathcote Amory combined honey, milk, and rum; Howe drank G&T; Lawson took his whisky with soda, while Clarke drank his neat. Callaghan, Cripps, Major, and Brown all chose to drink water (of varying carbonation) for their Budget speeches.

——————— 6 APRIL · THE TAX YEAR ———————

The British tax year (uniquely in the world) runs from 6 April to 5 April. The cause of this idiosyncrasy was the shift from the Julian to the Gregorian calendar. Since the Middle Ages (*c.*1152), the English legal and fiscal year had begun on the Quarter Day, 25 March – the Christian feast of the Annunciation of the Virgin Mary, known as Lady Day [see p.334]. Although much of Catholic Europe had adopted the Gregorian calendar in 1582, England only made the change in 1752 (after Chesterfield's Act of 1751). In order to correct the accumulated error of 11 days, 2 September 1752 was immediately followed by 14 September 1752. Many workers were convinced that they were being conned out of 11 days of life and 11 days of pay – and a popular cry of the time was 'Give us back our eleven days!' The authorities clearly felt similarly aggrieved, so the legal year was shifted 11 days forward from 25 March to 6 April. When Income Tax was reimposed in 1842 [see p.224] the tax year was firmly established as 6/4–5/4. [See pp.72–79 for other tax years.]

——— INCOME TAX · 2005–6 ———

Income tax was first levied in 1799 by Pitt the Younger, as a 'temporary measure' to finance the French Revolutionary War. The initial rate was 2 shillings in the pound. The tax was abolished in 1816, only to be re-imposed in 1842 by Robert Peel (again temporarily) to balance reductions in customs duties. By the end of the C19th, income tax was a permanent feature of the British economy [see p.223].

Income tax allowances	2004–5	2005–6
Personal allowance	4,745	4,895
Personal allowance (65–74)	6,830	7,090
Personal allowance (>75)	6,950	7,220
Income limit for age-related allowances	18,900	19,500
Married couple's allowance (born before 6·4·1935)	5,725	5,905
Married couple's allowance (aged ≤75)	5,795	5,975
Minimum amount of married couple's allowance	2,210	2,280
Blind person's allowance	1,560	1,610

The rate of relief for the continuing married couple's allowance and maintenance relief for people born before 6 April 1935, and for the children's tax credit, remains at 10%.

Income tax rates	*threshold*	%
Starting rate	£1–£2,090	10
Basic rate	£2,091–£32,400	22
Higher rate	>£32,401	40

Payment bands 0%	10%	22%	40%
Personal allowance	*from* 1–2,090	*from* 2,091–32,400	*after* 32,401

The 10% starting rate includes SAVINGS income. Where an individual has savings income in excess of the starting rate limit they will be taxed at 20% up to the basic rate limit, and at the higher rate for income above the basic rate limit. The tax rates for dividends are 10% for income up to the basic rate limit, and 32·5% thereafter.

——— STAMP DUTY ———

The thresholds below (in £) represent the 'total value of consideration' of the deal. The rate that applies to any given transfer applies to the whole value of that deal.

rate %	*Residential* not *in a disadvantaged area*	*Residential in a disadvantaged area*	*Non-residential*
0	0–120,000	0–150,000	0–150,000
1	120,001–250,000	150,001–250,000	150,001–250,000
3	250,001–500,000	250,001–500,000	250,001–500,000
4	>500,001	>500,001	>500,001

The rate of stamp duty on the transfer of SHARES and SECURITIES is set at 0·5%.

---------------- NATIONAL INSURANCE · 2005–6 ----------------

Although National Insurance dates from 1911, modern funding of social security
was proposed by Beveridge and established by the National Insurance Act (1946).

Lower earnings limit, primary Class 1	£82/w
Upper earnings limit, primary Class 1	£630/w
Primary threshold	£94/w
Secondary threshold	£94/w
Employees' primary Class 1 rate	11% of £94.01–£630/w · 1% >£630/w
Employees' contracted-out rebate	1·6%
Married women's reduced rate	4·85% of £94.01–£630/w · 1% >£630/w
Employers' secondary Class 1 rate	12·8% on earnings above £94/w
Employers' contracted-out rebate, salary-related schemes	3·5%
Employers' contracted-out rebate, money-purchase schemes	1·0%
Class 2 rate	£2·10/w
Class 2 small earnings exception	£4,345/w
Special Class 2 rate for share fishermen	£2·75/w
Special Class 2 rate for volunteer development workers	£4·10/w
Class 3 rate	£7·35/w
Class 4 lower profits limit	£4,895/y
Class 4 upper profits limit	£32,760/y
Class 4 rate	8% of £4,895–£32,760/y · 1% >£32,760/y

---------------- CAPITAL GAINS TAX ----------------

Annual exemptions 2005–6   Individuals &c. = £8,500 · Other trustees = £4,250

The amount chargeable to Capital Gains Tax is added onto the top of income
liable to income tax for individuals, and is charged to CGT at the following levels:

Below the Starting Rate limit	10%
Between the Starting Rate and Basic Rate limits	20%
Above the Basic Rate limit	40%

Capital gains arising on disposal of a 'principal private residence' remain exempt.

---------------- CORPORATION TAX ON PROFITS ----------------

2005–06	*£ per year*
Starting rate: 0%	0–10,000
Marginal relief	10,001–50,000
Small companies' rate: 19%	50,001–300,000
Marginal small companies' relief	300,001–1,500,000
Main rate: 30%	≥1,500,001
Non-corporate distribution rate	19%

——————————————— OTHER TAXES OF NOTE ———————————————

Value Added Tax (VAT*)

Standard rate	17·5%
Reduced rate (e.g. energy saving materials; women's sanitary products)	5%
Zero rate (e.g. young children's clothing and footwear; books & newspapers)	0%
VAT registration threshold (i.e. you must register if you turnover is…)	≥ £58,000

* When Arthur Daley ordered a 'large VAT' from Dave at the Winchester Club he was, of course, requesting a Vodka and Tonic – Arthur didn't do the other kind of VAT.

Inheritance Tax 2005–6
Threshold £275,000 · Rate 40%

Air Passenger Duty 2005–6	*standard*	*reduced*
Specified European destinations	£10	£5
All other destinations	£40	£20

Insurance Premium Tax 2005–6
Standard rate 5% · Higher rate (for travel and some vehicle & domestic) 17·5%

Fuel Duty (effective September 2005)	*per litre*
Sulphur-free petrol/diesel	48·32p
Ultra low sulphur petrol/diesel	48·32p
Biodiesel	28·32p
Bioethanol	28·32p
Rebated gas oil (red diesel)	6·44p
Rebated fuel oil	6·04p
Road fuel gas other than natural gas (e.g. LPG)	12·7p /kg
Natural gas used as road fuel	10·8p /kg

——————————— GRADUATED VEHICLE EXCISE DUTY ———————————

The new system of charging vehicle excise duty for private cars based on Carbon Dioxide (CO_2) emissions was introduced to encourage car manufacturers and purchasers to consider the environmental impact of engines. Cars first registered and licensed on or after 1 March 2001 will qualify; those registered prior to this will be charged the old rate based on engine size. Current bands and charges are:

Band	*CO_2 emissions g/km*	*diesel car*	*petrol car*	*alt. fuel*
A	≤100	£75	£65	£55
B	101–120	£85	£75	£65
C	121–150	£115	£105	£95
D	151–165	£135	£125	£115
E	166–185	£160	£150	£140
F	>185	£170	£165	£160

[Prices are for 12 months · Source: DVLA · www.vcacarfueldata.org.uk/ved/]

—— ADAM SMITH INSTITUTE'S TAX FREEDOM DAY ——

Each year the Adam Smith Institute [adamsmith.org] calculates the 'Tax Freedom Day'. This is the theoretical day in the calendar when the average tax-payer ceases to work 'for the Government' and starts to earn for themselves. The chart below shows how the Adam Smith Tax Freedom Day has moved over recent years:

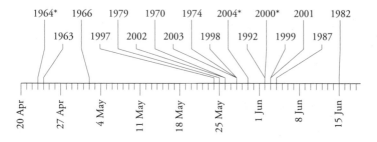

[* These are leap years that have the effect of making Tax Freedom Day a day early.]

———— TRIAL OF THE PYX ————

Dating back to 1249, the *Trial of the Pyx* is an annual examination of UK coins to ensure that they conform to the standards of weight, fineness, composition, and diameter now set by the 1971 Coinage Act. (Pyx is the name given to the chests in which sample coins are stored and transported – though it is also the name for the vessel in which the host or consecrated bread of the sacrament is reserved.) Throughout the year, the Deputy Master of the Mint selects at random a number of coins from each issue to be set aside for the Trial. (The number of each type of coin is set by Statutory Instrument, for example 1 out of every 5,000 cupro-nickel coins of a denomination of 10p or less.) Then, each February, the Treasury issues a warrant to the Queen's Remembrancer to convene and swear in a jury† (usually from the Goldsmiths' Company) at Goldsmiths' Hall in the City of London. The jury counts and weighs the coins, and sets aside a sample to be melted and tested by the Assay Office. Once all these tests have been completed the Verdict of the Jury is signed and delivered to the Queen's Remembrancer, who in turn signs it and delivers it to the Treasury, which then causes it to be publicly printed.

† The Oath: '*You shall well and truly, after your knowledge and discretion, make the assays of these moneys of gold, platinum, silver, gold-plated silver, cupro-nickel, nickel-brass and bimetal, and truly report if the said moneys be in weight and fineness or composition according to the standard weights for weighing and testing the coins of the realm, and the standard trial plates of gold, platinum, silver, copper, nickel and zinc in the custody of the* Secretary of State and used for determining the justness of the gold, platinum, silver, gold-plated silver, cupro-nickel, nickel-brass, and bimetallic coinage of the realm, and be in conformity with the Coinage Act 1971 or any proclamation in force in pursuance of that Act; and if the diameter of such of these coins as are of cupro-nickel, nickel-brass and bimetal be in conformity with that Act or any such proclamation as aforesaid; so help you God.'

INCOME DISTRIBUTION

The distribution bands of real UK/GB disposable household income per week:

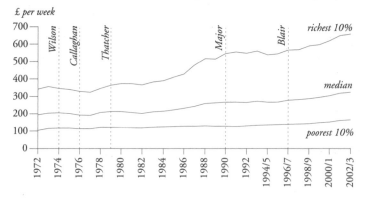

[Adjusted to 2002/03 prices using RPI less local taxes. Equivalised household disposable income before deduction of housing costs. Data from 1993/94 onwards are for financial years. Source of data changed in 1994/95: income definition changed and geographic coverage changed from UK to GB. Source: Social Trends 35 · Crown ©.]

BRITISH PAY

Median gross pay (Apr 2004)	♂	♀	*difference*	*average*
Per year full-time	£24,236·00	£18,531·00	£5,705·00	£22,060·00
Per week full-time	£462·00	£358·00	£104·00	£422·10
Per week part-time	£119·00	£130·70	-£11·70	£129·00
Per hour full-time	£11·04	£9·46	£1·58	£10·41
Per hour part-time	£6·01	£6·27	-£0·26	£6·24

Of all employees	*gross annual pay*		
10% earn less than	£5,373	30% earn more than	£25,379
20% earn less than	£9,222	20% earn more than	£30,341
30% earn less than	£12,500	10% earn more than	£38,877

[Anl. Survey of Hours & Earnings 2004]

Highest paid jobs (Apr 2004)	*£ per week*
Directors and chief executives of major organisations	1,791
Senior officials in national government	1,168
Medical practitioners	1,168
Aircraft pilots and flight engineers	1,094
Lowest paid jobs	*£ per week*
Waiters, waitresses	206
Launderers, dry cleaners, pressers	204
Floral arrangers, florists	197
Leisure and theme park attendants	191

INCOME TAX PAYABLE · 2004–5

Annual income (£)	No. of taxpayers (m)	Total tax liability (£m)	Average rate of tax (%)	Average amount of tax (£)
4,745–4,999	0·3	4	0·2	12
5,000–7,499	3·1	435	2·2	142
7,500–9,999	3·5	1,700	5·6	486
10,000–14,999	6·2	7,750	10·1	1,250
15,000–19,999	5·0	11,500	13·2	2,300
20,000–29,999	6·0	22,700	15·5	3,790
30,000–49,999	4·1	27,300	18·1	6,730
50,000–99,999	1·4	23,800	25·8	17,200
100,000 and over	0·4	31,800	33·6	73,300
ALL INCOMES	29·9	126,900	18·2	4,240

[Total annual income of the individual for income tax purposes including earned and investment income. Figures relate to taxpayers only. Projected estimates based upon the 2001–02 Survey of Personal Incomes, in line with March 2004 Budget. Here, total tax liability is the total liability after reductions which refer to allowances given at a fixed rate. Source: Inland Revenue. Crown ©]

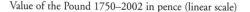

VALUE OF THE £

Value of the Pound 1750–2002 in pence (linear scale)

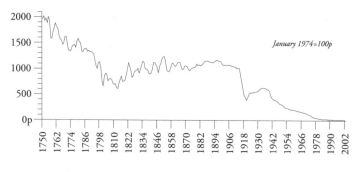

January 1974=100p

[Source: House of Commons Library · Crown ©]

DECIMALISATION

Although there was an attempt to decimalise the British currency in 1849 when Florins (worth £⅒) were introduced, it was only with the growth of the European Union that change became inevitable. Britain finally went decimal on 15·02·1971.

————————————— CHARITY —————————————

The 166,514 charities registered in England and Wales have a combined income of £36·29bn – of which 45·7% is generated by just 521 organisations (0·3%). >57% of charities have an annual income <£10,000; 34,313 raise <£1,000 a year.

No of charities	Annual income bracket	combined income
34,313 (20·6%)	<£1,000	£0·009bn (0·1%)
61,766 (37·1%)	£1,001–10,000	£0·279bn (0·8%)
47,773 (28·7%)	£10,001–100,000	£1·612bn (4·4%)
9,912 (5·6%)	£100,001–250,000	£1·596bn (4·4%)
8,004 (4·8%)	£250,001–1m	£3·935bn (10·9%)
4,225 (2·5%)	£1m–10m	£12·287bn (33·9%)
521 (0·3%)	>£10m	£16·572bn (45·7%)
166,514	ALL CHARITIES	£36·290bn

[Souce: The Charity Commission · Crown ©]

Research in 2004 by The Giving Campaign shows that the poor give to charity more often than the rich. The most charitable town in the UK, Sunderland, is also one of the poorest; Guildford, the UK's richest town, is the 8th most uncharitable.

Most charitable	Wealth rank	Least charitable	Wealth rank
(1=most givers; 114=least)	*(1=most wealthy; 114=least)*	*(1=most givers; 114=least)*	*(1=most wealthy; 114=least)*
1..............Sunderland..........100		114.............London.............23	
2...............Blackpool.............92		113.............Harrow.............10	
3...............Motherwell...........89		112.............Twickenham.........20	
4.................Dundee.............55		111...Kingston-upon-Thames......2	
5......Newcastle upon Tyne......72		110.............Ilford.............33	
6.............Kilmarnock...........60		109...........Croydon.............18	
7...............Liverpool.............69		108............Southall.............86	
8...............Oldham.............81		107...........Guildford.............1	

Additional research† indicates who gives, how much they give, how, and to whom:

[by sex and social grouping]	♂	♀	AB	C1	C2	DE
% who give to charity	60	71	76	70	66	58
Average donation (£/month)	10·81	13·55	28·63	12·49	7·56	6·11

Method of giving	% of population	Causes supported	% of population
Street collection	18·8	Medical research	24·4
Door-to-door	15·5	Children or young people	21·6
Raffle/lottery tickets (not NL)	12·2	Animals	11·1
Buying from charity shop	10·6	Other medical/healthcare	10·8
Shop-counter collection tins	10·2	Religious organisations	10·0
Church collection	10·0	Overseas relief	8·5
Sponsorship	9·0	Blind people	6·7
Collection at work	6·0		
Buying goods for a charity	5·5		

[† Source: Charities Aid Fdtn. & Nat. Cnl. for Vol. Orgs. 2003 · Only some methods and causes shown.]

———————— THE SUNDAY TIMES RICH LIST · 2005 ————————

No.	billionaire	age	£ billion	activity	last year
1	Lakshmi Mittal	54	14·8	steel	5
2	Roman Abramovich	39	7·5	industry, football	1
3	Duke of Westminster	53	5·6	property	2
4	Hans Rausing & family	79	4·9	packaging	3
5	Philip & Christina Green	53	4·7	retail	4
6	Oleg Deripaska	36	4·4	aluminium	new
7	Sir Richard Branson	55	3·0	various *Virgins*	6
8	Kirsten Rausing	49	2·6	inheritance	7
9	David & Simon Reuben	66, 62	2·5	property, trading	9
10	Spiro Latsis & family	68	2·4	banking, shipping	11=

———————————— MINIMUM WAGE ————————————

First introduced by Labour on 1 April 1999, the present minimum wage rates are:

Adult rate (aged ≥22) ....£5·05/h
Development rate (18–21 inclusive) ....£4·25/h
16- and 17-year-olds above compulsory school leaving age................£3·00/h

———————————— UK HOUSEHOLD SAVINGS ————————————

£	No savings at all	<1,500	1,500–10,000	10–20k	>20,000
%	33	20	25	8	13

[2002/3 data · Source: Social Trends 35 · Crown ©]

———————————— FORBES MAGAZINE RICH LIST · 2005 ————————————

No.	billionaire	age	$ billion	activity	last year
1	William Gates III	49	46·5[†]	Microsoft	1
2	Warren Buffett	74	44·0	investing	2
3	Lakshmi Mittal	54	25·0	Mittal Steel	62
4	Carlos Slim Helu	65	23·8	telecoms	17
5	Prince Alwaleed	48	23·7	investing	4
6	Ingvar Kamprad	78	23·0	Ikea	13
7	Paul Allen	52	21·0	Microsoft	5
8	Karl Albrecht	85	18·5	supermarkets	3
9	Lawrence Ellison	60	18·4	Oracle	12
10	S. Robson Walton	61	18·3	Wal-Mart	6

† *To put William Gates III's fortune in some perspective, it is > twice the GDP of Bolivia.*

INTEREST RATES & THE MPC

Since 1997, the Monetary Policy Committee (MPC) has been responsible for setting UK interest rates (though in exceptional circumstances the Government can issue instructions to the MPC for a limited period of time). Sitting on the MPC are: the Governor of the Bank of England, the two Deputy Governors, the Bank's Chief Economist, the Executive Director for Market Operations, and four external members appointed by the Chancellor. The MPC meets monthly and decisions are reached by one-member-one-vote with the Governor wielding the casting vote. Below is a chart of the changes in Bank of England interest rates since June 1997:

Date	change	rate	Date	change	rate	Date	change	rate
			04·10·01	-0·25	4·50%	08·04·99	-0·25	5·25%
			18·09·01	-0·25	4·75%	04·02·99	-0·5	5·50%
04·08·05	-0·25	4·50%	02·08·01	-0·25	5·00%	07·01·99	-0·25	6·00%
05·08·04	+0·25	4·75%	10·05·01	-0·25	5·25%	10·12·98	-0·5	6·25%
10·06·04	+0·25	4·50%	05·04·01	-0·25	5·50%	05·11·98	-0·5	6·75%
06·05·04	+0·25	4·25%	08·02·01	-0·25	5·75%	08·10·98	-0·25	7·25%
05·02·04	+0·25	4·00%	10·02·00	+0·25	6·00%	04·06·98	+0·25	7·50%
06·11·03	+0·25	3·75%	13·01·00	+0·25	5·75%	06·11·97	+0·25	7·25%
10·07·03	-0·25	3·50%	04·11·99	+0·25	5·50%	07·08·97	+0·25	7·00%
06·02·03	-0·25	3·75%	08·09·99	+0·25	5·25%	10·07·97	+0·25	6·75%
07·11·01	-0·5	4·00%	10·06·99	-0·25	5·00%	06·06·97		6·50%

AVERAGE MORTGAGE RATES

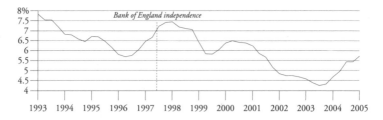

[Source: Survey of Mortgage Lenders · Council of Mortage Lenders · May 2005]

LARGEST MORTGAGE LENDERS

2004 Rank	Group	£b lent in 2004	2004 % of lending	2004 % of market	£b outstanding mortgages 2004
1	HBOS	68·4	23·4	21·6	189·0
2	Lloyds TSB	26·3	9·0	9·1	80·1
3	Abbey National	24·9	8·6	10·4	91·1
4	Nationwide BS	23·2	8·0	9·2	81·0

[Source: Council of Mortage Lenders · 2005]

--- INCOME vs HOUSE PRICES ---

The table below illustrates the growing gulf between the average income of house buyers and the average cost of properties. The data below are for all UK properties.

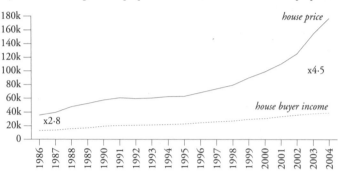

[Source: Survey of Mortgage Lenders · Office of the Deputy Prime Minister · 2005]

--- COUNCIL TAX BANDS ---

ENGLAND	value £	WALES	value £	SCOTLAND	value £
A	>40,000	A	>44,000	A	>27,000
B	40,001–52,000	B	44,001–65,000	B	27,001–35,000
C	52,001–68,000	C	65,001–91,000	C	35,001–45,000
D	68,001–88,000	D	91,001–123,000	D	45,001–58,000
E	88,001–120,000	E	123,001–162,000	E	58,001–80,000
F	120,001–160,000	F	162,001–223,000	F	80,001–106,000
G	160,001–320,000	G	223,001–324,000	G	106,001–212,000
H	>320,001	H	324,001–424,000	H	>212,001
		I	>424,001		

In September 2005, the Government announced that they were delaying plans to revalue the Council Tax bands of properties in England to reflect values at 1 April 2005. The Welsh bands came into effect from 1 April 2005, based on values at 1 April 2003.

--- GAZUMP & GAZUNDER ---

GAZUMPING
Where sellers increase the price of a property just before the exchange of contracts, so as to pressurise the buyer into paying more.

GAZUNDERING
Where buyers decrease their offer on a property just before the exchange of contracts so as to pressurise the seller into accepting less.

The inestimable *Oxford English Dictionary* traces *gazump* to the 1920s, and it may be that it derives from the Yiddish 'gezumph', meaning to swindle or overcharge.

——————ON TAXES——————

DIRECT TAX · taxes levied on income received (e.g. income tax). They are generally considered to be *progressive*, since the amount due is proportionate to income.

INDIRECT TAX · taxes levied on the purchase of goods and services (e.g. VAT). They are generally considered to be *regressive*, since all pay the same amount regardless of income.

STEALTH TAX · an informal term for taxation that is (often deliberately) obscured from those who pay it. This may be because the tax: is very complex (e.g. advanced corporation tax on pension funds); is levied in an unusual way (e.g. speed cameras); is introduced some time after its announcement (e.g. delayed increases in fuel duty); or is 'hidden' in the price (e.g. landfill tax). The most common type of stealth tax involves freezing the thresholds at which taxes are payable. For example, by not raising with inflation the rate at which the higher rate of income tax is paid, more people are drawn into paying the tax – and on a greater proportion of their income.

TAX AVOIDANCE · the legal organisation of one's financial affairs (e.g. by utilising tax allowances and reliefs) to minimise one's tax burden.

TAX EVASION · any illegal method of reducing tax (e.g. failing to declare income or falsely claiming tax reliefs).

WINDFALL TAX · a tax levied on unforeseen or unexpectedly large profits, especially those considered to have been garnered unfairly (e.g. Gordon Brown's taxation in 1997 of the profits of privatised utilities companies).

——————TOP BRANDS '05——————

Interbrand's analysis of the 10 largest global and UK brands of 2005 were :

Global brands	Value $m
Coca-Cola	67,525
Microsoft	59,941
IBM	53,376
GE	46,996
Intel	35,588
Nokia	26,452
Disney	26,441
McDonald's	26,014
Toyota	24,837
Marlboro	21,189

UK brands	Value $m
HSBC	10,429
Reuters	3,866
BP	3,802
Smirnoff	3,097

—TOP UK EMPLOYERS '05—

According to the *Sunday Times* the top companies to work for in the UK are:

W.L. Gore.......mnf. GORE-TEX &c.
St Ann's Hospice...............hospice
Beaverbrooks.........jewellery retailer
Pannone & Partners.........legal firm
Data Connection..computer software

Of the big companies in the UK who employ 5,000 or more, the top 10 are:

1 ....Nationwide
2 ....Asda
3 ....KPMG
4 ....Carphone Warehouse
5 ....Mothercare
6 ....Cadbury Schweppes
7 ....Compass
8 ....Pfizer
9 ....Severn Trent Water
10 .........................W.S. Atkins

MONOPOLY

In 2005 Hasbro issued a new London version of *Monopoly* to celebrate 70 years of the game, and reflect changes in the property market. The 'Here and Now' edition features new counters (roller-blade, skateboard, aeroplane, and mobile phone), and players receive £2m for passing Go. (All the prices have been inflated simply by adding 5 zeros). Below are some of the old and new properties on the board:

Old	New
Old Kent Road	Portobello Market
King's Cross	London City Airport
Pentonville Rd	GMTV Studios
Marylebone	Stansted Airport
Bow St	Science Museum
Marlborough St	Nat. Hist. Musm
Vine St	Tate Modern
Strand	London Eye
Fleet St	Hyde Park
Coventry St	Covent Garden
Piccadilly	Regent St
Regent St	Notting Hill
Oxford St	Soho
Bond St	Kings Rd
Liverpool St	Heathrow Airport
Park Lane	Canary Wharf
Mayfair	The City

2006 ISSUE COINS

The Queen graciously gave approval of the Chancellor of the Exchequer's recommendations that the following special coins be issued during 2006:

· A £5 coin to celebrate the 80th birthday of HM the Queen
· A pair of £2 coins for Isambard Kingdom Brunel's 200th birthday
· A series of three 50p coins to commemorate the 150th anniversary of the Victoria Cross

GAMBLING

CASINOS (2004–5)
Number operating	138
Casino visits (GB)	12·3m
Money exchanged for chips	£4,158m
House win	£715m (17%)
Number employed	c.15,300
Duty (tax) paid	£157m
Annual casino licence	£8,541

BINGO CLUBS (2004–5)
Number operating	676
Bingo admissions	c.78·5m
Money staked	£1,777m
Number employed	18,500
Duty (tax) paid	£81m

GAMING MACHINES (2004–5)
Number of machines	244,000
Cash staked	£10·71bn
Prizes paid out	£8·54·bn
Income for owners	£2·17bn
Number employed	c.21,996
Duty (tax) paid	£156m
Machines located in pubs	c.40%

The 1968 Gaming Act allows for a range of gaming machines in certain locations, each with a corresponding maximum stake and prize, for example:

Location	stake	prize
Casino	50p	£2,000
Bingo club	50p	£500
Other club	50p	£250
Pub; betting office	30p	£25
Café; family arcade	30p	£5 cash

[Figures for 2004–5
Source: Report of the Gaming Board for GB]

In 2005 a new Gambling Act was passed to update the 1968 Act and bring all commercial gambling (apart from the National Lottery and spread betting) under the aegis of a Gambling Commission.

─────────────── THE NATIONAL LOTTERY ───────────────

The National Lottery was established by Act of Parliament on 21 October 1993, and on 14 November 1994 the first tickets went on sale. Five days later, 22 million watched the first draw live on BBC1. (The first winning numbers were 30, 3, 5, 44, 14, 22, and [bonus] 10.) The Department for Culture, Media, and Sport appoints and directs the National Lottery Commission, which has twice awarded the lottery licence to Camelot, whose current 7 year licence expires on 31 January 2009. Although responsible for raising lottery funds, Camelot plays no part in their allocation. Rather, six 'good causes'† are designated (arts, sport, heritage, &c), to which about 28p in the £1 is given. The breakdown of lottery income is:

12% tax   *50% to winners*   *28% to good causes*

0·5% Camelot profit   *5% retailer commission*   *4·5% operating costs*

To celebrate its 10th birthday in 2004, the National Lottery commissioned a poll from MORI to explore the effects of winning on those who had won over *c.*£1m.:

❧ 1 in 7 had given £1m or more to a family member or friend, thereby creating >728 additional and 'indirect' millionaires ❧ 87% of jackpot winners had given a proportion of their winnings to charity ❧ 65% of winners said they were 'happier' having won the jackpot; 35% said they were 'as happy' ❧ 1 in 10 winners bought more than 10 cars since winning ❧ 35% of winners bought a new BMW; 27% a new Ford ❧ of those in work at the time of winnings, 27% remained employed ❧ 92% of winners who were married at the time of winning had remained in the same marriage ❧

After London won the 2012 Olympic bid [see p.292] it was announced that up to £1·5bn of the costs would be generated by the Lottery, of which half would come from new Olympic Lottery games. The rest would come from usual Lottery funds. ❧ Despite all numbers having an equal chance of being drawn, superstition surrounds certain numbers and combinations. Below is a graph of how many times each ball has been drawn in the Lotto from the first draw until 13·08·2005:

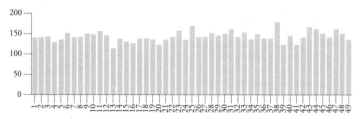

† Recently, concerns have been expressed, not least by John Major, the PM who set up the lottery, that funds were being used to replace normal Government spending, thus undermining the basic principle of 'additionality' upon which the lottery was premised.

———————————— THE COST OF LIVING ————————————

The 'cost of living' is measured by tracking the Retail Price Index (RPI), and the Consumer Price Index (CPI). The RPI measures a 'basket' of goods and services (modified annually to reflect changing spending patterns) bought by most households [see below]. The CPI is similar to the RPI with a few differences, such as the exclusion of mortgage repayments, house depreciation and insurance, council tax, and the like. The table below show historic changes in the RPI and CPI since 1971:

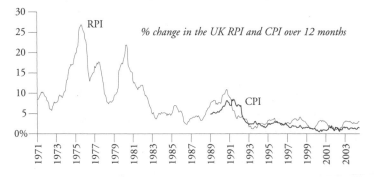

[Data prior to 1997 are estimates. Source: Social Trends 35 · Crown ©]

— RPI 'BASKET' CHANGES —

Some 2005 changes to the RPI basket:

items removed · French baguette; powdered baby formula; diet-aid drink; children's slippers; cycle helmets; plastic patio set; upholstered settee; smoke alarm; analogue camcorder; dumb-bells; liquid plant fertiliser; single serve cat food; disposable razors; gold bangle, &c.

items added · pre-packed vegetables; vended cigarettes; wooden patio set; leather settee; gardeners' fees; private surgery & chiropractors' fees; mobile phone handsets; wrapping paper; laptops; music concerts; cinema popcorn; champagne; razor cartridge blades; gemstone ring; cash-machine charges; self-storage fees; home delivery charges; solicitors' fees, &c.

— RECENT CPI/RPI DATA —

CPI & RPI % change over 12 months:

Year	month	CPI	RPI
2005	Aug	2·4	2·8
	Jul	2·3	2·9
	Jun	2·0	2·9
	May	1·9	2·9
	Apr	1·9	3·2
	Mar	1·9	3·2
	Feb	1·6	3·2
	Jan	1·6	3·2
2004	Dec	1·6	3·5
	Nov	1·5	3·4
	Oct	1·2	3·3
	Sep	1·1	3·1
	Aug	1·3	3·2
	Jul	1·4	3·0
	Jun	1·6	3·0
	May	1·5	2·8
	Apr	1·2	2·5
	Mar	1·1	2·6

UK POSTAL RATES · AT 1·9·2005

DOMESTIC	1ST	2ND			
≤60g	30p	21p	≤450	1·59	1·30
≤100	46	35	≤500	1·78	1·48
≤150	64	47	≤600	2·15	1·75
≤200	79	58	≤700	2·52	2·00
≤250	94	71	≤750	2·71	2·12
≤300	1·07	83	≤800	2·90	*first class*
≤350	1·21	94	≤900	3·27	*first class*
≤400	1·40	1·14	≤1kg	3·64	*first class*

Add 88p for each additional 250g over 1kg

Recorded Signed For = postage + 66p · Proof of Delivery = postage + £2·20

AIRMAIL	Letters Europe	Zone 1	Zone 2
Postcards	0·42	0·47	0·47
≤10g	0·42	0·47	0·47
≤20	0·42	0·68	0·68
≤40	0·60	1·05	1·12
≤60	0·78	1·42	1·56
≤80	0·96	1·79	2·00
≤100	1·14	2·16	2·44
≤120	1·32	2·53	2·88
≤140	1·50	2·90	3·32

To find a postcode call
08456 039 038
For further information see
www.royalmail.com

Small packets		Printed papers	
Europe	*Z 1/2*	*Europe*	*Z 1/2*
1·03	1·37	0·89	1·35
1·14	1·56	0·98	1·55
1·25	1·75	1·07	1·75

PRICING IN PROPORTION

On 1 January 2006 the UK postal market will be opened up to full competition. From 4 September 2006, the Royal Mail is proposing to replace the traditional weight tariff for postage (above) with 'Pricing in Proportion' that will take into account the size of the item sent as well as its weight. The three size categories are:

Category	size (mm)	thick (mm)	weight (g)	1st	2nd
Letter	≤240x165	≤5	0–100	30p	21p
Large Letter	≤353x250	≤25	0–100	42p	35p
			101–250	61p	53p
			251–500	85p	72p
			501–750	123p	105p
Packet	>353 long or >250 wide	or >25	0–100	94p	80p
			101–250	119p	104p
			251–500	159p	132p
			501–750	206p	166p
			751–1kg	253p	199p

At the time of writing, the prices quoted above are estimated prices only. All items >1kg will remain on the standard weight-based scale. The maximum weight for 2nd class post is set to rise to 1kg.

ROYAL MAIL STAMPS OF 2005

11 Jan	Farm animals	7 Jun	Trooping the Colour
8 Feb	South-west England	5 Jul	End of War
24 Feb	Jane Eyre	19 Jul	Motorcycles
15 Mar	Magic!	23 Aug	A Celebration of Food
22 Mar	Castles (Definitives)	15 Sep	Classic ITV
8 Apr	Charles & Camilla	18 Oct	Trafalgar
21 Apr	World Heritage Sites	1 Nov	Christmas

POSTCODE ANATOMY

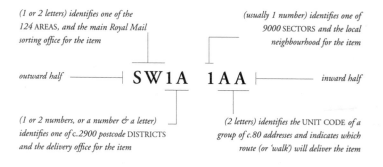

(1 or 2 letters) identifies one of the 124 AREAS, and the main Royal Mail sorting office for the item

(usually 1 number) identifies one of 9000 SECTORS and the local neighbourhood for the item

outward half — **SW1A 1AA** — inward half

(1 or 2 numbers, or a number & a letter) identifies one of c.2900 postcode DISTRICTS and the delivery office for the item

(2 letters) identifies the UNIT CODE of a group of c.80 addresses and indicates which route (or 'walk') will deliver the item

---

ROYAL MAIL PROHIBITED POST

Some of the items that are prohibited from being sent through the Royal Mail:

Aerosols · Alcoholic liquids with alcohol content higher than 70% · Asbestos
Batteries* · Butane lighters and refills · Clinical and medical waste
Flammable, non-flammable, toxic compressed gases · Corrosives
Counterfeit money or counterfeit postage stamps · Drugs of any description
Dry ice · Environmental waste · Explosives · Filth · Flammable liquids or solids
Lottery tickets except for UK tickets · Indecent or offensive material
Infectious substances§ · Items worth >£2,500 · Magnetised material†
Matches · Oxidising materials or organic peroxides · Pesticides
Toxic liquids, solids or gases · Poisons · All radioactive material and samples*
Weapons of war · Ammunition · Solvent-based paints, varnishes and enamels
Water-based paints, varnishes and enamels with volume >150ml
Any other item prohibited by law or judged by Royal Mail to be harmful

§ Listed by the *World Health Organisation* to be in risk Group 4, and the Group 3 substances listed in schedule 3 part 5 of the *Control of Substances Hazardous to Health Regulations* 1999 (COSHH). * Classed as dangerous by the ICAO. † Materials with a magnetic field strength ≥0.159A/m at 2·1m from the outside of the package.

CURRENCY SYMBOLS

£ The Pound sign derives from the capital L written in cursive script, with one or two horizontal bars bisecting it to indicate it is an abbreviation. (L stood for *libre*, the Latin for a pound in weight; a pound of silver was the standard on which the monetary unit is based.) The £ sign is also used for pounds in Syria, Egypt, Lebanon, Turkey, &c.

$ The origin of the the Dollar sign is controversial and a host of explanations had been given – some are more likely than others. For example: that it derives from the superimposition of the 'U' and 'S' of United States. One curious and highly unlikely theory is that the sign is linked to the slave trade, and the Spanish words for a slave (*esclavo*) and the nail (*clavo*) that locked the shackles. It is suggested that an 'S' with a nail ('S' and *clavo*), was written $. Perhaps the most plausible suggestion is that the sign was created when the letters 'P' and 'S' from the Spanish Pesos were conflated if written at speed. Oddly, neither US notes nor coins feature the $ sign.

€ The design of the euro sign was required to be 'a highly recognisable symbol of Europe; easy to write by hand; and to have an aesthetically pleasing design'. [Two out of three is not bad.] The EC claims that the symbol was 'inspired by the Greek letter epsilon, harking back to Classical times and the cradle of European civilisation'. The two parallel lines apparently 'indicate the stability of the euro'. At best this is fanciful twaddle. The EC claims that the euro symbol was the product of 'teamwork', but most agree that it is really the unsung work of Arthur Eisenmenger – graphic designer for the then EEC. Eisenmenger designed the European Union flag and the 'CE' logo [see p.267], and recalls that sometime in 1974 he simply fused the letters C and E using Indian ink on a 8" wide cardboard sheet 'without giving it much thought'. For type designers, the euro has proved problematic. Not only is it hard to 'retrofit' a new symbol into many existing fonts, but the strict design set by the EC has effectively to be ignored to make the clumsy logo work with any grace.

¥ The design of the Yen (the Japanese unit of currency since 1871) is much less problematic being, like the Pound, a letter slashed with lines to show it is an abbreviation. In the 1990s, London city traders knew it by the rhyming slang 'Bill & Ben'.

¤ This is a generic currency symbol, used with a three letter currency code or to indicate that a symbol is missing from a font.

SPECIAL DRAWING RIGHTS (SDR)

In 1969, the IMF created the SDR as an 'international reserve asset' in response to fears about an over-reliance on gold and the Dollar. The SDR is not actually a currency but a means of accounting by IMF members who agree to accept SDRs in settlement of accounts. SDRs are allocated to countries in proportion to their IMF quotas, and members can trade between themselves. The original SDR was 0·888671g of fine gold, or US$1, but it is now based upon a basket of major currencies. At present 1 SDR=*c*.$1·471.

ECONOMIC INDICATORS OF NOTE

Indicator	2004	2003	2002	2001	2000	1999	1998	1997	1996	1995	1994	(...) 1986
FTSE 100	4,814	4,477	3,940	5,217	6,222	6,930	5,883	5,136	4,119	3,689	3,066	1,679
RPI inflation (% year-on-year)	3·0	2·9	1·7	1·8	2·9	1·5	3·4	3·1	2·4	3·5	2·4	3·4
Real GDP (% year-on-year)	3·1	2·2	1·8	2·3	3·9	2·9	3·1	3·3	2·8	2·9	4·4	4·0
Average mortgage rate (%)	5·2	4·6	5·0	5·2	6·7	6·5	7·3	7·6	6·5	7·5	7·8	12·3
Average gross savers' rate (%)	4·3	3·4	3·6	3·8	5·5	5·0	6·0	6·1	4·5	5·2	5·6	10·9
Number of taxpayers (million)	29·5	28·9	28·6	29·3	27·0	26·9	26·2	25·7	25·8	25·3	25·0	23·7
Highest rate of income tax (%)	40	40	40	40	40	40	40	40	40	40	40	60
Higher-rate taxpayers (% of all taxpayers)	11	11	11	10	10	9	9	8	8	8	8	4
Unemployed (millions)	0·9	0·9	0·9	1·0	1·1	1·2	1·3	1·6	2·1	2·3	2·6	3·1
Unemployment rate (%)	2·7	3·0	3·1	3·2	3·6	4·1	4·5	5·3	7·0	7·6	8·8	10·5
Change in manufact. jobs year-on-year (%)	-4·2	-5·1	-5·4	-3·4	-2·4	-3·1	1·0	0·4	0·9	2·5	0·8	-2·0
Number of cars produced in UK (million)	1·65	1·66	1·63	1·49	1·64	1·79	1·75	1·70	1·19	1·53	1·47	1·02
Real annual disposable income/head (£)	12,491	12,258	11,971	11,814	11,386	10,907	10,610	10,540	10,203	9,987	8,777	7,426
Total consumer credit (£b)	23·0	20·2	21·1	17·7	14·2	14·8	14·4	12·0	11·2	8·1	5·7	4·4
Credit cards in issue (millions)	71·9	66·5	60·4	54·9	49·7	43·5	40·1	36·6	32·5	27·6	25·4	N/A
Change in average house price (%)	11·1	14·4	16·9	6·2	13·6	10·9	12·0	10·9	4·6	1·4	2·5	13·9
Change in average earnings (%)	4·4	3·3	3·6	4·4	4·5	4·8	5·2	4·2	3·6	3·1	3·7	8·1
Lending secured on houses (£b)	291·3	277·4	220·7	160·2	119·7	114·7	89·4	77·2	71·7	57·3	57·9	N/A
Properties repossessed (%)	0·05	0·07	0·11	0·16	0·20	0·27	0·31	0·31	0·40	0·47	0·47	0·30
Outstanding credit (% household income)	23·3	22·1	21·9	20·2	19·6	19·0	17·6	15·6	14·6	13·7	12·3	10·0
US Dollar/GB Pound ($/£)	1·83	1·63	1·50	1·44	1·52	1·62	1·66	1·64	1·56	1·58	1·53	1·47
Euro/GB Pound (€/£) [pre-1999 estimated]	1·47	1·45	1·59	1·61	1·64	1·52	(1·49)	(1·45)	(1·21)	(1·19)	(1·27)	(1·48)
Euro/US Dollar (€/$) [pre-1999 estimated]	0·80	0·89	1·06	1·12	1·09	0·94	(0·90)	(0·88)	(0·77)	(0·75)	(0·83)	(1·01)
Gold price 1 Troy Ounce = (£)	223·3	222·3	206·2	188·3	184·3	171·4	177·4	202·1	248·6	243·4	250·8	251·2

[Sources: Bank of England; ONS; Halifax Building Society; Council of Mortgage Lenders; HM Treasury; British Bankers' Association · Many figures have been rounded]

Parliament & Politics

*Politics are such a torment that I would advise
every one I love not to mix with them.*
— THOMAS JEFFERSON

THE HOUSE OF COMMONS

House of Commons, London, SW1A 0AA
Switchboard: 020 7219 3000 · www.parliament.uk

STATE OF THE PARTIES · as at 7 August 2005

Labour	353	Independent	2
Conservative	196	Ulster Unionist	1
Liberal Democrat	62	Respect	1
Scottish National Party	6	Speaker (Michael Martin)‡	1
Plaid Cymru	3	Deputy Speakers‡	3
Democratic Unionist	9	TOTAL	645
Sinn Féin [see below]	5	GOVERNMENT MAJORITY	65
Social Democratic & Labour	3	(‡ By tradition, these do not normally vote.)	

Oldest MP .... Piara Khabra [Lab; Ealing Southall] *b.* 20·11·24
Youngest MP.................. Jo Swinson [Lib Dem; East Dunbartonshire] *b.* 05·02·80
Largest majority........ 19,519; Thomas Clarke [Lab; Coatbridge, Chryston & Bellshill]
Smallest majority.................................... 37; Laura Moffatt [Lab; Crawley]

THE PARLIAMENTARY OATH

By law, MPs and Peers must swear an oath (or make an affirmation) of allegiance
before they can take their seat in Parliament, enter the Chamber, participate in
proceedings, or table motions or questions. The current Parliamentary Oath is:

I ———— (swear by Almighty God) *or* (do swear)
or (do solemnly, sincerely and truly declare and affirm)
that I will be faithful and bear true allegiance to Her Majesty Queen Elizabeth,
her heirs and successors, according to law. So help me God.

The Oath must be sworn by MPs and Peers at each new Parliament, and on the
accession of a new Monarch. Furthermore, the Oath must be said in English,
though MPs have been allowed to recite Gaelic and Welsh versions in addition.
Sinn Féin MPs have long refused to give the Oath or take their seats in Parliament.
In 1997, Speaker Boothroyd ruled that any MPs who refused to swear the Oath,
as well as getting no salary, would henceforth be denied the facilities of the House.

BRITISH PRIME MINISTERS

1997	Tony Blair L	1858	Viscount Palmerston Li
1990	John Major C	1858	Edward Stanley C
1979	Margaret Thatcher C	1855	Viscount Palmerston Li
1976	James Callaghan L	1852	G. Hamilton-Gordon C
1974	Harold Wilson L	1852	Edward Stanley C
1970	Edward Heath C	1846	John Russell W
1964	Harold Wilson L	1841	Sir Robert Peel T
1963	Alec Douglas-Home C	1835	William Lamb W
1957	Harold Macmillan C	1834	Robert Peel T
1955	Sir Anthony Eden C	1834	Arthur Wellesley T
1951	Winston Churchill C	1834	William Lamb W
1945	Clement Attlee L	1830	Charles Grey W
1940	Winston Churchill N/C	1828	Arthur Wellesley T
1937	Neville Chamberlain N/C	1827	Frederick Robinson T
1935	Stanley Baldwin N/C	1827	George Canning T
1931	Ramsay MacDonald N	1812	Robert Jenkinson T
1929	Ramsay MacDonald L	1809	Spencer Perceval T
1924	Stanley Baldwin C	1807	William Bentinck T
1924	Ramsay MacDonald L	1806	William Grenville W
1923	Stanley Baldwin C	1804	William Pitt [The Younger] T
1922	Andrew Bonar Law C	1801	Henry Addington T
1916	David Lloyd George Co	1783	William Pitt [The Younger] T
1908	Herbert Asquith Li & Co	1783	William Bentinck T
1905	H. Campbell-Bannerman Li	1782	William FitzMaurice W
1902	Arthur Balfour C	1782	C. Watson-Wentworth W
1895	Marquess of Salisbury C	1770	Frederick North T
1894	Earl of Rosebery Li	1767	Augustus Fitzroy W
1892	William Gladstone Li	1766	William Pitt [The Elder] W
1886	Marquess of Salisbury C	1765	C. Watson-Wentworth W
1886	William Gladstone Li	1763	George Grenville W
1885	Marquess of Salisbury C	1762	John Stuart T
1880	William Gladstone Li	1757	T. Pelham-Holles W
1874	Benjamin Disraeli C	1756	William Cavendish W
1868	William Gladstone Li	1754	T. Pelham-Holles W
1868	Benjamin Disraeli C	1743	Henry Pelham W
1866	Edward Stanley C	1742	Spencer Compton W
1865	John Russell Li	1721	Sir Robert Walpole W

Whig · Liberal · Tory · Labour · Conservative · National · Coalition

The term *Prime Minister* was initially one of abuse, with the position referred to formally as *First Lord of the Treasury*. Only in 1905 was the term used in a Royal Warrant. (The first Act of Parliament to refer directly to the *Prime Minister* was the Chequers Estate Act 1917.) On 2 August 2003, Blair became the longest continuously serving Labour PM, passing Attlee's record of 6 years and 92 days. Blair's 2005 election victory may allow him to surpass Thatcher's 11 years and 209 days.

THE CABINET

Prime Minister, First Lord of the Treasury, and Minister for the Civil Service

The Rt Hon TONY BLAIR MP

formed May 2005

Deputy Prime Minister & First Secretary of State	John Prescott
Chancellor of the Exchequer	Gordon Brown
SoS for Foreign & Commonwealth Affairs (Foreign Secretary)	Jack Straw
SoS for Work and Pensions	David Blunkett
SoS for Environment, Food and Rural Affairs	Margaret Beckett
SoS for Transport, & SoS for Scotland	Alistair Darling
SoS for Defence	John Reid
Lord Privy Seal & Leader of the Commons	Geoff Hoon
SoS for Health	Patricia Hewitt
SoS for Culture, Media and Sport	Tessa Jowell
Parliamentary Secretary to the Treasury & Chief Whip	Hilary Armstrong
SoS for the Home Department (Home Secretary)	Charles Clarke
SoS for Northern Ireland, and SoS for Wales	Peter Hain
Minister without Portfolio	Ian McCartney
Leader of the Lords & Lord President of the Council	Baroness Amos
SoS for Constitutional Affairs & Lord Chancellor	Lord Falconer
SoS for International Development	Hilary Benn
SoS for Trade and Industry	Alan Johnson
SoS for Education and Skills	Ruth Kelly
Chancellor of the Duchy of Lancaster	John Hutton
Chief Secretary to the Treasury	Des Browne
Minister for Communities & Local Government	David Miliband
Also attending Cabinet: Attorney General	Lord Goldsmith
Lords' Chief Whip; Captain of the Gentlemen-at-Arms	Lord Grocott
Minister of State for Europe	Douglas Alexander

CONSTITUTION OF THE GOVERNMENT

	Total	MPs ♀	♂	Peers ♀	♂	Unpaid
Cabinet	23	16	5	1	1	1
Ministers of State	27	15	9	2	1	0
Under Secs. of State & Parliamentary Secs.	37	21	8	6	2	2
Whips	23	12	3	5	3	0
Law Officers	3	1	0	1	1	0
TOTAL	113	65	25	15	8	3

The above total includes three unpaid positions; but not the Lord Chamberlain, the Lord Steward, the Master of the Horse, or the Church Estates Commissioner.

THE HOUSE OF LORDS

House of Lords, London, SW1A 0PW · 020 7219 3000 · www.parliament.uk

STATE OF THE PARTIES & COMPOSITION OF THE LORDS · 1 July 2005

Conservative	208	Bishops	25
Labour	215	Other	14
Liberal Democrat	74	Total	723
Crossbench	187		

8 Peers on leave of absence are excluded.

Archbishops and Bishops	25 [0]
Life Peers under the Appellate Jurisdiction Act 1876	28 [1]
Life Peers under the Life Peerages Act 1958	586 [129]
Peers under House of Lords Act 1999	92 [3]

[Numbers within brackets indicate the number of women included in the figure.]

Since Hereditary Peers ceased to sit or vote in the Lords in 1999, there have been four categories of Members:

LIFE PEERS · appointed for the whole of their lives, theoretically by the Queen but effectively by the PM. The title of Life Peer ceases on death.

ELECTED HEREDITARY PEERS · when the right of Hereditary Peers to sit and vote ended, 92 of the *c.*700 Hereditary Peers were allowed to remain until the next, unscheduled, stage of reform: 75 were elected by their party; 15 were office holders (e.g. Deputy Speakers) elected by the House; and 2 held Royal appointments (i.e. the Earl Marshal and the Lord Great Chamberlain).

ARCHBISHOPS & BISHOPS · Anglican Archbishops of Canterbury and York, the Bishops of Durham, London, and Winchester, and 21 senior Diocesan Bishops of the Church of England all have seats in the Lords. While most cease to be members when they retire, the two Archbishops are traditionally made Life Peers.

LORDS OF APPEAL IN ORDINARY ('LAW LORDS') · Lords appointed from senior figures in the judicial system to hear appeals from the lower courts [see p.283]. They retire at 75 but keep their seats. There are usually 12 active 'Law Lords' at any time. The judicial functions of the House of Lords are currently under review.

Oldest sitting member	The Lord Renton (*b.* 12·08·1908)
Longest serving member	The Rt Hon the Earl Jellicoe (took seat 1939)
Youngest member	The Lord Freyberg (*b.* 15.12.1970)
Leader of the House	The Rt Hon. the Baroness Amos
Average age of members	68

Some Life Peers in 2005

Andrew Adonis	Jack Cunningham	Estelle Morris
Donald Anderson	Derek Foster	Chris Patten
Tony Banks	Alastair Goodlad	David Ramsbotham
Virginia Bottomley	Neil Kinnock	Gillian Shepherd
	Brian Mawhinney	Chris Smith

———————————— THE SCOTTISH PARLIAMENT ————————————

Edinburgh EH99 1SP · www.scottish.parliament.uk · 0131 348 5000

The Scottish Parliament was formed by the Scotland Act (1998), but has its basis in the referendum held on 11 September 1997, at which the two questions were:

Question	Yes %	No %	Turnout %
There should be a Scottish Parliament	74·3	25·7	60·4
The Parliament should have tax raising powers	63·5	36·5	60·4

The first Parliamentary elections were held on 6 May 1999; the first meeting was held on 12 May; and the Scottish Parliament was officially opened on 1 July 1999. On 7 September 2004, Members (MSPs) moved from the Edinburgh Assembly Hall to their new purpose-built Parliament at Holyrood. The Parliament has 129 MSPs – 73 represent parliamentary constituencies and are elected by 'first past the post'; the remaining 56 are regional MSPs (7 for each of the 8 regions) who are elected by the Additional Member System (AMS) of proportional representation. Elections are held every four years – usually on the first Thursday in May. The second election was held in 2003, and the state of the parties at July 2005 was:

Number of MSPs	constituency	regional	total
Scottish Labour	45	4	49
Scottish National Party	8	17	25
Scottish Conservative & Unionist	3	15	18
Scottish Liberal Democrat	13	4	17
Scottish Green Party	0	7	7
Scottish Socialist Party	0	6	6
Scottish Senior Citizens' Unity Party	0	1	1
Independent MSPs/No affiliation	3	2	5
Presiding Officer (George Reid)	1	0	1

After the break from Westminster in 1999, the Scottish Parliament took control over a number of DEVOLVED MATTERS. These include education, health, local environment, housing, police, fire services, prisons, forestry, fisheries, sports, civil defence, food standards, tourism, criminal justice, planning, and heritage and the arts. The Scottish Parliament may introduce primary legislation and, significantly, has the power to raise or lower the basic rate of income tax by up to three pence in the pound. The Westminster Parliament kept control over certain RESERVED POWERS – for example foreign policy, defence, constitutional matters, the currency macro-economic decisions, and so on. The government of the Scottish Parliament is the Scottish Executive, which runs the day-to-day business of the devolved powers, manages a budget of c.£26bn, and is accountable to the Scottish Parliament (along with its Civil Service). Since 1999, the Executive has been a coalition between the Scottish Labour Party and the Scottish Liberal Democrats. The Executive is led by the First Minister (at present, Jack McConnell) who in turn appoints the Ministers.

——————— THE NATIONAL ASSEMBLY FOR WALES ———————

Cathays Park, Cardiff, CF1 3NQ · wales.gov.uk · 029 2082 5111

Welsh devolution was proposed in the Labour manifesto of 1997, and endorsed (by a slender majority) in the Welsh referendum of 18 September 1997: 50·3% endorsed the Assembly; turnout was 60·1%. The first elections were held on 6 May 1999, and are held every four years. The Assembly has 60 Members (AMs) – 40 are elected by 'first past the post' (1 AM for each constituency); the other 20 are elected by proportional representation (4 AMs for each of the 5 regions). The last election was held in May 2003, and the state of the parties at 1 Sep. 2005 was:

Number of AMs	*Constituency*	*Regional*	*Total*
Labour	29	0	29
Plaid Cymru	4	7	11
Conservative	1	10	11
Liberal Democrat	3	3	6
Others/Independents	2	0	2
Presiding Officer (Lord Dafydd Elis-Thomas)	1	0	1

The Welsh Assembly has no tax raising or varying powers, and is able to pass only secondary legislation on areas including agriculture, housing, industry, tourism, health, highways, the environment, and so on. The Assembly elects the First Minister (currently Rhodri Morgan) who in turn selects a Cabinet to perform the day-to-day business of government – all of whom are accountable to the Assembly.

——————— THE NORTHERN IRELAND ASSEMBLY ———————

Stormont, Belfast, BT4 3XX · www.niassembly.gov.uk · 028 9052 1333

The Northern Ireland Assembly was established as a result of the April 1998 Belfast ('Good Friday') Agreement, and endorsed by referenda in N. Ireland and the Republic of Ireland a month later. The Assembly has 108 members (6 from each of the 18 Westminster constituencies) elected by Single Transferable Votes. It enjoys a broad range of transferred powers (e.g. health and agriculture), with some powers (e.g. policing) that may be transferred later. However, since the first elections in June 1998, and actual devolution in 1999, the Assembly has been plagued by unrest over arms' decommissioning. Most recently, on 14 October 2002, the Assembly was suspended by the SoS for N. Ireland, John Reid, and direct rule from Westminster re-established. The Assembly was dissolved on 28 April 2003 for May elections that were postponed until November, at which the results were:

DUP ....33†	SDLP.................18	UKUP.................1
Sinn Féin............24	Alliance................6	Independent...........1
Ulster Unionists 24	PUP 1	†Includes 3 Ulster Unst. defectors.

After the elections, the Assembly was re-suspended – in which state it remains.

THE LONDON ASSEMBLY

The Greater London Authority (GLA), which consists of the Mayor and Assembly, was established by a referendum on 7 May 1998 (Yes: 72·0%; Turnout: 34·1%). The Mayor (currently Ken Livingstone) is directly elected by all London voters under the Supplementary Vote System (which allows for first and second choices). The 25-member Assembly (one for each of the 14 GLA constituencies, and 11 on a London-wide basis) is elected by the Additional Member System. Elections for Mayor and Assembly take place together, every four years. The GLA enjoys powers over eight areas of London life: transport; planning; economic development; the environment; police; fire and emergency planning; health; and culture. The last election was held in June 2004, and the state of the parties at July 2005 was this:

Conservative 9	Liberal Democrat 5	UK Independence..... 2
Labour................. 7	Green 2	(June 2004 turnout, 36·6%)

POLITICAL NICKNAMES OF NOTE

Tony Blair .... *Bambi; Bliar; Poodle*
George W. Bush .... *Dubya; 43; Shrub*
James Callaghan............ *Sunny Jim*
Bill Clinton .... *Slick Willie, Bubba*
Jack Cunningham .... *the Enforcer*
Edwina Currie .... *Cruella; Eggwina*
Frank Dobson .... *Dobbo; Uncle Albert*
Michael Heseltine ...... *Hezza; Tarzan*
Michael Howard.............. *Dracula*
Neil Kinnock....... *the Welsh Windbag*
Ken Livingstone.............. *Red Ken*
Harold Macmillan .... *Supermac*
Peter Mandleson ...... *Dome Secretary; Bobby; Mandy; the Prince of Darkness*

Reginald Manningham-Buller.........
Bullying-Manner
Colin Moynihan... *Miniature for Sport*
Richard Nixon .... *Tricky Dick(y)*
Michael Martin .... *Gorbals Mick*
Dudley Pound............ *Phoney Quid*
John Prescott .. *Two Jags; Prezza; Luigi*
Ronald Reagan.............. *the Gipper*
John Redwood .... *the Vulcan*
Dennis Skinner ... *the Beast of Bolsover*
Margaret Thatcher............. *Maggie; the Iron Lady*
Ann Widdecombe .... *Doris Karloff*
David Willetts.............. *Two Brains*

MINISTERIAL GIFTS

The Ministerial Code of ethics [see p.261] states that no Minister or public servant, or their families, should 'accept gifts, hospitality, or services from anyone which would, or might appear to, place them under an obligation'. Gifts worth less than £140 may be kept by the recipient, but those worth more must be given to the department for use, display, or disposal. Ministers may elect to purchase the gift at its cash value (minus £140). The Cabinet Office publishes an annual list of gifts received, from which we learn that in 2004–05 Tony Blair received a number of gifts worth >£140 including: a Segway transporter (King of Jordan); a porcelain dish (Govt. of Turkey); silver beakers (Longley Park Sixth Form College); an electric car (President of Ferrari); a bronze fox (Govt. of Belgium); and a Nativity scene (President, Palestinian National Authority). John Prescott declared no gifts.

———————— THE FATHER OF THE HOUSE ————————

The Father of the House is the MP who has enjoyed the longest unbroken service in the Commons (currently Alan Williams). Although the position affords little day-to-day power (except, perhaps, for conferring some respect), the Father of the House does preside at the election of the Speaker at the beginning of a Parliament or when the Speaker steps down. In addition, the Father of the House may be encouraged to move motions of a ceremonial nature (e.g. offering congratulations on a Royal marriage), or to speak on issues of historical precedent or perspective. A number of notable parliamentarians have been Fathers of the House, including Campbell-Bannerman, Lloyd George, Churchill, Callaghan, and Ted Heath who was widely criticised for presiding over the clumsy election of Speaker Martin.

———————— ELIGIBILITY FOR PARLIAMENT ————————

To be an MP a person must be over 21 and a citizen of Britain, the Republic of Ireland or a Commonwealth country. EU citizens cannot become MPs unless they meet the above requirements, although they may stand as candidates at local and European elections. The following are disqualified from sitting in the Commons:

Peers who sit in the House of Lords · undischarged bankrupts · those who hold offices of profit under the Crown† (including holders of judicial office, civil servants, members of the armed forces or the police forces, members of the legislature of any country or territory outside the Commonwealth, and Government nominated directors of commercial companies) · those found guilty of one or more offences and sentenced to more than 12 months in prison are disqualified while detained in the United Kingdom, Channel Islands, Isle of Man or the Republic of Ireland · those found guilty of certain electoral offences (corrupt or illegal practices).

† As the result of a resolution passed by the Commons in 1623, MPs cannot resign. Seats can only be vacated by an MP's death, elevation to the peerage, expulsion, or disqualification (as above), or by the dissolution of Parliament. Thus, an MP who wishes to leave the Commons is obliged to engineer disqualification by applying for a spurious 'office of profit under the Crown'. Traditionally, the two offices are:

Crown Steward and Bailiff of the three
Chiltern Hundreds of Stoke, Desborough, and Burnham
or
Crown Steward and Bailiff of the Manor of Northstead

Once an MP has applied for one of these posts, their Warrant of Office is signed by the Chancellor of the Exchequer, their parliamentary seat becomes vacant, and a by-election is called. Some who have left Parliament in this rococo manner are:

Betty Boothroyd [C100s] · Alastair Goodlad [C100s] · Neil Kinnock [C100s]
Leon Brittan [MoN] · Matthew Parris [MoN] · J. Enoch Powell [MoN]

———— PARLIAMENTARY SALARY & ALLOWANCES ————

Members of Parliament (from April 2005)
Members' Parliamentary Salary £59,095
Staffing Allowance (maximum) £84,081
Incidental Expenses Provision (IEP) £20,000
IT equipment (centrally provided) .... worth *c*.£3,000
London Supplement (for inner London seats) £2,613
Additional Costs Allowance (for those with seats outside London) £21,634
Winding up Allowance (maximum) £34,694
Car Mileage, first 10,000 miles .... 40p per mile
— thereafter .... 25p per mile
Motorcycle allowance .... 24p per mile
Bicycle allowance .... 20p per mile

Total Ministerial pay comprises Parliamentary salary (above) and Ministerial salary:

Position	Ministerial salary	total pay
Prime Minister†	£124,837	£183,932
Cabinet Minister	£74,902	£133,997
Cabinet Minister (Lords)	—	£101,668
Minister of State	£38,854	£97,949
Minister of State (Lords)	—	79,382
Parliamentary Under Secretary	£29,491	£88,586
Parliamentary Under Secretary (Lords)	—	£69,138
Government Chief Whip	£74,902	£133,997
Government Deputy Chief Whip	£38,854	£97,949
Government Whip	£25,005	£84,100
Leader of the Opposition	£68,662	£127,757
Leader of the Opposition (Lords)	—	£69,138
Opposition Chief Whip	£38,854	£97,949
Speaker	£74,902	£133,997
Lord Chancellor	—	£213,899
Attorney General	—	£106,358

(† 2005 research by the Hay Group shows that European Prime Ministers are paid only
10–25% of the salaries garnered by comparable Chief Executives in the private sector.)

Backbench Peers
Subsistence .... Day £75 · Overnight £150
Office secretarial allowance .... £65 per sitting day and <40 additional days
Travel .... as for MPs
Spouse/children's expenses .... 6 return journeys per year
Lords' Ministers and paid office holders
Ministers' Night Subsistence Allowance ... £33,000 for those with a second home in London
London Supplement .... £1,667 except those with official residence &c.
Secretarial allowance £4,884
Spouse/children's expenses .... 15 return journeys per year

—— SALARIES FOR DEVOLVED LEGISLATURES &c. ——

Scottish Parliament 2005–6	*additional salary*	*total salary*
Member of the Scottish Parliament (MSP)	—	£51,709
First Minister	£74,903	£126,612
Scottish Minister	£38,857	£90,566
Junior Scottish Minister	£24,338	£76,047
Presiding Officer	£38,857	£90,566

National Assembly for Wales 2005–6	*additional salary*	*total salary*
Assembly Member (AM)	—	£45,232
Assembly First Minister	£74,903	£120,135
Assembly Minister	£38,853	£84,085
Presiding Officer	£38,853	£84,085
Leader of the largest non-cabinet party	£38,853	£84,085
AMs who are also MPs or MEPs		£15,077

Northern Ireland Assembly	*total salary*
Members of the Legislative Assembly	£31,817
Presiding Officer	£48,850

The Assembly has been suspended since 14 October 2002. In December 2003, these salaries were introduced (at a lower rate than if the Assembly were sitting) to pay MLAs for constituency work.

European Parliament 2005–6	*total salary*
UK Members of the European Parliament	£59,095

Members of Parliament who are also members of a devolved legislature receive the full parliamentary salary (see above) and one third of the salary due to them for their other role. Since 2004, Westminster MPs are ineligible to serve additionally as MEPs. The devolved legislatures control their own expenses and allowances.

London Assembly 2005–6	*total salary*
Member of the London Assembly (MLA)	£49,266
Mayor of London	£115,793
Deputy Mayor	£71,995

Some other salaries of note (for 2005)	*total salary*
Director General of the BBC	£459,000
Governor of the Bank of England	£268,135
Lord Chief Justice	£211,399
Master of the Rolls	£191,276
Archbishop of Canterbury	£64,400

—— COST OF PRIME MINISTERIAL COSMETICS ——

In reponse to written a Parliamentary question, No. 10 revealed that between May 1997–July 2005, Tony Blair spent £1,841·42 on make-up and make-up artists.

―――――――――― TIMELINE OF ELECTORAL LAW ――――――――

1832 .... *property qualifications to vote introduced; 'rotten boroughs' abolished*
1872 .... *secret ballot introduced*
1885 .... *distribution of seats reorganised*
1911 .... *five-year Parliamentary terms introduced*
1918 .... *all men ≥21 entitled to vote; women ≥30 entitled to vote*
1928 .... *all women ≥21 entitled to vote*
1949 .... *'university vote' and 'business vote' abolished*
1969 .... *voting aged dropped to 18 for all*
1985 .... *British citizens overseas eligible to vote for ≤5 years after they leave*
1989 .... *qualifying period for overseas electors extended from 5 to 20 years*
1994 .... *EU residents in UK entitled to vote and stand in UK European elections*
1995 ... *EU residents in UK obliged to register and entitled to stand in local elections*
1998 .... *registration of political parties and symbols introduced*
2000 .... *registration rules changed; postal voting extended; disabled voters assisted;
       funding and spending of parties controlled; Electoral Commission established*
2002 .... *all-women shortlists for Parliamentary candidates permitted*

―――――――――――― GUESTS AT CHEQUERS ――――――――――

A relentless Freedom of Information campaign by Norman Lamb MP has coerced No.10 into releasing the names of those who have attended official dinners at Chequers [see p.260]. Some of those who have dined (July 1997–April 2005) include:

Clive Anderson	Stephen Fry	Esther Rantzen	Kevin Spacey
Dickie Bird	Bob Geldof	Simon Rattle	Patrick Stewart
Cilla Black	Mick Hucknall	Steve Redgrave	Sting
Bono	Jeremy Irons	Richard & Judy	Imogen Stubbs
David Bowie	Simon Mayo	Alan Rickman	Alan Sugar
Melvyn Bragg	John Mortimer	Anita Roddick	Emma Thompson
Richard Branson	John Motson	Alan Rusbridger	Pete Townshend
Richard Curtis	James Naughtie	Salman Rushdie	Michael Winner
Sinead Cusack	Trevor Nunn	Jimmy Savile	David Yelland
Dawn French	David Puttnam	Delia Smith	Kirsty Young

―――――――― CHANNEL 4 POLITICAL AWARDS · 2005 ――――――

The Channel 4 News award .... Boris Johnson [Con]
The politician's politician .... Alan Johnson (SoS Work and Pensions) [Lab]
Opposition politician of the year .... John Bercow [Con]
Hansard award for political innovation .... Steve Webb [Lib D]
Political humorist of the year .... Steve Bell, *The Guardian*
Campaigning politician .... Geraldine Smith (Morecambe cocklepickers) [Lab]
Peer of the year .... Baroness Mallalieu (Pres. Countryside Alliance) [Lab]
Political book of the year .... *An Honourable Deception* · Clare Short [Lab]

———————————— QUANGOS ————————————

QUANGOs are Quasi-Autonomous Non-Governmental Organisations: semi-public bodies funded in full or part by the taxpayer, whose appointed members are not directly accountable to the electorate. They are also known, less catchily, as Non-Departmental Public Bodies (NDPBs). Since QUANGOs began to flourish in the 1960s, they have come under almost constant attack for their reliance on patronage, their tendency to bureaucracy, and their unaccountability. Critics have accused governments in turn of devolving powers to QUANGOs in the false belief that they are more efficient than civil servants – and to diminish the perception of waste. However, QUANGOs are not necessarily as bureaucratic and incompetent as they tend to be painted. The Medical Research Council, Trinity House Lighthouse Service, the Victoria & Albert Museum, and the National Criminal Intelligence Service are some of the many QUANGOs performing vital public functions. However, the perceived redundancy of many such organisations (the Pig Production Development Committee, perhaps) does much to undermine public confidence. *The Essential Guide to British Quangos* (2005) by Dan Lewis casts a sceptical eye over the proliferation of QUANGOs, and names his 9 most 'useless':

> *British Potato Council · Milk Development Council · Energy Savings Trust*
> *Agricultural Wages Committees · Wine Standards Board*
> *Westminster Foundation for Democracy · Football Licensing Authority*
> *Investors in People UK · Economic and Social Research Council*

———————————— PARLIAMENTARY PERIODS ————————————

Parliament .... period from *election* to *dissolution* (maximum 5 years)
Session .... runs from *State Opening* to *Prorogation*
Recess .... a break within a *session* – e.g. Christmas, Easter
State Opening† .... heralds new *session* or new *parliament*
Prorogation .... heralds the end of a *session*
Dissolution .... the end of a *parliament* – heralds new elections
Week .... a long time in politics, according to Harold Wilson

† The State Opening of Parliament takes place when Parliament reconvenes after a general election, and then when each new session begins (normally in November). At the State Opening, members of the Commons are summoned to the Lords by Black Rod [see p.254] to hear the Queen's Speech. The speech, which outlines the government's proposed legislation for the session ahead, is read by the Sovereign but written by her Government. If the Monarch is unable to attend the State Opening (as the Queen was in 1959 and 1963), Parliament is opened by the Lords Commissioners (the Lord Chancellor, the Lord President of the Council, the Lord Privy Seal, the Lord Steward, and the Lord Chamberlain). The Lord Chancellor then delivers the Monarch's speech in the third person. (Before each State Opening, the cellars of the Palace of Westminster are searched by the Yeoman of the Guard to prevent a recurrence of the treasonous Gunpowder Plot that took place on 5 November 1605.)

—————————— PARLIAMENTARY MISCELLANY ——————————

ERSKINE MAY · refers to the *Treatise on the Law, Privileges, Proceedings & Usage of Parliament* – first published by Clerk of the House, Thomas Erskine May, in 1844 – which (now in its 22nd edition) is acknowledged as the authoritative text on the law and practice of both Houses of Parliament.

PARLIAMENTARY PRIVILEGE · the House of Commons enjoys various rights to protect its sovereignty, the most important of which is the immunity of MPs from prosecution for sedition, libel or slander for anything said during proceedings in the House.

ANOTHER PLACE · the term by which (according to convention) members of the Commons and Lords refer to the other Chamber.

BLACK ROD · or *The Gentleman Usher of the Black Rod,* is the Lords' equivalent of the Serjeant-at-Arms in the Commons. At the State Opening of Parliament he is sent to the Commons to summon MPs to the Lords for the Queen's Speech. (To symbolise the independence of the Commons, the door to the Chamber is slammed in his face, and he knocks three times to be admitted.)

SPEAKER · the Speaker is an MP elected by fellow members, who presides over and represents the Commons. MPs may only speak if they 'catch the Speaker's eye' and are called by him or her to speak.

OPPOSITION DAYS · 20 days per parliamentary session set aside for debates chosen by the Opposition – 17 for the Official Opposition, 3 for the third largest party.

NO CONFIDENCE MOTIONS · are those on the subject of confidence in a Government, or those central to a Government's agenda (such as the Budget). If such debates are lost, the Government is under the obligation of convention to resign. The last no confidence motion to be passed was in 1979, which the Labour Government lost by just 1 vote.

ADJOURNMENT DEBATES · half-hour debates introduced just before the end of the day's business. They have no likelihood of becoming law, and are used to raise awareness of certain subjects, often those of a local or personal interest to a backbench MP.

SITTING · the Commons usually sits during these hours of the week:

Mon..............	2:30pm – 10:30pm
Tue & Wed	11:30am – 7:30pm
Thur..............	11:30am – 6:00pm
Fri (some)	9:30am – 3:00pm

SNUFF · a snuffbox is kept at the door of the Commons, and MPs are entitled to take snuff when in the Chamber. (Smoking has been prohibited since 1693.)

USUAL CHANNELS · a colloquial term for negotiations between the Whips of different parties. It has often been said that the usual channels of British politics are the 'most polluted waterways in London'.

MAIDEN SPEECH · an MP's initial speech given on first being elected. By convention they are heard without interruption, and usually include tributes to the previous MP and to the delights of the people and environment of a new MP's constituency.

—————— PARLIAMENTARY MISCELLANY cont. ——————

AYE · a vote in favour of a motion, as opposed to 'NO'.

HANSARD · is the official edited 'substantially' verbatim report of proceedings in both Houses – Members' speeches are reproduced with repetitions and redundancies cut and clear mistakes corrected.

WEST LOTHIAN QUESTION · the dilemma, posed by Tam Dalyell, as to how, after devolution, an MP from Scotland could vote on matters affecting English seats, but not on matters that had been devolved to a Scottish Parliament.

GIVING WAY · when a speaking MP allows another member to interrupt.

ANNUNCIATOR · TV screens around the House which display current and future business and divisions.

QUORUM · the minimum number of MPs required for a vote: 40.

SHORT MONEY · funding allocated by Parliament to support the opposition parties in their official duties. It was introduced in 1975 by the Wilson Government, and is named after the architect of the scheme, Edward Short. ('Cranborne money' was introduced for opposition parties in the Lords in 1996 by the then leader of the Lords, Lord Cranborne.) The total amount of Short money paid to opposition parties for 2004–5 was £5,350,509·84.

HATS · male MPs are prohibited from addressing the House while wearing a hat. Until 1998, those wishing to raise a point of order during a division had to be wearing a hat.

UNPARLIAMENTARY LANGUAGE · in order to maintain the dignity of Parliament and its members, certain words have been declared 'unparliamentary' by Speakers over the years. Such words (which include *coward, git, swine, traitor, hooligan, rat,* and *liar*) tend to be those considered coarse or abusive, or those that imply an MP is lying or drunk. An MP using such language will be asked to withdraw the words and, if they refuse, may be 'named' and suspended. Winston Churchill famously employed the euphemism 'terminological inexactitude' instead of 'lie'.

GREEN PAPER · a consultative document issued by the Government to outline legislative options and invite comment from interested parties. WHITE PAPERS are a more conclusive statement of policy intent, detailing the proposed content of the Bill that is to be presented to Parliament. In an attempt to streamline the process of legislation, more Bills are being published in draft form to allow backbenchers and interested parties time to comment on the proposals.

DIVISION BELL · votes in the House of Commons are known as 'divisions'. Members 'divide' by walking through either the Aye or No lobby, where their names are recorded by tellers from each party. Divisions are signalled on the annunciator screens, and by the sounding of the 'Division Bell' in the Palace of Westminster. Since divisions can take place throughout the day and night, many local restaurants and bars are equipped with bells that warn MPs they must return to vote. (*The Division Bell* is also the name of the 1994 album by *Pink Floyd*.)

—————— UK POST-WAR ELECTION BREAKDOWN ——————

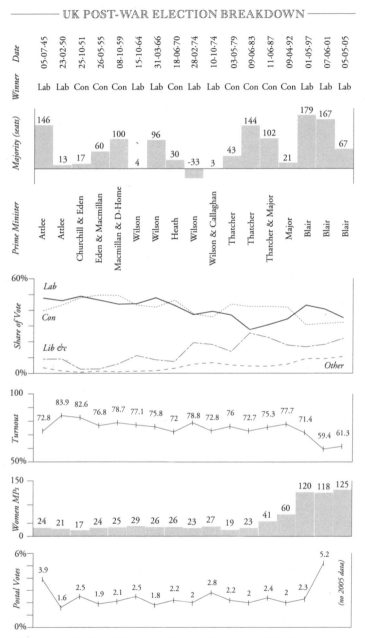

There is a surprising degree of dispute surrounding many of these figures, especially winning majorities.

─────── SHARE OF VOTE vs SHARE OF SEATS ───────

British general elections are run under the 'First Past The Post' system, where the candidate with the greatest number of votes in a given constituency is the winner. This system tends to produce results where the number of Parliamentary seats a party wins is disproportionate to the number of votes cast for it. In general terms, FPTP favours the Labour and Conservative parties, who enjoy strong local popularity, and penalises the Liberal Democrats whose support is more evenly spread across the country. Below is a breakdown of the percentage of votes cast for each party compared with the percentage of seats taken after each election. In the 2005 election, for example, the Labour party received 55·2% of the seats from 35·25% of votes. In contrast, a Lib Dem vote of 22·0% gave them 9·6% of seats.

Election	Conservative	Labour	Liberal	Other
	% vote → % seats	% vote → % seats	% vote → % seats	% vote → % seats
05·07·45	39·7 → 33·0	*47·7 → 61·4	9·0 → 1·9	3·6 → 3·8
23·02·50	43·3 → 47·7	*46·1 → 50·4	9·1 → 1·4	1·5 → 0·5
25·10·51	*48·0 → 51·4	48·8 → 47·2	2·6 → 1·0	0·7 → 0·5
26·05·55	*49·6 → 54·8	46·4 → 44·0	2·7 → 1·0	1·3 → 0·3
08·10·59	*49·4 → 57·9	43·8 → 41·0	5·9 → 1·0	1·0 → 0·2
15·10·64	43·3 → 48·3	*44·1 → 50·3	11·2 → 1·4	1·4 → 0·0
31·03·66	41·9 → 40·2	*47·9 → 57·6	8·5 → 1·9	1·7 → 0·3
18·06·70	*46·4 → 52·4	43·0 → 45·7	7·5 → 1·0	3·1 → 1·0
28·02·74	37·8 → 46·8	*37·2 → 47·4	19·3 → 2·2	5·8 → 3·6
10·10·74	35·7 → 43·6	*39·3 → 50·2	18·3 → 2·0	6·7 → 4·1
03·05·79	*43·9 → 53·4	37·0 → 42·4	13·8 → 1·7	5·3 → 2·5
09·06·83	*42·4 → 61·1	27·6 → 32·2	25·4 → 3·5	4·6 → 3·2
11·06·87	*42·4 → 57·8	30·8 → 35·2	22·6 → 3·4	4·4 → 3·5
09·04·92	*41·9 → 51·6	34·4 → 41·6	17·8 → 3·1	5·8 → 3·7
01·05·97	30·7 → 25·0	*43·2 → 63·6	16·8 → 7·0	9·3 → 4·4
07·06·01	31·7 → 25·2	*40·7 → 62·7	18·3 → 7·9	9·3 → 4·2
05·05·05	32·3 → 30·5	*35·2 → 55·2	22·0 → 9·6	10·5 → 4·7

* Indicates the party formed a goverment. No post-War government has had a majority of the vote.

─────── SUCCESSFUL PRIME MINISTERS ───────

In July 2005, a Populus Network survey of 216 'opinion formers' (chief executives, company chairmen, &c.) asked how successful various Prime Ministers had been:

	Successful		Neutral	Unsuccessful		time as
	very	fairly		fairly	very	PM
Thatcher	55	35	3	5	3	11y 209d
Blair	27	56	9	5	3	[see p.243]
Churchill	40	31	15	11	2	8y 240d
Macmillan	4	44	30	18	4	6y 281d
Wilson	2	35	20	33	11	7y 279d
Heath	1	10	22	40	28	3y 259d

––––––––––––––––– SOME ELECTORAL MISCELLANY –––––––––––––––––

THURSDAYS · the Prime Minister may call a general election on any day except those considered 'dies non' [see over]. However, since 1935 every General Election has been held on a Thursday. It seems that Thursdays were originally selected since they were the furthest day from any influence from the paypacket (Fridays), or the pulpit (Sundays).

MONTH · of the 16 general elections held since 1945, 3 have been in May; 4 in October; 4 in June; 2 in February; and 1 each in March, April and July. No election has been held in January since 1910, and the last election held in December followed the Armistice in 1918.

POLLING HOURS · are 7am–10pm in general elections.

MULTIPLE POLLS · candidates are allowed to stand for election in any number of seats. If they are elected to more than one, complex rules exist to decide which they will represent.

TACTICAL VOTING · the practice of voting for a candidate who you do not actually support, in order to deny victory to another. Such a tactic was first widely adopted in February 1974, where in some constituencies Labour supporters voted Liberal to undermine the Tories. It is suggested that First Past The Post encourages this kind of negative voting, whereas PR makes it easier to vote for one's preferred candidate.

DEAD HEAT · if two or more candidates poll an equal number of votes, the Returning Officer decides the result by lot, in any manner he likes.

DEATH · if a candidate dies prior to the publication of the statement of persons nominated, the election can proceed in the normal way. However, if a candidate dies *after* publication of this statement the Acting Returning Officer must countermand the notice of the poll or, if voting has already begun, must direct that polling be abandoned. Then, new elections must be arranged as if the writ for that election had been received 28 days after the day on which proof of the candidate's death was given to the Acting Returning Officer. This unusual situation occurred in the 2005 general election when the Lib Dem candidate for South Staffordshire, Jo Harrison, died on 30 April. The poll was abandoned, and a new election held on 23 June; the Tories held the seat.

COSTS · the administration of general elections is funded by the Treasury. Since WWII, elections have cost:

Year	£m		
1945	0·7	1974 Feb	5·0
1950	0·8	1974 Oct	6·0
1951	0·9	1979	13·8
1955	1·0	1983	23·4
1959	1·1	1987	36·1
1964	1·7	1992	38·0
1966	1·6	1997*	45·8
1970	3·7	2001*	51·0
		* *estimated cost*	

DEPOSITS · candidates must deposit £500 with the *Acting Returning Officer* when nomination papers are delivered. Any candidate who polls less than one-twentieth of the total votes cast forfeits this deposit, which goes into the Consolidated Fund (i.e. general taxation). Other deposits are returned. The number of deposits lost at the 2005 general election was 1,382.

—————— SOME ELECTORAL MISCELLANY cont. ——————

HOMELESS · the homeless or those with no permanent residence can register to vote (for a period of 1 year) by declaring a local connection and giving an address to which communications can be sent, or by undertaking to collect communications from the Electoral Registration Officer.

GENERAL ELECTION TIMETABLE · elections are held 17 working days (excluding 'dies non' [see below]) after the date of the Proclamation and the issue of the writs. Notice of an election must be published by the (Acting) Returning Officer no later than 4pm on the 3rd day after the day the writ is issued. Nomination papers must be received not later than the 6th working day after the issue of the writ (between 10am–4pm). Polling day is the 11th working day after the last day for receipt of nomination papers.

DIES NON · days that are excluded for certain legal calculations. In electoral terms they are: Saturdays, Sundays, Christmas Eve, Christmas Day, Maundy Thursday, Good Friday, Bank holidays in any part of the United Kingdom, and any day appointed for public thanksgiving or mourning.

EXIT POLLS · it is unlawful to publish before the polls have closed at 10pm any statement or forecast as to the result of the election which is based upon information supplied by voters after they have voted (i.e. exit polls). The maximum penalty for contravention of this rule is 6 months imprisonment and a fine of £5,000. However, unlike in some countries, the publication of opinion polls during an election and even on polling day is not prohibited.

RE-COUNTS · any candidate may ask for a re-count in their constituency, though the final decision rests with the Acting Returning Officer. In practice, re-counts occur when a counting error is suspected; the winning margin is very small; or if a candidate has only just failed to keep their deposit. In the latter case, only that candidate's votes are re-counted.

REGISTERED ELECTORS · as of 1 December 2004 there were 44,180,243 parliamentary electors. Of the 659 constituencies, the most populous are the Isle of Wight (108,253 voters) and SW Norfolk (88,774). The least are the Western Isles (21,346) and Orkney & Shetland (32,876). The average constituency in the UK has *c*.68,000 registered voters.

KHAKI ELECTION · the snap election called by Conservative PM, the Earl of Salisbury, in October 1900 in the wake of British victories in the 2nd Boer War. The tactic was marginally successful, and the Tories were returned with a slightly increased majority. 'Khaki' refers to the the colour of the army's uniform in South Africa, and the term has subsequently been applied to any election held in the wake of a military success (e.g. the 1983 post-Falklands election).

REJECTED VOTES · Acting Returning Officers will reject ballot papers for a number of reasons: [1] if they do not bear the official mark; [2] if votes are given for more than the maximum number of candidates; [3] if anything is written or marked by which the voter can be identified; or [4] if they are unmarked or if the intention of the voter is not certain.

─────SOME MINISTERIAL RESIDENCES OF NOTE─────

10 Downing Street, London...Prime Minister
11 Downing Street, London...........................Chancellor of the Exchequer
12 Downing Street, London..............................Government Chief Whip
Chequers, Buckinghamshire...Prime Minister
Dorneywood.......Chancellor of the Exchequer (but currently, the Deputy PM)
1 Carlton Gardens, London, and Chevening.....................Foreign Secretary
Hillsborough Castle..............Sec. State for Northern Ireland (and the Queen)
Bute House, Edinburgh...................................First Minister of Scotland

10 Downing St. was given to Walpole by George II. While Chancellors were regular inhabitants in the C19th, since Balfour it has been the home of all PMs. 11 Downing St. has housed Chancellors since 1828. The flats above Nos. 10 & 11 usually house PM and Chancellor respectively. However, to accommodate Blair's family, Gordon Brown swapped flats to move, amusingly, above No.10.

─────IMPEACHMENT─────

Although Britain has seen fewer than 70 impeachments, and no one has been impeached since Lord Melville was charged and acquitted in 1806, Parliament still retains the power to impeach MPs and Lords. The two Houses can prosecute for any crime they like – exercising, in the words of Erskine May [see p.254], 'the functions of a high court of justice and of a jury'. The procedure is complex, and varies depending whether the accused is a Commoner or Peer. In essence, the Commons determines if an impeachment is warranted, and prepares and prosecutes the case. The Lords questions the accused, summons witnesses and adjudicates. It is for the Commons to demand judgement be passed, or to pardon the accused (the Sovereign has no right of pardon in such cases). A number of recent reports into parliamentary privilege have called for impeachment to be abandoned, claiming that in the modern political culture it is effectively obsolete. Yet, in 2004, 11 MPs expressed an intention to impeach Tony Blair for taking Britain to war against Iraq [see www.impeach-blair.org]. These MPs will have to persuade the Commons that Blair has a case to answer – a task that failed the last time it was attempted, when some MPs tried to impeach the Foreign Secretary, Palmerston, in 1848 over an alleged secret treaty with Russia.

─────SPECTATOR PARLIAMENTARIAN AWARDS '05─────

Backbencher of the year..Vera Baird [Lab]
Minister to watch ....Alan Johnson [Lab]
Speech of the year............................(hunting speech) Barry Sheerman [Lab]
Survivor of the year ....John Redwood [Con]
Peer of the year ....Baroness Mallalieu [Lab]
Politician of the year ....Charles Kennedy [Lib D]
Parliamentarian of the year ....Sir Peter Tapsell [Con]

——CLASSES OF SECRET——

Sensitive government documents are classed into four categories of secrecy:

TOP SECRET

Material likely to: threaten directly the internal stability of the UK or friendly countries; lead to widespread loss of life; cause exceptionally grave damage to the effectiveness or security of UK or allied forces or to the effectiveness of extremely valuable security operations; cause exceptionally grave damage to relations with friendly governments; cause severe long-term damage to the UK economy.

SECRET

Material likely to: raise international tension; damage seriously relations with friendly governments; threaten life directly, or seriously prejudice public order, or individual security or liberty; cause serious damage to the operational effectiveness or security of UK or allied forces or the continuing effectiveness of highly valuable security or intelligence operations; cause substantial material damage to national finances or economic and commercial interests.

CONFIDENTIAL

Material likely to: materially damage diplomatic relations (i.e. cause formal protest or other sanction); prejudice individual security or liberty; cause damage to the operational effectiveness or security of UK or allied forces or the effectiveness of valuable security or intelligence operations; work substantially against national finances or economic and commercial interests; substantially undermine the financial viability of major organisations; impede the investigation or facilitate the commission of serious crime; impede seriously the development or operation of major government policies; shut down or otherwise substantially disrupt significant national operations.

RESTRICTED

Material likely to: affect diplomatic relations adversely; cause substantial distress to individuals; make it more difficult to maintain the operational effectiveness or security of UK or allied forces; cause financial loss or facilitate improper gain or advantage; prejudice the investigation or aid the commission of crime; breach proper undertakings to maintain the confidence of information provided by third parties; impede the effective statutory restrictions on disclosure of information; disadvantage government in commercial or policy negotiations with others; undermine the proper management of the public sector.

A range of 'descriptors' can also be added, for example:
BUDGET......... *pre-announcement Budget measures*
HONOURS ... *actual or potential award of an honour*
INVESTIGATION............ *into discipline or crime*
VISITS......... *by royalty, ministers or very senior staff*
MEDICAL.......... *confidential reports and material*
CONTRACTS..... *tenders and terms being considered*

——MINISTERS' CONDUCT——

from THE MINISTERIAL CODE
*a Code of Conduct and Guidance
on Procedures for Ministers*

SELFLESSNESS · *Holders of public office should act solely in terms of the public interest. They should not do so in order to gain financial or other material benefits for themselves, their family, or their friends.*

INTEGRITY · *Holders of public office should not place themselves under any financial or other obligation to outside individuals or organisations that might seek to influence them in the performance of their official duties.*

OBJECTIVITY · *In carrying out public business, including making public appointments, awarding contracts, or recommending individuals for rewards and benefits, holders of public office should make choices on merit.*

ACCOUNTABILITY · *Holders of public office are accountable for their decisions and actions to the public and must submit themselves to whatever scrutiny is appropriate to their office.*

OPENNESS · *Holders of public office should be as open as possible about all the decisions and actions that they take. They should give reasons for their decisions and restrict information only when the wider public interest clearly demands.*

HONESTY · *Holders of public office have a duty to declare any private interests relating to their public duties and to take steps to resolve any conflicts arising in a way that protects the public interest.*

LEADERSHIP · *Holders of public office should promote and support these principles by leadership and example.*

—————————— PARLIAMENTARY WHIPS ——————————

He will tell you how Sir Somebody Something, when he was whipper-in for the
Government, brought four men out of their beds to vote in the majority…
— CHARLES DICKENS, *Sketches by Boz,* 1835

Whips are MPs or Peers appointed by each party to act as intermediaries between the leadership and backbenchers. Their main functions are to maintain discipline; keep members informed of parliamentary business; and ensure that backbench MPs vote the 'right way'. Whips also organise the 'pairing' system, where MPs of one party are 'paired' with MPs from another, allowing them both to be absent without affecting a division. Each week, the Whips produce an agenda (known as the 'Whip') which details upcoming business and indicates by a code of lines (also known as 'Whips') the importance of each vote. Items underlined *once* are routine and attendance is optional; items underlined *twice* are important and attendance is required unless a 'pair' has been arranged; items underlined *three times* (the 'three line Whip') are vital (e.g. motions of no confidence) – pairing is not normally allowed and failure to attend can result in an MPs suspension from their parliamentary party. It seems that the parliamentary use of the term *whip* originates from the language of the fox-hunt, where the *whipper-in* is the huntsman's assistant who drives stray hounds back into the pack with his whip.

—————— HUMPHREY · THE DOWNING STREET CAT ——————

In October 1989, a one-year-old black and white stray cat ensconced himself in the Cabinet Office in Whitehall. Inevitably he was named Humphrey, in honour of the archetypal *Yes Minister* civil servant Sir Humphrey Appleby. A memo written in 1992 described Humphrey as 'a workaholic who spends nearly all his time at the office, has no criminal record, does not socialise a great deal or go to many parties, and has not been involved in any sex or drugs scandals that we know of'. After a minor kidney disorder in 1993 Humphrey was placed on a diet (no 'treats or titbits'), although his illness did not prevent him from accusations of attacking a nest of newborn robins. In 1995, Humphrey vanished, only to return from the Royal Army Medical

Humphrey

College after a few months where he had been 'on holiday'. When the Blairs entered No. 10 in 1997 rumours circulated that Cherie was allergic to cats, considered them unhygienic, and wanted Humphrey out. To counter these allegations a photocall was set up with Humphrey in Cherie's arms. However, Humphrey's illness worsened and late in 1997 a press release was issued that the Chief Mouser to the Cabinet Office had retired. The media, still of the opinion that harm had befallen Humphrey, were taken to a secret South London location to photograph him alongside newspapers of the day to prove he was alive. It has been pointed out that one anagram of 'Humphrey the Downing Street cat' is 'Cherie wants mog hurt? Thy end pet!'

———————————— BRITISH OVERSEAS TERRITORIES ————————————

The fourteen British Overseas Territories [with estimated populations (2003)] are:

Anguilla [12,200] · British Antarctic Territory [0] · Bermuda [64,500]
British Indian Ocean Territory [4,000] · British Virgin Islands [21,300]
Cayman Islands [42,000] · Falkland Islands [2,379, at 2001]
Gibraltar [28,231, at 2001]· Montserrat [4,483]
St Helena [4000] & dependencies (Ascension Is. [1000] & Tristan da Cunha [275])
Turks and Caicos Islands [20,014, at 2001] · Pitcairn Island [47]
South Georgia & South Sandwich Islands [0] · Sovereign Cyprus Base Areas [n/a]

———————————— BRITISH PASSPORT WORDING ————————————

*Her Britannic Majesty's Secretary of State requests and requires in the name of Her
Majesty all those whom it may concern to allow the bearer to pass freely without let or
hindrance and to afford the bearer such assistance and protection as may be necessary.*

Since British passports are issued in the name of Her Majesty, the Queen does not
possess one, although all other members of the Royal Family do – including the
Duke of Edinburgh. In other states where the Queen is Sovereign, similar wording
is used, except that the request is made in the name of the Queen's representative
in that realm – such as the Governor-General, or the Minister of Foreign Affairs.

———————————— THE COMMONWEALTH ————————————

The Commonwealth of Nations is a voluntary association of 53 sovereign states –
all of which, excepting Mozambique, have experienced direct or indirect British
rule. Although the Commonwealth has no formal constitution or charter, its
common goals are declared to be the promotion of 'democracy and good
governance, respect for human rights and gender equality, the rule of law, and
sustainable economic and social development'. The Commonwealth members are:

Antigua & Barbuda* · Australia* · Bahamas* · Bangladesh · Barbados*
Belize* · Botswana · Brunei Darussalam · Cameroon · Canada* · Cyprus
Dominica · Fiji Islands · The Gambia · Ghana · Grenada* · Guyana
India · Jamaica* · Kenya · Kiribati · Lesotho · Malaysia · Malawi
Maldives · Malta · Mauritius · Mozambique · Namibia · Nauru
New Zealand* · Nigeria · Pakistan · Papua New Guinea*
St Kitts & Nevis* · St Lucia* · St Vincent* · Samoa · Seychelles
Sierra Leone · Singapore · Solomon Islands* · South Africa
Sri Lanka · Swaziland · Tanzania · Tonga · Trinidad & Tobaga
Tuvalu* · Uganda · United Kingdom · Vanuatu · Zambia

In December 2003 Zimbabwe withdrew its membership after its suspension was not lifted.
* The Queen is not only Queen of the UK and its overseas territories, but also of these realms.

—————————— THE EUROPEAN UNION ——————————

The European Union (EU) has its roots in the European Coal & Steel Community (ECSC) formed in 1951 between Belgium, France, Germany, Italy, Luxembourg, and the Netherlands, who united to co-operate over production of coal and steel: the two key components of war. Since then, through a series of treaties, Europe as an economic and political entity has developed in size, harmonisation, and power. For some, the expansion in EU membership [see below] and the introduction of the euro (in 2002) are welcome developments in securing co-operation and peace; for others, the growth of the EU is a threat to the sovereignty of member nations.

MAJOR EU INSTITUTIONS

European Parliament · the democratic voice of the people of Europe, the EP approves the EU budget; oversees the other EU institutions; assents to key treaties and agreements on accession; and, alongside the Council of Ministers, examines and approves EU legislation. The EP sits in Strasbourg and Brussels, and its members are directly elected every 5 years.

Council of the EU · the pre-eminent decision-making body, the Council is made up of ministers from each national government. The Council meets regularly in Brussels to decide EU policy and approve laws, and every three months Presidents and PMs meet at European Councils to make major policy decisions.

European Commission · proposes new laws for the Council and Parliament to consider, and undertakes much of the EU's day-to-day work, such as oversee-ing the implementation of EU rules. Commissioners are nominated by each member state, and the President of the Commission is chosen by the national governments. It is based in Brussels.

European Court · ensures EU law is observed and applied fairly, and settles any disputes arising. Each state sends a judge to the Court in Luxembourg.

EU MEMBERSHIP

Since the founding of the European Economic Community [EEC] by the Treaty of Rome in 1957, the (now) EU membership has developed as follows:

Country	entry	members
Belgium		
France		
Germany	1958	6
Italy		
Luxembourg		
Netherlands		
Denmark		
Ireland	1973	9
UK		
Greece	1981	10
Portugal	1986	12
Spain		
Austria		
Finland	1995	15
Sweden		
Cyprus		
Czech Rep.		
Estonia		
Hungary		
Latvia	2004	25
Lithuania		
Malta		
Poland		
Slovakia		
Slovenia		
Bulgaria	*'on track'*	
Romania		
Turkey	*'negotiating'*	
Croatia		

─────────── UK EUROPE REFERENDUM · 1975 ───────────

The Europe referendum question, held on 6 June 1975, was 'Do you think that the UK should stay in the European Community (the Common Market)?'

Electorate 40,086,677 · *Votes cast* 29,453,194 · *Turnout* 64% · *Yes vote* 67·1%

─────────── THE EUROPEAN CONSTITUTION ───────────

A new EU constitution was agreed in 2004 to reflect changes in the size and complexity of the EU. The new constitution would 'streamline' and 'simplify' the EU; establish a full-time President of the Council; create a European Foreign Minister; change the voting systems; recognise devolved governments; and so on. However, before the treaty has effect it must be ratified by every member. Some states use a parliamentary vote for ratification, others employ a referendum. After voters in France and the Netherlands rejected the constitution, the ratification process was placed on hold in many states. The state of ratification [1·9·2005] is:

Country	ratification status		
Austria	*ratified by Parliament*	Italy	*ratified by Parliament*
Belgium	*awaiting ratification by Parl.*	Latvia	*ratified by Parliament*
Cyprus	*ratified by Parliament*	Lithuania	*ratified by Parliament*
Czech Rep.	*referendum on hold*	Luxembourg	*56% 'Yes' in referendum*
Denmark	*referendum on hold*	Malta	*ratified by Parliament*
Estonia	*awaiting ratification by Parl.*	Netherlands	*61% 'No' in referendum*
Finland	*awaiting ratification by Parl.*	Poland	*referendum on hold*
France	*55% 'No' in referendum*	Portugal	*referendum on hold*
Germany	*awaiting ratification by Parl.*	Slovakia	*ratified by Parliament*
Greece	*ratified by Parliament*	Slovenia	*ratified by Parliament*
Hungary	*ratified by Parliament*	Spain	*77% 'Yes' in referendum*
Ireland	*awaiting referendum*	Sweden	*awaiting ratification by Parl.*
		UK	*referendum on hold*

─────────── THE EUROPEAN MOTTO ───────────

United in diversity · Undod mewn amrywiaeth [*Welsh*]
Unyta yn dyversyta [*Cornish*] · Ae mynd, monie kynd [*Gaelic*]
Eenheid in verscheidenheid [*Dutch*] · Jednota v rozdielnosti [*Slovak*]
In Vielfalt geeint [*German*] · Unidade na diversidade [*Portuguese*]

─────────── EUROPE DAY ───────────

Europe Day is 'the occasion for activities and festivities that bring Europe closer to its citizens and peoples of the Union closer to one another'. It is celebrated every 9 May, to commemorate Robert Schuman's 1950 proposal to create an organised Europe that would be 'indispensable to the maintenance of peaceful relations'.

THE EURO

NOTES & COINS IN CIRCULATION

Coin	number	total value €	Note	number	total value €
€2	3,115m	6,230m	€500	332m	166,250m
€1	4,629m	4,630m	€200	144m	28,735m
50¢	4,083m	2,041m	€100	935m	93,451m
20¢	6,429m	1,286m	€50	3,235m	161,751m
10¢	7,860m	786m	€20	1,994m	39,888m
5¢	9,337m	467m	€10	1,643m	16,431m
2¢	10,662m	23m	€5	1,220m	6,101m
1¢	11,658m	127m	TOTAL	9,503m	512,607m
TOTAL	58,773m	15,780m			

[*Source: European Central Bank, 2005*]

Officially, *euro* and *cent* are written lowercase and, in English, the spelling does not change when plural (e.g. 100 euro; 100 cent). Oddly, the plural *euros* and *cents* are permitted with languages like French and Spanish. [See p.240 for the euro symbol.] Euro coins share common faces — there are three different versions, all of which were designed by Luc Luycx of the Royal Belgian Mint. All three designs show maps of Europe and apparently 'symbolise the unity of the EU'. The reverse faces of the coins are country-specific and designed by each country – although all are surrounded by the constellation of 12 stars from the European Union flag.

Denomination	common side design
€2, €1	EU map before enlargement of 2004
50¢, 20¢, 10¢	individual EU countries before enlargement of 2004
5¢, 2¢, 1¢	Europe in relation to Africa and Asia

Euro notes were designed by Robert Kalina, from Austria's national bank, on the theme of 'ages and styles of Europe'. Each denomination has a single design that is common to all euro area countries, depicting one of seven architectural periods. Windows and gateways adorn the front of each note; bridges are on the reverse:

Note	colour	size (mm)	architecture	Note	colour	size (mm)	architecture
€5	grey	120x62	Classical	€50	orange	140x77	Renaissance
€10	red	127x67	Romanesque	€100	green	147x82	Baroque/Rococo
€20	blue	133x72	Gothic	€200	yellow	153x82	C19th iron/glass
				€500	purple	160x82	C20th modern

CURRENT CIRCULATION OF THE EURO

OFFICIAL CURRENCY
Belgium, Germany, Greece, Spain, France, Ireland, Italy, Luxembourg, the Netherlands, Austria, Portugal, Finland

DE FACTO CURRENCY
without formal agreement
Andorra, Kosovo, Montenegro

SPECIAL ARRANGEMENTS
Monaco, the Vatican City, San Marino

OVERSEAS TERRITORIES
Guadeloupe, French Guiana, Martinique, Mayotte, Réunion, Saint Pierre and Miquelon, French Southern & Antarctic Territories

THE FIVE ECONOMIC TESTS

Government policy on Economic and Monetary Union (EMU) was set out by the Chancellor Gordon Brown in a statement to Parliament on 27 October 1997. The Government asserts that a successful single currency within a single European market would in principle be of benefit to Europe and the UK. The Government states that the constitutional issues are 'factors' to be taken into consideration – but they are not overriding so long as: membership is in the national interest; the case is clear and unambiguous; and, there is popular consent. The current basis for deciding whether or not there is a clear and unambiguous economic case for membership, and whether the question be put to a national referendum, are Gordon Brown's 'five economic tests':

Are business cycles and economic structures compatible, so that we and others could live comfortably with euro interest rates on a permanent basis?

If problems emerge is there sufficient flexibility to deal with them?

Would joining EMU create better conditions for firms making long-term decisions to invest in Britain?

What impact would entry into EMU have on the competitive position of the UK's financial services industry, particularly the City's wholesale markets?

In summary, will joining EMU promote higher growth, stability and a lasting increase in jobs?

THE CE MARK

The CE mark indicates that a product has been manufactured to all of the relevant standards laid down by EU directives. It must be affixed to all products sold in EU markets (whether imported or not) that fall within the scope of EU directives.

THE EUROPEAN ANTHEM

The European Anthem is Beethoven's setting of Friedrich von Schiller's *Ode to Joy* in his 9th Symphony (1823). The tune was adapted by Herbert von Karajan (for piano, wind band, and orchestra), and it was adopted as the anthem in 1985.

THE EU'S LANGUAGES

The 20 official languages:

Español .... Spanish	Italiano .... Italian	Latviski .... Latvian
Dansk .... Danish	Nederlands ...... Dutch	Lietuvikai ... Lithuanian
Deutsch .... German	Português .... Portuguese	Magyar ...... Hungarian
Elinika .... Greek	Suomi .... Finnish	Malti .... Maltese
English .... English	Svenska .... Swedish	Polski .... Polish
Français .... French	Cestina........... Czech	Slovencina....... Slovak
	Eesti........... Estonian	Slovenscina...... Slovene

Establishment & Faith

*The mystic reverence, the religious allegiance, which are essential to
a true monarchy, are imaginative sentiments that no legislature can
manufacture in any people.* — WALTER BAGEHOT

THE SOVEREIGN

ELIZABETH II
*by the Grace of God, of the United Kingdom of Great Britain
and Northern Ireland and of her other Realms and Territories Queen,
Head of the Commonwealth, Defender of the Faith*

Born at 17 Bruton Street, London W1, on 21 April 1926, at *c.*2·40am
Ascended the throne, 6 February 1952 · Crowned, 2 June 1953

ORDER OF SUCCESSION

The Prince of Wales	The Earl of Wessex
Prince William of Wales	The Lady Louise Windsor
Prince Henry of Wales	The Princess Royal
The Duke of York	Mr Peter Phillips
Princess Beatrice of York	Miss Zara Phillips
Princess Eugenie of York	Viscount Linley [&c...]

*The eldest son of the monarch is heir to the throne followed by his heirs. After that come any
other sons of the monarch and their heirs, followed by any daughters of the monarch and
their heirs. Roman Catholics are barred from succession under the Act of Settlement (1701).*

ROYAL CONGRATULATIONS

The tradition of sending messages of royal congratulations to subjects on certain
auspicious days was inaugurated in 1917 by George V, who sent telegrams to those
celebrating their 60th wedding anniversary or 100th birthday. Nowadays, on
request, the Queen sends congratulatory cards, via the Royal Mail, to citizens of
Her Realms or UK Overseas Territories, on the following celebratory occasions:

WEDDING ANNIVERSARIES	BIRTHDAYS
60th, 65th, & 70th anniversaries	100th & 105th birthdays
and then every year thereafter	and then every year thereafter

Contact: Private Sec.'s Office, Buckingham Palace, London SW1A 1AA, 020 7930 4832.

—————————— ENGLISH MONARCHS ——————————

We're not a family; we're a firm.
— GEORGE VI (1895–1952)

Danish Line

Svein Forkbeard	1014
Canute the Great	1016–35
Harald Harefoot	1035–40
Hardicanute	1040–42
Edward the Confessor	1042–66
Harold II	1066

Norman Line

William the Conqueror	1066–87
William II Rufus	1087–1100
Henry I Beauclerc	1100–35
Stephen	1135–54
Henry II Curtmantle	1154–89
Richard I Coeur de Lion	1189–99
John (Lackland)	1199–1216
Henry III	1216–72
Edward I	1272–1307
Edward II	1307–27
Edward III	1327–77
Richard II	1377–99

Plantagenet, Lancastrian Line

Henry IV	1399–1413
Henry V	1413–22
Henry VI	1422–61, 1470–71

Plantagenet, Yorkist Line

Edward IV	1461–70, 1471–83
Edward V	1483
Richard III Crookback	1483–85

House of Tudor

Henry VII Tudor	1485–1509
Henry VIII	1509–47
Edward VI	1547–53
Lady Jane Grey	[9 days] 1553
Mary I Tudor	1553–8
Elizabeth I	1558–1603

House of Stuart

James I	1603–25
Charles I	1625–49

Commonwealth & Protectorate

Oliver Cromwell	1649–58
Richard Cromwell	1658–59

House of Stuart, Restored

Charles II	1660–85
James II	1685–88

House of Orange and Stuart

William III, Mary II	1689–1702

House of Stuart

Anne	1702–14

House of Brunswick, Hanover

George I	1714–27
George II	1727–60
George III	1760–1820
George IV	1820–30
William IV	1830–37
Victoria	1837–1901

House of Saxe-Coburg-Gotha

Edward VII	1901–10

House of Windsor

George V	1910–36
Edward VIII	1936
George VI	1936–52
Elizabeth II	1952– *Whom God Preserve*

MONARCH MNEMONIC

Willy, Willy, Harry, Stee, Harry, Dick, John, Harry III. I, II, III Neds, Richard II, Harrys IV, V, VI... then who? Edwards IV, V, Dick the bad, Harrys (twain) & Ned the Lad, Mary, Bessie, James the vain, Charlie, Charlie, James again ... William & Mary, Anne Gloria, 4 Georges, William & Victoria; Edward VII next & then George V in 1910; Edward VIII soon abdicated: George the VI was coronated; After which Elizabeth who is our Queen until her death.

—————————————— ROYAL FINANCES ——————————————

The Queen receives income from public funds to meet expenditure that relates to her duties as Head of State and the Commonwealth. This derives from 4 sources:

Source (year ending 31 March)	2004	2005
The Queen's Civil List	£9·9m	£10·6m
Parliamentary Annuities	£0·4m	£0·4
Grants-in-Aid	£21·6m	£20·2m
Expenditure met directly by Government		
Departments and the Crown Estate	£4·9m	£5·5m
TOTAL	£36·8m	£36·7m

The Queen's Civil List is provided by Parliament on a 10-year cycle to meet the central staff costs and expenses of HM's household. The Parliamentary Annuity is paid to the Duke of Edinburgh to meet official expenses; annuities paid to other members of the Royal Family are reimbursed by The Queen. Grants-in-Aid are paid by the Departments of Transport, & Culture, Media, and Sport.

The Queen has always been subject to indirect taxes (such as VAT) and has volunteered to pay council tax. Although the Sovereign is exempt from income tax, since 1993 the Queen has paid income and capital gains tax on a voluntary basis (the Civil List and the Grants-in-Aid are not considered personal income, and are disregarded for tax). On her death, the Queen's assets will be subject to inheritance tax – although all bequests from Sovereign to Sovereign are exempt. Some miscellany from the Royal Public Annual Report 2003–4 is given below:

❦ Buckingham Palace employs 6 full-time telephone operators. In 2004–5 they answered 315,000 incoming calls. ❦ >2,800 people received honours at 27 investitures. ❦ 6 garden parties were held at Buckingham Palace and the Palace of Holyroodhouse, attended by >38,000 guests. ❦ On average, 32 carriage horses are stabled in the Royal Mews. ❦ 91% of the Queen's suppliers are paid within 30 days of invoice. ❦ The 'occupied Royal palaces' have an aggregate floor area of c.160,000m². ❦ The Queen sent 28,000 anniversary messages [see p.268] and sent >55,000 items of correspondence. ❦ A fibre-optic link connects Buckingham Palace with St James's Palace. ❦ The Buckingham Palace gardens are c.39 acres (including the lake); c.30,000 walk through them every year. ❦ The Royal Train made 19 journeys. ❦

—————————————— UNION FLAG SPECIFICATIONS ——————————————

The official sizes of the Union Flag, as laid down by the Foreign Office List, 1900:

For use on shore...8 breadths (12'x6')
For use on shore *when specially ordered* ....4 breadths (6'x3'); 12 breadths (18'x9')
For use on boats..4 breadths (6'x3')
For use on board ship...8 breadths (12'x6')

——————— ROYAL FAMILY ENGAGEMENTS ———————

Mr Tim O'Donovan compiled a list of official engagements undertaken by the Royal Family during 2004 – as reported in the pages of the Court Circular:

	Official visits, openings, &c	Receptions, lunches, dinners, &c	Other, e.g. investitures, meetings	Total official engagements UK	Total official engagements abroad
The Queen	119	65	203	387	49
Duke of Edinburgh	159	137	60	356	67
Prince of Wales	226	87	165	478	94
Duke of York	172	73	27	272	309
Earl of Wessex	130	50	19	199	232
Countess of Wessex	119	20	10	149	34
Princess Royal	271	102	95	468	131
Duke of Gloucester	107	48	17	172	43
Duchess of Gloucester	86	30	14	130	36
Duke of Kent	117	33	16	166	25
Princess Alexandra	72	30	33	135	—

——————— THE UNION FLAG ———————

Government buildings are obliged to fly the Union Flag on the these days:

BD Countess of Wessex......... 20 Jan
Queen's Accession................. 6 Feb
BD of the Duke of York........ 19 Feb
St David's Day (Wales*) .... 1 Mar
Commonwealth Day .... 13 Mar
BD Earl of Wessex .... 10 Mar
BD The Queen .... 21 Apr
St George's Day (England*)...... 23 Apr

Europe Day† .... 9 May
Coronation Day .... 2 Jun
BD Duke of Edinburgh .... 10 Jun
Official BD The Queen .... 11 Jun
BD Duchess of Cornwall........ 17 Jul
BD The Princess Royal......... 15 Aug
Remembrance Day .... 11 Nov
BD Prince of Wales .... 14 Nov
Queen's Wedding Day......... 20 Nov
St Andrew's Day (Scotland*) .... 30 Nov
Also, the Opening & Prorogation of Parliament‡.

The Union flag must be flown with the wider diagonal white stripe above the red diagonal strip in the half nearest to the flag pole. (To fly the flag upside-down is a signal of distress.) On the above days, flags should be flown 8am–sunset. *If a building has more than one flagstaff, the appropriate national flag may be flown with the Union Flag but not in a superior position. † The Union Flag should fly alongside the European flag, though always taking precedence. ‡ In London only, whether the Queen performs the ceremony or not. ❦ The Union flag should be flown at HALF-MAST (i.e. ⅔ up) from the announcement of the death of the Sovereign, except on Proclamation Day, when it is flown at full-mast from 11am–sunset; and, subject to special command from the Queen at half-mast: for the funeral of members of the Royal Family, foreign rulers, Prime Ministers and ex-PMs, and any other occasions commanded. ❦ The ROYAL STANDARD is hoisted only when the Queen is actually present in any given building.

—————————————— ROYAL WARRANTS ——————————————

Royal Warrants are awarded, on the advice of the Lord Chamberlain, to people or companies who have regularly supplied goods or services to The Queen, The Duke of Edinburgh, or The Prince of Wales for at least five consecutive years. (The Warrants of the late Queen Mother lapse on 31 December 2007). Warrants are initially granted for a five year period, after which their status is reviewed. Complex rules govern how companies may use the Royal Arms and the legend 'By Appointment' – and Warrants automatically lapse if the grantee dies or leaves, or if the firm is sold or becomes bankrupt. The following hold all 4 Royal Warrants:

Ede & Ravenscroft (*robe makers*) · Land Rover · Jones Yarrell (*newsagents*)
The General Trading Company (*suppliers of fancy goods*) · Smythson (*stationers*)
Blossom and Browne's Sycamore (*launderers & dry-cleaners*)
Gerald Benney (*gold and silversmiths*) · Halcyon Days (*suppliers of objets d'art*)

—————————————— ESQUIRE ——————————————

Formerly, an Esquire was a high order – ranking immediately below a knight. Although sources vary, it seems that there were traditionally five classes of Esquire:

Younger sons of Peers and their eldest sons
Eldest sons of Knights and their eldest sons
Chiefs of ancient families (by prescription)
Esquires by creation or office (e.g. judges; QCs; JPs)
Esquires who attend the Knight of the Bath on his installation

Nowadays, Esquire is used as a courtesy for those without a higher title or religious rank with the intention, it seems, of conveying some notion of gentlemanliness. If Esquire is added post-nominally, the usual prefix title (Mr, Dr, &c.) is dropped.

—————————————— ROYAL GUN SALUTES ——————————————

Royal gun salutes are fired to mark special anniversaries and constitutional events:

Accession Day · The Queen's Birthday · Coronation Day
The Duke of Edinburgh's Birthday · The Queen's Official Birthday
State Opening and Prorogation of Parliament · Royal Births
– and when a visiting Head of State meets the Sovereign
in London, Windsor, or Edinburgh.

The Royal Salute is 21 rounds – though 41 are fired at Hyde Park (a Royal Park), and the Tower of London (a Royal Palace and Fortress). On Royal anniversaries the Tower fires 62 rounds – the additional 21 'for the City of London'. When the Queen's official birthday coincides with The Duke of Edinburgh's actual birthday the Tower of London fires a total of 124 rounds — i.e. 62 rounds twice.

—— THE QUEEN'S CHRISTMAS BROADCAST 2004 ——

'Christmas is for most of us a time for a break from work, for family and friends, for presents, turkey and crackers. But we should not lose sight of the fact that these are traditional celebrations around a great religious festival, one of the most important in the Christian year. Religion and culture are much in the news these days, usually as sources of difference and conflict, rather than for bringing people together. But the irony is that every religion has something to say about tolerance and respecting others. For me, as a Christian, one of the most important of these teachings is contained in the parable of the Good Samaritan, when Jesus answers the question, 'Who is my neighbour?'. … Everyone is our neighbour, no matter what race, creed or colour. The need to look after a fellow human being is far more important than any cultural or religious differences. … We have only to look around to recognise the benefits of this positive approach in business or local government, in sport, music and the arts. There is certainly much more to be done and many challenges to be overcome. Discrimination still exists. Some people feel that their own beliefs are being threatened. Some are unhappy about unfamiliar cultures. They all need to be reassured that there is so much to be gained by reaching out to others; that diversity is indeed a strength and not a threat. We need also to realise that peaceful and steady progress in our society of differing cultures and heritage can be threatened at any moment by the actions of extremists at home or by events abroad. … I believe tolerance and fair play remain strong British values and we have so much to build on for the future. It was for this reason that I particularly enjoyed a story I heard the other day about an overseas visitor to Britain who said the best part of his visit had been travelling from Heathrow into central London on the tube. His British friends were, as you can imagine, somewhat surprised, particularly as the visitor had been to some of the great attractions of the country. "What do you mean?" they asked. "Because" he replied "I boarded the train just as the schools were coming out. At each stop children were getting on and off – they were of every ethnic and religious background, some with scarves or turbans, some talking quietly, others playing and occasionally misbehaving together – completely at ease and trusting one another." "How lucky you are," said the visitor, "to live in a country where your children can grow up this way. I hope they will be allowed to enjoy this happy companionship for the rest of their lives."'

… peaceful and steady progress in our society of differing cultures and heritage can be threatened at any moment …

When the text of the Queen's Christmas broadcast is entered into *Microsoft Word's* 'Auto Summarize' feature and is condensed down to just 3 sentences, the result is:

Everyone is our neighbour, no matter what race, creed or colour.
Discrimination still exists. Some are unhappy about unfamiliar cultures.

———————— CURIOUS OFFICES OF STATE ————————

Earl Marshall
THE DUKE OF NORFOLK

Originally a military appointment first made by William the Conqueror, the Earl Marshall is now responsible for organising a host of State ceremonies including weddings, funerals, the State Opening of Parliament, Coronations, and the like.

Queen's Remembrancer
ROBERT TURNER

The oldest judicial post in continuous existence (dating to 1164), the Queen's Remembrancer has a number of roles, including Trial of the Pyx [see p.227] the nomination of High Sheriffs, and the Quit Rents Ceremony.

Queen's Swan Marker
DAVID BARBER

Responsible for marking swans during Swan Upping, as well as monitoring the swan population and advising on swan welfare.

Lord Chamberlain
LORD LUCE

The senior member and overseer of the Royal Household. Among other duties he is the conduit of communication between the Queen and the Lords. His symbols of office, used on ceremonial occasions, are a white staff and a key. On the death of the Sovereign, the staff is symbolically broken over the monarch's grave to signify that the Household has been dissolved.

Yeoman Warder Ravenmaster, Tower of London
DERRICK COYLE

Ensures that Charles II's decree – that there are always six ravens at the Tower of London – is adhered to; responsible for the care and feeding of the ravens.

Master of the Horse
LORD VESTEY

The formal head of the Royal Mews, who attends ceremonial occasions such as Trooping the Colour and the State Opening of Parliament.

Mistress of the Robes
THE DUCHESS OF GRAFTON

Senior lady of the Royal Household (usually a Duchess), responsible for arranging the rota of Ladies in Waiting Upon the Queen. When established by Elizabeth I the Mistress of the Robes was responsible for the Queen's jewellery and clothes.

Master of the Queen's Music
SIR PETER MAXWELL DAVIES

An honourary position conferred on 'a musician of distinction'. Since the time of George V, the Master has had no formal duties, although they may compose pieces for State or Royal occasions.

The Sovereign's Piper
MAJOR JIM STOUT

When staying at one of her official residences, the Queen is serenaded for fifteen minutes each morning, at 9am, with bagpipes played by her Piper, who paces back and forth under her window. The office was established by Queen Victoria in 1843.

The Keeper of the Privy Purse
ALAN REID

Responsible for the management of the Queen's financial affairs.

Surveyor of the Queen's Pictures
DESMOND SHAWE-TAYLOR

Enjoys curatorial responsibility over the paintings (c.7,000) and miniatures (c.3,000) in the Royal Collection.

——————————WHO'S NEW IN WHO'S WHO——————————

Published annually since 1849, *Who's Who* is one of the most respected biographical reference books in the world. When, during WWII, paper rationing threatened its publication, Churchill personally intervened to ensure the book continued to be printed. Below are some of those who were added to the 2005 edition (those who have died during the year enter the companion *Who Was Who*):

Matthew Carter .... *Gen. Sec. Lab. Pty*	Elizbeth McColgan .... *athlete*
Shami Chakrabati .... *Dir. Liberty*	Edward McLachlan .... *cartoonist*
Eric Clapton .... *musician*	Stuart Murphey ...... *Controller BBC3*
Eoin Colfer...................... *author*	Martin Newland .. *Ed. Daily Telegraph*
Rosemary Conley........... *food expert*	Bill Nighy .... *actor*
James Culloty .... *jockey*	Jamie Oliver....................... *chef*
Kevin Curran.......... *Gen. Sec. GMB*	Julie & Stephen Pankhurst ....
Lawrence Dallaglio........ *rugby player*	*founders Friends Reunited*
Alan Davies .... *comedian*	Rowan Pelling.. *Fmr Ed. Erotic Review*
Frank Dickens .... *cartoonist*	Vince Power .... *Mean Fiddler*
Roger Draper .... *Sport England*	David Prentis .... *Gen. Sec. Unison*
Hugh Fearnley-Whittingstall...... *chef*	Corin Redgrave .... *actor*
Bryan Ferry.................... *musician*	Chris Riddell.................. *cartoonist*
Philippa Funnell .... *event rider*	José Rodríguez Zapatero...............
Mel Gibson .... *actor*	*Prime Minister, Spain*
Parmjit Singh Gill..... *MP Leic. South*	Martin Rowson .... *cartoonist*
Julian Glover..................... *actor*	Mikhail Saakashvili.... *Pres. of Georgia*
Michael Golding............ *yachtsman*	Adam Sampson ..... *Director of Shelter*
Phillip Green .... *retailer*	Kristin Scott Thomas............. *actor*
Matt Groening........ *Simpsons creator*	Rufus Sewell .... *actor*
Joanne Harris .... *author*	Alan Shearer.................. *footballer*
Tim Heald .... *author*	Matthew Syed...... *table-tennis player*
John Hegley........................ *poet*	Peter Tatchell......... *gay-rights activist*
Tim Henman................ *sportsman*	Louise Taylor ...... *Dir. Crafts Council*
Alan Hollinghurst.............. *author*	Colm Tóibín .... *author*
Peter Jackson .... *film director*	Steven Tomkins .... *Dir. RIBA*
John Kerry .... *US Senator*	Brian Tuner .... *chef*
Nicole Kidman .... *actress*	Jack Vettriano..................... *artist*
Justin King.......... *CEO J. Sainsbury*	Edmund de Waal......... *potter, writer*
Kirit Kumar Pathak ...... *Patak's Foods*	Venetia Williams.......... *horse trainer*
David Lynch .... *film director*	Debbie Wiseman .... *composer*
Iain Martin....... *Editor The Scotsman*	Stephen Woodhams............. *florist*

A few recreations – LEO BAXENDALE 'seeping into the woodwork and rotting it' · JOHN CROYDEN 'restacking the dishwasher' · JOANNE HARRIS 'mooching, lounging, strutting, strumming, priest-baiting and quiet subversion of the system' · GARY MCDOWELL 'mint juleps' · DAVID SEARS 'watching and working with heavy horses' · JAMES SKEA 'losing keys' · ANNE TEMPEST 'inventing labour-saving devices' · CHARLES VALENTINE BETTS 'making watercress sandwiches' · MAJOR GEN. MICHAEL WILSON 'molecatcher' · BARON WINSTON 'festering'

ORDERS OF CHIVALRY

British honours are awarded twice a year: New Year, and the Queen's birthday in June. On each occasion around 1,350 are ennobled, divided into three lists: Prime Minister's; Diplomatic & Overseas; and Armed Forces. Awards are also announced on the resignation of a Prime Minister. Although some awards are in the personal gift of the Queen (e.g. Order of the Garter), the Monarch is the 'fountain of honour' for all awards. There are no fixed criteria for deciding which type or class of order is awarded; recently new committees have been set up to vet candidates.

THE MOST NOBLE ORDER OF THE GARTER
'Honi soit qui mal y pense'
(Shame on him who thinks evil of it)
Knight/Lady of the Garter........... KG/LG
Est. 1348 · *blue ribbon*
Membership 25

THE MOST ANCIENT & NOBLE ORDER OF THE THISTLE
'Nemo me impune lacessit'
(No one provokes me with impunity)
Knight/Lady of the Thistle........... KT/LT
Revived 1687 · *green ribbon*
Membership 16 (usually Scottish)

THE MOST HONOURABLE ORDER OF THE BATH
'Tria Juncta in Uno' (Three joined in one)
Est. 1725 · *crimson ribbon*
Knight/Dame Grand Cross .... GCB
Knight/Dame Commander....... KCB/DCB
Companion .... CB

THE ORDER OF MERIT
Est. 1902 · *blue & crimson ribbon*
Member of the Order of Merit .... OM
Membership 24

THE MOST DISTINGUISHED ORDER OF ST MICHAEL AND ST GEORGE
'Auspicium Melioris Aevi'
(Token of a better age)
Est. 1818 · *blue & scarlet ribbon*
Knight/Dame Grand Cross.......... GCMG
Knight/Dame Cmdr........ KCMG/DCMG
Companion .... CMG

THE ROYAL VICTORIAN ORDER
'Victoria'
Est. 1896 · *blue, red, & white ribbon*
Knight/Dame Grand Cross .... GCVO
Knight/Dame Commander... KCVO/DCVO
Commander .... CVO
Lieutenant........................... LVO
Member.............................. MVO

THE MOST EXCELLENT ORDER OF THE BRITISH EMPIRE
'For God and the Empire'
Est. 1917 · *pink & grey ribbon*
Knight/Dame Grand Cross............. GBE
Knight/Dame Commander .... KBE/DBE
Commander .... CBE
Officer.............................. OBE
Member .... MBE

THE ORDER OF THE COMPANIONS OF HONOUR
'In Action Faithful & in Honour Clear'
Est. 1917 · *carmine & gold ribbon*
Companion........................... CH
Membership 65

Other orders include
THE DISTINGUISHED SERVICE ORDER (1866) · DSO

THE IMPERIAL SERVICE ORDER (1902) · ISO

THE ROYAL VICTORIAN CHAIN (1902)

THE MOST EMINENT ORDER OF THE INDIAN EMPIRE (1878)

SOME HONOURS OF NOTE · 2005

New Year's Honours

KNIGHT BACHELOR
Robert Davies .... historian
Brian Harrison .... scholar
Alan Jones .... Chairman Toyota
Digby Jones .... Director CBI
Matthew Pinsent .... rower

GBE
Elizabeth Butler-Sloss .... judge

DBE
Tanni Grey-Thomspon .... athlete
Kelly Holmes .... athlete

CBE
Quentin Blake .... illustrator
Roger Daltry .... musician
Lisa Jardine .... academic
John Lill .... pianist
Anna Massey .... actor
Alan Plater .... playwright
Eric Sykes .... comic
Alan Whicker .... broadcaster

OBE
James Clarke .. London marathon Ch.
Ray Cooney .... playwright
James Cracknell .... rower
Paul Lamplugh .. Susy Lamplugh Trust
Colin Montgomery .... golfer
Geoffrey Palmer .... actor
Alexandra Shulman .... Ed. *Vogue*
John Sullivan .... writer
Leslie Thomas .... writer
Pete Waterman .... impresario
Tom Wilkinson .... actor

MBE
Barry Davies .... commentator
David Gelly .... musician
Emily Johnston .... cleaner
Leslie Law .... equestrian
Hugh Lloyd .... actor, writer
George Wyllie .... sculptor

Queen's Birthday Honours

KNIGHT BACHELOR
Michael Barber ..... PM's delivery unit
Rod Eddington .... British Airways
Clive Gillinson ... Ldn. Symph. Orch.
David Jason .... actor
Jonathan Sacks .... Chief Rabbi
Iqbal Sacranie ... Muslim Council GB
Pritpal Singh .... headteacher
John Tomlinson .... opera singer
Terry Wogan [Hon.] .... radio presenter

DCB
Elizabeth Manningham-Buller ... MI5

CBE
Tim Bevan .... Working Title films
William Boyd .... novelist
Eric Fellner .... Working Title films
Jocelyn Hay .... Voice of Lstnr & Vwr
Brian May .... musician
Christopher Wright ..... Chrysalis Grp

OBE
Frank Gardener .... journalist
John Mayall .... Bluesbreaker
Suzy Menkes .... fashion writer
Jimmy Page .... musician
Jonathan Ross .... radio presenter
Albert Sewell ...... football statistician
David Sexton .... football manager
Midge Ure .... musician
Sylvia Young .... theatre school

MBE
Ade Adepitan .... basketball player
Les Ferdinand .... footballer
Pippa Funnell .... equestrian
Fergus Henderson .... restaurateur
Sarah Kennedy .... radio presenter
Basil D'Oliveira .... cricketer
Peter Seabrook .... broadcaster

COMPANION OF HONOUR
Judy Dench .... actor

SOME NOTES ON ETIQUETTE

The origin of the word *etiquette* is not clear. It might derive from the French for a ticket, or from a Spanish word for a book of ceremonies. Either way, etiquette prescribes a set of rules for behaviour which, as society evolves, can quickly seem outdated. Below are a few formal traditions of etiquette.

Formal INVITATION envelopes to a couple are traditionally addressed just to the lady, whereas the invitation itself is made out to both parties. ❦ Prompt REPLY is essential. The usual forms are:

Mr Wooster thanks Mr and Mrs Glossop for their kind invitation to dinner on Friday 26th May and has much pleasure in accepting.

or

Mr Wooster thanks Mr and Mrs Glossop for their kind invitation to dinner on Friday 26th May but regrets he is unable to accept due to a previous engagement.

THANK-YOU LETTERS may be brief, but should be heartfelt and prompt. It is traditional to address thank-you letters for a party to the hostess. ❦ When faced at a meal with complex PLACE SETTING involving a panoply of knives and forks, work from the outside in. ❦ At dessert after a formal meal, port and other wines are PASSED TO THE LEFT and guests usually serve themselves. It is sometimes acceptable to give a 'BACKHANDER' and fill the glass of the person sitting to your right. ❦ If SMOKING is allowed at formal dinners, it should not commence until after the 'Loyal Toast' to the Queen. ❦ FUNERAL CARDS attached to flowers should read *In Loving Memory* and not *With Deepest Sympathy*.

LETTERS should always be dated. ❦ If a typed or wordprocessed letter is sent, it may be more informal to 'top and tail' the letter by writing the *Dear* — and *Yours sincerely* by hand. ❦ Personal letters should ideally be handwritten; letters of condolence should always be handwritten. ❦ EMAIL is a curiously detached form of communication best suited to business transactions. It should be avoided in all formal social situations, and rejected out of hand for the communication of any serious emotion – especially congratulations or condolences. ❦ TEXT MESSAGING is suitable only for the transmission of logistical data – and, of course, for flirtation. ❦ The formality of SIGNING OFF LETTERS has relaxed over the years. The traditional sign-off would have followed the form:

I beg (or have the honour) to remain, Sir, Your obedient servant.

Nowadays, the formal sign-off to a letter where the addressee's name is known is *Yours sincerely*. Where the name is not known (letters that start Dear Sir or Madam) the sign-off is *Yours faithfully*. Sign-offs to informal letters are more personal, and range from *Yours ever* to *With love*. ❦ The formal sign-off for a letter addressed to the Queen is:

I have the honour to remain, Madam, Your Majesty's most humble and obedient subject.

❦ When addressing the Queen in person [see p.280] the word MA'AM should be said to rhyme with 'psalm' not 'ham'. ❦ When formally presented to Royalty, men should BOW from the neck and not from the waist.

─────────────────── THE CUT ───────────────────

To 'cut' is to affect not to know someone when passing or meeting them. An Edwardian dandy (or 'knut') would have recognised four different forms of cut:

THE CUT DIRECT	THE CUT SUBLIME
To look an acquaintance straight in the face and pretend not to know him.	*To admire some object or distant scene until the acquaintance has passed.*
THE CUT INDIRECT	THE CUT INFERNAL
To glance another way and pretend not to see an acquaintance.	*To stop and attend to your shoes until the acquaintance has walked by.*

─────────── ON THE FOLDING OF VISITING CARDS ───────────

In the C19th an elaborate taxonomy developed regarding how visiting (or calling) cards should be left, folded, and inscribed when those of 'quality' paid social calls:

Nature of call	style of fold
Visit	*right-hand upper corner folded down*
Felicitation	*left-hand upper corner folded down*
Condolence	*left-hand lower corner folded down*
PPC, PDA*	*right-hand lower corner folded down*
Made on all members of a family	*the lady's card folded in the middle*
Delivered in person	*right-hand side folded down*

*When persons were going abroad or were to be absent for a long period, if they had not the time or inclination to take leave of their friends by making formal calls, they would send cards folded in this manner, or inscribed 'PPC' which stood for *pour prendre congé* (although many assumed the initials to stand for presents parting compliments) or 'PDA' which stood for *pour dire adieu*. Other card inscriptions included: 'PC' – *pour condoler*; 'PF' – *pour féliciter*; 'PR' – *pour remercier*; or 'PP' – *pour présenter*. In each case, these inscriptions would be made in ink, in upper case letters, in the lower left-hand corner. If a card was enclosed within an envelope it usually indicated that communication between the two parties was at an end. The three exceptions to this rule were: [a] when they were sent to a newly married couple; [b] when they were in reply to a wedding invitation and sent by someone absent from their usual home; [c] when they were PPC or PDA cards. In 1857, the Duke of Parma started the custom of leaving Cartes de Visite with his portrait for the albums of friends. Visiting cards were sometimes nicknamed Paste Boards. So, to 'shoot a PB' was to leave one's card.

─────────────── TERMS OF ENDEARMENT ───────────────

2 Glances make 1 Bow ☞ 2 Bows make 1 How d'ye do ☞
6 How d'ye do's make 1 Conversation ☞ 4 Conversations make 1 Acquaintance

AN ELEMENTARY GUIDE TO FORMS OF ADDRESS

Personage	envelope	start of letter	verbal address
The Queen	The Queen's Most Excellent Majesty†	Madam/May it please your Majesty	Your Majesty/Ma'am
The Duke of Edinburgh	HRH The Duke of Edinburgh†	Sir	Your Royal Highness/Sir
The Queen Mother	Her Majesty Queen —— The Queen Mother†	Madam	Your Majesty/Ma'am
Royal Prince	HRH The Prince ——, (The Prince of ——)†	Sir	Your Royal Highness/Sir
Royal Princess	HRH The Princess (of) ——†	Your Royal Highness	Your Royal Highness/Madam
Royal Duke	HRH The Duke of ——†	Your Royal Highness	Your Royal Highness/Sir
Royal Duchess	HRH The Duchess of ——†	Your Royal Highness	Your Royal Highness/Madam
Duke	His Grace the Duke of ——	My Lord Duke/Dear Duke	Your Grace/Duke
Duchess	Her Grace the Duchess of ——	Dear Madam/Dear Duchess	Your Grace/Duchess
Marquess	The Most Honourable The Marquess of ——	My Lord/Dear Lord	My Lord/Lord
Marchioness	The Most Honourable The Marchioness of ——	Madam/Dear Lady	Madam/Lady
Earl	The Rt Hon The Earl of ——	My Lord/Dear Lord	My Lord/Lord
Earl's wife	The Rt Hon The Countess of ——	Madam/Dear Lady	Madam/Lady
Countess	The Rt Hon The Countess of ——	Madam/Dear Lady	Madam/Lady
Viscount	The Rt Hon The Viscount ——	My Lord/Dear Lord	Lord
Viscount's wife	The Rt Hon The Viscountess ——	Madam/Dear Lady	Lady
Baron	The Rt Hon Lord ——	My Lord/Dear Lord	Lord
Baron's wife	The Rt Hon Lady ——	My Lady/Dear Lady	Lady
Baroness	The Rt Hon The Lady —— (or The Baroness) ——	My Lady/Dear Lady	Madam/Lady
Baronet	Sir Bertie Wooster Bt (or Bart).	Dear Sir Bertie	Sir Bertie
Baronet's wife	Lady ——	Dear Madam/Dear Lady ——	Lady ——
Knight of an Order	Sir Bertie Wooster (and order)	Dear Sir Bertie	Sir Bertie
Knight Bachelor	Sir Bertie Wooster.	Dear Sir Bertie	Sir Bertie
Knight's wife	Lady ——	Dear Madam/Dear Lady ——	Lady ——
Dame	Dame ——	Dear Madam/Dear Dame ——	Dame ——

— AN ELEMENTARY GUIDE TO FORMS OF ADDRESS —

Personage	envelope	start of letter	verbal address
Life Peer	The Rt Hon Lord —— (of ——)	My Lord/Dear Lord ——	—— Lord ——
Life Peeress	The Rt Hon The Lady (*or* Baroness) —— (of ——)	My Lady/Dear Lady ——	—— Lady ——
Archbishop	The Most Rev & Rt Hon the Lord Archbishop of ——	Dear Archbishop	Your Grace/Archbishop
Bishop	((The Rt Rev) (and Right Hon)) The Bishop of ——	Dear Bishop	Bishop
Lord Chancellor	The Rt Hon The Lord Chancellor	*by rank*	*by rank*
Prime Minister	The Rt Hon The Prime Minister PC MP	Dear Prime Minister.	Prime Minister/Sir
Deputy PM	The Rt Hon The Deputy Prime Minister PC MP	Dear Deputy Prime Minister	Deputy Prime Minister/Sir
Chancellor of the Exchequer	The Rt Hon The Chancellor of the Exchequer PC MP	Dear Chancellor.	Chancellor/Sir
Foreign Secretary	The Rt Hon The SoS for Foreign & Comwlth Affairs	Dear Foreign Secretary	Foreign Secretary/*by rank*
Home Secretary	The Rt Hon The SoS for the Home Department	Dear Home Secretary	Home Secretary/*by rank*
Secretary of State	The Rt Hon The SoS for ——	Dear Secretary of State	Secretary of State/*by rank*
Minister	(The Rt Hon) Bertie Wooster Esq. (PC) MP	Dear Minister	Minister/*by rank*
MP‡	Bertie Wooster Esq. MP	Dear Mr Wooster	Mr Wooster
MP Privy Councillor	The Rt Hon Bertie Wooster PC MP	Dear Mr Wooster	Mr Wooster
Privy Councillor	The Rt Hon Bertie Wooster PC	Dear Mr Wooster.	Mr Wooster
High Court Judge	The Hon Mr Justice ——	Dear Sir —— /Dear Judge	Sir/My Lord/Your Lordship
Ambassador (British)	His Excellency —— HM Ambassador to ——	*by rank*	Your Excellency
Lord Mayor	The Rt Hon the Lord Mayor of ——	My (Dear) Lord Mayor	Lord Mayor
Mayor	The Worshipful Mayor of ——	(Dear) Mr Mayor	Mr Mayor

It is hard to overstate the complexity of 'correct' form which (especially in the legal and clerical fields as well as Chivalry) can become extremely rococo, and is the subject of considerable dispute between sources. Consequently, the above tabulation can only hope to provide a very elementary guide. ❦ Readers interested in the correct formal styling of the wives of younger sons of Earls, for example, are advised to consult specialist texts on the subject. † It is usual to address correspondence to members of the Royal Family in the first instance to their Private Secretary. ‡ A similar styling is used for Members of the European Parliament [MEP]; Scottish Parliament [MSP]; National Assembly for Wales [AM]; and Northern Ireland Assembly [MLA]. From the moment Parliament is dissolved [see p.253] there are no Members of Parliament, and consequently the letters MP should not be used. By convention medical doctors are styled Dr ——, whereas surgeons use the title Mr ——; many gynaecologists, although surgeons, are styled Dr.

——————————— THE LEGAL YEAR & LAW TERMS ———————————

The legal year starts in October when judges process two miles (nowadays by car) from Temple Bar to Westminster Abbey for a service conducted by the Dean of Westminster, at which the Lord Chancellor reads the lesson. This is followed by a 'breakfast' in Westminster Hall. The legal year is divided into these four terms:

HILARY† .... 11 Jan – 12 Apr | TRINITY .... 6 Jun – 31 Jul
EASTER.............. 25 Apr – 26 May | MICHAELMAS .... 2 Oct – 21 Dec

The origin of these terms is thought to derive from a prohibition by the church of swearing any form of oath between these three periods: Advent and Epiphany; Septuagesima and fourteen days after Easter; and Ascension and Corpus Christi.

[† This term is so named after St Hilary whose feast is celebrated on 13 January.]

——————————————— JURY SERVICE ———————————————

The range of those liable to be called for jury service was extended by the Criminal Justice Act (2003), which abolished what had become regarded as a 'middle-class opt-out'. Previously, 'professionals' such as dentists, doctors, and lawyers were excused from service, as were members of the clergy, MPs, and the judiciary. Now, anyone on the electoral register is liable to random selection to serve on a jury.

To be ELIGIBLE for jury service you must be at older than 18 and younger than 70 on the day your service is to start; a registered parliamentary or local government elector; and you must have lived in the United Kingdom, the Channel Islands or the Isle of Man for any period of at least 5 years since you were 13 years old.

INELIGIBLE individuals include: those on bail or involved in criminal proceedings; those sentenced to life imprisonment; those who have in the previous 10 years served any part of a sentence of imprisonment or had passed on them a suspended sentence of imprisonment; and those with mental disorders.

Individuals may request DEFERRAL of service to another date within 12 months (if, for example, the date clashes with an examination), or EXCUSAL* from the summons (if, for example, they do not speak English). Jurors may claim for loss of earnings, travel costs, and daily subsistence, based upon these current rates:

Loss of earnings (max) ..... £55·19 for first 10 days; £110·40 for subsequent days
General subsistence rate .... £4·73 per day

Certain expenses are also paid. For more details call the *Jury Central Summoning Bureau* 0845 3555567. * In July 2005, after the second trial of Sion Jenkins for the murder of his foster daughter Billie-Jo, the Judge excused the jury from ever having to serve again. Under *s.*8 of the Contempt of Court Act 1981 it is illegal to 'obtain, disclose or solicit any particulars of statements made, opinions expressed, arguments advanced or votes cast by members of a jury in the course of their deliberations in any legal proceedings'.

——— COURT STRUCTURE IN ENGLAND & WALES ———

HOUSE OF LORDS
hears appeals from the Court of Appeal and, occasionally, the High Court

COURT OF APPEAL

Criminal Division	Civil Division
hears appeals from the Crown Court	*hears appeals from the High Court &c.*

HIGH COURT

Queen's Bench Division	Family Division	Chancery Division
contract, tort, &c.	*Matrimonial*	*Equity, trusts, &c.*
Commercial Court	*Proceedings relating to*	*bankruptcy, tax partners*
Admiralty Court	*children*	*Companies & Patents*
	Probate Service	
Administrative Court		Divisional Court
oversees inferior courts,	Divisional Court	*appeals from the*
tribunals, Local Auth.,	*appeals from*	*County Courts on*
Ministers, officials &c.	*Magistrates' Courts*	*bankruptcy & land*

CROWN COURT	COUNTY COURT
tries indictable offenses,	*tries the majority of civil*
cases from Magistrates' courts	*litigation, subject to the*
cases for sentence	*nature of the claim*

MAGISTRATES' COURT	TRIBUNALS
tries summary offences,	*hear appeals from decisions on:*
committals to Crown Court,	*immigration, social security,*
family and youth courts	*child support, pensions, tax, land, &c.*

[Source: The Court Service · Crown ©]

——— JURY OATHS & AFFIRMATIONS ———

Some of the various oaths that can be sworn by those of different faiths

General Oath
I swear by Almighty God that I will faithfully try the defendant and give a true verdict according to the evidence.

Affirmation
I do solemnly, sincerely and truly declare and affirm that I will faithfully try the defendant and give a true verdict according to the evidence.

Hindu / Sikh / Islamic Oath
I swear by *(The Gita)* / *(Waheguru)* / *(Allah)* that I will faithfully try the defendant and give a true verdict according to the evidence.

Moravian / Quaker Oath
I, being one of the *(United Brethren called Moravians)* / *(people called Quakers)* do solemnly, sincerely and truly declare and affirm that I will faithfully try the defendant and give a true verdict according to the evidence.

——————————— UK FORCES STRENGTH ———————————

The graph below illustrates the strength of UK Regular Armed forces since 1974.

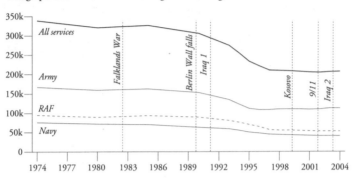

[Figures are for trained and untrained personnel; they exclude Gurkhas, mobilised reservists,
and others not counted as the UK Regular Forces. Source: DASA. Crown ©]

——————————————— THE SA80 ———————————————

The SA80 is a family of weapons that forms the basis of personal firepower for
British forces. Soldiers use three versions of the SA80: the L85 Individual Weapon
[IW]; the L86 Light Support Weapon [LSW]; and a shorter carbine version of the
SA80 issued primarily to those (like tank drivers) who do not have small arms as
a primary weapon system. An infantry section comprises of two four-man fire-
teams with 2 IWs (one with underslung grenade launcher); 1 LSW; and, recently
introduced, 1 Minimi belt-fed light machine gun. The SA80's specifications are:

L85 Individual Weapon		*L86 Light Support Weapon*
5·56mm NATO	*calibre*	5·56mm NATO
4·98kg	*loaded weight*	6·58kg
785mm	*length*	900mm
518mm	*barrel length*	646mm
940m/s	*muzzle velocity*	970m/s
30 round magazine	*feed*	30 round magazine
400m	*effective range*	1,000m
610–775rpm	*cyclic rate of fire (rounds/min)*	610–775rpm

The SA80 has been dogged by problems from its inception – including an early
fault where some guns went off when dropped. Indeed, the SA80's design means
it cannot safely be fired from the left shoulder (vital for left-handers and if moving
round corners). Trials proved the SA80 impressively accurate, but unreliable and
prone to mechanical failure; in 1997 NATO suspended the weapon after a series of
'jams'. Numerous overhauls later, including a complete redesign by the German
manufacturer Heckler & Koch, British forces now carry the more reliable SA80A2.

UK SERVICE RANKS

service	ROYAL NAVY	ROYAL MARINES†	ARMY	ROYAL AIR FORCE	NATO
OFFICERS	Admiral of the Fleet	—	Field Marshall	Marshall of the RAF	OF-10
	Admiral	General	General	Air Chief Marshall	OF-9
	Vice Admiral	Lieutenant General	Lieutenant General	Air Marshall	OF-8
	Rear Admiral	Major General	Major General	Air Vice-Marshall	OF-7
	Commodore	Brigadier	Brigadier	Air Commodore	OF-6
	Captain	Colonel	Colonel	Group Captain	OF-5
	Commander	Lieutenant Colonel	Lieutenant Colonel	Wing Commander	OF-4
	Lieutenant Commander	Major	Major	Squadron Leader	OF-3
	Lieutenant	Captain	Captain	Flight Lieutenant	OF-2
	Sub-Lieutenant	Lieutenant/2nd Lieutenant	Lieutenant/2nd Lieutenant	Flying Officer/Pilot Officer	OF-1
	Midshipman	—	Officer Cadet	Officer Designate	OF-(D)
OTHER RANKS	Warrant Officer Class 1	Warrant Officer Class 1	Warrant Officer Class 1	Warrant Officer	OR-9
	Warrant Officer Class 2	Warrant Officer Class 2	Warrant Officer Class 2	—	OR-8
	Chief Petty Officer	Colour Sergeant	Staff Sergeant	Flight Sergeant/Chief Technician	OR-7
	Petty Officer	Sergeant	Sergeant	Sergeant	OR-6
	Leading Rate	Corporal	Corporal	Corporal	OR-4
	—		Lance Corporal		OR-3
	Able Rating	Marine	Private (Class 1–3)	Junior Technician / Leading & Senior Aircraftman	OR-2
	—	—	Private (Class 4)/Junior	Aircraftman	OR-1

[Source:DASA] The Naval rank of Warrant Officer Class 2 was introduced in 2004. † The Royal Marines were established in 1664 as a corps of sea soldiers to be raised and disbanded as required. In 1755 they became a permanent part of the Navy trained as soldiers and seamen to fight and to maintain discipline on ships. The Royal Marines gained their tough fighting reputation during the capture of Gibraltar in 1704, and have since played a decisive role in military deployment across the world.

———————————— THE 'SEASON' ————————————

Is there anything so splendid; so jaded; so welcoming; so elitist;
so meritorious; so meretricious; as the English social Season?
— WILFRED GOWERS-ROUND

Traditionally, the 'Season' ran from April to August, during which time the key
social events would take place, and débutantes would be presented at Court.
Nowadays, the Season is much more informal and runs throughout the year.
Below are some of Society events during 2006 [see pp.316–7 for more sporting events]:

Lord Mayor's New Year's Parade · 020 8566 8586 .... 1 Jan
Burns' Night · various local parties and balls.................................... 25 Jan
RSC Stratford Season · 0870 609 1110 · rsc.org.uk .... *starts* 6 Apr
Oxford *vs* Cambridge Boat Race · 01225 383518 · theboatrace.org .... 2 Apr
Crufts · 020 7518 1012 · crufts.org.uk... 9–12 Mar
Cheltenham Festival · 01242 513014 · cheltenham.co.uk .... 14–17 Mar
Grand National · 0151 523 2600 · aintree.co.uk .... 8 Apr
Royal Caledonian Ball · 020 8940 8079 · royalcaledonianball.com .... Apr
Glyndebourne · 01273 813 813 · glyndebourne.com........................ *starts* 19 May
Badminton Horse Trials · 01454 218375 · badminton-horse.co.uk.............. 4–7 May
Chelsea Flower Show · 0870 906 3781 · rhs.org.uk/chelsea .... 22–27 May
Royal Windsor Horse Show · 01753 860633 · rwhs.co.uk .... 11–14 May
Royal Academy Summer Exhib. · 020 7300 8000 · royalacademy.org.uk .... Jun–Aug
Trooping the Colour · 020 7414 2479.. 17 Jun
Epsom Derby · 01372 470 047 · epsomderby.co.uk............................... 3 Jun
Garsington Opera · 01865 361636 · garsingtonopera.org................... 10 Jun–11 Jul
Royal Ascot · 01344 876 876 · ascot.co.uk .... 20 Jun
Cartier International Polo · 01784-434 212 · guardspoloclub.com................ 24 July
Wimbledon · 020 8946 2244 · wimbledon.org .... 26 Jun–9 Jul
Glorious Goodwood · 01243 755030 · goodwood.co.uk........................ 1–5Aug
Henley Royal Regatta · 01491 572153 · hrr.co.uk........................ 28 Jun–2 Jul
The Proms · 020 7589 8212 · bbc.co.uk/proms .... 15 Jul–10 Sep
Cowes Week · 01983 295 744 · cowesweek.co.uk .... 29 Jul–5 Aug
Edinburgh Festival · 0131 473 2001 · eif.co.uk .... Aug–Sep
Notting Hill Carnival · 0870 059 22 22 · lnhc.org.uk .... 26–28 Aug
Braemar Highland Gathering · 01339 755377 · braemargathering.org .... 2 Sep
Horse of the Year Show · 020 8900 9282 · hoys.co.uk......................... 4–8 Oct
Louis Vuitton Classic · 020 7399 4050 · vuitton.com .... tba
Lord Mayor's Show · 020 7332 1456 · lordmayorsshow.org .... Nov
Varisty Rugby Match · thevarsitymatch.com....................................... Dec
Carols at King's Chapel · kings.cam.ac.uk/chapel .... 24 Dec

The *Silly Season* (traditionally, the *Big Gooseberry Season*) lasts for the months of
summer – or when Parliament is not sitting. During this time, any old story is good
enough for the newspapers especially, in the past, those about large gooseberries. The
Oyster Season was traditionally September–April; hence the saying 'Who eats oysters on
St James's Day will never want', since to afford oysters in August was a sign of wealth.

——————— RELIGIOUS COMPOSITION OF THE UK ———————

The 2001 Census was the first census to include a voluntary question on religious identity and affiliation – which *c.*92% of respondents were willing to answer. (The question had been included in previous censuses in N. Ireland.) The results were:

religion	thousands	%	religion	thousands	%
Christian	42,079	71·6	No religion	9,104	15·5
Muslim	1,591	2·7	Not stated	4,289	7·3
Hindu	559	1·0	(All religions	45,163	76·8)
Sikh	336	0·6	(All No or Not	13,626	23·2)
Jewish	267	0·5	TOTAL	58,789	100
Buddhist	152	0·3			

[Source: Census 2001 · Crown ©]

At the time of the Census, following similar events in New Zealand, an internet rumour spread claiming that if enough people declared 'Jedi Knight' as their religion, being a 'Jedi' would receive official legal status. Astonishingly, 390,127 people (0·7%) actually did declare their religion as Jedi. And, it seems from the regional breakdown that Jedi Knights are most likely to be found in Brighton and Hove (2·6%), and Oxford (2%). *'For over a thousand generations, the Jedi Knights were the guardians of peace and justice'.*

——————— SINS, GIFTS, & VIRTUES ———————

According to a BBC survey of *c.*2000 Radio 4 listeners, the traditional Seven Deadly Sins are in need of modernisation to reflect the evolution of moral values:

TRADITIONAL SINS	21st-CENTURY SINS
Anger · Gluttony · Sloth	*Cruelty · Adultery · Bigotry · Greed*
Envy · Pride · Lust · Greed	*Dishonesty · Hypocrisy · Selfishness*

It is said that Mahatma Gandhi considered these to be his Seven Deadly Sins:

Wealth without works · Pleasure without conscience
Knowledge without character · Commerce without morality
Science without humanity · Worship without sacrifice
Politics without principle

And, Evagrius Ponticus (AD*c.*346–399), the Deacon of Constantinople, declared in *On the Eight Evil Thoughts* that there were Eight Principal Sins, which were:

Gluttony · Fornication · Avarice · Dejection (lack of pleasure)
Anger · Weariness (acedia) · Vainglory · Pride

THE 7 GIFTS OF THE HOLY GHOST	THE 7 HEAVENLY VIRTUES
Counsel · Fear of the Lord · Fortitude	*Charity · Faith · Fortitude*
Knowledge · Righteousness	*Hope · Justice*
Understanding · Wisdom	*Prudence · Temperance*

———————————— THE TEN COMMANDMENTS ————————————

Exodus [chapter 20, verses 1–17] ❧ And God spake all these words, saying, ❧ I am the Lord thy God, which have brought thee out of the land of Egypt, out of the house of bondage. ❧ Thou shalt have no other gods before me. ❧ Thou shalt not make unto thee any graven image, or any likeness of any thing that is in heaven above, or that is in the earth beneath, or that is in the water under the earth: ❧ Thou shalt not bow down thyself to them, nor serve them: for I the Lord thy God am a jealous God, visiting the iniquity of the fathers upon the children unto the third and fourth generation of them that hate me; ❧ And shewing mercy unto thousands of them that love me, and keep my commandments. ❧ Thou shalt not take the name of the Lord thy God in vain; for the Lord will not hold him guiltless that taketh his name in vain. ❧ Remember the sabbath day, to keep it holy. ❧ Six days shalt thou labour, and do all thy work: ❧ But the seventh day is the sabbath of the Lord thy God: in it thou shalt not do any work, thou, nor thy son, nor thy daughter, thy manservant, nor thy maidservant, nor thy cattle, nor thy stranger that is within thy gates: ❧ For in six days the Lord made heaven and earth, the sea, and all that in them is, and rested the seventh day: wherefore the Lord blessed the sabbath day, and hallowed it. ❧ Honour thy father and thy mother: that thy days may be long upon the land which the Lord thy God giveth thee. ❧ Thou shalt not kill. ❧ Thou shalt not commit adultery. ❧ Thou shalt not steal. ❧ Thou shalt not bear false witness against thy neighbour. ❧ Thou shalt not covet thy neighbour's house, thou shalt not covet thy neighbour's wife, nor his manservant, nor his maidservant, nor his ox, nor his ass, nor any thing that is thy neighbour's. ❧

A Channel 4 survey (Feb 2005) asked the public to create a new set of Ten Commandments that reflected the moral issues of the 21st-century. They suggested:

1 .... Treat others as you would have them treat you
2 .. Take responsibility for your actions
3 .... Don't kill
4 .... Be honest
5 .... Don't steal
6 .... Protect and nurture children
7 .... Protect the environment
8 .... Look after the vulnerable
9 .... Never be violent
10 .... Protect your family

———————————— THE THREE JEWELS OF JAINISM ————————————

To achieve the goal of the liberation of the soul, Jains attempt to live by the tripartite rules of their ethical code. The 'three jewels' of Jain ethics are as follows:

SAMYAK DARSHANA (right perception) · attempting to perceive the truth clearly without being swayed by superstition or prejudice.

SAMYAK JNANA (right knowledge) · having accurate knowledge of the universe and scripture, and the mental attitude to use this knowledge.

SAMYAK CHARITRA (right conduct) · to live according to Jain ethics, and avoid doing any harm to other living creatures.

―――――――――― THE HINDU TRINITY ――――――――――

All Hindu Gods are part of the Supreme Being Brahman, but beneath him are the Trimurti – three gods who represent the perpetual cycle of creation – Brahma creates the world; while Vishnu sustains it; and Shiva destroys it.

God	*consort*	*vehicle*
Brahma *(creator)*	Saraswati *(learning)*	Hamsa – the swan
Vishnu *(preserver)*	Lakshmi *(wealth)*	Garuda – the bird
Shiva *(destroyer)*	Parvati *(mother goddess)*	Nandi – the bull

Vishnu's avatars, below, have appeared in 9 times of crisis, the 10th is yet to come:

Matsya	the fish God	*saved the world from flood*
Kurma	the tortoise God	*created liquid of immortality for Gods*
Varaha	the wild boar	*rescued earth from a demon*
Nara-Simha	the man-lion	*killed evil king*
Vamana	the dwarf	*defeated Bali; regained Heaven and Earth*
Parashurama	Rama with an axe	*defeated oppressor of the people*
Rama	hero of the Ramayana	*killed demon Ravana*
Krishna	the blue God	*lifted mountain; saved village from storm*
Buddha	Siddartha Gautama	*all deities are manifestations of Vishnu*
Kalkin	the horse God	*will come in 428898CE*

―――――――――― RASTAFARIANISM & GANJA ――――――――――

For Rastafarians, the smoking of Ganja (marijuana) is central to their faith. Ganja, the 'wisdom weed', is considered the herb of life which brings believers closer to God. For some its use is based upon Biblical references, including Genesis I:

11 · *And God said, Let the earth bring forth grass, the herb yielding seed, and the fruit tree yielding fruit after his kind, whose seed is in itself, upon the earth: and it was so.*

12 · *And the earth brought forth grass, and herb yielding seed after his kind, and the tree yielding fruit, whose seed was in itself, after his kind: and God saw that it was good.*

―――――――――― SHINTO & KAMI ――――――――――

Central to Shinto is the worship of KAMI, which might tentatively be translated as 'spirits', except that features such as oceans and forces such as earthquakes are also Kami. There are many millions of Kami which influence natural and human events and can themselves be influenced by prayer. Kami are not believed to be divine, omnipotent, or supernatural, but are part of the human world and, as such, make mistakes and 'misbehave'. Three types of Kami are worshipped in particular: the ancestors of the clans; the kami of natural objects, creatures, and forces; and the souls of dead humans who are noted for outstanding achievements.

THE FIVE PILLARS OF ISLAM

SHAHADA .. to affirm there is only one God, and Muhammad was his messenger
SALAT .... to pray five times a day
ZAKAH .... to give alms and charity to the poor
SAUM.............................. to fast during the month of Ramadan [see p.336]
HAJJ.............................. to pilgrimage to Mecca at least once in a lifetime

BUDDHA'S FOUR NOBLE TRUTHS

Life involves suffering, and is inevitably sorrowful
Suffering has its roots in desire and craving which arise from ignorance
The end of suffering comes with the cessation of desire
Nirvana can be reached by the Noble Eightfold Path

The Noble Eightfold Path further outlines a method of disciplined behaviour:

Right view .... understanding the Four Noble Truths
Right aspiration............ having caring thoughts and intent for all living things
Right speech..................... speaking kindly, truthfully, without bad language
Right bodily action..................... following the Five (or Ten) Moral Precepts
Right livelihood .... undertaking work that will harm nothing living
Right endeavour.............. practise meditation and work to stop bad thoughts
Right mindfulness .... giving full attention and best effort to one's actions
Right concentration .... which leads to enlightenment

SIKHISM'S FIVE ARTICLES OF FAITH

The 5 *Panj Kakas*, or articles of faith, worn by many Sikhs are: KESH (uncut hair)
KIRPAN (sword) · KARA (steel bangle) · KACHHA (under-shorts) · KANGHA (comb)

MORMON LIVING PROPHETS

The Church of Jesus Christ of Latter-Day Saints (the Mormons) was founded in
1830 by Joseph Smith, who is believed by Mormons to have been chosen by God
as a Prophet. In 1844, Smith was killed in jail by a mob while facing charges of
conspiracy. Since then, the Church has been led by the following Prophets:

Brigham Young	1844–77	David O. McKay	1951–70
John Taylor	1877–87	Joseph Fielding Smith	1970–72
Wilford Woodruff	1887–98	Harold B. Lee	1972–73
Lorenzo Snow	1898–1901	Spencer W. Kimball	1973–85
Joseph F. Smith	1901–18	Ezra Taft Benson	1985–94
Heber J. Grant	1918–45	Howard W. Hunter	1994–95
George Albert Smith	1945–51	Gordon B. Hinckley	1995–

──── SCIENTOLOGY ────

Scientology is the legal trademark for a quasi-religious philosophy founded in the 1950s by the science-fiction writer L(afayette) Ron(ald) Hubbard (d.1986). Premised on Hubbard's 1950 book *Dianetics*, the Church of Scientology preaches that an individual's immortal spirit (or 'thetan') may be attained by the elimination of mental and physical stresses through a process of 'auditing'. It is claimed that as individuals pass through Scientology's programme they attain spiritual freedom and enlightenment. From its creation, Scientology has faced suspicion and criticism from doctors, psychologists, the media, and even governments. The Church's status as a religion has been challenged in a number of countries, and some critics have alleged that the organisation is more akin to a cash-raising cult than a faith. Yet, despite this scepticism, the Church claims to be growing, and currently receives high-profile advocacy from celebrity believers like Tom Cruise and John Travolta.

──── KABBALAH ────

Kabbalah is a mystical Jewish faith that focuses on the nature of God, miracles, and the cosmos. Belief in Kabbalism reached a peak in C13th Spain, when Moses of Leon wrote its holy Aramaic text, the *Zohar*. Recently, a new form of Kabbalah has emerged, expounded by the ex-insurance agent turned rabbi Feivel Shraga Gruberger – now known as 'The Rav'. He and his wife Karen run the Kabbalah Center from where they preach the word of the *Zohar* – 'the authentic Holy Grail ... the ultimate instrument for generating endless miracles'. (So powerful is the *Zohar,* 'just by being in the presence of the [22] volumes creates an impenetrable shield of spiritual protection'.) Other aspects of The Rav's teaching focus on the wearing of a (£20) bracelet of red string to ward-off the 'evil eye'; and the drinking of Kabbalah water (£4/*l*). In recent years Kabbalah has attracted curiosity through followers such as Madonna; and controversy because of its apparent financial acquisitiveness.

──── KWANZAA ────

Kwanzaa is a secular holiday celebrated from 26 December – 1 January by African-Americans. Kwanzaa was proposed in 1966 by Dr Maulana Karenga in response to the race riots of 1965. Dr Karenga felt that Christmas was an overtly 'white' and Eurocentric festival. Consequently, there was a need to create a 'black' festival that would resonate with the African roots of black Afro-Americans. Kwanzaa is based on traditional African harvest festivals with the additional themes of strong community and family. At the heart of the festival are the *Nguzo Saba,* the seven principles, each of which is celebrated in turn over the course of the festival week:

UMOJA (*unity*) · KUJICHAGULIA (*self-determination*)
UJIMA (*collective work and responsibility*) · UJAMAA (*cooperative economics*)
NIA (*purpose*) · KUUMBA (*creativity*) · IMANI (*faith*)

A seven-tiered candelabra is employed: one candle is lit for each day of the festival. The celebrations close with a Karamu, a special meal at which gifts are given. Since 1966 Kwanzaa has become one of America's principal end of year celebrations.

Sport

The Olympic Games profoundly and positively influenced my life.
I want to give that opportunity to others and leave a legacy for future generations.
— SEBASTIAN COE

LONDON 2012 OLYMPICS

Despite being considered an underdog (and much to the horror of Paris), London
was awarded the 2012 Olympics by IOC President Jacques Rogge on 6 July 2005.
Lord Coe was universally praised for a politically astute bid that focused on the
inspirational quality of the Games, and the sporting legacy they will bequeath.

Voting round 1	*round 2*	*round 3*	*round 4*
LONDON: 22	MADRID: 32	LONDON: 39	LONDON: 54
Paris: 21	London: 27	Paris: 33	Paris: 50
Madrid: 20	Paris: 25	Madrid: 31	
New York: 19	New York: 16		
Moscow: 15			

The London 2012 Games will be centred around a new Olympic Park to be built
in Stratford, East London. ❦ The Olympic Stadium will cost an estimated £250m.
❦ The Olympic Village will have 17,320 beds, and, after the Games, the Village
will be converted into 3,600 apartments, most of which will be affordable housing. ❦ 9·6 million tickets for the Games will be available, with 75% of the tickets
priced at under £50. ❦ £7bn will be spent improving London's transport system.
❦ After the Games, four of the newly-built arenas will be dismantled and then
rebuilt in other parts of the country. ❦ The Games will be paid for by: Olympic
Lottery (£1.5b); IOC TV and marketing deals (£560m); sponsorship (£450m);
ticket revenues (£300m); licensing (£60m); London Development Agency
(£250m); and a London Council Tax increase of £20 per household (£625m) for
6 years. ❦ Work on the Aquatics Centre began in 2005, and is expected to finish
in 2008. ❦ The Stratford Olympic Park should be finished by December 2011.❦

Events such as athletics, cycling, swimming, diving and hockey will be held in
Stratford. Existing sporting venues and landmarks will be utilised for other events:

Mlnm. Dome	*gymnastics, basketball*	Lord's Cricket Ground	*archery*
Eton Dorney	*rowing, canoe, kayak*	Regent's Park	*road cycling*
ExCel	*boxing, table tennis*	Royal Artillery Barracks	*shooting*
	taekwondo, weightlifting, wrestling	Weald Country Park	*mountain bikes*
Greenwich Park	*equestrian*	Wembley Stadium	*football*
Horse Guards Parade	*beach volleyball*	Weymouth–Portland	*sailing*
Hyde Park	*triathlon*	Wimbledon	*tennis*

──────────── ELLEN MacARTHUR'S RECORD ────────────

At 22:29 GMT, on Monday 7 February 2005, Ellen MacArthur sailed across the finish-line off Ushant and set a new solo non-stop round-the-world record time:

71 DAYS · 14 HOURS · 18 MINUTES · 33 SECONDS
[27,354 miles · average speed 15·9 knots]

This was 1 day, 8 hours, 35 minutes, 49 seconds faster than the previous sailing record set by Francis Joyon in 2004 – and an astonishing 242 days faster than the first record of 313 days set by Robin Knox-Johnston in 1969. A schematic of Ellen MacArthur's route is below, along with some of the key events of her journey:

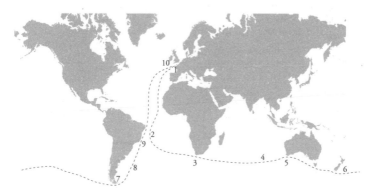

1 .... *crosses start-line off Ushant, France* · 28·11·04
2 .... *switches generators because of excess fuel consumption* · 12·12·04
3 .... *sets new Ushant–Cape of Good Hope record* (19d 9h 46m) · 17·12·04
4 .... *boat slows when it collides with unknown object* · 23·12·04
5 .... *sets new Ushant–Cape Leeuwin record* (29d 14h 5m) · 27·12·04
6 .... *badly burns her arm on generator and seeks medical advice* · 06·01·05
7 .... *sets new Ushant–Cape Horn record* (44d 23h 36m) · 12·01·05
8 .... *hit on head and wounded by gennaker* · 15·01·05
9 .... *equipment to hoist mainsail damaged and needs to be repaired* · 20·01·05
10 .... *crosses finish-line to break record* · 07·02·05

──────── INTERNATIONAL HOT DOG EATING CONTEST ────────

Nathan's Famous Fourth of July International Hot Dog Eating Contest is one of the year's highlights for the International Federation of Competitive Eating. In 2005, Takeru 'Tsunami' Kobayashi of Japan (weighing a modest 52kg) took his fifth straight title after cramming down 49 hot dogs in an impressive 12 minutes. The UK's entrant, first-timer Rob Burns, came 16th managing only a disappointing 10 hot dogs in the allotted time. Burns had earned his place in the final after winning the UK Eating Championship, at which he consumed 18 pork pies in 12 minutes.

LONDON MARATHON · 2005

On Sunday 17 April 2005, *c.*30,000 took part in the 25th London Marathon.

♂ *race results*
M. Lel [KEN] 02h 07m 26s
J. Gharib [MOR]...............02·07·49
H. Ramaala [RSA] ....02·08·32

♂ *wheelchair race results*
S. Mendoza [MEX] ....01·35·51
J. Adams [CAN] ....01·35·54
D. Weir [GBR].................01·36·03

♀ *race results*
P. Radcliffe [GBR] ....02·17·42
C. Tomescu-Dita [ROM] ......02·22·50
S. Chepkemei [KEN] ....02·24·00

♀ *wheelchair race results*
F. Porcellato [IT] ....01·57·00
S. Woods [GBR] ....01·57·03
T. Grey Thompson [GBR] ....02·02·39

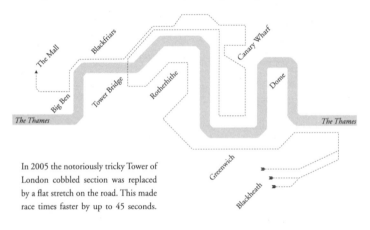

In 2005 the notoriously tricky Tower of London cobbled section was replaced by a flat stretch on the road. This made race times faster by up to 45 seconds.

LANCE ARMSTRONG & THE TOUR DE FRANCE

To the cynics and the sceptics, I'm sorry you cannot believe in miracles …
this is a hard sporting event and hard work wins it. Vive le Tour *for ever!*
— LANCE ARMSTRONG

On 24 July 2005, Lance Armstrong won his seventh consecutive *Tour de France* – a record-breaking achievement made more impressive by his battle against cancer. He had earlier announced his retirement. The 2005 *Tour* final results were these:

Results
Lance Armstrong 86h 15m 02s
Ivan Basso ....at 4:40
Jan Ullrich......................at 6:21

Yellow Jersey......... Lance Armstrong
Green Jersey............. Thor Hushovd
Polka-dot Jersey... Mickael Rasmussen
White Jersey........ Yaroslav Popovych

The Yellow Jersey is for the over all fastest time; the Green for the most points; the white and red Polka-dot Jersey is for the King of the Mountains; and the White for the best young rider (≤25).

─SPORTING INTRIGUE─

{JAN} · Arsenal's Ashley Cole was spotted with Chelsea manager Jose Mourinho in a London hotel – the *News of the World* alleged 'tapping-up'. {FEB} · Wayne Rooney was dropped as a guest from a school's match for being a poor role model. {MAR} Arsenal's Jermaine Pennant was jailed for 3 months for drink-driving while banned. ❦ Jose Mourinho was fined £5,000 for accusing Man. Utd of cheating. ❦ A student who claimed Wayne Rooney hit him in a nightclub dropped his allegations. {APR} · Newcastle's Lee Bowyer was

Wayne Rooney

fined £200,000 by his club for starting a fight with team-mate Kieron Dyer during Newcastle's 3–0 defeat by Aston Villa. ❦ Paula Radcliffe was photographed 'relieving' herself during her victorious London Marathon. {MAY} · Sprinter Mark Lewis-Francis was issued with a public warning after traces of cannabis were found in his system; he claimed he had passively inhaled the drug. ❦ Days after receiving a driving ban after overtaking a police car at 105mph, Rio Ferdinand was questioned by police after a disturbance at a hotel during Jody Morris' stag weekend; no one was charged over the incident. ❦ Wayne Rooney faced charges of driving without due care and attention after a collision at a shopping centre. ❦ Jenson Button and the BAR team were banned for 2 races after running an underweight car at the San Marino Grand Prix. {JUN} · Colin Montgomerie caused controversy at the Indonesian Open after failing to mark where his ball lay after a thunderstorm halted play. The next day he seemed to replace the ball in a more advantageous position. {JUL} ·

The Royal & Ancient faced criticism for altering the Open course, supposedly to make it harder for long-hitters. ❦ Sir Alex Ferguson was found guilty by the FA of improper conduct after implying that there were 'sinister' reasons behind refereeing decisions during a match against Newcastle in April 2005. ❦ Rumours abounded that Roy Keane's absence from a Man. Utd tour of Asia was due to disciplinary action rather than injury as claimed. Whispers persisted that Keane and Alex Ferguson had argued over the presence of family at a training camp. ❦ Four men pleaded guilty before a San Francisco court to distributing performance-enhancing steroids, in the 'BALCO scandal'. Their plea bargains meant that some of the world's top athletes implicated in the affair would be saved from testifying. {AUG} · French newspaper *L'Équipe* accused Lance Armstrong of drug-taking, after samples taken from Armstrong in 1999 were said to show traces of the illegal drug EPO, for which a test did not exist until 2000. Armstrong vehemently denied the claims calling them a 'witch-hunt'. ❦ Ricky Ponting and Simon Katich were fined a percentage of their match fees (75% and 50% respectively) following outbursts on being dismissed in the 4th Ashes Test. Ponting caused further controversy by claiming England were breaching the 'spirit' of cricket by using fielding substitutes to rest their bowlers. In the 4th Test, Ponting was run out by substitute fielder Gary Pratt. {SEP} · Wayne Rooney was sent off during a Champions League tie against Villarreal after clapping the referee's decision to yellow-card him.

─────────── MOST WATCHED SPORTING EVENTS ───────────

Event · [Source: BBC]	*date*	*channel*	*viewers*
England *vs* Argentina, World Cup '98	30·06·98	ITV	23.78m
England *vs* Romania, World Cup '98	22·06·98	ITV	19.48m
England *vs* Colombia, World Cup '98	26·06·98	BBC1	19.13m
Barry McGuigan *vs* Denilo Cabrera	15·02·86	BBC1	18.3m
Barry McGuigan *vs* Eusebio Pedroza	08·06·85	BBC1	18m
[*for comparison*] Liverpool *vs* AC Milan	25·05·05	ITV	14.6m

─────────── THE WORLD SERIES OF POKER ───────────

The 36th World Series of Poker final was played in *Benny's Bullpen* in Binion's Gambling Hall and Hotel, Las Vegas. Lasting nearly 14 hours, the 2005 final was the longest in the tournament's history. 5,619 players entered the $10,000 buy-in no-limit Texas Hold 'Em tournament, of which nine survived through to the final. Each finalist was guaranteed at least $1m prize money. The final head-to-head was between Australian ex-chiropractor Joseph Hacham and American amateur Steven Dannenmann. After 232 hands, Hacham won with a 7-high Straight that beat Dannenmann's paired Aces. Joseph Hacham won $7·5m, the title of World Series Champion, and a lovely diamond-encrusted white-gold Championship bracelet.

─────────── TV RIGHTS FOR SPORTS ───────────

Rights	*channel*	*until*
England football international home matches	BBC & Sky	2008
FA Cup	BBC & Sky	2008
Champions League	ITV & Sky	2006
UEFA Cup	ITV	2006
Football World Cup	ITV & BBC	2006
Premiership highlights	BBC	2006
Wimbledon	BBC	2008
UK domestic athletics fixtures	BBC	2008
Rugby Six Nations	BBC	2010
Home Test & one day international cricket	Sky	2009
Formula One	ITV	tbc
Oxford *vs* Cambridge boat race	ITV	2009

In 1996, the Government created a list of the 'Crown Jewels' of British sport protected under the Broadcasting Act (1996) so they are broadcast for free on terrestrial TV. They include: FIFA World Cup finals; FA Cup final; Scottish FA Cup final; the Grand National; the Derby; Wimbledon finals; European football Championship finals; Rugby League Challenge Cup final; and the Rugby World Cup final. Some events may be shown on pay-per-view TV if secondary coverage is given to a free terrestrial channel, including: Test Match Cricket in England World Athletics Championship; Ryder Cup; Open Championship; Commonwealth Games; and home side Rugby Six Nations. After England's 2005 Ashes victory, Test cricket's move from Channel 4 to Sky became controversial.

—————— SPORTSPEOPLE & THEIR SPONSORS · 2005 ——————

David Beckham.................Adidas	Paula Radcliffe.....................Nike
Darren Campbell ....Reebok	Maria Sharapova..................Nike
Roger Federer.....................Nike	Johnny Wilkinson..............Adidas
Tim Henman....................Adidas	Serena Williams....................Nike
Kelly Holmes ....Reebok	Venus Williams ....Reebok
Michael Owen ....Umbro	Tiger Woods ....Nike

————————————— DARTS AS SPORT —————————————

In March 2005, *Sport England* officially classified darts as a sport on the grounds that: it is played by thousands of people across the country; it is contested both nationally and internationally; and it requires both physical and mental skills.

I get fed up of the snobbery. I do. It does wear you down. All over the world, China, Japan, coast to coast across America, they see this for what it is: a sport. How I'd love to stick two fingers up to all those who knocked us. I'm World Champion, but people say I'm not a sportsman. Ridiculous. All you've got up there is your hand, your eye and your brain. There's no hiding behind a bat, or a car, or a racket.

— PHIL *'The Power'* TAYLOR, 12-times World Darts Champion

————————————— THE LAUREUS AWARDS · 2005 —————————————

The *Laureus World Sporting Academy* encourages the 'positive and worthwhile in sport', presenting awards to athletes in all disciplines. Some 2005 winners were:

World sportsman of the year.................................Roger Federer (tennis)
World sportswoman of the year ....Kelly Holmes (athletics)
Comeback of the year ....Alessandro Zanardi (motor racing)
Sportsperson with a disability................Chantal Peticlerc (wheelchair racing)
Alternative sportsperson of the year ....Ellen MacArthur (sailing)

————————————————— RED SHIRTS —————————————————

Research undertaken by scientists at Durham University [*Nature 2005; 425:293*] suggests that sportsmen wearing red shirts are more likely to win. In an analysis of wrestling, boxing, and taekwondo competitors at the 2004 Athens Olympics, (who are randomly assigned either a red or blue shirt), those wearing red won 55% of the matches. The researchers also studied Euro 2004, and found that teams who played in a variety of shirt colours during the tournament tended to perform better when playing in red. Russell Hill, one of the researchers, suggested that wearing red gave players an advantage because throughout the animal kingdom the colour red was associated with male dominance, testosterone, and strength.

Schott's Almanac 2006

THE PREMIERSHIP · 2004/05

Team	won	drew	lost	goals for	goals against	prize money	points
Chelsea	29	8	1	72	15	£9·5m	95
Arsenal	25	8	5	87	36	£9·025m	83
Man. Utd	22	11	5	58	26	£8·55m	77
Everton	18	7	13	45	46	£8·075m	61
Liverpool	17	7	14	52	41	£7·6m	58
Bolton	16	10	12	49	44	£7·125m	58
Middlesbrough	14	13	11	53	46	£6·65m	55
Man. City	13	13	12	47	39	£6·175m	52
Tottenham	14	10	14	47	41	£5·7m	52
Aston Villa	12	11	15	45	52	£5·225m	47
Charlton	12	10	16	42	58	£4·75m	46
Birmingham	11	12	15	40	46	£4·275m	45
Fulham	12	8	18	52	60	£3·8m	44
Newcastle	10	14	14	47	57	£3·325m	44
Blackburn	9	15	14	32	43	£2·85m	42
Portsmouth	10	9	19	43	59	£2·375m	39
West Brom.	6	16	16	36	61	£1·9m	34
Crystal Palace	7	12	19	41	62	£1·425m	33
Norwich	7	12	19	42	77	£950,000	33
Southampton	6	14	18	45	66	£475,000	32

Top scorer...Thierry Henry (Arsenal): 25 goals
Most red cards...Fulham: 7
Most yellow cards...Blackburn Rovers: 69
Best average goals per game...Arsenal: 2·19
Worst average goals conceded per game............................Norwich: 1·92

OTHER DIVISIONS – UP & DOWN

Up	2004–05	Down
Sunderland, Wigan West Ham	*Championship*	Rotherham, Gillingham Nottingham Forest
Luton, Hull, Sheffield Wednesday	*League One*	Stockport, Peterborough, Wrexham, Torquay
Yeovil, Scunthorpe Swansea, Southend	*League Two*	Cambridge United Kidderminster Harriers
Barnet Carlisle	*Conference*	Leigh RMI, Farnborough, Forest Green

TEAM OF THE SEASON

The Professional Footballers' Association annually nominates a Premiership 'team' of the season. In 2004/05 they selected the following players:

Petr Cech [CHE] · Gary Neville [MAN U] · John Terry [CHE] · Rio Ferdinand [MAN U]
Ashley Cole [ARS] · Frank Lampard [CHE] · Steven Gerrard [LIV] · Arjen Robben [CHE]
Shaun Wright-Phillips [MAN C] · Thierry Henry [ARS] · Andrew Johnson [C PAL]

SOME FOOTBALL AWARDS OF NOTE · 2004/05

FIFA world player of the year.................................Ronaldinho [Barcelona]
European footballer of the year......................Andriy Shevchenko [AC Milan]
Prof. Footballers' Assoc. player of the year.......................John Terry [Chelsea]
PFA young player award ....Wayne Rooney [Man. Utd]
PFA special merit award..................Shaka Hislop (for anti-racism campaign)
Football Writers' Assoc. player of the year.................Frank Lampard [Chelsea]
FA women's football awards: best international player........Rachel Yankey [Birm]
FA women's football awards: players' player of the year......Julie Fleeting [Arsenal]

DELOITTE FOOTBALL MONEY LEAGUE · 2003/04

The Deloitte Football Money League is based on club income, including: ticket sales, television revenue, merchandising, and hospitality. It does not factor players' wages or transfer fees paid by the club – thus Chelsea's £87·8m deficit last season is not reflected in the figures. Below are the 2003/04 season top earning clubs:

Club	£m				
Man. Utd (1)	171·5	Chelsea (10)	143·7	Inter Milan (6)	110·3
Real Madrid (4)	156·3	Juventus (2)	142·4	Bayern Munich (5)	110·1
AC Milan (3)	147·2	Arsenal (7)	115·0	Liverpool (8)	92·3
		Barcelona (13)	112·0	[Last season's rank in brackets.]	

PREMIERSHIP SHIRT SPONSORS · 2005/06

Team	sponsor	value/season			
Arsenal	O2	£5m	Man. City	Thomas Cook	£1m
Aston Villa	DWS	£1m	Man. Utd	Vodafone	£9m
Birmingham	Flybe	£750k	Middlesbr.	888.com	£1m
Blackburn	Lonsdale	n/a	Newcastle	Northern Rock	£5m
Bolton	Reebok	£2m	Portsmouth	OKI	n/a
Charlton	all:sports	£1·1m	Spurs	Thomson	£2·5m
Chelsea	Samsung	£11m	Sunderland	Reg Vardy	n/a
Everton	Chang Beer	£1·5m	West Brom	T-Mobile	£500k
Fulham	PIPEX	£1·25m	West Ham	Jobserve	n/a
Liverpool	Carlsberg	£5m	Wigan	JJB sports	n/a

[Sources: *The Times* & various]

—————— HOME NATIONS' FOOTBALL RECORD · 2005 ——————

Date		result		type	venue
09·02·05	England	0–0	Holland	F	Villa Park, England
09·02·05	Wales	2–0	Hungary	F	Millennium Stad., Cardiff
09·02·05	N. Ireland	0–1	Canada	F	Windsor Park, Belfast
26·03·05	England	4–0	N.Ireland	WCQ	Old Trafford, Manchester
26·03·05	Wales	0–2	Austria	WCQ	Millennium Stad., Cardiff
26·03·05	Italy	2–0	Scotland	WCQ	San Siro, Milan
30·03·05	Austria	1–0	Wales	WCQ	Ernst Happel Stad, Vienna
30·03·05	England	2–0	Azerbaijan	WCQ	St James' Park, Newcastle
30·03·05	Poland	1–0	N. Ireland	WCQ	Legia Stadium, Warsaw
28·05·05	USA	1–2	England	F	Soldier Field, Chicago
31·05·05	Columbia	2–3	England	F	Giants Stadium, New York
04·06·05	Scotland	2–0	Moldova	WCQ	Hampden Park, Glasgow
04·06·05	N. Ireland	1–4	Germany	F	Windsor Park, Belfast
08·06·05	Belarus	0–0	Scotland	WCQ	Dinamo Stadium, Minsk
17·08·05	Denmark	4–1	England	F	Parken, Copenhagen
03·09·05	Wales	0–1	England	WCQ	Millennium Stad., Cardiff
03·09·05	Scotland	1–1	Italy	WCQ	Hampden Park, Glasgow
03·09·05	N. Ireland	2–0	Azerbaijan	WCQ	Windsor Park, Belfast
07·09·05	N. Ireland	1–0	England	WCQ	Windsor Park, Belfast
07·09·05	Norway	1–2	Scotland	WCQ	Ullevaal Stadium, Oslo
07·09·05	Poland	1–0	Wales	WCQ	Wojska Polskiego, Warsaw

KEY TO TYPE: F – Friendly · WCQ – World Cup Qualifier

—————— FOOTBALL WORLD RANKING ——————

The FIFA/Coca-Cola world ranking system enables comparisons to be made between international teams, based on past performance. The ranking formula is:

RANKING = (*points for win, draw or loss*) + (*points for no. of goals scored*)
  – (*points for goals conceded*) + (*bonus for the away team*)
  × (*importance of match*) × (*by regional strength*)

Each variable has its own complicated subset of criteria to determine the weighting of points awarded. Only results from the 7 best matches of the year are given full weighting, though results from the previous 8 years are taken into account. The rankings are published monthly, and at the end of each year FIFA awards a 'Team of the Year' prize for the most points (awarded to Brazil in 2004), and 'Best Mover of the Year' prize for progress (China in 2004). The rankings for September 2005:

1. Brazil.........839 *pts*	5. Mexico 771	*11. England.........738*
2. Netherlands......785	6. France 770	*74. Scotland.........542*
3. Argentina.........778	7. USA 768	*82. Wales.............521*
4. Czech Rep........777	8. Spain 750	*101. N. Ireland 464*

GOLF MAJORS · 2005

♂	course	winner
MASTERS	Augusta, Georgia	Tiger Woods [USA] -12
US OPEN	Pinehurst Resort, N. Carolina	Michael Campbell [NZ] par
THE OPEN	St Andrews	Tiger Woods [USA] -14
USPGA	Baltusrol Golf Club, New Jersey	Phil Mickelson [USA] -4
♀		
KRAFT NABISCO	Rancho Mirage, California	Annika Sorenstam [SWE] -15
LPGA	Havre de Grace, Maryland	Annika Sorenstam [SWE] -11
US OPEN	Cherry Hills Village, Colorado	Birdie Kim [KOR] +3
WOMEN'S OPEN	Royal Birkdale, Southport	Jeong Jang [S. KOR] -16

THE 'ALL STAR' GOLF CUP · 2005

In August 2005, Ant and Dec organised the All Star Cup: a celebrity golf contest between Europe and USA, staged at the Celtic Manor Resort, Newport, and televised on SKY. Europe beat America 91 to 89 – the teams were as follows:

EUROPE – Chris Evans, Boris Becker, James Nesbitt, Steve Redgrave, Ronan Keating, Jodie Kidd, Ian Wright, Peter Schmeichel, Matt Dawson, Damian Lewis, Gavin Henson, Catherine Zeta-Jones, Colin Montgomerie (Cpt)

USA – Michael Douglas, Rob Lowe, Haley Osment, Michael Chang, Patrick Duffy, Steve Hytner, Kenny G, Cheryl Ladd, George Lopez, Cheech Marin, Mark Spitz, Boomer Esiason, Mark O'Meara (Cpt)

EMBASSY WORLD SNOOKER CHAMPIONSHIP · 2005

22-year-old Shaun Murphy became the first qualifier since Terry Griffiths in 1979 to win the *Embassy World Championship*, in a thrillingly close final against 'nearly-man' Matthew Stevens. After a 30-year association, Embassy stepped down as the World Championship's main sponsor because of the ban on tobacco advertising.

THE FINAL · FRAME-BY-FRAME
Shaun Murphy [ENG] 18–16 Matthew Williams [WAL]

DAY ONE		DAY TWO	
Frame.............tally	53–58 (52 Mur.) 3–6	*Frame.............tally*	72–35 (55) ...13–12
67–30 1–0	38–70 3–7	78–22 (51)....7–10	0–95 (95).....13–13
0–98 (54 break).1–1	125–0 (125).....4–7	84–11 (56)....8–10	81–4 (64).....14–13
20–103 (60).....1–2	79–6 (66) 5–7	5–64 8–11	68–37 (68) ...15–13
68–55 2–2	24–105 (80).....5–8	80–60 (80, 60) 9–11	1–83 (68).....15–14
29–65 2–3	5–86 (86) 5–9	137–0 (137)..10–11	85–35 (64) ...16–14
22–65 2–4	103–9 (84)......6–9	64–57.........11–11	0–124 (124)..16–15
76–34 (56)......3–4	58–68 (41).....6–10	20–88 (52) ...11–12	1–71 (52).....16–16
46–56 3–5		131–0 (107)..12–12	97–0 (97).....17–16
			83–28 (83) ...18–16

WISDEN CRICKETER OF THE YEAR

Awarded since 1889 by the cricketing bible *Wisden Almanack*, the Cricketer of the Year has been presented to such luminaries as W.G. Grace, Don Bradman, and Ian 'Beefy' Botham. No player can win the award twice. Recent winners include:

2005	A. Giles; S. Harmison; R. Key; A. Strauss; M. Trescothick
2004	C. Adams; A. Flintoff; I. Harvey; G. Kirsten; G. Smith
2003	M. Hayden; A. Hollioake; N. Hussain; S. Pollock; M. Vaughan
2002	A. Flower; A. Gilchrist; J. Gillespie; V. Laxman; D. Martyn
2001	M. Alleyne; M. Bicknell; A. Caddick; J. Langer; D. Lehmann
2000	C. Cairns; R. Dravid; L. Klusener; T. Moody; S. Mushtaq
1999	I. Austin; D. Gough; M. Muralitharan; A. Ranatunga; J. Rhodes
1998	M. Elliott; S. Law; G. McGrath; M. Maynard; G. Thorpe
1997	S. Jayasuriya; M. Ahmed; S. Anwar; P. Simmons; S. Tendulkar

TEST MATCH NATIONS

Ten nations enjoy 'Test Status', which is gained by applying to the International Cricket Council. The ICC's decision is based on: the applying team's performance; their level of organisation; and their commitment to the development of cricket in their country. Below are the Test Nations and the year they gained Test Status:

England (1877) · Australia (1877) · South Africa (1889)
West Indies† (1930) · New Zealand (1930) · India (1932) · Pakistan (1954)
Sri Lanka (1982) · Zimbabwe (1992) · Bangladesh (2000)

† The West Indies includes the following countries: Jamaica, Barbados, Guyana, Trinidad & Tobago, Antigua & Barbuda, St Kitts & Nevis, Dominica, St Lucia, St Vincent & the Grenadines, Anguilla, Montserrat, and Grenada.

ICC TEST & ODI WORLD RANKINGS

Test matches	rating	rank	rating	One Day Internat.
Australia	127	1	136	Australia
England	119	2	123	Sri Lanka
India	111	3	116	New Zealand
South Africa	100	4	116	Pakistan
New Zealand	100	5	111	South Africa
Sri Lanka	98	6	109	England
Pakistan	95	7	97	India
West Indies	74	8	90	West Indies
Zimbabwe	28	9	44	Zimbabwe
Bangladesh	6	10	14	Bangladesh

[Rankings and points as of September 2005]

─────────────── THE ASHES ───────────────

England *vs* Australia is the oldest international fixture in cricket's history, dating back to March 1877, when Australia beat England by 45 runs in Melbourne. However, the Ashes were born when Australia beat England by 7 runs at the Oval in 1882. A mock obituary announcing the death of English cricket was published in the *Sporting Times*, and a group of Melbourne Ladies presented the English team with the burnt remains of a bail in a 4" wooden urn. [See p.27 for coverage of the 2005 Ashes.]

Test results 1877–2005

─────────────── ICC AWARDS · 2004 ───────────────

Cricketer of the year	Rahul Dravid [IND]
Test player of the year	Rahul Dravid [IND]
One day international player of the year	Andrew Flintoff [ENG]
Emerging player of the year	Irfan Pathan [IND]
Umpire of the year	Simon Taufel [AUS]
Spirit of cricket award	New Zealand

─────────────── TWENTY20 CUP FINAL · 2005 ───────────────

Over half a million watched the 3rd year of Twenty20 games. The final day saw:

Semi-final 1	Lancashire *bt* Surrey by 22 runs
Semi-final 2	Somerset *bt* Leicestershire by 4 runs
Cup Final	Somerset *bt* Lancashire by 7 wickets

─────── SPORTING COMMENTARIES & RICHIE BENAUD ───────

In August 2005, BBC Radio 5 Live listeners voted for their favourite sporting commentary. The winner (with 78%) was the interaction between Jonathan Agnew and Brian Johnstone during the England *vs* West Indies Test Series of 1991. When Botham failed to hook an Ambrose bouncer and knocked off a bail while straddling his stumps, Aggers quipped 'he just couldn't quite get his leg over', reducing Johnners to fits of laughter, punctuated by a plaintive 'do stop it, Aggers…'. Ian Robertson's commentary of Jonny Wilkinson's 2003 World Cup-winning drop-goal was second; and third was Kenneth Wolstenholm's 1966 World Cup line 'they think it's all over – it is now!' ❦ In 2005, one of cricket's best-loved commentators retired from working in England. Richie Benaud, a leg-spinning all-rounder, captained Australia in 28 Tests, never losing a series while at the helm. In 1963 he became the first Test player to take 200 wickets and score 2,000 runs. As a commentator, he is admired for eloquent silences punctuated by a dry wit.

————— RUGBY LEAGUE CHALLENGE CUP · 2005 —————

27·08·05 MILLENNIUM STADIUM, CARDIFF
HULL 25–24 LEEDS

Hull – *Tries*: Tony, Raynor, Whiting, Cooke · *Goals*: Brough (4) · *Drops*: Brough
Leeds – *Tries*: penalty, Calderwood, Ward, Bai · *Goals*: Sinfield (4)

74,000 watched Hull beat Super League Champions Leeds in a closely contested
final. Hull's victory, their first Challenge Cup final for 23 years, was celebrated
throughout Rugby League, especially since it marked the end of the domination
by the big four (Leeds, Bradford, Wigan, & St Helens) who, apart from a win by
Sheffield in 1998, have held a monopoly on lifting the Challenge Cup since 1988.

————— MAN OF STEEL · 2004 —————

In 2004 Wigan Warriors' Andy Farrell was presented with the Man of Steel prize,
awarded by journalists to the outstanding player in Rugby League's Super League.

————— RUGBY UNION SIX NATIONS · 2005 —————

Date		result		venue
05·02·05	France	16–9	Scotland	Stade de France
05·02·05	Wales	11–9	England	Cardiff Millennium Std.
06·02·05	Italy	17–28	Ireland	Stadio Flaminio
12·02·05	Italy	8–38	Wales	Stadio Flaminio
12·02·05	Scotland	13–40	Ireland	Murrayfield
13·02·05	England	17–18	France	Twickenham
26·02·05	France	18–24	Wales	Stade de France
26·02·05	Scotland	18–10	Italy	Murrayfield
27·02·05	Ireland	19–13	England	Lansdowne Road
12·03·05	Ireland	19–26	France	Lansdowne Road
12·03·05	England	39–7	Italy	Twickenham
13·03·05	Scotland	22–46	Wales	Murrayfield
19·03·05	Wales	32–20	Ireland	Cardiff Millennium Std.
19·03·05	England	43–22	Scotland	Twickenham
19·03·05	Italy	13–56	France	Stadio Flaminio

FINAL TABLE 2005 — TOTAL EVER HONOURS

points	w	d	l	pd	country	triple crowns	grand slams	titles
10	5	0	0	74	Wales	17	8	22
8	4	0	1	52	France	n/a	8	14
6	3	0	2	25	Ireland	7	1	10
4	2	0	3	44	England	23	12	25
2	1	0	4	-71	Scotland	10	3	14
0	0	0	5	-124	Italy	n/a	0	0

—— INTERNATIONAL RUGBY BOARD AWARDS · 2004 ——

International player of the year .... Schalk Burger [RSA]
International team of the year .... South Africa
International coach of the year .... Jake White [RSA]
International Sevens team of the year .... New Zealand
International Sevens player of the year .... Simon Amor [ENG]
Spirit of Rugby award .... Jarrod Cunningham [NZ]
Vernon Pugh award for distinguished service .... Ronnie Dawson [IRE]
International women's personality of the year .... Donna Kennedy [SCO]

—— BRITISH & IRISH LIONS TOUR OF NZ · 2005 ——

Lions' coach Sir Clive Woodward originally selected a 45-man squad to tour New Zealand, including 21 English players, 11 Irish, 10 Welsh, and just 3 Scots. However, a flurry of injuries caused the squad to grow to an unwieldy 51 – 48 of whom played. As the Lions were beaten by the All Blacks in each of their three tests, many commentators became critical of Woodward's player selection policy, which seemed to favour experience over form. This was exacerbated by the absence of skipper Brian O'Driscoll, who was stretchered off after a tour-ending tackle in the first minute of the first test. Press interest in the tour was inevitably raised by the presence of Tony Blair's former 'spin doctor', Alistair Campbell, as the Lions' media consultant. The fixtures and results from the 2005 New Zealand tour were:

Date		result		venue
04·06·05	Bay of Plenty	20–34	Lions	Rotorua
08·06·05	Taranaki	14–36	Lions	New Plymouth
11·06·05	NZ Maori	19–13	Lions	Hamilton
15·06·05	Wellington	6–23	Lions	Wellington
18·06·05	Otago	19–30	Lions	Dunedin
21·06·05	Southland	16–26	Lions	Invercargill
25·06·05	New Zealand	21–3	Lions	Christchurch
28·06·05	North Manawatu	6–109	Lions	Palmerston
02·07·05	New Zealand	48–18	Lions	Wellington
05·07·05	Auckland	13–17	Lions	Auckland
09·07·05	New Zealand	38–19	Lions	Auckland

—— ZURICH PREMIERSHIP · 2004/5 ——

Champions	Wasps [see p.315]
Heineken Cup qualifiers	Wasps, Leicester, Sale, Bath, Saracens, Leeds
European Challenge Cup qualifiers	Gloucester, Newcastle, Worcester, London Irish, Northampton, Bristol
Relegated	Harlequins

Because of a new sponsorship deal, the 2005/06 Premiership will become the Guinness Premiership.

——SOME ATHLETICS WORLD RECORDS OF NOTE——

Event	set by	when	record
♂ 100m	Asafa Powell [JAM]	2005	9·77s
♀ 100m	Florence Griffith-Joyner [USA]	1988	10·49s
♂ 110m hurdles	Colin Jackson [GBR], Xiang Liu [CHN]	1993, 2004	12·91s
♀ 100m hurdles	Yordanka Donkova [BUL]	1988	12·21s
♂ 200m	Michael Johnson [USA]	1996	19·32s
♀ 200m	Florence Griffith-Joyner [USA]	1988	21·34s
♂ 400m	Michael Johnson [USA]	1999	43·18s
♀ 400m	Marita Koch [GER]	1985	47·60s
♂ 400m hurdles	Kevin Young [USA]	1992	46·78s
♀ 400m hurdles	Yuliya Pechonkina [RUS]	2003	52·34s
♂ 800m	Wilson Kipketer [DEN]	1997	1:41·11
♀ 800m	Jarmila Kratochvilova [TCH]	1983	1:53·28
♂ 1,500m	Hitcham El Guerrouj [MAR]	1998	3:26·00
♀ 1,500m	Yunxia Qu [CHN]	1993	3:50·46
♂ Mile	Hitcham El Guerrouj [MAR]	1999	3:43·13
♀ Mile	Svetlana Masterkova [RUS]	1996	4:12·56
♂ 5,000m	Kenenisa Bekele [ETH]	2004	12:37·35
♀ 5,000m	Elvan Abeylegesse [TUR]	2004	14:24·68
♂ 10,000m	Kenenisa Bekele [ETH]	2005	26:17·53†
♀ 10,000m	Junxia Wang [CHN]	1993	29:31·78
♂ Marathon	Paul Tergat [KEN]	2003	2:04·55
♀ Marathon	Paula Radcliffe [GBR]	2003	2:15·25
♂ High jump	Javier Sotomayor [CUB]	1993	2·45m
♀ High jump	Stefka Kostadinova [BUL]	1987	2·09m
♂ Long jump	Mike Powell [USA]	1991	8·95m
♀ Long jump	Galina Christiakova [URS]	1988	7·52m
♂ Triple jump	Jonathan Edwards [GBR]	1995	18·29m
♀ Triple jump	Inessa Kravets [UKR]	1995	15·50m
♂ Pole vault	Sergey Bubka [UKR]	1994	6·14m
♀ Pole vault	Yelena Isinbayeva [RUS]	2005	5·01m†
♂ Shot put	Randy Barnes [USA]	1990	23·12m
♀ Shot put	Natalya Lisovskaya [URS]	1987	22·63m
♂ Discus	Jürgen Schult [GER]	1986	74·08m
♀ Discus	Gabriele Reinsch [GER]	1988	76·80m
♂ Hammer	Yuriy Sedykh [URS]	1986	86·74m
♀ Hammer	Tatyana Lysenko [RUS]	2005	77·06m†
♂ Javelin	Jan Zelezny [CZE]	1996	98·48m
♀ Javelin	Osleidys Menéndez [CUB]	2005	71·70m†
♂ Decathlon	Roman Sebrle [CZE]	2001	9,026pts
♀ Heptathlon	Jackie Joyner-Kersee [USA]	1988	7,291pts
♂ 4x100m relay	USA	1992	37·40s
♀ 4x100m relay	Germany	1985	41·37s
♂ 4x400m relay	USA	1998	2:54·20
♀ 4x400m relay	USSR	1988	3:15·17

[Records correct as of 21·09·05 · †=awaiting ratification]

———————— IAAF WORLD CHAMPIONSHIPS · 2005 ————————

The World Athletics Championship in Helsinki saw Great Britain gain just one gold medal and two bronzes. Some of the gold medal-winning athletes follow:

Men	*event*	*Women*
J. Gatlin [USA] 9·88s	100m	L. Williams [USA] 10·93s
L. Doucouré [FRA] 13·07s	110/100m hurdles	M. Perry [USA] 12·66s
J. Gatlin [USA] 20·04s	200m	A. Felix [USA] 22·16s
J. Wariner [USA] 43·93s	400m	T. Williams-Darling [BAH] 49·55s
R. Ramzi [BRN] 1:44·24s	800m	Z. Calatayud [CUB] 1:58·82s
R. Ramzi [BRN] 3:37·88s	1,500m	T. Tomashova [RUS] 4:00·35s
B. Limo [KEN] 13:32·55s	5,000m	T. Dibaba [ETH] 14:38·59
K. Bekele [ETH] 27:08·33	10,000m	T. Dibaba [ETH] 30:24·02
J. Gharib [MAR] 2:10·10	Marathon	P. Radcliffe [GBR] 2:20·57
Y. Kyrmarenko [UKR] 2·32m	High jump	K. Bergqvist [SWE] 2·02m
D. Phillips [USA] 8·60m	Long jump	T. Madison [USA] 6·89m
A. Nelson [USA] 21·73m	Shot put	N. Ostapchuk [BLR] 20·51m
W. Davis [USA] 17·57m	Triple jump	T. Smith [JAM] 15·11m
R. Blom [NED] 5·80m	Pole vault	Y. Isinbayeva [RUS] 5·01m WR
B. Clay [USA] 8,732pts	Dec-/Heptathlon	C. Kluft [SWE] 6,887pts

———————— THE EUROPEAN ATHLETICS CUP · 2005 ————————

The European Athletics Cup is an event in which national teams compete in leagues to win promotion into the elite top 8, which then battle for the title. Each country fields one representative per event, who accumulates points for their team (8 points for 1st place down to 1 point for 8th). At the end of the competition, the lowest-scoring two teams are relegated. In 2005 the event was held in Florence: GB's men's team was in the elite 8 competing for the Cup, whereas GB's women were in a lower league, fighting for promotion. Below are the top team results:

♂ country	points	♀ country	points
1…Germany	113	1…Russia	131·5
2…France	104	2…Poland	94
3…Italy	98	3…Germany	93
4…Poland	94·5	4…France	90·5
5…Russia	88	5…Ukraine	86
6…Spain	86·5	6…Romania	85
7…Great Britain	70	7…Italy	77
8…Czech Republic†	63	8…Greece†	62

† Most athletics stadia have eight lanes. However, in 2006 the Spanish Stadium hosting the event will have nine – allowing for an extra team to take part. This means that instead of the usual two relegations, only one team will be dropped; thus GB's men and Italy's women will compete. After securing promotion in 2005, Finland and Ukraine's men and Sweden and GB's women will join the elite group (now numbering 9) in 2006.

WIMBLEDON WINNERS · 2005

MEN'S SINGLES
Roger Federer [SUI]
bt Andy Roddick [USA]
6–2, 7–6 (7–2), 6–4

———

*'I'm very, very proud. This is the third
time so it's very special. I came here with
huge expectations and to be standing
here with the trophy is almost a dream.'*
ROGER FEDERER
reacting to his 3rd successive victory

LADIES' SINGLES
Venus Williams [USA]
bt Lindsay Davenport [USA]
4–6, 7–6 (7–4), 9–7

MEN'S DOUBLES
Stephen Huss [AUS] &
Wesley Moodie [RSA]
bt Bob Bryan [USA]
& Mike Bryan [USA]
7–6 (7–4), 6–3, 6–7 (2–7), 6–3

LADIES' DOUBLES
Cara Black [ZIM]
& Liezel Huber [RSA]
bt Svetlana Kuznetsova [RUS]
& Amelie Mauresmo [FRA]
6–2, 6–1

MIXED DOUBLES
Mary Pierce [FRA]
& Mahesh Bhupathi [IND]
bt Paul Hanley [USA]
& Tatiana Perebiynis [USA]
6–4, 6–2

BOYS' SINGLES
Jeremy Chardy [FRA]
bt Robin Haase [NED]
6–4, 6–3

GIRLS' SINGLES
Agnieszka Radwanska [POL]
bt Tamira Paszek [AUT]
6–3, 6–4

BOYS' DOUBLES
Jesse Levine [USA] &
Michael Shabaz [USA]
bt Samuel Groth [AUS]
& Andrew Kennaugh [GBR]
6–4, 6–1

GIRLS' DOUBLES
Viktoria Azarenka [BLR] &
Agnes Szavay [HUN]
bt Marina Erakovic [NZL]
& Monica Niculescu [ROM]
6–7 (5–7), 6–2, 6–0

WIMBLEDON 2005 PRIZE MONEY & MISC.

Round (No. prizes)	♂ singles	♀ singles
Winner (1)	£630,000	600,000
Runner-up (1)	£315,000	300,000
Semi-final (2)	£157,500	145,690
Quarter-final (4)	£81,900	73,710
4th round (8)	£44,100	37,480
3rd round (16)	£25,100	20,400
2nd round (32)	£15,440	12,350
1st round (64)	£9,450	7,560

[Doubles winnings are different]

Strawberries consumed	28,000kg
Rackets strung	2,150
No. GB men in 1st round	9
No. GB men in 2nd round	4
No. GB women in 1st round	6
No. GB women 2nd round	1

Highest TV viewing figure	9·3m
	A. Murray *vs* D. Nalbandian
Tim Henman out in	R2
Best performing Brit	A. Murray, R3
Chocolate tennis balls sold	3,900
Total attendance	467,188

———————————— THE DAVIS CUP ————————————

The Davis Cup began in 1900 and now involves 134 countries, of which only 16 qualify to play in the World Group. The rest fight it out in continental leagues in an effort to gain promotion into the elite World Group. Great Britain currently plays in the Europe–Africa Zone Group 1. British results for 2005 follow:

5–6 March · Europe/Africa Zone Group 1 2nd round
Ramat Hasharon, Tel Aviv, Israel (surface: hard – outdoors)
Great Britain *bt* Israel 3–2

Greg Rusedski [GBR] *bt* Harel Levy [ISR] 6–4, 6–3, 6–0
Noam Okun [ISR] *bt* Alex Bogdanovic [GBR] 7–6 (7–3), 6–2, 6–2
Andrew Murray and David Sherwood [GBR]
bt Jonathan Erlich and Andy Ram [ISR] 6–4, 7–6 (7–5), 7–6 (7–5)
Greg Rusedski [GBR] *bt* Noam Okun [ISR] 6–3, 6–4, 6–2
Harel Levy [ISR] *bt* David Sherwood [GBR] 6–7 (1–7), 6–4, 6–3

————————————

23–5 September · Davis Cup World Group Play-Offs,
Palexpo Arena, Geneva, Switzerland (surface: clay)
Switzerland *bt* Great Britain 5–0 *(GB failed to gain promotion to World Group)*

Roger Federer [SUI] *bt* Alan Mackin [GBR] 6–0, 6–0, 6–2
Stanislas Wawrinka [SUI] *bt* Andrew Murray [GBR] 6–3, 7–6 (7–5), 6–4
Roger Federer [SUI] & Yves Allegro [SUI]
bt Greg Rusedski [GBR] & Andrew Murray [GBR] 7–5, 2–6, 7–6 (7–1), 6–2
George Bastl [SUI] *bt* David Sherwood [GBR] 6–3, 6–0
Stanislas Wawrinka [SUI] *bt* Alan Mackin [GBR] 7–5, 7–6 (7–5)

Previous winners	2001......France	1997.....Sweden	1993...Germany
2004.......Spain	2000.......Spain	1996......France	1992........USA
2003....Australia	1999....Australia	1995........USA	1991......France
2002......Russia	1998.....Sweden	1994.....Sweden	1990........USA

————— TENNIS GRAND SLAM TOURNAMENTS · 2005 —————

Event	month	surface	♂	winner ♀
Australian Open	Jan	Rebound Ace	Marat Safin	Serena Williams
French Open	May/Jun	clay	Rafael Nadal	J. Henin-Hardenne
Wimbledon	Jun/Jul	grass	Roger Federer	Venus Williams
US Open	Aug/Sep	cement	Roger Federer	Kim Cljisters

Winning all four Grand Slam games in one year is exceedingly rare; the only people to have achieved the feat are: Don Budge [USA] (1938), Maureen Connoly [USA] (1953), Rod Laver [AUS] (1962 & '69), Margaret Smith Court [AUS] (1970), Steffi Graf [GER] (1988) – Steffi Graf also won the Olympic Gold in that year, making a 'Golden Slam'.

——————FORMULA ONE TEAMS & DRIVERS · 2005——————

Ferrari . . . . Michael Schumacher [GER] & Rubens Barichello [BRA]
BAR. . . . . Jenson Button [GBR] & Takuma Sato [JAP]
Renault . . . . Fernando Alonso [SPA] & Giancarlo Fisichella [ITA]
BMW Williams . . . . Mark Webber [AUS] & Nick Heidfeld [GER]
McLaren Mercedes . . . . Kimi Raikkonen [FIN] & Juan Pablo Montoya [COL]
Sauber. . . . . Jacques Villeneuve [CAN] & Felipe Massa [BRA]
Red Bull. . . . . David Coulthard [GBR] & Christian Klien [AUT]
Toyota . . . . Jarno Trulli [ITA] & Ralf Schumacher [GER]
Jordan . . . . Narain Karthikeyan [IND] & Tiago Monteiro [POR]
Minardi . . . . Christijan Albers [NED] & Patrick Friesacher [AUT]

——————FORMULA ONE WORLD CHAMPIONSHIP · 2005——————

Date	Grand Prix	track	winning driver	car
06·03·05	Australia	Albert Park	Giancarlo Fisichella	Renault
20·03·05	Malaysia	Sepang	Fernando Alonso	Renault
03·04·05	Bahrain	Manama	Fernando Alonso	Renault
24·04·05	San Marino	Imola	Fernando Alonso	Renault
08·05·05	Spain	Barcelona	Kimi Raikkonen	McLaren
22·05·05	Monaco	Monte Carlo	Kimi Raikkonen	McLaren
29·05·05	Germany	Nürburgring	Fernando Alonso	Renault
12·06·05	Canada	Gilles Villeneuve	Kimi Raikkonen	McLaren
19·06·05	America	Indianapolis	Michael Schumacher	Ferrari
03·07·05	France	Magny-Cours	Fernando Alonso	Renault
10·07·05	Britain	Silverstone	Juan Pablo Montoya	McLaren
24·07·05	Germany	Hockenheim	Fernando Alonso	Renault
31·07·05	Hungary	Hungaroring	Kimi Raikkonen	McLaren
21·08·05	Turkey	Istanbul Otodrom	Kimi Raikkonen	McLaren
04·09·05	Italy	Monza	Juan Pablo Montoya	McLaren
11·09·05	Belgium	Spa-Francorchamps	Kimi Raikkonen	McLaren
25·09·05*	Brazil	Interlagos	Juan Pablo Montoya	McLaren
09·10·05	Japan	Suzuka		
16·10·05	China	Shanghai		

During this race Fernando Alonso became Spain's first (and the youngest) world driver's champion.

——————SUPERBIKES, RALLY & MOTORSPORT——————

Isle of Man TT (senior) [2005]. . . . . John McGuinness
Isle of Man TT (junior) [2005]. . . . . Ian Lougher
Moto GP [2004]. . . . . Valentino Rossi
British Superbikes [2004]. . . . . John Reynolds
World Superbikes [2004] . . . . James Toseland
World Rally [2004]. . . . . Sebastian Loeb
Le Mans [2005]. Tom Kristensen, JJ Lehto, Marco Werner

─────── WORLD BOXING CHAMPIONS · AT 1·9·2005 ───────

Weight	WBC	WBA	IBF	WBO
Heavy	Klitschko, V [UKR]	Ruiz [PR]	Byrd [USA]	Brewster [USA]
Cruiser	Mormeck [FRA]	Mormeck [FRA]	Bell [JAM]	Nelson [GBR]
Light heavy	Adamek [POL]	Tiozzo [FRA]	Woods [GBR]	Erdei [HUN]
Super middle	Beyer [GER]	Kessler [DEN]	Lacy [USA]	Calzaghe [GBR]
Middle	Taylor [USA]	Taylor [USA]	Taylor [USA]	Taylor [USA]
Light middle	Mayorga [NCA]	Simms [USA]	Karmazin [RUS]	Santos [PUR]
Welter	Judah [USA]	Collazo [USA]	Judah [USA]	Margarito [MEX]
Light welter	Mayweather [USA]	Maussa [COL]	Hatton [GBR]	Cotto [PUR]
Light	Corrales [USA]	Diaz, J [USA]	*vacant*	Corrales [USA]
Super feather	Barrera [MEX]	Mosquera [PAN]	Peden [AUS]	Barrios [ARG]
Feather	Chi [KOR]	John [INA]	*vacant*	Harrison [GBR]
Super bantam	Larios [MEX]	Monshipour [FRA]	Vazquez [MEX]	Guzman [DOM]
Bantam	Hasegawa [JAP]	Sidorenko [UKR]	Marquez [MEX]	Vorapin [THA]
Super fly	Tokuyama [JAP]	Castillo [MEX]	Perez [NCA]	Hernandez [MEX]
Fly	Wonjongkam [THA]	Parra [USA]	Darchinyan [AUS]	Narvaez [ARG]
Light fly	Ortiz [MEX]	Vasquez [PAN]	Grigsby [USA]	Cazares [MEX]
Straw	Junlaphan [THA]	Niida [JAP]	Rachman [INA]	Calderon [PUR]

─────── WORLD SWIMMING CHAMPIONSHIP · 2005 ───────

In July 2005 the World Swimming Championships were held in Montreal. Nine world records were broken over the course of the meet. Britain's performance was disappointing, with a total of only 3 bronze medals. Some selected results follow:

Event	*winner*	*record*	*time*
♂ 50m butterfly	Roland Schoeman [RSA]	WR	22·96
♀ 50m butterfly	Danni Miatke [AUS]		26·11
♀ 50m breaststroke	Jade Edmistone [AUS]	WR	30·45
♂ 100m freestyle	Filippo Magnini [ITA]	CR	48·12
♀ 100m freestyle	Jodie Henry [AUS]		54·18
♂ 100m breaststroke	Brendan Hansen [USA]	CR	59·37
♀ 100m breaststroke	Leisel Jones [AUS]		1:06·25
♂ 100m butterfly	Ian Crocker [USA]	WR	50·40
♀ 100m butterfly	Jessica Schipper [AUS]	CR	57·23
♂ 200m backstroke	Aaron Peirsol [USA]	WR	1:54·66
♀ 200m breaststroke	Leisel Jones [AUS]	WR	2:21·72
♂ 200m freestyle	Michael Phelps [USA]		1:45·20
♀ 200m freestyle	Solenne Figues [FRA]		1:58·60
♀ 200m butterfly	Otylia Jedrzejczak [POL]	WR	2:05·61
♂ 400m freestyle	Grant Hackett [AUS]		3:42·91
♀ 400m freestyle	Laure Manaudou [FRA]		4:06·44
♂ 800m freestyle	Grant Hackett [AUS]	WR	7:38·65

Key: CR – Championship Record · WR – World Record

BBC SPORTS PERSONALITY OF THE YEAR · 2004

Sports personality of the year............................... Kelly Holmes
Team of the year.................................. GB Olympic men's coxless four
Overseas personality .... Roger Federer (Swiss)
Coach of the year... Arsene Wenger
Lifetime achievement .... Ian Botham
Young personality .... Andrew Murray
Unsung hero .... Abdullah Ben-Kmayal
Helen Rollason award 'for courage and achievement in the face of adversity' ...... Kirsty Howard

Finally after 20 years of dreaming, having seven out of nine years injured, I've got my dream – not once but twice. It's been an emotional rollercoaster. Winning erased the nights of crying my eyes out and the pain I've been going through … I feel it's the biggest sporting honour your country can give you so I'd like to thank the public.
— DAME KELLY HOLMES

Previous Personalities		
'03.... Jonny Wilkinson	'87 .. Fatima Whitbread	'70 ...... Henry Cooper
'02 ...... Paula Radcliffe	'86 .... Nigel Mansell	'69 .... Ann Jones
'01..... David Beckham	'85.... Barry McGuigan	'68 ...... David Hemery
'00 ...... Steve Redgrave	'84 ..... Torvill & Dean	'67 ...... Henry Cooper
'99 .... Lennox Lewis	'83.......... Steve Cram	'66 .... Bobby Moore
'98 ..... Michael Owen	'82 ... Daley Thompson	'65.... Tommy Simpson
'97....... Greg Rusedski	'81 .... Ian Botham	'64.......... Mary Rand
'96......... Damon Hill	'80 ...... Robin Cousins	'63.... Dorothy Hyman
'95... Jonathan Edwards	'79 .... Sebastian Coe	'62 .. Anita Lonsbrough
'94......... Damon Hill	'78.......... Steve Ovett	'61........ Stirling Moss
'93..... Linford Christie	'77....... Virginia Wade	'60 ...... David Broome
'92 .... Nigel Mansell	'76.......... John Curry	'59......... John Surtees
'91....... Liz McColgan	'75......... David Steele	'58 .... Ian Black
'90...... Paul Gascoigne	'74..... Brendan Foster	'57............. Dai Rees
'89 .... Nick Faldo	'73 ...... Jackie Stewart	'56............ Jim Laker
'88.......... Steve Davis	'72 .... Mary Peters	'55........ Gordon Pirie
	'71 .... Princess Anne	'54..... Chris Chataway

SOME SPORTING THEME TUNES

Wimbledon......................... *Light and Tuneful* · Keith Prowse
Ski Sunday........................... *Pop Looks Bach* · Sam Fonteyn
BBC Test Match cricket .... *Soul Limbo* · Booker T and The MGs
Channel 4 Test Match cricket............................ *Mambo No.5* · Lou Bega
Match of the Day .... *Match of the Day* · Barry Stoller
Pot Black................... *The Black and White Rag* · Winifred Atwell
BBC snooker .... *Drag Racer* · Doug Wood
Rugby Special.. *Holy Mackerel* · Brian Bennet
Superstars.. *Heavy Action* · Johnny Pearson
International showjumping............................. *A Musical Joke* · Mozart

─────────────── MODERN OLYMPICS ───────────────

Season & host		year	sports	athletes	nations	most golds
S	Athens	1896	9	241	14	11 USA
S	Paris	1900	18	997	24	25 FRA
S	St Louis	1904	17	645	12	77 USA
S	London	1908	22	2008	22	56 GBR
S	Stockholm	1912	14	2407	28	25 USA
S	Antwerp	1920	22	2606	29	41 USA
S	Paris	1924	17	3089	44	45 USA
W	Chamonix	1924	6	258	16	4 NOR
S	Amsterdam	1928	14	2883	46	22 USA
W	St Moritz	1928	4	464	25	6 NOR
S	Los Angeles	1932	14	1332	37	41 USA
W	Lake Placid	1932	4	252	17	6 USA
S	Berlin	1936	19	3963	49	33 GER
W	Garmisch-Partenkirchen	1936	4	646	28	7 NOR
S	London	1948	17	4104	59	38 USA
W	St Moritz	1948	4	669	28	4 NOR
S	Helsinki	1952	17	4955	69	40 USA
W	Oslo	1952	4	694	30	7 NOR
S	Melbourne	1956	17	3114	72	37 USSR
W	Cortina d'Ampezzo	1956	4	821	32	7 USSR
S	Rome	1960	17	5338	83	43 USSR
W	Squaw Valley	1960	4	665	30	7 USSR
S	Tokyo	1964	19	5151	93	36 USA
W	Innsbruck	1964	6	1091	36	11 USSR
S	Mexico City	1968	20	5516	112	45 USA
W	Grenoble	1968	6	1158	37	6 NOR
S	Munich	1972	23	7134	121	50 USSR
W	Sapporo	1972	6	1006	35	8 USSR
S	Montreal	1976	21	6084	92	79 USSR
W	Innsbruck	1976	6	1123	37	13 USSR
S	Moscow	1980	21	5179	80	80 USSR
W	Lake Placid	1980	6	1072	37	10 USSR
S	Los Angeles	1984	23	6829	140	83 USA
W	Sarajevo	1984	6	1272	49	7 GER
S	Seoul	1988	25	8391	159	55 USSR
W	Calgary	1988	6	1423	57	11 USSR
S	Barcelona	1992	28	9356	169	45 USSR†
W	Albertville	1992	7	1801	64	10 GER
W	Lillehammer	1994	6	1737	67	11 RUS
S	Atlanta	1996	26	10318	197	44 USA
W	Nagano	1998	7	2176	72	12 GER
S	Sydney	2000	28	10651	200	40 USA
W	Salt Lake City	2002	7	2399	77	13 NOR
S	Athens	2004	28	?	202	35 USA

ˢ Summer Olympic · ᵂ Winter Olympic · † the former USSR

─────── READY RECKONER OF OTHER RESULTS · 2005 ───────

For other major sporting results, see the appropriate pages within this section.

AMERICAN FOOTBALL · Superbowl	New Eng. Patriots *bt* Phil. Eagles 24–21
ANGLING · National Coarse Ch. Div.1	Steve Clark 72·92 kg
BADMINTON · World Ch.	♂ Taufik Hidayat [INA] *bt* Dan Lin [CHI] 15–3, 15–7
	♀ Xingfang Xie [CHI] *bt* Ning Zhang [CHI] 11–8, 9–11, 11–3
English National Ch.	♂ Aamir Ghaffar *bt* Nicholas Kidd 15–3, 15–4
	♀ Elizabeth Cann *bt* Tracey Hallam 11–8, 11–3
BASEBALL · World Series [2004]	Boston Red Sox *bt* St Louis Cardinals 4–0
BASKETBALL · BBL Trophy final	Newcastle Eagles 85–60 Brighton Bears
NBA finals	San Antonio Spurs *bt* Detroit Pistons 4–3
THE BOAT RACE	Oxford *bt* Cambridge [by two lengths, in 16min 42s]
BOG SNORKELLING · World Championships	Iain Hawkes [GBR]
CHEESE ROLLING · Cooper's Hill	♂ Chris Anderson [GBR] ♀ Dione Carter [NZ]
CHESS · British Championship	Jonathan Rowson
CRICKET · Test series – South Africa *vs* England	England won 2–1
Test series – England *vs* Bangladesh	England won 2–0
NatWest Series (Eng, B'gladesh, Aus)	England and Australia drew in the final
County Championship	Nottinghamshire
Womens' cricket World Cup	Australia *bt* India by 98 runs
Womens' Ashes series	England *bt* Australia 1–0
CROQUET · World Croquet Championship	Reg Bamford [RSA]
CYCLING · *Tour de France*	Lance Armstrong [USA]
Tour of Britain	Nick Nuyens [BEL] 19:04·32
DARTS · Ladbrokes W. Ch. [PDC]	Phil 'The Power' Taylor *bt* Mark 'Flash' Dudbridge
Lakeside World Championship [BDO]	Raymond van Barneveld *bt* Martin Adams
ELEPHANT POLO · World Championships	Scotland *bt* Thailand 6–5
ENDURANCE RACES · Marathon des Sables	♂ Lahcen Ahansal [MOR] 19:09·04
	♀ Simone Kayser Diederich [LUX] 29:36·03
Devil o' The Highlands	♂ John Kennedy 6:08·06 · ♀ Helen Johnson 7:04·37
EQUESTRIANISM · Badminton	Primmore's Pride *ridden by* P. Funnell [GBR] 44.5 pen
FOOTBALL · FA Cup	Arsenal 0–0 Man. Utd (Arsenal win 5–4 on penalties)
FA Cup · Womens'	Charlton Women 1–0 Everton Ladies
UEFA Cup	Sporting Lisbon 1–3 CSKA Moscow
Champions League	Liverpool 3–3 AC Milan (Liverpool win 3–2 on penalties)
Community Shield	Chelsea 2–1 Arsenal
Carling Cup	Liverpool 2–3 Chelsea (after extra time, 1–1 at 90 mins)
LDV Vans Trophy	Southend 0–2 Wrexham
Premiership	Chelsea
Championship	Sunderland
League 1	Luton
League 2	Yeovil
Scottish Premiership	Rangers
Scottish Cup	Celtic 1–0 Dundee United
Women's Euro 2005	Germany 3–1 Norway
FORMULA ONE · World Drivers Champion	Fernando Alonso

—— READY RECKONER OF OTHER RESULTS · 2005 cont. ——

GOLF · Solheim Cup	USA *bt* Europe 15.5 – 12.5
World Match Play Championship	Michael Campbell [NZ]
GREYHOUND RACING · William Hill Greyhound Derby	Westmead Hawk
HORSE RACING · Grand National	Hedgehunter *trained by* W. Mullins *ridden by* R.Walsh
Epsom Derby	Motivator *trained by* Michael Bell *ridden by* Johnny Murtagh
Cheltenham Gold Cup	Kicking King *trained by* T. Taaffe, *ridden by* B. Geraghty
1,000 Guineas	Virginia Waters *trained by* A. O'Brien, *ridden by* K. Fallon
2,000 Guineas	Footstepsinthesand *trained by* A. O'Brien, *ridden by* K. Fallon
The Oaks	Eswarah *trained by* Michael Jarvis *ridden by* Richard Hills
St Leger	Scorpion *trained by* A. O'Brien, *ridden by* F. Dettori
RUGBY LEAGUE · Super League	Leeds
Challenge Cup	Hull 25–24 Leeds
RUGBY UNION · Zurich Premiership	Leicester
Zurich Premiership Championship	Leicester 14–39 Wasps
Powergen Cup	Bath 12–20 Leeds
Wildcard Final	Gloucester 16–24 Saracens
Celtic Cup	Munster 27–16 Llanelli
Heineken Cup	Stade Français 12–18 Toulouse
European Challenge Cup	Sale 27–3 Pau
Varsity Match [2004]	Oxford 18–11 Cambridge
Celtic League	Ospreys
RUNNING · Chicago Marathon [OCT 2004]	♂ Evans Rutto [KEN] 02:06·16
	♀ Constantina Tomescu-Dita [ROM] 02:23·45
New York City Marathon [NOV 2004]	♂ Hendrik Ramaala [RSA] 2:09·28
	♀ Paula Radcliffe [GBR] 2:23·10
Paris Marathon	♂ Salim Kipsang [KEN] 02:08·02
	♀ Lydiya Grigoryeva [RUS] 02:27·00
London Marathon	♂ Martin Lel [KEN] 2:07·26
	♀ Paula Radcliffe [GBR] 2:17·42
Boston Marathon	♂ Hailu Negussie [ETH] 2:11·45
	♀ Catherine Ndereba [KEN] 2:25·13
Great North Run	♂ Zersenay Tadesse [ERI] 0:59:05
	♀ Deratu Tulu [ETH] 1:07:03
Mascot Grand National	*The Sun* Scoop 6 Squirrel
TENNIS · Australian O.	Marat Safin [RUS] *bt* Lleyton Hewitt [AUS] [1–6, 6–3, 6–4, 6–4]
	Serena Williams [USA] *bt* Lindsay Davenport [USA] [2–6, 6–3, 6–0]
French Open	Rafael Nadal [ESP] *bt* Mariano Puerta [ARG] [6–7, 6–3, 6–1, 7–5]
	Justine Henin-Hardenne [BEL] *bt* Mary Pierce [FRA] [6–1, 6–1]
US Open	Roger Federer [SUI] *bt* Andre Agassi [USA] [6–3, 2–6, 7–6 (7–1), 6–1]
	Kim Clijsters [BEL] *bt* Mary Pierce [FRA] [6–3, 6–1]
SAILING · Star European Ch.	Iain Percy [GBR] & Steve Mitchell [GBR]
Rolex Fastnet race	Iromiguy *sailed by* Jean-Yves Chateau [FRA]
SNOOKER · The Masters	Ronnie O'Sullivan *bt* John Higgins 10–3
SQUASH · The World Games	♂ P. Nicol [GBR] *bt* T. Lincou [FRA] 9–4, 9–0, 9–4
	♀ N. David [MAS] *bt* R. Grinham [AUS] 9–4, 10–8, 9–1

(No NHL ice hockey results, as a labour dispute caused the entire 2004/05 season to be scrapped.)

─────── SELECTED SPORTING CALENDAR · 2006 ───────

JANUARY · 19 Dec–2 Jan ....Ladbrokes' Darts World Championship
7–15 ....Lakeside World Professional Darts Championship
16–29 ....Tennis · Australian Open
FEBRUARY · 4 .... Rugby Union · Six Nations · Ireland *vs* Italy; England *vs* Wales
5 ....Rugby Union · Six Nations · Scotland *vs* France
11 ....Rugby Union · Six Nations · France *vs* Ireland; Italy *vs* England
12 ....Rugby Union · Six Nations · Wales *vs* Scotland
25 ....Rugby Union · Six Nations · France *vs* Italy; Scotland *vs* England
26 ....Rugby Union · Six Nations · Ireland *vs* Wales
26 ....Football · Carling Cup Final
MARCH · 12 ....Formula One · Grand Prix, venue tbc
10-12 ....Athletics · World Indoor Championships, Moscow
11 ....Rugby Union · Six Nations · Wales *vs* Italy; Ireland *vs* Scotland
12 ....Rugby Union · Six Nations · France *vs* England
14–17 ....Horse racing · Cheltenham Festival
15-26 ....Commonwealth Games, Melbourne, Australia
18 ...Rugby Union · Six Nations · Italy *vs* Scot.; Wales *vs* France; Eng. *vs* Ireland
19 ....Formula One · Grand Prix, venue tbc
APRIL · 2 ....Rowing · The Boat Race
2 ....Formula One · Grand Prix, venue tbc
8 ....Horse racing · The Grand National, Aintree
8/9 ....Rugby Union · Powergen Cup Final
16 ....Formula One · Grand Prix, venue tbc
16–1 May ....Snooker · World Championships, Sheffield
23 ....Flora London Marathon
30 ....Formula One · Grand Prix, venue tbc
MAY · 4–7 ....Equestrian · Badminton Horse Trials
6 ....Horse racing · 2,000 Guineas, Newmarket
7 ....Horse racing · 1,000 Guineas, Newmarket
10 ....Football · UEFA Cup Final · Phillips Stadion, Eindhoven
11–15 ....Cricket · England *vs* Sri Lanka, 1st Test, Lords
13 ....Football · FA Cup Final, Wembley Stadium
13 ....Football · Scottish Cup Final
14 ....Formula One · Grand Prix, venue tbc
27 ....Rugby Union · Zurich Premiership Final, Twickenham
17 ....Football · Champions League Final, Stade de France, Paris
20/21 (tbc) ....Rugby Union · Heineken Cup Final, Millennium Stadium
25–29 ....Cricket · England *vs* Sri Lanka, 2nd Test, Edgbaston
28 ....Formula One · Grand Prix, venue tbc
29–11 June ....Tennis · French Open
JUNE · 2–6 ....Cricket · England *vs* Sri Lanka, 3rd Test, Trent Bridge
2–3 ....Horse racing · Derby meeting, Epsom
4 ....Formula One · Grand Prix, venue tbc
9 ....Football · World Cup, Germany, opening ceremony
15 ....Cricket · Twenty20 ODI · England *vs* Sri Lanka, The Rose Bowl
15–18 ....Golf · US Open, Winged Foot Golf Club, Mamaroneck, NY

─────── SELECTED SPORTING CALENDAR · 2006 cont. ───────

JUNE (cont.) · 17 .... Cricket · 1st ODI, England *vs* Sri Lanka, Lord's
18 .... Formula One · Grand Prix, venue tbc
20 .... Cricket · 2nd ODI, England *vs* Sri Lanka, The Oval
24 .... Cricket · 3rd ODI, England *vs* Sri Lanka, Riverside
25 .... Formula One · Grand Prix, venue tbc
26–10 July.. Tennis · Wimbledon
28 .... Cricket · 4th ODI, England *vs* Sri Lanka, Old Trafford
28–29.............................. Athletics · European Cup, Malaga, Spain
28–2 July .... Rowing · Henley Regatta
tbc.. Horse racing · Royal Ascot
JULY · 1 .... Cricket · 5th ODI, England *vs* Sri Lanka, Headingley
2.. Formula One · Grand Prix, venue tbc
2–23... Cycling · Tour de France
9 .... Football · World Cup Final, Germany
13–17.............................. Cricket · 1st Test, England *vs* Pakistan, Lord's
16 .... Formula One · Grand Prix, venue tbc
20–23........................... Golf · The Open Championship, Royal Liverpool
27–31........................ Cricket · 2nd Test, England *vs* Pakistan, Old Trafford
29–5 Aug....................................... Sailing · Cowes Week
30 .... Formula One · Grand Prix, venue tbc
AUGUST · 1–5 .... Horse racing · Glorious Goodwood
4–8.............................. Cricket · 3rd Test, England *vs* Pakistan, Headingley
6.. Formula One · Grand Prix, venue tbc
8–13 .... Athletics · European Athletics Championship, Gothenburg
14–20.......... Golf · US PGA Championship, Medinah Country Club, Illinois
17–21 .... Cricket · 4th Test, England *vs* Pakistan, the Oval
27 .... Formula One · Grand Prix, venue tbc
28................. Cricket · Twenty20 International, England *vs* Pakistan, Bristol
28–11 Sep................................... Tennis · US Open, Flushing Meadows
30 .... Cricket · 1st ODI, England *vs* Pakistan, Cardiff
tbc .... Rugby League · Powergen Challenge Cup final, Millennium Stadium
SEPTEMBER · 2–4 .... Athletics · IAAF World Cup
2................................ Cricket · 2nd ODI, England *vs* Pakistan, Lord's
5.............................. Cricket · 3rd ODI, England *vs* Pakistan, Rose Bowl
7–10 .... Horse racing · St Leger meeting, Doncaster
8 .... Cricket · 4th ODI, England *vs* Pakistan, Trent Bridge
10 .... Cricket · 5th ODI, England *vs* Pakistan, Edgbaston
10 .... Formula One · Grand Prix, venue tbc
17 .... Formula One · Grand Prix, venue tbc
OCTOBER · 1 .... Formula One · Grand Prix, venue tbc
15 .... Formula One · Grand Prix, venue tbc
22 .... Formula One · Grand Prix, venue tbc
NOVEMBER · 5 .... New York City Marathon
DECEMBER · 1–3 .... Tennis · Davis Cup final

Inevitably, at the time of going to press, some entries were tentative or yet to be confirmed.

Ephemerides

*That Kalendar or Ephemerides which he maketh of the
diversities of times and seasons for all actions and purposes.*
— FRANCIS BACON

―――――――――――――――― 2006 ――――――――――――――――

Roman numerals.................MMVI		Indian (Saka) year ......1928 (22 Mar)	
Regnal year[1].................54th (6 Feb)		Sikh year ....538 Nanakshahi Era (14 Mar)	
Dominical Letter[2].........................A		Jewish year.................5767 (23 Sep)	
Epact[3]..............................✱ (XXX)		Roman year [AUC].......2759 (21 Apr)	
Golden Number (Lunar Cycle)[4] XII		Masonic year[5] ....6006 Anno Lucis	
Chinese New Year . *Dog* 4704 (29 Jan)		Knights Templar year.........888 (AO)	
Hindu New Year........2063 (30 Mar)		Baha'i year.................163 (21 Mar)	
Islamic year...............1427 (31 Jan)		Queen bee colour ......white [see below]	

[1] The number of years from the accession of a monarch; traditionally, legislation was dated by the
Regnal year of the reigning monarch. [2] A way of categorising years to facilitate the calculation of
Easter. If 1 January is a Sunday, the Dominical letter for the year will be A, if 2 January is a Sunday
it will be B, and so on. [3] The number of days by which the solar year exceeds the lunar year. [4]
The number of the year (1–19) in the 19 year Metonic cycle; it is used in the calculation of Easter,
and is found by adding 1 to the remainder left after dividing the number of the year by 19.
[5] For some Freemasons, AU stands for *Anno Lucis*, the 'Year of Light' when the world was formed.

―――――――― ANNUAL QUEEN BEE COLOUR CODING ――――――――

Around the world, apiculturists (bee-keepers) employ a series of colour codes to
identify queen bees and indicate their age. A smudge of harmless quick-drying
paint is applied to the thorax of the queen bee so that she stands out within the
hive's population. It seems that the origin of this colour coding derives from the
work of the Nobel Laureate Austrian zoologist Karl Von Frisch, who researched
the language, orientation, and direction-finding of bees – as well as their senses of
hearing, smell, and taste. The queen bee colour coding system operates as follows:

Colour	*last digit of year*	*example*	*mnemonic*
White	1 or 6	2006/2011	Will
Yellow	2 or 7	2007/2012	You
Red	3 or 8	2008/2013	Raise
Green	4 or 9	2009/2014	Good
Blue	5 or 0	2010/2015	Bees?

A number of bee-keeping journals change their jacket colour annually to match.

─────────────── RED LETTER DAYS ───────────────

Red Letter Days are those of ecclesiastical or civil significance, so named because they were marked out in red ink on early religious calendars. (The Romans marked unlucky days with black chalk, and auspicious days with white.) When these days falls within law sitting [see p.282], Judges of the Queen's Division sit wearing elegant scarlet robes. The Red Letter Days in Great Britain are as follows:

Conversion St Paul	25 Jan	St Barnabas	11 Jun
Purification	2 Feb	Official B/D HM the Queen†	17 Jun
Accession HM the Queen	6 Feb	St John the Baptist	24 Jun
Ash Wednesday	1 Mar	St Peter	29 Jun
St David's Day	1 Mar	St Thomas	3 Jul
Annunciation	25 Mar	St James	25 Jul
B/D HM the Queen	21 Apr	St Luke	18 Oct
St Mark	25 Apr	SS Simon & Jude	28 Oct
SS Phillip & James	1 May	All Saints	1 Nov
St Matthias	14 May	Lord Mayor's Day†	—
Ascension	25 May	B/D HRH Prince of Wales	14 Nov
Coronation HM the Queen	2 Jun	St Andrew's Day	30 Nov
B/D HRH Duke Edinburgh	10 Jun	*(† indicates the date varies by year)*	

─────────────── THIRTY DAYS... ───────────────

30 days hath November,
April, June and September,
February hath 28 alone,
And all the rest have 31

or

30 days hath November,
April, June and September,
Of 28 there is but one
And the rest 30 and 1

Dirty days hath September,
April, June, and November,
From January up to May
The rain it raineth every day.
February hath twenty-eight alone,
· And all the rest have thirty-one.
If any of them had two and thirty
They'd be just as wet and dirty.

THOMAS HOOD (1799–1845)

─────────────── KEY TO SYMBOLS USED OVERLEAF ───────────────

[ʙₕ✳]	UK Bank Holiday	[£]	Union Flag to be flown
[ᴅ̃]	National Day	[ᵂ1900]	Wedding Anniversary
[ʜ̃]	National Holiday	[Ꞵ1900]	Admission Day [US States]
[ᵇ1900]	Independence Day	◗	Full Moon
[ᴮ1900]	Birthday	[⚘]	Annual meteor shower
[†1900]	Anniversary of death	[ᴺ̃]	United Nations Day
[®]	Religious holiday	[☛]	Hunting season (traditional)
[§*patronage*]	Saint's Day	[O]	Eclipse

Italicised entries indicate dates subject to change or those tentative at the time of printing.

─────────────────── JANUARY ───────────────────

Capricorn [♑]   *Birthstone* · GARNET   **Aquarius** [♒]
(Dec 22–Jan 20)   *Flower* · CARNATION   (Jan 21–Feb 19)

1 ....New Year's Day [♯♭*] · Solemnity of Mary [®]................Su
2 ....Haiti – Ancestor's Day [ℵ] · David Bailey [β1938]..............M
3 ....St Genevieve [§ *protector of Paris*] · Alaska [β1959]................Tu
4 ......................T.S. Eliot [†1965] · Quadrantids [☄]......................W
5 ....Twelfth Night [®] · St Edward the Confessor [†1066]..............Th
6 ....Epiphany [®] · Armenia – Christmas Day [ℵ]................F
7 ....Gerald Durrell [β1925]..........................Sa
8 ....Greece – Midwife's Day [ℵ] · Elvis Presley [β1935]..............Su
9 ....Richard Nixon [β1913]..........................M
10 ....Rod Stewart [β1945] · Coco Chanel [†1971]................Tu
11 ....*traditionally, the day on which lambs start to appear*..............W
12 ....Des O'Connor [β1932] · Dame Agatha Christie [†1976]..........Th
13 ....St Hilary of Poitiers [§ *against snake bites*]................F
14 ....◐ · Humphrey Bogart [†1957]......................Sa
15 ....Venezuela – Teacher's Day [ℵ] · Martin Luther King [β1929]........Su
16 ......USA – Martin Luther King Day [ℵ] · Japan – Coming of Age [ℵ]......M
17 ....Al Capone [β1899]..........................Tu
18 ....................A.A. Milne [β1882] hence, 'Pooh Day'....................W
19 ....Dolly Parton [β1946]..........................Th
20 ....Presidential Inauguration Day, USA..................F
21 ....St Agnes [§ *children of Mary*] · George Orwell [†1950]..............Sa
22 ....Lord Byron [β1788] · Queen Victoria [†1901]............Su
23 ....Salvador Dali [†1989]..........................M
24 ....St Francis de Sales [§ *journalists*]................Tu
25 ....Scotland – Burns' Night · Conversion of St Paul [®]............W
26 ....Australia – Australia Day [ℵ]................Th
27 ....Wolfgang Amadeus Mozart [β1756]................F
28 ....St Thomas Aquinas [§ *students*] · Charlemagne [†814]........Sa
29 ....Chinese New Year – the Dog [ℵ]....................Su
30 ....Mahatma Gandhi [†1948 *assassinated*] · Phil Collins [β1951]..........M
31 ....Guy Fawkes [†1606 *executed*]....................Tu

French Rev. calendar ..... *Pluviôse* (rain)	Dutch month ...... *Lauwmaand* (chilly)
Angelic governor................ *Gabriel*	Saxon month .... *Wulf-monath* (wolf)
Epicurean calendar ..... *Marronglaçaire*	Talismanic stone .... *Jasper*

❦ The Latin month *Ianuarius* derives from *ianua* ('door'), since it was the opening of the year. It was also associated with the *Janus*, two-faced Roman god of doors and openings who guarded the gates of heaven. Janus could simultaneously face the year just past and the year to come. ❦ *If January Calends be summerly gay, 'Twill be winterly weather till the calends of May.* ❦ *Janiveer – Freeze the pot upon the fier.* ❦ *He that will live another year, Must eat a hen in Januvere.* ❦ On the stock-market, the *January Effect* is the trend of stocks performing especially well that month. ❦

─────────────── FEBRUARY ───────────────

Aquarius [♒]   *Birthstone* · AMETHYST   *Pisces* [♓]
(Jan 21–Feb 19)   *Flower* · PRIMROSE   (Feb 20–Mar 20)

1..........National Freedom Day, USA · St Bride [§ *poets, blacksmiths, & healers*] ....W
2.....................Candlemas [®] · Groundhog Day, USA....................Th
3....................St Blaise [§ *sore throats*] · Val Doonican [♭1927]....................F
4..................Sri Lanka [♭1948] · Norman Wisdom [♭1915] ....Sa
5............................St Agatha [§ *protection against fire*]............................Su
6.........................New Zealand – Waitangi Day [ℵ].........................M
7................................Charles Dickens [♭1812]................................Tu
8 ....Mary, Queen of Scots [†1587 *beheaded*] · James Dean [♭1931] ....W
9..........Carmen Miranda [♭1909] · Gordon Strachan [♭1957] ....Th
10 ....Queen Victoria & Prince Albert [⚭1840].....................F
11.................Scottish salmon fishing season opens [❤].................Sa
12..........Charles Darwin [♭1809] · Abraham Lincoln [♭1809] ....Su
13....................◑ · Catherine Howard [†1542 *beheaded*].....................M
14...........St Valentine [§ *lovers*] · Arizona [♭1912] · Oregon [♭1859] ....Tu
15.........................Sir Ernest Shackleton [♭1874].........................W
16.............................John McEnroe [♭1959].............................Th
17..............Molière (Jean-Baptiste Poquelin) [†1673]..............F
18 ....Nepal [ℵ] · Gambia [♭1965] · John Travolta [♭1954]..............Sa
19............................Prince Andrew [♭1960] [£]............................Su
20 ....USA – President's Day [ℵ] · Sidney Poitier [♭1927].............M
21..............Robert Mugabe [♭1924] · Malcolm X [†1965 *assassinated*].............Tu
22.............Feast of Chair of St Peter [®] · Bruce Forsyth [♭1928] ....W
23....................Brunei [ℵ] · Samuel Pepys [♭1633]....................Th
24.................Estonia [♭1918] · Alain Prost [♭1955] ....F
25.................Kuwait [ℵ] · Sir Christopher Wren [†1723] ....Sa
26...................Victor Hugo [♭1802] · Levi Strauss [♭1829]...................Su
27...............................Paddy Ashdown [♭1941]...............................M
28 ....Shrove Tuesday [®] · Hind stalking season closes [❤] ....Tu

French Rev. calendar ..... *Ventôse* (wind)	Dutch month . *Sprokelmaand* (vegetation)
Angelic governor .... *Barchiel*	Saxon month........... *Solmonath* (Sun)
Epicurean calendar .... *Harrengsauridor*	Talismanic stone................... *Ruby*

❦ Much mythology and folklore considers February to have the bitterest weather: *February is seldom warm.* ❦ *February, if ye be fair, The sheep will mend, and nothing mair; February, if ye be foul, The sheep will die in every pool.* ❦ *As the day lenghtens, the cold strengthens.* ❦ That said, a foul February is often said to presage a fine year: *All the moneths in the year curse a fair Februeer.* ❦ The word February derives from *februa* – which means cleansing or purification, and reflects the rituals undertaken before Spring. ❦ Having only 28 days in non-leap years [see p.342], February was known in Welsh as '*y mis bach*' – the little month. ❦ February is traditionally personified in pictures either by an old man warming himself by the fireside, or as 'a sturdy maiden, with a tinge of the red hard winter apple on her hardy cheek'. ❦

———————— MARCH ————————

Pisces [♓]   *Birthstone* · BLOODSTONE   *Aries* [♈]
(Feb 20–Mar 20)   *Flower* · JONQUIL   (Mar 21–Apr 20)

1 .... Ash Wednesday [®] · St David [§ *Wales*] .... W
2 .... St Chad [§ *medicinal springs*] · Mikhail Gorbachev [ʙ 1931] .... Th
3 .... Morocco [ɴ] · Florida [ʙ 1845] .... F
4 .... St Casimir [§ *Poland & Lithuania*] · Antonio Vivaldi [ʙ 1678] .... Sa
5 .... Joseph Stalin [†1953] .... Su
6 .... Ghana [ʙ 1957] · Michelangelo [ʙ 1475] .... M
7 .... Sir Ranulph Fiennes [ʙ 1944] · Stanley Kubrick [†1999] .... Tu
8 .... St John of God [§ *booksellers*] .... W
9 .... St Dominic Savio [§ *wrongly accused*] · Napoleon & Josephine [⚭1796] ...... Th
10 .... Prince Edward [ʙ 1964] [£] .... F
11 .... Rupert Murdoch [ʙ 1931] · Sir Alexander Fleming [†1955] .... Sa
12 .... Liza Minelli [ʙ 1946] .... Su
13 .... Tsar Alexander II [†1881 *assassinated*] .... M
14 .... ◑ · Penumbral lunar eclipse [◯] · Albert Einstein [ʙ 1879] .... Tu
15 .... Hungary [ɴ] · Julius Caesar [†44BC *assassinated*] .... W
16 .... *first day of Bacchanalia in Ancient Rome* .... Th
17 .... St Patrick's Day [§ *Ireland*] · World Maritime Day [ɴ] .... F
18 .... Ivan the Terrible [†1584] · Neville Chamberlain [ʙ 1869] .... Sa
19 .... St Joseph [§ *fathers & carpenters*] · Bruce Willis [ʙ 1959] .... Su
20 .... Tunisia [ʙ 1956] · Sir Isaac Newton [†1727] .... M
21 ..... International Day for the Elimination of Racial Discrimination [ɴ] ..... Tu
22 .... Marcel Marceau [ʙ 1923] · William Shatner [ʙ 1931] .... W
23 .... World Metereological Day [ɴ] · Pakistan [ɴ] .... Th
24 .... Queen Elizabeth I [†1603] .... F
25 .... Annunciation Day [®] · Greece [ʙ 1821] .... Sa
26 .... Bangladesh [ʙ1971] · Noël Coward [†1973] .... Su
27 .... Quentin Tarantino [ʙ 1963] .... M
28 .... Virginia Woolf [†1941 *suicide*] · Neil Kinnock [ʙ 1942] .... Tu
29 .... Total solar eclipse [◯] · Robert Falcon Scott [†1912] .... W
30 .... Queen Mother [†2002] .... Th
31 .... Charlotte Brontë [†1855] · Jesse Owens [†1980] .... F

French Rev. Cal. .... *Germinal* (budding) | Dutch month .... *Lentmaand* (spring)
Angelic governor .... *Machidiel* | Saxon month .... *Hrèth-monath* (rough)
Epicurean calendar .... *Oeufalacoquidor* | Talismanic stone .... *Topaz*

❦ The first month of the Roman year, March is named for Mars, the god of war but also an agricultural deity. ❦ The unpredictability of March weather leads to some confusion (*March has many weathers*), though it is generally agreed that March *comes in like a lion, and goes out like a lamb*. Yet, because March is often too wet for crops to flourish, many considered *a bushel of Marche dust* [a dry March] *is worth a ransom of gold*. ❦ March hares are 'mad' with nothing more than lust, since it is their mating season. ❦ The *Mars* bar is named after its creator Frank Mars. ❦

---APRIL---

Aries [♈]	*Birthstone* · DIAMOND	*Taurus* [♉]
(Mar 21–Apr 20)	*Flower* · SWEET PEA	(Apr 21–May 21)

1 ....April Fool's Day [except in Scotland] · Roe buck season opens [☙] ....Sa
2.............St Urban of Langres [§ *vine dressers*] · Alec Guinness [♭1914]...........Su
3 ....Marlon Brando [♭1924] · Graham Greene [†1991]...............M
4...............Senegal [♭1960] · Martin Luther King [†1968 *assassinated*]............Tu
5.............................St Vincent Ferrer [§ *builders*] ....W
6 ....Harry Houdini [♭1874] · Paul Daniels [♭1938].................Th
7 ....World Health Day [♮] · Jackie Chan [♭1954] ....F
8.........Japan – flower festival [♮] · Cuckoos start to appear ....Sa
9.............Palm Sunday [®] · Isambard Kingdom Brunel [♭1806]...........Su
10.............................Omar Sharif [♭1932].............................M
11 ....Harry Secombe [†2001] ....Tu
12 ....Bobby Moore [♭1941] · Franklin D. Roosevelt [†1945]...........W
13 ....◑ · Chad [♮] · Samuel Beckett [♭1906] · Gary Kasparov [♭1963]......Th
14 ....Good Friday [♮✱] [®] · Abraham Lincoln [†1865 *assassinated*] ....F
15.................Jeffrey Archer [♭1940] · Tommy Cooper [†1984].................Sa
16 ....Easter Sunday [®] · St Drogo [§ *shepherds*].....................Su
17 ....Easter Monday [♮✱] [®] · Syria [♭1946]...............M
18 ....Zimbabwe [♭1980] · Albert Einstein [†1955] ....Tu
19 ....Prince Rainier III of Monaco & Grace Kelly [⚭1956].............W
20...................Adolf Hitler [♭1889] · Leslie Phillips [♭1924]...................Th
21 ....Queen Elizabeth [♭1926][£] · Lyrids [.☄] ....F
22............Vladimir Ilyich Lenin [♭1870] · Jack Nicholson [♭1937] ....Sa
23 ....St George [§ *England*] · World Book & Copyright Day [♮]..........Su
24 ....Daniel Defoe [†1731] · Clement Freud [♭1924] ....M
25....................Australia & New Zealand – Anzac Day ....Tu
26.......................Tanzania [♮] · Sid James [†1976] ....W
27...............South Africa [♮] · Sierra Leone [♭1961]...................Th
28...............Arbor Day, USA · Benito Mussolini [†1945 *executed*] ....F
29 ....Japan [♮] · Saddam Hussein [♭1937].....................Sa
30...............Netherlands [♮] · Stag stalking season closes [☙] ....Su

French Rev. Calendar .. *Floréal* (blossom)	Dutch month......... *Grasmaand* (grass)
Angelic governor...............*Asmodel*	Saxon month........... *Easter-monath*
Epicurean calendar ....*Petitpoisidor*	Talismanic stone................ *Garnet*

❦ April, T.S. Eliot's 'cruellest month', heralds the start of Spring and is associated with new growth and sudden bursts of rain. ❦ Its etymology might derive from the Latin *aperire* ('to open') – although in Old English it was known simply as the *Eastre-monath*. ❦ *April with his hack and his bill, Plants a flower on every hill.* ❦ The custom of performing pranks and hoaxes on April Fool's Day (or *poisson d'avril* as it is known in France) is long established, although its origins are much disputed. ❦ According to weather folklore, *If it thunders on All Fools' day, it brings good crops of corn and hay.* Usually, cuckoos will first appear in *The Times* around 8 April. ❦

——————————— MAY ———————————

Taurus [♉]   *Birthstone* · EMERALD   *Gemini* [♊]
(Apr 21–May 21)   *Flower* · LILY OF THE VALLEY   (May 22–Jun 22)

1 ....May Day · Ayrton Senna [†1994].........................M
2.............................Leonardo da Vinci [†1519].............................Tu
3...........World Press Freedom Day [℟] · Henry Cooper [♭1934]...........W
4.............St Florian [§ *against fire & water*] · Audrey Hepburn [♭1929]............Th
5....................Japan – Children's Day · Eta Aquarids [•]....................F
6................Sigmund Freud [♭1856] · Marlene Dietrich [†1992]................Sa
7 ....Robert Browning [♭1812] · Pyotr Tchaikovsky [♭1840].............Su
8.....................VE Day · Czech Republic [℟].........................M
9.....................Glenda Jackson [♭1936].........................Tu
10.........................Fred Astaire [♭1899].........................W
11................Jeremy Paxman [♭1950] · Minnesota [♭1858]................Th
12...............Florence Nightingale [♭1820] · St Pancras [§]...............F
13.........◑ · Daphne du Maurier [♭1907] · Stevie Wonder [♭1950]..........Sa
14.................Mother's Day, USA · Paraguay [℟].................Su
15.................International Day of Families [℟].........................M
16 ....Louis XVI & Marie Antoinette [⚭1770] ....Tu
17 ....World Telecommunication Day [℟] · Norway [℟] ....W
18 ....Pope John Paul II [♭1920] ....Th
19 ....Anne Boleyn [†1536 *executed*] · Robert Kilroy-Silk [♭1942].............F
20................Cameroon [℟] · Christopher Columbus [†1506] ....Sa
21................St Eugene de Mazenod [§ *dysfunctional families*]...................Su
22 ....International Day for Biological Diversity [℟] · Yemen [℟]..........M
23 ....Joan Collins [♭1933] ....Tu
24........Queen Victoria [♭1819] · Bob Dylan [♭1941] ....W
25.................Argentina [♭1810] · Jordan [♭1946] ....Th
26.................Samuel Pepys [†1703] · John Wayne [♭1907]...................F
27 ....Cilla Black [♭1943] · Paul Gascoigne [♭1967].................Sa
28....................Azerbaijan [℟] · Eric Morecambe [†1984]...................Su
29.....................USA – Memorial Day [℟].........................M
30 ......Joan of Arc [†1431 *executed*] · Henry VIII & Jane Seymour [⚭1536] ......Tu
31 ....The Visitation of the Blessed Virgin Mary [®]................W

French Rev. Cal. ...... *Prairial* (meadow)	Dutch month....... *Blowmaand* (flower)
Angelic governor ....*Ambriel*	Saxon month ...... *Trimilchi* [see below]
Epicurean calendar............*Aspergial*	Talismanic stone ....*Emerald*

❦ Named after *Maia*, the goddess of growth, May is considered a joyous month, as Milton wrote: 'Hail bounteous May that dost inspire Mirth and youth, and warm desire.' ❦ However, May has long been thought a bad month in which to marry: *who weds in May throws it all away.* ❦ Anglo-Saxons called May *thrimilce*, since in May cows could be milked three times a day. ❦ May was thought a time of danger for the sick; so to have *climbed May hill* was to have survived the month. ❦ Kittens born in May were thought weak, and were often drowned. ❦

--- JUNE ---

Gemini [Ⅱ]	**Birthstone** · PEARL	**Cancer** [♋]
(May 22–Jun 22)	**Flower** · ROSE	(Jun 23–Jul 23)

1 .... Samoa [♭1962] · Marilyn Monroe [♭1926] .... Th
2 .... Coronation of Elizabeth II [1953] [£] · Italy [♭] .... F
3 .... Duke of Windsor & Wallis Simpson [⚲1937] .... Sa
4 .... Tonga [♭1970] .... Su
5 .... World Environment Day [♮] · Denmark [♭] .... M
6 .... Sweden [♭] · Björn Borg [♭1956] .... Tu
7 .... Robert the Bruce [†1329] · Tom Jones [♭1940] .... W
8 .... The Prophet Muhammad [†632] .... Th
9 .... Emperor Nero [†AD68 *suicide*] · Charles Dickens [†1870] .... F
10 .... HRH Prince Philip [♭1921] [£] .... Sa
11 .... ☽ · Henry VIII & Catherine of Aragon [⚲1509] .... Su
12 .... Phillipines [♭1898] · George Bush (Snr) [♭1924] .... M
13 .... Alexander the Great [†323BC] · William Butler Yeats [♭1865] .... Tu
14 .... Flag Day, USA · Che Guevara [♭1928] .... W
15 .... St Vitus [§*epileptics*] · Arkansas [♭1836] .... Th
16 .... Freshwater fishing season opens [☙] · Bloom's Day (Ulysses) .... F
17 .... Iceland [♭1944] · Ken Livingstone [♭1945] .... Sa
18 .... Delia Smith [♭1941] · Sir Paul McCartney [♭1942] .... Su
19 .... J.M. Barrie [†1937] .... M
20 .... World Refugee Day [♮] · Errol Flynn [♭1909] .... Tu
21 .... Prince William [♭1982] .... W
22 .... St Thomas More [§*lawyers*] · Esther Rantzen [♭1940] .... Th
23 .... Midsummer's Eve · Luxembourg [♭] .... F
24 .... Midsummer's Day .... Sa
25 .... Croatia [♭] · Mozambique [♭1975] .... Su
26 .... United Nations Charter Day [♮] .... M
27 .... Djibouti [♭1977] · Helen Keller [♭1880] .... Tu
28 ...... Henry VIII [♭1491] · Archduke Franz Ferdinand [†1914 *assassinated*] ...... W
29 .... St Peter [§*keeper of the keys of heaven*] · Jayne Mansfield [†1967] .... Th
30 .... Mike Tyson [♭1966] .... F

French Rev. Cal. .... *Messidor* (harvest)	Dutch month ... *Zomermaand* (Summer)
Angelic governor. .... *Muriel*	Saxon month. .... *Sere-monath* (dry)
Epicurean calendar .... *Concombrial*	Talismanic stone .... *Sapphire*

❧ June is probably derived from *iuvenis* ('young'), but it is also linked to the goddess *Juno*, who personifies young women. In Scots Gaelic the month is known as *Ian t-Òg-mbìos*, the 'young month'; and in Welsh as *Mehefin*, the 'middle'. ❧ According to weather lore, *Calm weather in June, Sets corn in tune*. ❧ To 'june' a herd of animals is to drive them in a brisk or lively manner. ❧ Wilfred Gowers-Round asserts that 'June is the reality of the Poetic's claims for May'. ❧ In parts of South Africa the verb 'to june-july' is slang for shaking or shivering with fear – because these months, while summer in the north, are midwinter in the south. ❧

———————————— JULY ————————————

🦀 *Cancer* [♋]	*Birthstone* · RUBY	*Leo* [♌] 🦁
(Jun 23–Jul 23)	*Flower* · LARKSPUR	(Jul 24–Aug 23)

1 ....Canada – Canada Day [ɴ] · Princess Diana [β 1961] ....Sa
2 ....Ernest Hemingway [†1961 *suicide*] ....Su
3 ....St Thomas [§ *architects*] · Belarus [ɴ]........................M
4 ....USA – Independence Day [ɴ] ....Tu
5 ....Venezuela [β 1811] · P.T. Barnum [β 1810] ....W
6 ....Dalai Lama [β 1935] · George W. Bush [β 1946]..............Th
7 ....Solomon Islands [β 1978] · Sir Arthur Conan Doyle [† 1930]...........F
8 ....Percy Bysshe Shelley [†1822 *drowned*]........................Sa
9 ....Dame Barbara Cartland [β 1901] · Barbara Woodhouse [†1988] ....Su
10 ....The Bahamas [β 1973] · Wyoming [β 1890] ....M
11 .... ☽ · World Population Day [ɴ] · Mongolia [ɴ] ....Tu
12 ....Henry VIII & Catherine Parr [⚭ 1543] ....W
13 ....St Henry [§ *the childless*] · Harrison Ford [β 1942] ....Th
14 ....St Swithin's Day · Billy the Kid [†1881].................F
15 ....St Swithin's Day · Rembrandt [β 1606] ....Sa
16 ....Ginger Rogers [β 1911] · Tsar Nicholas & family [†1918 *executed*] ....Su
17 ....Donald Sutherland [β 1934] · Tim Brooke-Taylor [β 1940] ....M
18 ....Nelson Mandela [β 1918] ....Tu
19 ....Thomas Cook [†1892] · Ile Nastase [β 1946] ....W
20 ....Columbia [β 1819] ....Th
21 ....Belgium [ɴ] · Robert Burns [†1796] ....F
22 ....Jimmy Hill [β 1928] · Bonnie Langford [β 1964].................Sa
23 ....Egypt [ɴ] · St Bridget of Sweden [§ *Sweden*] ....Su
24 ....Captain Matthew Webb [†1883 *drowned*] · Peter Sellers [†1980].........M
25 ....St James [§ *labourers*] · Samuel Taylor Coleridge [†1834] ....Tu
26 ....Liberia [ɴ] · Sir Mick Jagger [β 1943] · New York [β 1788] ....W
27 ....Alexandre Dumas fils [β 1824]........................Th
28 ....Henry VIII & Catherine Howard [⚭ 1540] ....F
29 ....Prince Charles & Lady Diana [⚭ 1981] ....Sa
30 ....Arnold Schwarzenegger [β 1947] ....Su
31 ...........................J.K. Rowling [β 1965] ....M

French Rev. Cal........ *Thermidor* (heat)	Dutch month .... *Hooymaand* (hay)
Angelic governor............... *Verchiel*	Saxon month... *Mæd-monath* (meadow)
Epicurean calendar ....*Melonial*	Talismanic stone.............. *Diamond*

❦ July was originally called *Quintilis* (from *Quintus* – meaning fifth), but it was renamed by Mark Anthony to honour the murdered Julius Caesar, who was born on 12 July. ❦ *A swarm of bees in May is worth a load of Hay; A swarm of bees in June is worth a silver spoon; But a swarm of bees in July is not worth a fly.* ❦ *If the first of July be rainy weather, 'Twill rain mair or less for forty days together.* ❦ *Bow-wow, dandy fly – Brew no beer in July.* ❦ July used to be known as the thunder month, and some churches rang their bells in the hope of driving away thunder and lightning. ❦

———————————— AUGUST ————————————

Leo [♌]
(Jul 24–Aug 23)

Birthstone · AGATE
Flower · GLADIOLUS

Virgo [♍]
(Aug 24–Sep 23)

1	Stag and buck stalking season begins [♥]	Tu
2	Alan Whicker [♭1925] · Alexander Graham Bell [†1922]	W
3	Terry Wogan [♭1938] · Jack Straw [♭1946]	Th
4	Queen Mother [♭1900] · St Sithney [§ *mad dogs*]	F
5	Neil Armstrong [♭1930] · Marilyn Monroe [†1962 *suicide*]	Sa
6	Delta Aquarids (North) [☁] · Bolivia [♭1825]	Su
7	Mata Hari [♭1876] · Oliver Hardy [†1957]	M
8	St Dominic [§ *astronomers*] · Princess Beatrice [♭1988]	Tu
9	☽ · International Day of the World's Indigenous People [◈]	W
10	Ecuador [♭1822] · Missouri [♭1821]	Th
11	St Clare [§ *sore eyes*] · Enid Blyton [♭1897]	F
12	Glorious Twelfth– grouse season begins [♥] · Perseids [☁]	Sa
13	Alfred Hitchcock [♭1899] · Florence Nightingale [†1910]	Su
14	Steve Martin [♭1945] · Bertolt Brecht [†1956]	M
15	VJ Day · Assumption Day [◉] · Princess Anne [♭1950] [£]	Tu
16	Madonna [♭1958] · Elvis Presley [†1977]	W
17	Indonesia [♭1945] · Gabon [◈]	Th
18	Genghis Khan [†1227]	F
19	St Sebald [§ *Nuremburg*] · Julius 'Groucho' Marx [†1977]	Sa
20	Leon Trotsky [†1940 *murdered*]	Su
21	Princess Margaret [♭1930] · Hawaii [♭1959]	M
22	Richard III [†1485] · Dorothy Parker [♭1893]	Tu
23	William Wallace [†1305 *executed*] · Gene Kelly [♭1912]	W
24	St Bartholomew [§ *tanners*] · Ukraine [♭1991]	Th
25	Uruguay [◈] · Sean Connery [♭1930]	F
26	Prince Albert [♭1819]	Sa
27	Confucius [♭551BC] · Mother Teresa [♭1910]	Su
28	St Augustine of Hippo [§ *brewers*]	M
29	Ingrid Bergman [♭1915] · Ingrid Bergman [†1982]	Tu
30	Cleopatra [†30BC *suicide*]	W
31	Kyrgyzstan [◈] · Princess Diana [†1997]	Th

French Rev. Cal......... *Fructidor* (fruits)	Dutch month....... *Oostmaand* (harvest)
Angelic governor.............. Hamaliel	Saxon month ...... *Weod-monath* (weed)
Epicurean calendar .... *Raisinose*	Talismanic stone .... *Zircon*

❦ Previously called *Sextilis* (as the sixth month of the old calendar), August was renamed in 8BC, in honour of the first Roman Emperor, Augustus, who claimed this month to be lucky as it was the month in which he began his consulship, conquered Egypt, and had many triumphs. ❦ *Greengrocers rise at dawn of sun, August the fifth – come haste away, To Billingsgate the thousands run, Tis Oyster Day! Tis Oyster Day!* ❦ *Dry August and warme, Dothe harvest no harme.* ❦ *Take heed of sudden cold after heat.* ❦ *Gather not garden seeds near the full moon.* ❦ *Sow herbs.* ❦

——————— SEPTEMBER ———————

Virgo [♍]   *Birthstone* · SAPPHIRE   *Libra* [♎]
(Aug 24–Sep 23)   *Flower* · ASTER   (Sep 24–Oct 23)

1 ...... Partridge shooting season opens [♥] · St Giles [§ *cripples & blacksmiths*] ...... F
2 .... Vietnam [ℕ] · J.R.R. Tolkien [†1973] .... Sa
3 .... Oliver Cromwell [†1658] .... Su
4 .... USA Labor Day [ℕ] · Vicomte de Chateaubriand [β1768] .... M
5 .... Jesse James [β1847] .... Tu
6 .... Swaziland [ℕ] · Hendrik Verwoerd [†1966 *assassinated*] .... W
7 .... ◑ · Partial Lunar Eclipse [◯] · Brazil [♭1822] .... Th
8 ...... International Literacy Day [ℕ] · Nativity of Blessed Virgin Mary [®] ...... F
9 .... Japan – Chrysanthemum Day · Tajikistan [ℕ] .... Sa
10 .... Mungo Park [β1771] · Charles Cruft [†1938] .... Su
11 .... D.H. Lawrence [β1885] · Georgi Markov [†1978 *assassinated*] .... M
12 .... John F. Kennedy & Jacqueline Bouvier [♔1953] .... Tu
13 .... Roald Dahl [β1916] .... W
14 .... Exaltation of the Holy Cross [®] · Grace Kelly [†1982] .... Th
15 .... Battle of Britain Day · Costa Rica [ℕ] .... F
16 .... International Day for the Preservation of the Ozone Layer [ℕ] .... Sa
17 .... Stirling Moss [β1929] · Des Lynam [β1942] .... Su
18 .... St Joseph of Cupertino [§ *astronauts*] .... M
19 .... George Cadbury [β1839] · Jeremy Irons [β1948] .... Tu
20 .... Alexander the Great [β356BC] .... W
21 .... International Day of Peace [ℕ] · St Matthew [§ *accountants*] .... Th
22 .... Mali [ℕ] · Michael Faraday [β1791] .... F
23 .... Saudi Arabia [ℕ] · Julio Iglesias [β1943] .... Sa
24 .... F. Scott Fitzgerald [β1896] .... Su
25 .... St Mewrog [§ *cats*] · Ronnie Barker [β1929] .... M
26 .... T.S. Eliot [β1888] · George Gershwin [β1898] .... Tu
27 .... St Vincent de Paul [§ *charitable societies*] .... W
28 .... Brigitte Bardot [β1934] · Arthur 'Harpo' Marx [†1964] .... Th
29 .... Michaelmas Day [®] · Lord Sebastian Coe [β1956] .... F
30 .... Trout fishing season ends [♥] · Botswana [ℕ] .... Sa

French Rev. Cal.... *Vendémiaire* (vintage)	Dutch month..... *Herstmaand* (Autumn)
Angelic governor .... *Uriel*	Saxon month...... *Gerst-monath* (barley)
Epicurean calendar............ *Huîtrose*	Talismanic stone .... *Agate*

❦ September is so named as it was the seventh month in the Roman calendar. ❦ *September blows soft, Till the fruit's in the loft. Forgotten, month past, Doe now at the last.* ❦ *Eat and drink less, And buy a knife at Michaelmas.* ❦ To be 'Septembered' is to be multihued in autumnal colours, as Blackmore wrote: 'His honest face was Septembered with many a vintage.' ❦ Poor Robin's Almanac (1666) states 'now *Libra* weighs the days and night in an equal balance, so that there is not an hairs breadth difference betwixt them in length; this moneth having an R in it, Oysters come again in season.' ❦ The Irish name *Meán Fómhair* means 'mid-Autumn'. ❦

─OCTOBER─

♎ *Libra* [♎]	*Birthstone* · OPAL	*Scorpio* [♏]
(Sep 24–Oct 23)	*Flower* · CALENDULA	(Oct 24–Nov 22)

1 ...... Int. Day of Older Persons [♫] · Pheasant shooting season opens [❤] ..... Su
2 .... Mahatma Gandhi [♭1869] .... M
3 .... Germany [♫] · William Morris [†1896] .... Tu
4 .... St Francis of Assisi [§ *animals*] · Ann Widdecombe [♭1947] .... W
5 .... International Teacher's Day [♫] · Sir Bob Geldof [♭1954] .... Th
6 .... Children's Day [♫] .... F
7 .... ◑ · Edgar Allan Poe [†1849] · Desmond Tutu [♭1931] ..... Sa
8 .... Chevy Chase [♭1943] .... Su
9 .... USA – Columbus Day [♫] · Che Guevara [†1967] .... M
10 .... Fiji Day [♫] · Orson Welles [†1985] .... Tu
11 .... Ulrich Zwingli [†1531] · Bobby Charlton [♭1937] .... W
12 .... Spain [♫] · Magnus Magnusson [♭1929] .... Th
13 .... Margaret Thatcher [♭1925] · Edwina Currie [♭1946] .... F
14 .... Cliff Richard [♭1940] · Bing Crosby [†1977] .... Sa
15 .... St Teresa of Avila [§ *headache sufferers*] .... Su
16 .... World Food day [♫] · Marie Antoinette [†1793 *executed*] .... M
17 .... International Day for the Eradication of Poverty [♫] .... Tu
18 .... St Luke [§ *doctors*] · Elizabeth Arden [†1966] .... W
19 .... Jonathan Swift [†1745] .... Th
20 .... Jackie Kennedy & Aristotle Onassis [♏1968] .... F
21 .... Orionids [●] · Horatio Nelson [†1805 *in battle*] .... Sa
22 .... The Vatican [♫] · Paul Cézanne [†1906] .... Su
23 .... Brutus [† 42BC *suicide*] · Pelé [♭1940] .... M
24 .... United Nations Day [♫] · Zambia [♫] .... Tu
25 .... Geoffrey Chaucer [†1400] · Pablo Picasso [♭1881] .... W
26 .... Austria [♫] · François Mitterand [♭1916] .... Th
27 .... Captain James Cook [♭1728] · Simon le Bon [♭1958] .... F
28 .... St Jude of Thaddaeus [§ *desperate cases*] · Alfred the Great [†901] .... Sa
29 .... Sir Walter Raleigh [†1618 *executed*] .... Su
30 .... Michael Winner [♭1935] · Henry Winkler [♭1945] .... M
31 .... Halloween · Sir Jimmy Savile [♭1926] .... Tu

French Rev. Cal..... *Brumaire* (fog; mist)	Dutch month......... *Wynmaand* (wine)
Angelic governor .... *Barbiel*	Saxon month .... *Win-monath* (wine)
Epicurean calendar .... *Bécassinose*	Talismanic stone............... *Amethyst*

❦ October was originally the eighth month of the calendar. ❦ *Dry your barley land in October, Or you'll always be sober.* ❦ October was a time for brewing, and the month gave its name to a 'heady and ripe' ale: 'five Quarters of Malt to three Hogsheads, and twenty-four Pounds of Hops'. Consequently, *often drunk and seldom sober falls like the leaves in October.* ❦ In American politics, an *October surprise* is an event thought to have been engineered to garner political support just before an election (like the release of US hostages in Tehran in October 1980). ❦

─────────── NOVEMBER ───────────

Scorpio [♏]   *Birthstone* · TOPAZ   *Sagittarius* [♐]
(Oct 24-Nov 22)   *Flower* · CHRYSANTHEMUM   (Nov 23-Dec 21)

1.........All Saints' Day [®] · Hind and doe stalking season opens [❦] ....W
2..............All Souls' Day [®] · George Bernard Shaw [†1950].............Th
3...............Panama [℟] · St Martin de Porres [§ *barbers*]...................F
4............Wilfred Owen [†1918] · St Charles [§ *learning & the arts*].............Sa
5............ ◗ · Guy Fawkes Night · Taurids [☄] ....Su
6.......................Pytor Tchaikovsky [†1893 *suicide*]...................M
7..................Albert Camus [฿1913] · John Barnes [฿1963] ....Tu
8......................Ken Dodd [฿1931] · Montana [฿1889] ....W
9................Cambodia [฿1953] · Charles de Gaulle [†1970]............Th
10 ....Martin Luther [฿1483] · Richard Burton [฿1925] ....F
11 ....Remembrance Day · USA – Veterans' Day.............Sa
12 ....Grace Kelly [฿1929] ....Su
13 ....St Frances Xavier Cabrini [§ *immigrants*].................M
14 ....Prince Charles [฿1948] [£] · Claude Monet [฿1840].............Tu
15 ....Brazil – Republic Day · William Pitt the Elder [฿1708]...........W
16 ....International Day for Tolerance [℟] · Frank Bruno [฿1961] ....Th
17 ....Leonids [☄] · Jonathan Ross [฿1960] ....F
18 .... Latvia [฿1918] · Oman [℟] ....Sa
19 ....Calvin Klein [฿1942] · Jodie Foster [฿1962] ....Su
20 ....Queen Elizabeth II & Prince Philip [⚭1947] [£] ....M
21 ....World Television Day [℟] · North Carolina [฿1789]............Tu
22 ....John F. Kennedy [†1963 *assassinated*]..................W
23 ....USA – Thanksgiving [℟] · Boris Karloff [฿1887] ....Th
24 ....Ian Botham [฿1955] · Freddie Mercury [†1991] ....F
25 ....Suriname [฿1975] · St Catherine [§ *philosophers*].................Sa
26 ....Tina Turner [฿1938]....................Su
27 ....Ernie Wise [฿1925] · Jimi Hendrix [฿1942]...................M
28 ....Albania [℟] · Enid Blyton [†1968] ....Tu
29 .............C.S. Lewis [฿1898] · George Harrison [†2001] ....W
30 ....St Andrew [§ *Scotland & Russia*] · Oscar Wilde [†1900]............Th

French Rev. Calendar ... *Frimaire* (frost)	Dutch month .... *Slagtmaand* [see below]
Angelic governor.............*Advachiel*	Saxon month...... *Wind-monath* (wind)
Epicurean calendar.......*Pommedetaire*	Talismanic stone.................*Beryl*

❧ Originally, the ninth (*novem*) month, November has long been associated with slaughter, hence the Dutch *Slaghtmaand* ('slaughter month'). The Anglo Saxon was *Blotmonath* ('blood' or 'sacrifice month'). ❧ A dismal month, November has been the subject of many writers' ire, as J.B. Burges wrote: 'November leads her wintry train, And stretches o'er the firmament her veil Charg'd with foul vapours, fogs and drizzly rain.' ❧ Famously, Thomas Hood's poem *No!* contains the lines 'No warmth, no cheerfulness, no healthful ease ... No shade, no shine, no butterflies, no bees, No fruits, no flowers, no leaves, no birds, —— November!' ❧

—— DECEMBER ——

Sagittarius [♐]   *Birthstone* · TURQUOISE   *Capricorn* [♑]
(Nov 23-Dec 21)   *Flower* · NARCISSUS   (Dec 22–Jan 20)

1 .... World AIDS Day [ℵ] · Romania [ℵ] .... F
2 .... Laos [ℵ] · Philip Larkin [†1985] .... Sa
3 ...... International Day of Disabled Persons [ℵ] · Ozzy Osbourne [ℬ1948] ..... Su
4 .... Ronnie Corbett [ℬ1930] .... M
5 .... ☽ · Thailand [ℵ] · Wolfgang Amadeus Mozart [†1791] .... Tu
6 .... St Nicholas [§ *bakers & pawnbrokers*] · Finland [ℵ] .... W
7 .... Pearl Harbor Day, USA · Delaware [ℬ1787] .... Th
8 .... John Lennon [†1980 *murdered*] · The Immaculate Conception [®] .... F
9 .... Dame Judi Dench [ℬ1934] .... Sa
10 .... Nobel Prizes awarded · Human Rights Day [ℵ] .... Su
11 .... Indiana [ℬ1816] · Willie Rushton [†1996] .... M
12 .... Kenya [ℵ] · Princess Anne & Timothy Laurence [⚭1992] .... Tu
13 .... Japan – Soot Sweeping Day · Dick Van Dyke [ℬ1925] .... W
14 .... Geminids [☄] · Nostradamus [ℬ1503] .... Th
15 .... Walt Disney [†1966] .... F
16 .... Jane Austen [ℬ1775] · Noël Coward [ℬ1889] .... Sa
17 .... Orkney – Sow Day · USA – Wright Brothers Day .... Su
18 .... International Migrants Day [ℵ] · Betty Grable [ℬ1916] .... M
19 .... Emily Brontë [†1848] · Edith Piaf [ℬ1915] .... Tu
20 .... Bo Diddley [ℬ1928] · Uri Geller [ℬ1946] .... W
21 .... Benjamin Disraeli [ℬ1804] .... Th
22 .... First Day of Winter · Maurice & Robin Gibb [ℬ1949] .... F
23 .... Ursids [☄] · Carol Smillie [ℬ1961] .... Sa
24 .... Christmas Eve · Vasco da Gama [†1524] .... Su
25 .... Christmas Day [ℵ] · Quentin Crisp [ℬ1908] .... M
26 .... Boxing Day [ℵ] · St Stephen [§ *stonemasons*] .... Tu
27 .... Louis Pasteur [ℬ1822] · Janet Street-Porter [ℬ1946] .... W
28 .... Childermass [®] · Iowa [ℬ1846] .... Th
29 .... Thomas à Becket [†1170 *assassinated*] .... F
30 .... Rudyard Kipling [ℬ1865] · Heidi Fleiss [ℬ1965] .... Sa
31 .... New Year's Eve · Scotland – Hogmanay .... Su

French Rev. Calendar ..... *Nivôse* (snow)	Dutch month .... *Wiutermaand* (Winter)
Angelic governor .... Hanael	Saxon month ...... *Mid-Winter-monath*
Epicurean calendar .... *Boudinaire*	Talismanic stone .... *Onyx*

❦ *If the ice will bear a goose before Christmas, it will not bear a duck afterwards.* ❦ Originally the tenth month, December now closes the year. ❦ *If Christmas Day be bright and clear there'll be two winters in the year.* ❦ The writer Saunders warned in 1679 'In December, Melancholy and Phlegm much increase, which are heavy, dull, and close, and therefore it behoves all that will consider their healths, to keep their heads and bodies very well from cold'. ❦ Robert Burns splendidly wrote in 1795 – 'As I am in a complete Decemberish humour, gloomy, sullen, stupid'. ❦

DESCRIPTION OF THE MONTHS

Snowy, Flowy, Blowy, Showery, Flowery, Bowery, Hoppy,
Croppy, Droppy, Breezy, Sneezy, Freezy — GEORGE ELLIS (1753–1815)

ANNIVERSARIES OF 2006

25th Anniversary (1981)
Prince Charles married Lady Diana
Spencer ❦ Arthur Scargill elected
President of the National Union of
Mineworkers

50th Anniversary (1956)
Great Britain ended the 74-year
occupation of the Suez Canal zone ❦
Third-class abolished on British Rail

75th Anniversary (1931)
The BBC began broadcasting
television ❦ *The New Statesman* first
published ❦ The Empire State
Building opened ❦ Al Capone
sentenced to 11 years in jail for tax
evasion ❦ The USA adopts *The Star
Spangled Banner* as its national
anthem

100th Anniversary (1906)
SOS adopted internationally as a
distress signal ❦ The Bakerloo Line
opened ❦ The London Ritz opened
its doors for the first time

150th Anniversary (1856)
Queen Victoria established the
Victoria Cross ❦ End of the Crimean
War ❦ National Portrait Gallery
established

200th Anniversary (1806)
Ralph Wedgewood patented the
invention of carbon paper ❦ The
foundation stone of Dartmoor Prison
laid ❦ Lord Horatio Nelson buried in
St Paul's Cathedral, London

250th Anniversary (1756)
The start of the Seven Years' War
❦ Accademia, the principal art
gallery in Venice, opened

500th Anniversary (1506)
Construction of Fulham Palace,
London, commenced ❦ Construction
of St Peter's Basilica, Rome,
commenced

600th Anniversary (1406)
Isle of Man under English control

A RIDDLE FOR THE YEAR

'There is a father with twice six sons; these sons have thirty daughters a
piece (give or take), party-coloured, having one cheek white and the other
black, who never see each other's face, nor live above twenty-four hours.'

BRITISH SUMMER TIME

BST starts and ends at 1am on these Sundays (*'spring forward – fall back'*):
2006.......... clocks forward 1 hour, 26 March · clocks back 1 hour, 29 October
2007.......... clocks forward 1 hour, 25 March · clocks back 1 hour, 28 October

FLORA'S CLOCK

Below is one of the fanciful, and essentially theoretical, floral clocks based on the hour certain plants open and close (bracketed names indicate an hour of closing):

SUPERSTITIONS OF THE YEAR

January .... *Of this first month the opening day, and 7th like a sword will slay*
February.... *The 3rd day bringeth down to death, the 4th will stop a strong man's breath*
March............. *The 1st the greedy glutton slays, the 4th cuts short the drunkard's days*
April .... *The 10th day and the 11th too, are ready Death's fell work to do*
May................. *The 3rd to slay poor men had power, the 7th destroyeth in an hour*
June .... *The 10th a pallid visage shows, no faith nor truth the 15th knows*
July.............................. *The 13th is a fatal day, the 10th alike will mortals slay*
August..................... *The first kills strong men at a blow, the 2nd lays a cohort low*
September.... *The 3rd day of the month September, and 10th bring evil to each member*
October............ *The 3rd and 10th will poisèd breath, to men are foes as foul as death*
November.... *The 5th bears scorpion stings of pain, the 3rd comes with distraction's train*
December............. *The 7th is bad for human life, the 10th with serpent's sting is rife*
The lucky have whole days in which to choose; the unlucky have but hours & these they lose.

— ASTRA CIELO, *Signs, Omens, and Superstitions,* 1919

CARDINAL DAYS & THE SEASONS

The adjective *cardinal* derives from the Latin for 'hinge', and tends to be employed for those concepts upon which other things depend. For example, the cardinal points of the compass (N, S, E, W); the cardinal humours of the body (blood, phlegm, yellow bile, and black bile); the cardinal virtues and sins [see p.287]; and so on. In astronomy, the Cardinal Days are the two solstices and the two equinoxes.

SOLSTICES occur when the Sun is at its furthest point from the equator. In the northern hemisphere the sun's northernmost position occurs at the Summer Solstice (*c.*21 June) – the 'longest day'; and its southernmost position occurs at the Winter Solstice (*c.*22 December) – the 'shortest day'. EQUINOXES occur when the Sun is directly overhead at the equator and the hours of daylight and darkness are of equal length at all latitudes. This occurs twice yearly: the Spring or Vernal equinox (*c.*21 March); and the Autumn Equinox (*c.*23 September).

QUARTER DAYS

Quarter Days are those days traditionally employed to divide the year for legal, financial, or contractual purposes such as tenancies, interests, rents, &c. They are:

QUARTER DAYS – *England & Wales*
25 March (Lady Day) · 24 June (Midsummer Day)
29 September (Michaelmas) · 25 December (Christmas Day)

QUARTER DAYS – *Scotland*
2 February (Candlemas Day) · 15 May (Whitsuntide)
1 August (Lammas) · 11 November (Martinmas)

FINDING TIME

The Chancellor of France, Henri François d'Aguesseau (1668–1751), realised that his wife always kept him waiting a quarter of an hour after the dinner-bell had rung, and resolved to devote this time to writing a book on jurisprudence. He completed this great task in a work of four quarto volumes.

When asked how he found the time to write books, Archbishop Michael Ramsey (1904–88) is said to have replied: 'Monday, a quarter of an hour; Tuesday, 10 minutes; Wednesday, rather better, half an hour; Thursday, not very good, but 10 minutes; Friday, a lull, an hour; Saturday, half an hour.'

——————— NOTABLE CHRISTIAN DATES 2006 ———————

Epiphany · *manifestation of the Christ to the Magi*..6 Jan
Presentation of Christ in the Temple ....2 Feb
Ash Wednesday · *1st day of Lent*..1 Mar
The Annunciation · *when Gabriel told Mary she would bear Christ* ....25 Mar
Good Friday · *Friday before Easter; commemorating the Crucifixion*...................14 Apr
Easter Day (Western churches) · *commemorating the Resurrection* ....16 Apr
Easter Day (Eastern Orthodox) · *commemorating the Resurrection*......................23Apr
Rogation Sunday · *the Sunday before Ascension Day* ....1 May
Ascension Day · *commemorating the ascent of Christ to heaven*......................25 May
Pentecost (Whit Sunday) · *commemorating the descent of the Holy Spirit*..............4 Jun
Trinity Sunday · *observed in honour of the Trinity* ....11 Jun
Corpus Christi · *commemorating the institution of the Holy Eucharist*..............15 Jun
All Saints' Day · *commemorating all the Church's saints collectively*......................1 Nov
Advent Sunday · *marking the start of Advent* ....3 Dec
Christmas Day · *celebrating the birth of Christ* ....25 Dec

A few other terms from the Christian Calendar:

Bible Sunday.................2nd in Advent	Passion Sunday ....5th in Lent
Black/Easter Monday.....the day after Easter	Plough Monday..............after Epiphany
Collop/Egg Monday.........first before Lent	Quadragesima............1st Sunday in Lent
Egg Saturday ....day prior to Quinquagesima	Quinquagesima..........Sunday before Lent
Fig/Yew Sunday ....Palm Sunday	Refreshment.............4th Sunday in Lent
Holy Saturday.................before Easter	Septuagesima ....3rd Sunday before Lent
Holy Week....................before Easter	Sexagesima..........2nd Sunday before Lent
Low Sunday ....Sunday after Easter	Shrove Tuesday ('pancake day') ...before Lent
Maundy Thursday ...day before Good Friday	Shrovetide ....period preceding Lent
Mothering Sunday ....4th in Lent	St Martin's Lent.....................Advent
Palm Sunday ....before Easter	Tenebrae...........last 3 days of Holy Week
	[See also Calendar Miscellany on pp.340–41]

——————— CHRISTIAN CALENDAR MOVEABLE FEASTS ———————

Year	Ash Wednesday	Easter Day	Ascension	Pentecost	Advent Sunday
2007	21 Feb	8 Apr	17 May	27 May	2 Dec
2008	6 Feb	23 Mar	1 May	11 May	30 Nov
2009	25 Feb	12 Apr	21 May	31 May	29 Nov
2010	17 Feb	4 Apr	13 May	23 May	28 Nov
2011	9 Mar	24 Apr	2 Jun	12 Jun	27 Nov
2012	22 Feb	8 Apr	17 May	27 May	2 Dec
2013	13 Feb	31 Mar	9 May	19 May	1 Dec
2014	5 Mar	20 Apr	29 May	8 Jun	30 Nov
2015	18 Feb	5 Apr	14 May	24 May	29 Nov
2016	10 Feb	27 Mar	5 May	15 May	27 Nov
2017	1 Mar	16 Apr	25 May	4 Jun	3 Dec
2018	14 Feb	1 Apr	10 May	20 May	2 Dec

NOTABLE RELIGIOUS DATES FOR 2006

HINDU

Makar Sankrant · *Winter festival*	14 Jan
Vasant Panchami · *dedicated to Saraswati and learning*	2 Feb
Maha Shivaratri · *dedicated to Shiva*	26 Feb
Holi · *spring festival of colours dedicated to Krishna*	14 Mar
Varsha Pratipada (Chaitra) · *Spring New Year*	3 Mar
Hindu New Year & Ramayana Week	30 Mar
Rama Navami · *birthday of Lord Rama*	6 Apr
Hanuman Jayanti · *birth of Hanuman, the Monkey God*	13 Apr
Raksha Bandhan · *festival of brotherhood and love*	4 Aug
Janmashtami · *birthday of Lord Rama*	16 Aug
Ganesh Chaturthi · *birthday of Lord Ganesh*	27 Aug
Navarati & Durga-puja · *celebrating triumph of good over evil*	starts 23 Sep
Saraswati-puja · *dedicated to Saraswati and learning*	starts 29 Sep
Dassera (Vijay Dashami) · *celebrating triumph of good over evil*	2 Oct
Diwali (Deepvali) · *New Year festival of lights*	21 Oct
New Year	22 Oct

JEWISH

Purim (Feast of Lots) · *commemorating defeat of Haman*	14 Mar
Pesach (Passover) · *commemorating exodus from Egypt*	13 Apr
Shavuot (Pentecost) · *commemorating relevation of the Torah*	2 Jun
Tisha B'Av · *day of mourning*	3 Aug
Rosh Hashanah (New Year)	23 Sep
Yom Kippur (Day of Atonement) · *fasting and prayer for forgiveness*	2 Oct
Sukkoth (Feast of Tabernacles) · *marking the time in wilderness*	7 Oct
Simchat Torah · *9th day of Sukkoth*	15 Oct
Hanukkah · *commemorating rededication of Jerusalem Temple*	16 Dec

ISLAMIC

Eid al-Adha · *celebrating the faith of Abraham*	10 Jan & 31 Dec
Al Hijra (New Year)	31 Jan
Ashura · *celebrating Noah leaving the Ark, and the saving of Moses*	9 Feb
Milad Al-Nabi · *Muhammad's birthday*	11 Apr
Ramadan · *the month in which the Koran was revealed*	starts 24 Sep
Eid al-Fitr · *marks end of Ramadan*	24 Oct

SIKH

Birthday of Guru Gobind Singh · *founder of the Khalsa*	5 Jan
Sikh New Year (Nanakshahi calendar)	14 Mar
Hola Mahalla · *festival of martial arts*	14/15 Mar
Vaisakhi (Baisakhi) · *founding of the Khalsa*	13/14 Apr
Birthday of Guru Nanak (founder of Sikhism)	14 Apr
Martyrdom of Guru Arjan	16 Jun
Martyrdom of Guru Tegh Bahadur	24 Nov
Divali · *festival of light*	21 Oct

—————— NOTABLE RELIGIOUS DATES FOR 2006 cont. ——————

BAHA'I

Nawruz (New Year) .... Mar 21	Day of the Covenant........... 26 Nov
Ridvan................. Apr 21–2 May	Ascension of Abdu'l-Baha ..... 28 Nov
Declaration of the Báb .... 23 May	*World Religion day*.............. 15 Jan
Ascension of Baha'u'llah .... 29 May	*Race Unity Day*................. 11 Jun
Martyrdom of the Báb........... 9 July	*World Peace Day*................ 21 Nov
Birth of the Báb .... 20 Oct	*In addition, the eve of each of the*
Birth of Baha'u'llah .... 12 Nov	*nineteen Baha'i months is celebrated.*

JAIN

Mahavira Jayanti · *celebrates the day of Mahavira's birth* .... 11 Apr
Paryushan · *time of reflection and repentance* .... 20–27 Aug
Divali · *Mahavira gave his last teachings and attained ultimate liberation* .... 21 Oct
New year .... 22 Oct
Kartak Purnima · *time of pilgrimage* .... 5 Nov

BUDDHIST

Losar · *Tibetan New Year* .... 28 Feb
Parinivana Day· *marks the death of the Buddha* .... 15 Feb
Wesak (Vesak) · *marks the birth, death & enlightenment of the Buddha* .... 13 May
Dharma Day · *marks the start of the Buddha's teaching* .... 11 Jul
Sangha Day (Magha Puja Day) · *celebration of Buddhist community* .... 7 Oct

RASTAFARIAN

Ethiopian Christmas.............. 7 Jan	Marcus Garvey birthday ...... 17 Aug
Ethiopian Constitution.......... 16 Jul	Ethiopian New Year's Day...... 11 Sep
Haile Selassie birthday........... 23 Jul	Crowning of Haile Selassie...... 2 Nov

PAGAN

Imbolc · *fire festival anticipating the new farming season* .... 1/2 Feb
Spring Equinox · *celebrating the renewal of life* .... 20/21 Mar
Beltane · *fire festival celebrating Summer and fertility*........................ 30 Apr/1 May
Summer Solstice (Midsummer; Litha) · *celebrating the sun's power*.............. 21 Jun
Lughnasadh · *harvest festival* .... 2–4 Aug
Autumn Equinox (Harvest Home; Mabon) · *reflection on the past season*....... 23 Sep
Samhain (Halloween; All Hallows Eve) · *pagan new year* .... 31 Oct/1 Nov
Winter Solstice (Yule) · *celebrating Winter*................................ 20/21 Dec

CHINESE LUNAR NEW YEAR · 29–31 Jan

[Every effort has been taken to validate these dates. However, readers should be aware that there is a surprising degree of debate and dispute. This is caused by the interplay of: regional variations; differing interpretations between religious authorities; seemingly arbitrary changes in dates when holidays conflict; avoidance of days considered for one or other reason inauspicious; as well as the inherent unpredictability of the lunar cycle. Many festivals, especially Jewish holidays, start at sundown on the preceding day.]

───────── PUBLIC & BANK HOLIDAYS ─────────

England, Wales, & N. Ireland	2006	2007	2008
New Year's Day	2 Jan	1 Jan	1 Jan
[NI *only*] St Patrick's Day	17 Mar	19 Mar	17 Mar
Good Friday	14 Apr	6 Apr	21 Mar
Easter Monday	17 Apr	9 Apr	24 Mar
Early May Bank Holiday	1 May	7 May	5 May
Spring Bank Holiday	29 May	28 May	26 May
[NI *only*] Battle of the Boyne	12 July	12 July	14 July
Summer Bank Holiday	28 Aug	27 Aug	25 Aug
Christmas Day	25 Dec	25 Dec	25 Dec
Boxing Day	26 Dec	26 Dec	26 Dec

Scotland	2006	2007	2008
New Year's Day	3 Jan	1 Jan	1 Jan
2nd January	2 Jan	2 Jan	2 Jan
Good Friday	14 Apr	6 Apr	21 Mar
Early May Bank Holiday	1 May	7 May	5 May
Spring Bank Holiday	29 May	28 May	26 May
Summer Bank Holiday	7 Aug	6 Aug	4 Aug
Christmas Day	25 Dec	25 Dec	25 Dec
Boxing Day	26 Dec	26 Dec	26 Dec

These are the expected dates of holidays; some are subject to proclamation by the Queen.

───────── THE DIVISION OF MAN'S AGES ─────────

The Ape, the Lion, the Fox, the Ass, Thus sets forth man as in a glass.
APE — Like apes we be toying, till twenty-and-one;
LION — Then hasty as lions, till forty be gone;
FOX — Then wily as foxes, till threescore-and-three;
ASS — Then after for asses accounted we be.

───── TRADITIONAL WEDDING ANNIVERSARY SYMBOLS ─────

1st .... Cotton	10th .... Tin	35th .... Coral
2nd .... Paper	11th .... Steel	40th .... Ruby
3rd............. Leather	12th .... Silk, Linen	45th........... Sapphire
4th....... Fruit, Flowers	13th .... Lace	50th................. Gold
5th .... Wood	14th............... Ivory	55th .... Emerald
6th................ Sugar	15th............... Crystal	60th.......... Diamond
7th .... Wool, Copper	20th............... China	70th .... Platinum
8th.............. Pottery	25th .... Silver	75th.......... Diamond
9th.............. Willow	30th .... Pearl	*American symbols differ.*

[Debate rages about the order of cotton and paper for 1st and 2nd anniversaries.]

PHASES OF THE MOON 2006

NEW MOON			FIRST QUARTER			FULL MOON			LAST QUARTER		
d	*h*	*m*	*d*	*h*	*m*	*d*	*h*	*m*	*d*	*h*	*m*
			Jan....6...18...56			Jan....14...9...48			Jan....22...15...14		
Jan....29...14...15			Feb....5...6...29			Feb....13...4...44			Feb....21...7...17		
Feb....28....0...31			Mar....6...20...16			Mar....14...23...35			Mar...22...19...11		
Mar...29...10...15			Apr....5...12...01			Apr....13...16...40			Apr...21....3...28		
Apr...27...19...44			May....5...5...13			May....13...6...51			May...20....9...21		
May...27....5...26			Jun....3...23...06			Jun....11...18...03			Jun....18...14...08		
Jun....25...16...05			Jul....3...16...37			Jul....11...3...02			Jul....17...19...13		
Jul.....25....4...31			Aug....2....8...46			Aug....9...10...54			Aug....16....1...51		
Aug...23...19...10			Aug...31...22...57			Sep....7...18...42			Sep....14...11...15		
Sep....22...11...45			Sep....30...11...04			Oct....7....3...13			Oct....14....0...26		
Oct....22....5...14			Oct....29...21...25			Nov....5...12...58			Nov....12...17...45		
Nov...20...22...18			Nov...28....6...29			Dec....5....0...25			Dec....12...14...32		
Dec...20...14...01			Dec...27...14...48			[Key: *d*ays, *h*ours, and *m*inutes of Universal Time]					

new moon · *waxing crescent* · *first quarter* · *waxing gibbous* · *full moon* · *waning gibbous* · *last quarter* · *waning crescent* · *new moon*

FULL MOON NICKNAMES

Month	*nickname of full moon*
January	Moon after Yule
February	Wolf Moon
March	Lent(en) Moon
April	Egg Moon
May	Milk Moon
June	Flower Moon
July	Hay Moon
August	Grain Moon
September	Fruit Moon
October	Harvest Moon
November	Hunter's Moon
December	Moon before Yule

A 'Blue Moon' is usually defined as the second of two full moons that happens to appear in the same month.

EPOCHS & ERAS

An EPOCH is a fixed point in time (e.g. the birth of Christ), and the succession of events in the period following is an ERA. Some common epoch abbreviations are:

AD .... Anno Domini (*year of the Lord*) · after the birth of Christ

AH.................... Anno Hegirae (*year of the Hegira*) · the Muslim era is dated from the day of Muhammad's flight from Mecca (July 16, 622AD)

AUC....... Ab Urbe Condita (*since the founding of the city* [Rome]) · after 753BC

BC .... Before Christ · before the birth of Christ

BCE.............. Before the Christian/Common Era · before the birth of Christ

CE.............................. Christian/Common Era · after the birth of Christ

—————————— CALENDRICAL MISCELLANY ——————————

DOG DAYS · the hot, muggy days of sultry summer, associated by the Romans (*dies caniculares*) with the influence of the dog star Sirius which is high in the sky during summer days. Dog days are said to last for 'more than one month but less than two', from July until early September.

SALAD DAYS · days of inexperience (between youth and maturity) when people are 'green'. As Shakespeare wrote in *Antony & Cleopatra*: 'My salad days, When I was green in judgement, cold in blood, To say as I said then!'.

COLLAR DAYS · days upon which Knights wear the collar of their Order when taking part in any court ceremony. (For example, collars are worn when Her Majesty opens or prorogues Parliament.) Unless instructed by the Queen, collars are never worn after sunset, nor if on horseback during ceremonial parades.

Day	Old English	Roman
Sunday	Moon	Luna
Monday	Tiw/Tyr	Mars
Tuesday	Odin	Mercury
Thursday	Thor	Jupiter
Friday	Freya	Venus
Saturday	Saeternes	Saturn

ORBITS · the earth orbits the sun in 365 days, 5hr, 48m, 46s, which is the length of the solar year. The moon passes through its phases in about 29½ days; thus, a lunar year (12 lunar months) amounts to more than 354 days, 8hr, 48m.

HALCYON DAYS · generally a time of happiness and prosperity; in nautical terms, a period of two weeks of calm seas at the winter solstice.

HANDSEL MONDAY · the first Monday of the New Year when gifts were given and received. (From the Old English *handselen* – 'delivery into the hand'.)

HOLOCAUST MEMORIAL DAY · observed across Europe on 27 January each year, the anniversary of the liberation of Auschwitz-Birkenau. (It is also the European Day Against Genocide.)

ANNUS HORRIBILIS   *terrible year*
ANNUS MIRABILIS   *miraculous year*

BANIAN DAYS · the nautical term for those days when no meat would be served to a ship's crew. (Deriving from Hindu traders who eschewed the eating of meat.)

MEDICINAL DAYS · according to Hippocrates, these are the 6th, 8th, 10th, 12th, 16th, 18th, &c. days of a disease, when no 'crisis' will occur, and medicine may be safely administered. Similarly, MEDICINAL HOURS are those suitable for taking medicine: apparently, an hour before dinner, four hours after dinner, and bed-time.

EMBER DAYS · (*quatuor tempora*) the Wednesday, Friday, and Saturday of the weeks (Ember Weeks) following the first Sunday in Lent, Whitsunday, Holy Cross Day (14 Sep), and St Lucy's Day (13 Dec).

BORROWED DAYS · 12–14 February were traditionally said to be 'borrowed' from January. If these days were stormy, the year would be favoured with good weather; but if fine, the year's weather would be foul. The last three days of March were said to be 'borrowed' from April. They were expected to be stormy.

─────CALENDRICAL MISCELLANY cont.─────

EQUATION OF TIME · the difference between the time as shown by a clock and the time as shown by a sundial – greatest in November when the sun is 'slow'.

LUSTRUM · a period of five years.

PLOUGH MONDAY · the Monday after Epiphany when agricultural labourers traditionally resumed their toil.

SHROVETIDE · time preceeding Lent.

CALENDS · in the Roman calendar, the first day of the month.

IDES · in the Roman calendar, ides were the 15th day of March, May, July, and October, and the 13th day of all other months. (Julius Caesar was assassinated on the Ides of March 44BC).

NONES · in the Roman calendar, nine days before the Ides.

JOUR MAIGRE · a fast-day *(French)*.

HOCKTIDE · the second Monday and Tuesday after Easter, when money was raised for church, parish and charitable funds. These were also days of festivity, japes, and general merriment.

HEXAMERON · the 6 days of creation.

CAP & FEATHER DAYS · childhood.

TENEBRAE · ('darkness') · last three days of Holy Week.

HISTORICAL YEAR · the modern historical convention of measuring the year from 1 January, regardless of the system used in the time or culture of the location under discussion.

A YEAR AND A DAY · a set period of time in civil and legal custom. For example, if a person wounded did not die within a year and a day, their assailant could not be guilty of murder. [*This was amended by the Law Reform (Year and a Day Rule) Act 1996.*]

OAK AND ASH SEASONS · it was believed that if the oak leafed before the ash, the year would be fine and productive; whereas if the ash leafed before the the oak, there would be a cold Summer and an unproductive Autumn.

THE ATOMIC SECOND · is defined as the period of time taken for 9,192,631,770 oscillations of the cesium-133 atom exposed to a suitable excitation [see p.194].

CLIMACTERIC YEARS · the 7th and 9th years and their multiples by the odd numbers 3, 5, 7, 9 (i.e. 7, 9, 21, 27, 35, 45, 49, 63, and 81) which astrologers thought would be especially dismal since they were presided over by Saturn. [Climacteric is another name for the menopause.]

SHROVE TUESDAY or MARDI GRAS · the Tuesday before Lent – famous in the past for cock-fighting and louche behaviour, and nowadays for flipping pancakes and indigestion.

BEGINNING OF THE DAY · varies across history and by culture: modern Western and Chinese cultures follow Roman tradition by starting new days at *midnight*; Egyptians, Armenians, and Persians began their day at *dawn*; Greeks, Jews, Muslims started their day at *sunset*; some sailors, astronomers and other cultures began days at *noon*.

———————— HOURS FOR SLEEP ————————

Nature requires 6 · *Custom* 7 · *Laziness* 9 · and *Wickedness* 11

———————— THE CAD'S AMOROUS WEEK ————————

El lunes me enamro,	On Monday I fall in love,
martes lo digo,	On Tuesday I say so,
miércoles me declaro,	On Wednesday I make a declaration,
jueves consigo;	On Thursday I succeed;
viernes doy celos,	On Friday I make her jealous,
y sábado y domingo,	On Saturday and Sunday,
busco amor nuevo.	I look for new love.

———————— LEAP YEARS ————————

In the Gregorian calendar, Leap Years have 366 days, with the addition of an extra day: 29 February. Any year whose date is a number exactly divisible by four is a leap year, except years ending in '00', which must be divisible by 400. The extra day is added every four years to allow for the difference between a year of 365 days and the actual time it takes the Earth to circle the Sun. The table below shows the recent leap years, as well as the day of the week upon which each 29 February falls:

Monday	1932	1960	1988	2016	2044
Saturday	1936	1964	1992	2020	2048
Thursday	1940	1968	1996	2024	2052
Tuesday	1944	1972	2000	2028	2056
Sunday	1948	1976	2004	2032	2060
Friday	1952	1980	2008	2036	2064
Wednesday	1956	1984	2012	2040	2068

Tradition dictates that the normal conventions of gallantry are suspended during 29 February, and a woman may ask for a man's hand in marriage. By custom, if the man declines this request he is then bound by honour to buy the woman a silk gown by way of recompense. Of course, those born on 29 February (including Pope Paul III and Rossini) celebrate only one birthday in four – which, as Frederic discovered in *The Pirates of Penzance,* can lead to all sorts of elaborate difficulties.

———————— TRADITIONAL FASTING TERMS ————————

Term	*type of fast*
Jejunium generalé	a fast binding on all
Jejunium consuetudinarium	a local fast
Jejunium poenitentialé	a fast by way of penance
Jejunium votivum	a fast consequent on a vow

Index

Should not the Society of Indexers be know as Indexers, Society of, The?
— KEITH WATERHOUSE

─────── THINGS TO DO – BILLS, BROBDINGNAGIAN ───────

—————— BINGE DRINKING – COURT STRUCTURE ——————

─────HOUSE OF LORDS – MERCURY MUSIC PRIZE─────

—————— MICHELIN STARS, UK – PEACEKEEPERS, UN ——————

–SAFFIR-SIMPSON SCALE – TELEPHONE SHORT CODES–

–TEMPERATURE CONVERSIONS – ZEITGEIST, GOOGLE–

─────── ACKNOWLEDGMENTS ───────

The author would like to thank:

Jonathan, Judith, and Geoffrey Schott

Richard Album, Sarah Beal, Joanna Begent, Martin Birchall,
Andrew Cock-Starkey, James Coleman, Martin Colyer, Victoria Cook,
Gordon Corera, Aster Crawshaw, Rosemary Davidson, Jody & Liz Davies,
Will Douglas, Stephanie Duncan, Jennifer Epworth, Kathleen Farrar,
Minna Fry, Catherine Gough, Charlotte Hawes, Mark & Sharon Hubbard,
Max Jones, Robert Klaber, Alison Lang, Rachel Law, John Lloyd, Ruth Logan,
Chris Lyon, Jess Manson, Michael Manson, Sarah Marcus, Susannah McFarlane,
Lauren Mechling, Colin Midson, David Miller, Polly Napper, Nigel Newton,
Sarah Norton, Cally Poplak, Dave Powell, Alexandra Pringle, Bill Swainson,
Caroline Turner, David Ward, and Michael Winawer.

Schott's Almanac

2 0 0 7

LIBER PRAETERITORUM ET POSTERITATIS CARMEN

Published November 2006 · To reserve your copy, visit

www.schottsalmanac.com